Crispina and Her Sisters

Crispina and Her Sisters

Women and Authority in Early Christianity

CHRISTINE SCHENK, CSJ

FORTRESS PRESS
MINNEAPOLIS

CRISPINA AND HER SISTERS
Women and Authority in Early Christianity

Cover image: Tomb portrait of deceased Crispina cradling a codex embellished with Christogram. Lid of mid-fourth century Christian sarcophagus housed in Pio Cristiano museum at the Vatican. Vatican Pio Cristiano Museum
Cover design: Laurie Ingram

Print ISBN: 978-1-5064-1188-0
eBook ISBN: 978-1-5064-1189-7

The paper used in this publication meets the minimum requirements of American National Standard for Information Sciences — Permanence of Paper for Printed Library Materials, ANSI Z329.48-1984.

Manufactured in the U.S.A.

To the sisters and associates of the Congregation of the
Sisters St. Joseph

Let the sisters so live that they will be known
as the Congregation of God's Great Love.

(*Primitive Constitutions* ca. 1653)

Contents

Acknowledgments

The idea for this book first arose during a 2007 pilgrimage to Rome to visit sites of women leaders in the early church. Academic consultant Dr. Janet Tulloch suggested our group visit the Pio Cristiano Museum in the Vatican Museums, which contains the most comprehensive collection of early Christian archaeological discoveries in the world. There we found a number of beautiful fourth-century sarcophagi with sculpted portraits of deceased women surrounded by biblical scenes. The women hold scrolls, and their hands are held in teaching or proclaiming gestures, an iconography similar to that of Jesus figures on nearby tombs. I found the women's sarcophagi both fascinating and compelling. For over ten years, I had been working to retrieve information about women in the early church, yet I had never seen such tombs before. Did they supply persuasive evidence of women's ministerial involvement in the early church? A quick bit of research revealed that the sarcophagi had never been studied from the point of view of female ecclesial roles. After failing to persuade other scholars to study these mysterious "tomb ladies," I decided to undertake the challenge myself. An in-depth investigation of these unknown women was long overdue. And so began an arduous but surprisingly enjoyable three-year odyssey.

A multidisciplinary work of this nature never gets written without the help of many people. My religious community, the Congregation of St. Joseph, gave me the time and space I needed to complete the exhaustive research this book required. I owe a profound debt of gratitude to Dr. Carolyn Osiek, RSCJ, whose support and vast knowledge of the early church—particularly Christian women in the early centuries—gave me the courage to jump in where wiser heads might hesitate. Her suggestion to frame this study in terms of female authority rather than female leadership brought clarity and nuance to this exploration of women's ministries in the early church. In addition to interpreting many Greek and Latin inscriptions, Dr. Osiek's valuable feedback never failed to complicate my thinking even as it heightened my respect for the complexities of early church history. This book would not have happened without her conscientious, careful mentoring. In her capacity as a cultural historian in ancient religions and material culture, Dr. Tulloch provided needed precision to my efforts to determine what may or may not be inferred from early Christian funerary iconography. I am in her debt. Special thanks are also owed to Dr. Diana Culbertson, OP, who provided early editing assistance and blessed me with her erudition and keen interest.

I am especially touched by the generosity of experts in Greco-Roman and Christian sarcophagi, particularly Dr. Stine Birk, Dr. Jutta Dresken-Weiland, and Dr. Janet Huskinson, who graciously responded to my technical questions, particularly about *orans* figures. Archbishop Joseph Augustine Di Noia, OP, introduced me to Dr. Umberto Utro at the Vatican Museums, who affirmed my initial impressions of several sarcophagus motifs and pointed me to invaluable references. I am very grateful to Dr. Rosanna DiPinto and Msgr. Paolo Nicolini at the Vatican Museums for expediting acquisition of numerous rare images, making it possible for readers to contemplate early Christian funerary art for themselves. Thomas H. Short, PhD, PStat, provided statistical consultation, calculations, and interpretations to meaningfully compare various iconographical characteristics of male and female sarcophagus portraits. Alan Rome, librarian at St. Mary Seminary and Graduate School of Theology, patiently tracked down more than a few obscure tomes and greatly aided my research. The Ingalls Library at the Cleveland Museum of Art provided important technical and research support. Despite the blessing of abundant erudite consultation, mistakes sometimes happen. These belong to me alone.

As any writer knows, without the personal support and encouragement of friends and family, most books would never see the light of day. I am blessed by the unconditional support and love of my sisters, Constance Thoele, Paula Lantz, and Dr. Elizabeth Schenk, as well as brothers-in-law, Philip Lantz and Chip Wasson, and my adored niece, Sarah Lantz Ramsay, her spouse, Mack, and four equally adored nephews and their spouses, Jon Lantz, Benjamin Thoele (Jill), Tyler Schenk-Wasson, and Spencer Schenk-Wasson. Cousin Bev Thompson is a much-beloved cheerleader. I am also deeply grateful for the encouragement of long time Medical Mission Sister friends: Estelle Demers, Margaret McKenna, Loretta Whalen, and especially Miriam Therese Winter, who first helped me believe that I was capable of writing a book, any book, let alone this book. Other dear friends sustained me though long months of research and writing: Dr. Joan Nuth, Rose Torrence, Dr. Sallie Latkovich, CSJ, Sr. Jane Pank, HM, and my college chums, Mary Ellen Grady, Ellen and John Brztywa, and Polly Seitz.

The board and staff of FutureChurch first provided the incentive to take on a book of this magnitude. A special shout-out to board members Jocelyn Collens, James Connell, Marie Vidmar Graf, Mary Louise Hartman, Rita Houlihan, Eugene Kramer, and especially FutureChurch executive director Deborah Rose-Milavec, whose unstinting belief in me and in this project meant more than she probably realizes. My long-suffering CSJ-sister housemates—Jeanne Cmolik, Marcella Clancy, Ann LeTourneau, and Paula Therese Pilon—put up with weird writer hours and even weirder conversations about obscure iconographic motifs. I owe you!

I am blessed to have been accompanied all along the way by my spiritual director, Sr. Francis Therese Woznicki, SSJ-TOSF. Fran's discerning heart gave me the confidence I needed to shape a narrative that respected both the scientific analysis of the sarcophagi and the belief in a saving Christ that animated, and emanated from, these faithful women of the church.

Abbreviations

CIL   *Corpus Inscriptionum Latinarum*

RS 1   Deichmann, Friedrich W., Giuseppe Bovini, and Hugo Brandenburg, eds. *Rom und Ostia*. Repertorium Der Christlich-Antiken Sarkophage 1. Wiesbaden: Franz Steiner, 1967.

RS 2   Dresken-Weiland, Jutta, ed. *Italien: mit einem nachtrag; Rom und Ostia, Dalmatien, Museen der Welt*. Repertorium Der Christlich-Antiken Sarkophage 2. Mainz am Rhein: Philipp von Zabern, 1998.

RS 3   Christern-Briesenick, Brigitte, ed. *Frankreich, Algerien, Tunesien*. Repertorium Der Christlich-Antiken Sarkophage 3. Mainz am Rhein: Philipp von Zabern, 2003.

Introduction

On February 14, 2007, Pope Benedict XVI made the rather remarkable statement that "the history of Christianity would have turned out very differently without the contribution of women" and the "female presence was anything but secondary."[1] This observation from, arguably, the most erudite of contemporary popes could be interpreted as another way of saying that the influence of early Christian women was either primary or equal to that of Christian men.

This book explores the extent to which early Christian women can be said to have exercised authority in the first five centuries of Christianity. Understandings of authority can vary and often seem to depend on context. The first definition listed by most dictionary sources is about governance or jurisdiction: "The power or right to give orders, make decisions, and enforce obedience."[2] Both women and men exercised this type of authority in the early church. Church orders such as bishops, priests, deacons (male and female), and the orders of widows and virgins gradually became normative in the late first and early second centuries. By the fifth century, however, with the exception of monastic settings, the female exercise of governance in the mainstream church had all but disappeared. The second definition of authority listed by our dictionary sources is less restrictive: "The power to influence others, especially because of one's commanding manner or one's recognized knowledge about something"[3]

1. "Pope: History of Christianity Would Be Very Different without Women," *Asia News*, February 14, 2007, http://tinyurl.com/yb2v3e6s.
2. *Oxford English Dictionary* (online), s.v. "authority."
3. Ibid.

and "the confident quality of someone who knows a lot about something or who is respected or obeyed by other people."[4] This second type of authority is less tied to governance, although without it, governing would be difficult. I suggest that, in addition to some governance functions, early Christian women frequently exercised this second definition of authority within their social networks. In doing so, they catalyzed the growth and development of the early church to a much greater extent than is generally appreciated.

Discovering the extent to which Christian women exercised both types of authority named above is a challenging enterprise. Most people have never heard of Bitalia, Veneranda, Crispina, Petronella, Marcia Romania Celsa, Sofia the Deacon, and many other early women, even though their catacomb and tomb art suggest their authority was influential and valued by early Christian communities. This book explores visual imagery found on burial artifacts of prominent late third- and fourth-century Christian women. A review of women's history in the first four centuries of Christianity provides important context, as does a careful study of the meaning of funerary art within customary Roman commemorations. A fascinating picture emerges of women's authority in the early church, a picture either not available or sadly distorted in the written history. In the first two chapters, a concerted effort is made to situate the history of early Christianity within its own Greco-Roman culture without diminishing the distinctly Christian contributions that would gradually transform that culture, at least in part. Christian women were undeniably catalysts for significant social change. Readers who are already familiar with the roles of women in Greco-Roman culture, patronage, and social networks in late antiquity, and biblical and historical women in early Christianity may wish to skim or skip these two chapters. It would be helpful, however, to read the conclusion of chapter 2 before reading subsequent chapters.

Since most history relies heavily on the writings of men, historical data about the lives of women can be exceedingly hard to come by. Even though there were many female patrons of male leaders in the early church, such as Mary of Magdala, Phoebe, Lydia, Bassilla,

---

4. *Merriam Webster Learner's Dictionary* (online), s.v. "authority."

Paula, Olympias, and others, their presence is barely discernible in the literary sources. It did not take feminist scholars long to recognize that visual imagery, inscriptions, and funerary artifacts could provide important information about women in the early church that was not available elsewhere. Chapter 3 briefly explores the history of early Christian art and the role of art in religion. It includes a broad overview of methods used by art historians to analyze early Christian art and the interpretive challenges of relating it to the history of early Christian women.

Chapter 4 explores portrait frescos of women found in the catacombs of Priscilla and Domitilla in Rome and at San Gennaro in Naples. At the Priscilla catacomb, most scholars now believe the *Fractio Panis* fresco represents a woman's funerary meal rather than a Christian Eucharist. A fresh interpretation of the controversial female *orans* figure in the *Velata* cubiculum posits that the deceased woman exercised authority as an enrolled widow. Portrait frescos of women holding scrolls and codices at the catacombs of Domitilla and San Gennaro provide substantial evidence that they were remembered, at the least, as influential teachers and "women of the Word." Roman funerary practices and sarcophagus motifs found in late antiquity are discussed at length in chapter 5. Christians were part of their Greco-Roman culture, and so Christian funerary art is rooted in Greco-Roman artistic conventions. In the past, scholars studied Christian and non-Christian sarcophagi as two separate disciplines. Today, they are studied together since both were "produced in the same places by the same workshops for very similar patrons and clients."[5] For Romans, whether Christian or not, a sarcophagus was a monument filled with meaning, not just a container for a corpse. Planning for how one wished to be remembered was an important process. Many sarcophagi were purchased beforehand by an owner or patron who chose iconographical motifs to best represent the departed, often a spouse, a child, or, in many cases, the owners themselves. This chapter contextualizes an investigation into how and why Christians,

---

5. Jaś Elsner, introduction to *Life, Death and Representation: Some New Work on Roman Sarcophagi*, ed. Jaś Elsner and Janet Huskinson (New York: de Gruyter, 2011), 9.

especially Christian women, chose and interpreted their own sarcophagus art.

Chapters 6 and 7 discuss outcomes of original research analyzing 2119 images and descriptors of third- to early fifth-century sarcophagi and fragments, which comprise all currently available images of Christian sarcophagi and loculus plates. A special focus is Christian portraits and what can be discovered from the iconography chosen by the deceased person and/or patron who commissioned it. Conducted over a three-year period, this investigation builds upon earlier work by art historian Janet Huskinson, as well as Stine Birk's seminal research into portraits on Roman (non-Christian) sarcophagi. Chapter 6 pays special attention to individual commemorations of Christian women. An in-depth analysis of iconographical features such as scrolls, speech gestures, and in-facing "apostle" figures suggests that many women were commemorated as persons of status, influence, and authority within their Christian social networks. One highly significant finding is that there are three times as many individual portraits of Christian women compared to individual portraits of Christian men. Chapter 7 discusses analyses of male, couple, and child portraits. It concludes with a preliminary investigation of embedded portraits previously believed to be nonexistent on Christian tombs.

Since most of the sarcophagi and catacomb art discussed in this book dates to the fourth century, the concluding chapter explores what can be known from the literary record about contemporaneous Christian women who lived during this dramatically transformative time for church and empire. What we know about early "mothers of the church" such as Marcella, Paula, Melania the Elder, Macrina, and Olympias comes to us solely through the writings of men. Two other "mothers"—Egeria and Proba—wrote literary texts of their own. The lives of these "literary sources women" provide helpful context for the women commemorated on Christian sarcophagus and catacomb depictions. Chapter 8 asks (and tries to answer) some tantalizing questions: Does the literary record corroborate or oppose what the iconic portrayals in catacomb frescos and sarcophagi suggest? Were contemporaneous women from the literary record role models for the women buried in the sarcophagi and catacombs? Or were the catacomb/tomb women role models for their literary contemporaries? Did fourth-century Christian women exercise biblical and spiritual authority?

Late antique catacomb frescos and portrait tombs of Christian women suggest that they viewed themselves or were viewed by their loved ones as persons of authority with significant religious influence. Literary sources about the lives of fourth-century women corroborate the archaeological evidence. My findings, based on a careful review of the extant archaeological remains, confirm what contemporary scholars such as Carolyn Osiek and Peter Lampe have already surmised: women were considerably more influential in the spread of early Christianity than is generally appreciated. It is my hope that this study will bring nuance to the common assumption that only men were influential in early Christianity. While men predominate in the literary record, funerary portraits point to a preponderance of influential women. Few women are remembered in the literary sources as persons with authority. Yet, sarcophagus portraits of Christian women outnumber portraits of Christian men by three to one. Female portraits are shown with scrolls, speech gestures, and in-facing apostle figures, which enhance the ecclesial authority of the deceased. These findings suggest that women exercised ecclesial authority to a greater degree than previously recognized.

Some caveats may be in order. A small part of this book includes a summation of archaeological and literary evidence indicating that some early Christian women held titles such as *presbytera* (priest), *diakonos* (deacon), and *episcopa* (bishop or overseer). I wish to be clear that what is being presented here is not primarily a theological work. While I will offer some theological reflections about what early Christians may have been communicating via their funerary art, this book is mainly a discussion of the evidence from history and archaeology for women's exercise of authority, including some governance functions, in early Christianity. It may be helpful to emphasize that the meaning and functioning of priests, deacons, and bishops was quite different in different historical periods (see Gary Macy, *The Hidden Tradition of Women's Ordination*). It should not be assumed, therefore, that a fourth-century "priest" is the same entity as a twenty-first-century man with this title. Yet, there is significant epigraphical and literary evidence that some women in early Christian communities held titles that were similar or equivalent to those of men. This book should not be viewed as arguing one way or the other about the theology of ordaining women, as important as that conversation is for our day. It has the far deeper goal of allowing men, and especially women, to retrieve the memory of influential women whose witness has for too long been invisible or distorted in Christian memory. It is my hope that drawing attention to these ancient images of early Christian women in iconic authority portrayals may help us reset our preconceived mental models. If they also help women to see themselves in early Christian history, my work is doubly blessed.

1.

Women and Early Christianity: Sociocultural Context

In just over three centuries, Christianity grew from an obscure sect in a Palestinian backwater to the official religion of a far-flung, if decaying, Roman Empire. This rapid growth was due in no small measure to the ministry and patronage of women who welcomed early Christian missionaries, both male and female, into the complex social network of Greco-Roman households. It is one of the ironies of history that despite their early prominence in proclaiming the Christian message, the ecclesial leadership of Christian women in the fifth century was significantly more circumscribed than in the first.

INTERPRETIVE CHALLENGES

Scholars seeking to discover women's roles in late antiquity face formidable challenges. Like all history until the mid-twentieth century, Christian history was written by men with preconceived notions about women. Philosophical treatises viewed females as created subordinate to males.

"The male is by nature superior and the female inferior, the male ruler and the female subject," said Aristotle.[1] Since women's primary

---

1. Aristotle, *On Politics*, 1.1254 b (H. Rackham [Cambridge MA: Harvard University Press, 1944], http://tinyurl.com/yd8kxkd5).

roles were understood to belong to the household and reproduction, participation in political, cultural, and religious life was frowned upon. Classical Jewish, Christian, and non-Christian texts are dense with declarations that men are made to rule and women are made to obey.[2] For centuries, selected literary sources, including church synodal canons and writings by church fathers, were believed to be both normative and descriptive of early church life. However, in evaluating historical data, feminist biblical scholars and church historians now recognize the importance of differentiating between "gender ideology" and "the reality of women's lives."[3] Special mention must be made of the interpretive challenges posed by those seeking to uncover "the reality of women's lives."

As in modern English, the Greek and Latin masculine plurals often function grammatically as gender neutral in describing groups composed of both women and men. Scholars maintain that in interpreting ancient writings, it is often incorrectly assumed that only men are referred to when, in fact, women were included. Because of these grammatical conventions, women effectively become invisible in these texts. For example, in the New Testament, words describing both ordinary believers and leaders holding special offices are almost always rendered in the masculine plural. When translated from Greek into English, words for believers such as "saints," "elect," and "righteous" are interpreted inclusively, applying therefore to both men and women. But words signifying leadership offices such as apostles (*apostoloi*), teachers (*didaskaloi*), or bishop/overseer (*episcopoi*) are invariably interpreted as applying only to men. This occurs even though individual women leaders such as Phoebe (deacon/*diakonos*) and Junia (apostle/*apostolos*) are described in the New Testament by masculine nouns (Rom 16:1–16). Therefore, masculine plural descriptions of leadership offices should not necessarily be interpreted

---

2. E.g., Gen 3:16: "To the woman he said, I will greatly increase your pangs in childbearing; in pain you shall bring forth children, yet your desire shall be for your husband, and he shall rule over you." 1 Tim 2:11–12: "Let a woman learn in silence with full submission. I permit no woman to teach or to have authority over a man; she is to keep silent."

3. Ute E. Eisen, *Women Officeholders in Early Christianity: Epigraphical and Literary Studies*, trans. Linda M. Maloney (Collegeville, MN: Liturgical Press, 2000), 3.

as excluding women since there is clear evidence that women also served the church as deacons, apostles, overseers, and teachers.[4]

Care must also be taken to avoid portraying Jesus as liberating women from a Judaism that restricted and subordinated them any more than other ancient cultures. Jewish women shared the lot of all women in late antiquity. Patriarchy restricted both Jewish and gentile women, but the extent of that restriction depended more on a woman's socioeconomic status, cultural context, and geography than her religious affiliation. Jesus was an observant Jew. His movement arose from faith that just as God brought Israel out of slavery in Egypt, so God would act to remove Roman oppression in Israel and bring about a new time of justice and right relationship among nations and peoples. Jesus's inclusive practice should be viewed as emerging from his Judaism, not apart from it.

ORIGINS OF THE JESUS MOVEMENT

Many know a good deal about the miracle-working, crucified Jesus who loved the poor and challenged the rich. But until recently, few knew much about the sociopolitical and cultural realities surrounding his execution by the Roman authorities. Rome's ingenious political strategy delegated client kings (in Israel, the Herodians) to collect taxes and keep the peace. The imperium excelled at co-opting elite local families to rule on its behalf. As long as peace prevailed and taxes flowed into the imperial treasury, these elite rulers retained their power. The dynasty of Herod the Great (37–4 BCE) would rule Israel until the destruction of the Jerusalem temple in 70 CE. For most of the first century, it was obvious to many (including Jesus) that Israel, led by militant religious zealots, was on a collision course with Rome. The underlying causes were both political and religious. Politically, Roman economic practices, especially in Galilee, were responsible for the systematic eviction of agrarian families from their ancestral lands. Israelites paid a threefold tax: a tithe to the local Herodian rulers, a tithe to Rome, and a tithe to the temple. This regressive system

---

4. Carolyn Osiek and Margaret Y. MacDonald with Janet Tulloch, *A Woman's Place: House Churches in Earliest Christianity* (Minneapolis: Fortress Press, 2006), 6.

benefited the elite at the expense of peasant farmers and poor artisans whose labor kept the empire's wealthy fed and clothed. Regressive economies were common to agrarian communities throughout the empire where "taxes and rents flowed relentlessly away from the rural producers to the storehouses of cities (especially Rome), private estates, and temples."[5]

In Israel, an increasingly impoverished rural peasantry rose up in a series of popular rebellions that were brutally suppressed by Rome's legions. After Herod's death in 4 CE, Judas the Galilean (whose father had been killed by Herod) led such a rebellion. He raided the Greco-Roman city of Sepphoris in Galilee and armed his followers with weapons from the royal fortress. Rome retaliated by sending three legions from Syria under the legate Varus to quell the uprising. Varus crucified two thousand men, women, and children outside the city walls of Jerusalem. The point of this draconian form of capital punishment was to terrorize subject peoples into submission. Varus recaptured Sepphoris, burned surrounding rural villages, and sold their families into slavery. Miriam (Mary) of Nazareth, Jesus's mother, would have been about fifteen or sixteen at the time, and since most women married between ages twelve and fifteen, Jesus himself was probably a toddler.[6] Painful memories of lost loved ones would reverberate in Galilean villages for generations.

From a religious perspective, observant Jews were outraged that the land promised and given to them by God was occupied and polluted by idolaters. There arose a widespread expectation that God would decisively intervene to expel the Roman overlords and inaugurate the eschaton, the end of days, when the promised land would be restored and God's justice would prevail forever. Pious, suffering Jews were constantly on the lookout for a messiah, God's prophetic servant, who would redeem Israel. Since oppressed peoples frequently name their children after liberators, it is no accident that we find many Miriams (Marys) in the New Testament. The sister of Moses,

---

5. Douglas Oakman, "The Countryside in Luke-Acts," in *The Social World of Luke-Acts: Models for Interpretation*, ed. Jerome H. Neyrey (Peabody, MA: Hendrickson, 1991), 155, as cited in Elizabeth A. Johnson, *Truly Our Sister: A Theology of Mary in the Communion of Saints* (New York: Continuum 2003), 144.

6. Johnson, *Truly Our Sister*, 153.

Miriam exercised important leadership in the events of Exodus, although later redactors would downplay her role.[7] Jesus's Hebrew name is actually Jeshua for the biblical Joshua who claimed the promised land for the Jewish peoples.

Such was the political-religious world into which Jesus of Nazareth was born. Culturally, Jesus was a member of a poor agrarian family that settled in the small village of Nazareth in Galilee, the most fertile agricultural region in Israel. Excavations at Nazareth suggest an agrarian subsistence society.[8] Just three to four miles away was the large Greco-Roman city of Sepphoris. After Judas the Galilean's rebellion, Herod Antipas (son of Herod the Great) made Sepphoris the region's capital and began new building projects. Most of the citizens in this city of eight to ten thousand people were Jews. Excavations have uncovered many purification pools (*miqva'oth*) but no public statues or temples to the gods.[9] Affluent members of the Herodian family as well as other ruling elites lived at Sepphoris. They owned private homes decorated with frescos and elaborate mosaics, and unlike rural villages such as Nazareth, the city had a sewage system. Poor villages normally had just one *miqva'ot* for everyone to use (see figure 1.1).

This "tale of two cities"—Sepphoris and Nazareth—throws into sharp relief the differences that existed between rural and urban societies throughout the Roman Empire. Jesus's prophetic criticism of Jewish elites complicit with Roman practices that impoverished Israel would cost him his life. Elisabeth Schüssler Fiorenza points out, however, that Jesus's proclamation did not directly address the structures of oppression:

> It implicitly subverts them by envisioning a different future and different human relationships on the grounds that all persons in Israel are created and elected by the gracious goodness of Jesus' Sophia-God. Jesus and his movement set free those who are dehumanized and in bondage to evil powers, thus implicitly subverting economic or patriarchal-androcentric

---

7. Wilda C. Gafney, *Daughters of Miriam: Women Prophets in Ancient Israel* (Minneapolis: Fortress Press, 2008), 81–85.

8. Johnson, *Truly Our Sister*, 142–44.

9. Ibid., 155.

structures, even though the people involved in this process might not have thought in terms of social structures.[10]

Figure 1.1. This first century *miqva'ot* (ritual bath) is found at Qumran in southern Israel. At the time of Jesus, the city was inhabited by a Jewish sect called the Essenes who awaited a final apocalyptic battle between good and evil. The Dead Sea Scrolls were found here. Todd Bolen/BiblePlaces.com.

WOMEN IN PALESTINIAN JUDAISM

Discovering the "realities of women's lives" in first-century Palestine is challenging largely because much of the historical data about first-century Judaism is extrapolated backward to the first century from later second to fourth-century rabbinic sources. Even so, recent archaeological excavations and the discovery of the Dead Sea Scrolls have been helpful in providing a broader picture of first-century Palestinian Judaism than previously available. The following summary portrait is derived from multiple sources.

Galilean Hebrew women such as Mary of Nazareth may have been among the poorest in the world in Jesus's day. As we

10. Elisabeth Schüssler Fiorenza, *In Memory of Her: A Feminist Theological Reconstruction of Christian Origins* (New York: Crossroad, 1983), 142.

have seen, economic policies divested Israelite families of their ancestral lands and impoverished artisan families such as Joseph's as well. Despite significant economic obstacles, agrarian families were remarkably self-sufficient. Village families grew, harvested, processed, and preserved basic foodstuffs such as barley, wheat, olives, olive oil, grapes, wine, legumes, and vegetables. Goats and the occasional cow provided dairy products, sheep were sheared, and flax harvested to spin cloth for clothing. These diverse products could also be sold or bartered at market to obtain goods such as metal for tools that could not be produced in the village. Inexorable taxation, even in the face of a bad harvest, meant that those who grew and harvested crops for the empire could be left on the brink of destitution.

Since subsistence cultures relied on extended family units working together in close quarters, women were not segregated and secluded as was typical in higher status families.[11] In such a context, it is probable that low-status rural women had greater freedom to move about in public than did their higher status sisters.[12] Because everyone's work was needed to survive, Johnson finds that agrarian women "exercised control over critical aspects of household life and may well have achieved a more relatively balanced form of social unity with men in household settings."[13]

An agrarian Jewish mother probably exercised parental authority with her husband, including arranging marriages, especially for daughters who "were valuable in view of the array of tasks facing female members of a household."[14] Hebrew women were not allowed to divorce their husbands but could be divorced for anything from burning the dinner (Rabbi Hillel) to adultery (Rabbi Shammai).[15] In a culture in which a woman's survival often depended on the patriarchal household, divorce could be disastrous. Seen in this light, Jesus's proscription of divorce is protective of women. Most Hebrew

11. Johnson, *Truly Our Sister*, 192.

12. Kathleen E. Corley, *Private Women, Public Meals: Social Conflict in the Synoptic Tradition* (Peabody, MA: Hendrickson, 1993).

13. Johnson, *Truly Our Sister*, 203.

14. Ibid.

15. Ben Witherington III, *Women in the Ministry of Jesus* (New York: Cambridge University Press, 1984), 3. The comment by Rabbi Hillel is widely quoted, however divorce over a burnt meal was not widespread (Carolyn Osiek, personal correspondence with author, October 22, 2015).

women had minimal property rights. Theoretically women could inherit land, but in practice male heirs had precedence. Even if a woman did inherit property, her husband had the right to its use and its fruits.[16] As was common in all first-century patriarchal cultures, Jewish girls were betrothed at a very young age.

There is no evidence that first-century Jewish women led synagogue worship in Palestine. Ross Kraemer's seminal study of epigraphic, papyrological, and archaeological sources, however, found that in the second century, both women and men in the Jewish diaspora (Jews who had their homes outside of Israel) held synagogal office. Whether a woman should be educated in the Torah was widely debated.[17] Women were not normally accepted as witnesses in Jewish law.[18] Jesus's behavior toward women, even viewed through the androcentric lens of the Gospel texts, is significant. Jesus welcomed women into his closest discipleship:

> Soon afterwards he went on through cities and villages, proclaiming and bringing the good news of the kingdom of God. The twelve were with him, as well as some women who had been cured of evil spirits and infirmities: Mary, called Magdalene, from whom seven demons had gone out, and Joanna, the wife of Herod's steward Chuza, and Susanna, and many others, who provided for them out of their resources. (Luke 8:1–3)

Women were rarely named in ancient texts unless they had social prominence. The clear implication of the Lukan text is that Jewish women of means supported Jesus's Galilean mission.[19] In Luke's portrayal, Mary Magdalene, Joanna, Susanna, "and many others" are the first in a long line of female patrons who supported the Christian mission financially and helped it prosper. Matthew, Mark, and John also name women disciples from Galilee as members of Jesus's itinerant group of disciples.[20] All four Gospels attest that Jesus welcomed

16. Witherington, *Women in the Ministry*, 1–6.

17. Ross Shepard Kraemer, "Jewish Women and Women's Judaism(s) at the Beginning of Christianity," in *Women and Christian Origins*, ed. Ross Shepard Kraemer and Mary Rose D'Angelo (New York: Oxford University Press, 1999), 71.

18. Witherington, *Women in the Ministry*, 6–10.

19. Mary R. Thompson, *Mary of Magdala: Apostle and Leader* (Mahwah, NJ: Paulist, 1995), 50.

20. Mark 15:40–41, 47; 16:1; Matt 27:55–56, 61; 28:1; John 19:25; 20:1–2. For a comprehensive review of the women who accompanied Jesus through cross, burial, death, and resurrec-

women as well as men into his discipleship to learn about the imminent "reign of God."[21]

Since it was not customary for men to speak to women outside their kinship circles, much less travel around the countryside with them, Jesus's behavior would have been shocking to elite Greco-Roman and Jewish sensibilities.[22] This being said, social expectations for rural women were probably quite different from expectations for urban women in high status households. Jesus's inclusion of married and single women in his travelling band and his special compassion for widows and the landless poor testified to his fidelity to Israel's God who throughout history upheld the lowly. Throughout the Gospels, we see Jesus challenge deep-seated patriarchal assumptions: that only women bear the burden of sexual sin (John 8:1–11), that Samaritan and Canaanite women are to be shunned and discounted (John 4; Matt 15:21–28), and that prodigal sons are to be disowned (Luke 15:11–32). Instead, men are challenged to own their complicity in adultery; the Samaritan woman becomes a missionary, bringing her whole town to belief in Jesus; the Canaanite woman's fierce love for her daughter succeeds in broadening Jesus's own understanding of those to whom the good news is sent; and the wayward son is welcomed home with a huge party thrown by a prodigal father.

Women's call to discipleship is most evident in the resurrection accounts, for it is upon the testimony of women that the proclamation of the resurrection depends. All four Gospels show Mary of Magdala leading the other women disciples in accompanying Jesus to his death, anointing and burying his body, viewing the empty tomb, and experiencing his risen presence. That the message of the resurrection was first given to women is regarded by scholars as significant evidence for the historicity of the resurrection accounts.

tion, see Raymond E. Brown, *The Death of the Messiah*, vol. 2 (New York: Doubleday, 1994), 1013–25.

21. John P. Meier, *A Marginal Jew: Rethinking the Historical Jesus*, vol. 3, *Companions and Competitors* (New York: Doubleday, 2001), 73–80.

22. Ibid., 76. Meier argues convincingly against the opinion that Luke introduces wealthy women in anticipation of later female patrons who supported nascent Christianity: "Granted Luke's desire to present Christianity as a 'respectable' religion that does not threaten the Roman order, it hardly seems likely that he would have created the potentially shocking picture of women, some married, traveling around Galilee with Jesus and his twelve male disciples without benefit of husbands."

Had overzealous disciples fabricated these texts, it is unlikely they would have included female testimony in a society that did not accept women as legal witnesses.

Figure 1.2. Excavation of an early first-century synagogue in Magdala with ornamented square table in center. A coin minted in Tiberias in 29 CE was found here, attesting that the synagogue dates to the time of Mary of Magdala and Jesus. It is likely that both prayed at this site. Todd Bolen/BiblePlaces.com.

Literary and social conventions in antiquity dictated that if women were mentioned (a very rare occurrence), they were nearly always named by their relationship to the patriarchal household, for example: "Joanna the wife of Herod's steward Chuza" (Luke 8:3). Atypically, Mary of Magdala was named according to the town she was from (Migdal), not by her relationship to a man (see figure 1.2). The scholarly consensus is that she was an independent woman of means not bound to a patriarchal household. After the events of the resurrection, we hear very little about Mary of Magdala except in extracanonical writings.[23] By the sixth century, Gregory the Great, without any scriptural basis, portrayed her as a prostitute. A common

23. See, for example, the Gospel of Mary, Gospel of Thomas, Pistis Sophia, Gospel of Philip, Dialogue of the Savior, and Sophia of Jesus Christ.

misreading of Luke's gospel attributes the "seven demons" that Jesus expelled from Mary Magdalene to grave sinfulness (Luke 8:2). But Thompson explains, "For people in the first century of the Christian era, the expression, 'from whom seven devils had gone out,' would have meant that she had been cured of a serious illness. The number seven would accentuate the seriousness of her condition or possibly its recurrent nature."[24] Gregory's powerful sermon on repentance meant that henceforth in the West Mary Magdalene would be remembered as a forgiven prostitute, rather than the influential woman of faith who underwrote Jesus's Galilean mission and first proclaimed the resurrection.[25] The Eastern church never viewed her as a prostitute but honored her throughout history as the "Apostle to the Apostles." Since one important criterion for "apostolic authority" in the early church was whether a person was an eyewitness to Jesus's life and resurrection, a gender gap arose when early male leaders designated requirements for leadership. Ann Graham Brock supplies convincing evidence of tension over women's apostolic leadership in early Christian texts.[26] Brock grapples with the question of how and why Mary Magdalene's apostolic authority was suppressed. In the Gospel of Luke, eyewitnesses to Jesus's death and resurrection are portrayed quite differently than in Matthew, Mark, and John. Matthew, Mark, and John show Mary Magdalene and the other women arriving first at the empty tomb. Only in Luke does Peter arrive first. The examples in table 1.1 indicate that the author of Luke had an agenda, and that agenda was to raise up the authority and

24. Thompson, *Mary of Magdala*, 14. Thompson cites George A. Buttrick, *Interpreter's Dictionary of the Bible* (Nashville: Abingdon, 1962), 288.

25. According to Thompson, scholars suggest that the interpretation of Luke 8:2 as immoral behavior can be traced to the early fourth-century writings of Ephraim the Syrian (306–73). Ephraim apparently conflated Mary of Magdala with Luke's anointing by Mary of Bethany: "Mary by the oil showed forth the mystery of his mortality who by his teaching mortified the concupiscence of her flesh." Philip Schaff and Henry Wace, eds., *Nicene and Post-Nicene Fathers of the Christian Church*, vol. 13 (Grand Rapids: Eerdmans, 1983), 326–27, as cited by Thompson, *Mary of Magdala*, 14.

26. Ann Graham Brock, *Mary Magdalene, The First Apostle: The Struggle for Authority* (Cambridge, MA: Harvard Divinity School Press, 2003), chs. 2 and 9. Other canonical texts studied by Brock include Matthew, Mark, and John. Extracanonical texts include Gospel of Peter, Gospel of Thomas, Gospel of Mary, Pistis Sophia, Gospel of Philip, Acts of Paul, Dialogue of the Savior, and Sophia of Jesus Christ. She also examines Theodoret and selected Syriac and Coptic texts.

prominence of Peter, at least in part by diminishing the apostolic witness of Mary Magdalene and the other women disciples.[27]

Table 1.1. Citations from Luke that Enhance the Role of Peter and Diminish Those of Mary of Magdala and the Other Women Disciples[28]

1. Matthew, Mark, and John report that Christ first appeared to Mary Magdala.

2. Only Luke shapes his material to claim that the risen Lord first appeared exclusively to Peter (Luke 24:34).

3. Luke omits the anointing at Bethany that in the other three Gospels occurs just before Jesus's passion. Instead, he places it earlier in Jesus's Galilean ministry (Luke 7:36–50). This place-ment diminishes the anointing woman's prophetic initiative evoking Samuel's anointing of David as king. Only Luke iden-tifies the woman as a penitent sinner.

4. While the other gospels describe the male disciples as fleeing, in Luke they are subtly woven into the crucifixion scene: "But all his acquaintances, including the women who had followed him from Galilee, stood at a distance, watching these events" (Luke 23:49).

5. Luke alone omits the resurrection appearance and commission-ing to Mary of Magdala and the other women to go and tell the good news of the resurrection to the other disciples.

6. Luke regularly omits or mitigates unflattering traditions about Peter. In Mark and Matthew Jesus tells Peter to "get behind me Satan" after Peter rebukes him (Mark 8:33; Matt 16:23). Luke omits both Peter's rebuke and Jesus's harsh reply (Luke 9:22–23). Luke also omits Peter's promise never to deny Jesus "even though they all fall away." (Matt 26:33; Mark 14:29).

27. Brock, *Mary Magdalene*, ch. 5.
28. Ann Graham Brock, *Mary Magdalene, the First Apostle: The Struggle for Authority* (Cam-bridge, MA: Harvard University Press, 2003), ch. 5.

But why? It can only be that eyewitnesses to the resurrection had a strong claim to exercise leadership and authority in the early church. It would follow that Jesus's women disciples also had a claim to exercise leadership, and this was a problem for at least some early Christians. According to Elaine Pagels: "From Luke through Irenaeus, respect for the apostles as eyewitnesses for Jesus and the resurrection translates into respect for the bishops and presbyters, whom ecclesiastical Christians consider the apostles' only legitimate heirs."[29] Luke's writings and subsequent early texts examined by Brock reveal that the apostleship and leadership role of Mary Magdalene was suppressed while the person and leadership of Peter were intentionally brought to the fore in order to establish, without competition, one body of leadership within the early church.[30]

The canonical gospels show only two individuals receiving an exclusive resurrection experience of the risen Christ: Mary Magdalene (John 20:13–17) and Simon Peter (Luke 24:34). Such an experience had great significance for one's status as an "apostle." Paul, writing between 40 and 60 CE, uses the word inclusively to describe his own mission to the gentiles as well as that of other missionaries. In Romans 16:7, he calls Andronicus and Junia (a married missionary couple) "prominent among the apostles." Writing twenty years later, after the fall of Jerusalem (80–85), Luke names three requirements for replacing the apostle Judas:

> Therefore it is necessary to choose one of the men who have been with us the whole time the Lord Jesus was living among us, beginning from John's baptism to the time when Jesus was taken up from us. For one of these must become a witness with us of his resurrection. (Acts 1:21–22).

Luke's new criteria guarantee that the individual title of apostle will die out as the original witnesses die and that prominent leaders such as Paul, Mary Magdalene, James of Jerusalem, and Junia and Andronicus no longer qualify as "apostles." Ironically, third- and fourth-century churchmen will claim the authority of the twelve apostles in imposing new church orders excluding women from leadership. According to Brock, "An examination of early Christian texts reveals

29. Ibid., 141.
30. Ibid., ch. 9.

that Mary Magdalene's prominence had to be dealt with, her position either as an apostle or an eyewitness of the resurrection is often altered, weakened, or eradicated from the narrative altogether."[31]

Biblical scholars have long noted that the writer of Luke and Acts is concerned with presenting the Christian message as compatible with values and mores of the aristocratic class in the Greco-Roman world. Accusations by the second-century critic Celsus denigrating Christianity as a religion of women, children, and slaves were probably already circulating when Luke wrote his gospel. Luke's material seems to have been carefully shaped to respond to these critiques.[32] While the authority of Mary Magdalene and the other women witnesses was discounted in the early church, it was impossible to extinguish their memory. The other canonical gospels acknowledge their primary role in events surrounding the resurrection, and male church leaders from Hippolytus in the third century and Gregory of Antioch in the sixth acknowledged her apostolic witness. Hippolytus refers to Mary as "the Apostle to the Apostles" and Gregory the Great describes Jesus as saying to the women at the tomb: "Be the first teachers to the teachers. So that Peter who denied me learns that I can also choose women as apostles."[33]

Christianity expanded rapidly outside Palestine and soon flourished in Hellenist cultures surrounding the Mediterranean. This expansion was due in no small part to the influence of prominent women patrons such as Phoebe, Prisca (Rom 16:1–5), and Lydia (Acts 16:11–15, 40). Within fifteen years of Jesus's death, nascent Christian communities had already formed in urban areas including Rome, Corinth in Greece, Paphos in Cyprus, Alexandria in Egypt, Antioch in Syria, and Ephesus and Antioch in Pisidia (both in Asia Minor —modern Turkey).[34]

---

31. Ibid., 141.

32. Ross Shepherd Kraemer, *Her Share of the Blessings: Women's Religions among Pagans, Jews, and Christians in the Greco-Roman World* (Oxford: Oxford University Press, 1992), 128–29.

33. Brock, *Mary Magdalene*, 15.

34. Sheila E. McGinn, *The Jesus Movement and the World of the Early Church* (Winona, MN: Anselm Academic, 2014), 118.

GRECO-ROMAN CULTURE AND THE FINANCIAL
INDEPENDENCE OF WOMEN

To understand the sociocultural complexities surrounding Christian women who sought to exercise authority, it is important to know something about the world into which Christianity spread. Rome's legendary roads, built so that the military could quickly quell uprisings or conquer new territories, also permitted rapid dissemination of Roman cultural values. These same roads would also permit travelling evangelists to preach Christianity throughout the empire. After the senate granted Octavian the quasi-religious title "Augustus" in 27 BCE, the once proud republic would gradually be replaced with monarchical rule by emperors deemed to be godlike. Henceforth, cities would vie with one another for permission to build temples for imperial religious rites.[35] Offering sacrifice on behalf of the emperor was understood to be everyone's patriotic duty, for upon such sacrifices the well-being of the empire was thought to rest. This cultural expectation would bring sporadic, localized persecution to followers of the Jesus movement for four centuries.[36] As we shall see, the threat of such persecution is one factor that impacted women's religious leadership in the early churches.

In antiquity, all women, except vestal virgins and priestesses of various cults, were expected to marry and bear children to continue the family line and secure its economic well-being. Girls usually entered an arranged marriage in their midteens with a husband commonly ten to twenty years older. Only freeborn Roman citizens could legally marry. Elite women were discouraged from marrying below their status, although such unions are commonly attested in funerary inscriptions.[37] Once married, an elite woman became a respectable matron (*matrona*) and was expected to run the household, spin wool or flax for clothing, oversee household slaves, and manage her husband's estate. Many matrons were active in Roman politics,

---

35. Lynn R. LiDonnici, "Women's Religions and Religious Lives in the Greco-Roman City," in Kraemer and D'Angelo, *Women and Christian Origins*, 85.

36. Joseph Kelly, *The World of the Early Christians* (Collegeville, MN: Liturgical Press, 1997), 186.

37. Osiek and MacDonald, *A Woman's Place*, 101.

albeit usually behind the scenes. Roman aristocratic women also engaged in religious and philosophical pursuits. Even though all women were expected to be subordinate to men, aristocratic women had access to considerable wealth. They used it to influence political issues as well as to exercise public patronage by building public theaters, sports arenas, fountains, and temples.

Freeborn women lived in diverse economic circumstances. Some were merchants, small property owners, and tradespeople. Others could be innkeepers, weavers, shoemakers, or prostitutes. Many probably ran small businesses with their husbands in the cities or helped manage small farms in the countryside. After manumission, freedwomen led lives similar to freeborn women. They started small businesses and worked in the trades, including prostitution, which was one way of earning their freedom. Like freedmen, freedwomen still had client obligations to their former owners, who now became their patrons. Freed and enslaved women and men did enter into stable unions even though they were not permitted to legally marry. Within the Jewish community, such marriages would have been considered licit, regardless of their social status.[38] These unions would also be recognized within Christian communities, although women embracing the continent lifestyle praised by Paul would eventually have a profound impact on church polity.[39]

As may now be obvious, marriage laws were designed to assure that Roman wealth and property remained as far as possible in aristocratic control. Since *patria potestas* (father rule) was the ideological norm regardless of social status, women, children, and slaves were subject to male heads of household. There were two kinds of marriage contracts *cum manu* and *sine manu*. In *cum manu* contracts, the wife was legally under her husband's control and could not own property.[40] Everything acquired before her marriage was transferred to her husband, although she retained some rights to her dowry in case of divorce. In *sine manu* contracts, the woman and her property remained legally under the control of her father (or a

---

38. Kraemer, *Her Share*, 137.

39. Osiek and MacDonald, *A Woman's Place*, 23.

40. Jane F. Gardner, *Women in Roman Law and Society* (Bloomington: Indiana University Press, 1991), 11.

family appointed guardian), though any offspring belonged legally to the husband. In this arrangement, a woman could inherit from her father's estate when he died, giving her increasing control over her own affairs.[41] By the Christian period, *sine manu* marriages were the norm. Fathers preferred them because they made it easier to keep the family fortune intact. Daughters chose them to retain their property and, since fathers normally died before husbands, to hasten the day when they might independently manage their own affairs.

By the first century BCE, elite Roman women had the right to initiate divorce, own property, and inherit land and money. Divorce was frequent among the elite classes, often owing to social maneuvering for greater status. Still, the ever-present double standard existed. Male infidelity with concubines, high-class prostitutes, and slaves was commonplace, although some stoic philosophers did argue, to little avail, that men should be faithful to their wives.[42] Female infidelity, on the other hand, was, according to Augustan marriage laws, a criminal offense, punishable by divorce, exile, loss of half her dowry, and loss of one third of any remaining property. A convicted adulteress could never again enter into a valid marriage, and her husband was required to divorce her or face stiff legal penalties.[43] The intent of such laws was to assure the legitimacy and aristocratic bloodlines of heirs.

In the late republic and early Christian periods, some elite Roman women began to challenge the double standard by claiming the same sexual freedoms enjoyed by men. Greater financial and social independence also made divorce a viable option for women. The greatest threat to a woman's life was pregnancy and childbirth, and high maternal mortality rates made elite women reluctant to risk pregnancy. A child born in the second century CE had an average life expectancy of less than twenty-five years, and only four of one hundred men, and fewer women, would reach age fifty.[44] To maintain a stable population, each woman would theoretically need to produce

41. Susan Treggiari, *Roman Marriage: Iusti Coniuges from the Time of Cicero to the Time of Ulpian* (Oxford: Clarendon, 1993), 3.

42. The stoic philosopher Musonius Rufus (ca. 20–100 CE) was one, as quoted by Bruce Winter, *Roman Wives, Roman Widows* (Grand Rapids: Eerdmans, 2003), 68–71.

43. Winter, *Roman Wives, Roman Widows*, 42.

44. Bruce W. Frier, "Roman Life Expectancy; Ulpian's Evidence," *Harvard Studies in Classical*

five offspring. Younger men delayed marriage via long betrothals to female children. In this way, they could delay family responsibilities and continue unencumbered sexual liaisons with older Roman matrons.

All of these factors led to a decreased birth rate, especially in the elite populations, and, in Augustus's view, a shameful decline in Roman morality. In 17 BCE, Augustus passed legislation to discourage promiscuous behavior and to provide incentives for bearing children. These laws would change the lives of women, both freeborn and freed, for centuries to come. While freeborn women had the right to inherit, under Roman law they theoretically could not administer property without the legal guardianship of a male relative called a *tutela*. Augustus ruled that freeborn women who gave birth to three children and freedwomen who had borne four children would no longer be required to have a legal guardian in the management of their property. Claudius later abolished the *tutela* completely, "thus essentially doing away with male control of the property of citizen women. This meant that on the death of her father, every such woman became capable of freely administering her own property."[45]

As is often the case, this legislation followed actual practice. In the years before Augustus's legislation, the freeborn elite observed the conventions of male guardianship only loosely. Abolishing it for freedwomen with four children, however, greatly expanded opportunities for nonelites to become financially independent and even prosperous. Freeborn and freedmen also benefitted from the new law because having more children reduced the monies they were required to contribute for public services. Nevertheless, women were affected the most by the new legislation because they were now permitted to manage their own affairs.

Until recently, most interpreters of early Christian texts assumed that women in the Roman world were not active in business or public affairs but concerned themselves only with domestic and child-rearing duties. Classical writings, written by men describing elite

Philology 86 (1982): 213–51, as cited in Peter Brown, *The Body and Society: Men, Women and Sexual Renunciation in Early Christianity* (New York: Columbia University Press, 1988), 6.

45. Carolyn Osiek and David L. Balch, *Families in the New Testament World: Households and House Churches* (Louisville: Westminster John Knox, 1997), 57.

populations, did little to disabuse them of this notion. The Roman historian Dio Cassius depicts Augustus epitomizing the ideal marriage as one in which "a wife is of chaste conduct, domestic, mistress of the house, its good stewardess, a rearer of children."[46] Concerns about population stability led Augustus and his successors to make marriage mandatory for Roman citizens between the ages of twenty and fifty years of age or risk losing inheritance and tax privileges. The widowed and divorced were expected to remarry after brief mourning periods of six months to two years.[47] In Greco-Roman culture, the stability of the patriarchal household, and patriarchal marriage, increasingly came to signify the stability of the body politic.[48] This cultural understanding had a negative impact on female leadership in early Christianity, especially as continence and virginity came to be increasingly valued within the early communities.

The Christian Scriptures provide the best literary evidence available that independent women such as Lydia the purple-dye merchant (Acts 16:14–40), Mary in Jerusalem (Acts 12:12–17), and Nympha of Laodicea (Col 4:15) were heads of their own household without reference to any male relative. In fact, the lives of many, if not most, women in late antiquity did not fit the idealized model painted in classical writings by Greek and Roman men. While these independent women are all but invisible in ancient texts, they are commonly attested in archaeological and epigraphical artifacts. For example, excavations at Pompeii identified two women, Julia Felix and Eumachia, who owned businesses and leased large estates. Eumachia's family business shipped goods in large pottery jars (amphorae), later found by archaeologists as far away as Carthage. Her first-century tomb bears this inscription: "Eumachia, daughter of Lucius, [built this] for herself and her household."[49] Archaeologists identified Julia Felix's large residence through this inscription: "In the property of

---

46. Winter, *Roman Wives Roman Widows*, 53.

47. Gardner, *Women in Roman Law*, 77–78, as cited in Kraemer and D'Angelo, *Women and Christian Origins*, 212.

48. See Virginia Burrus, *Chastity as Autonomy: Women in the Stories of the Apocryphal Acts* (Lewiston, NY: Edwin Mellen, 1987), 94; and Mary Rose D'Angelo, "(Re)Presentations of Women in the Gospel of Matthew and Luke-Acts," in Kraemer and D'Angelo, *Women and Christian Origins*, 188.

49. *Corpus Inscriptionum Latinarum* (*CIL*) 10.8.13, as cited by Osiek and Balch, *Families*, 27.

Julia Felix, daughter of Spurius, to lease: the Venus baths fitted up for the best people, tavern shops and second story rooms."[50] According to Carolyn Osiek and David L. Balch:

> Eumachia and Julia Felix are independent women, whose inscriptions do not defer to any male authority figure, running their businesses, exercising their feminine influence within their own households and in the city. . . . They are specific examples of what is possible for wealthy women in Roman cities, possible for women householders like Prisca with her husband Aquila (1 Cor. 16:19, Rom. 16:3–5), Phoebe (Rom. 16:1–3), and Nympha (Col. 4:15).[51]

Contemporary readers might assume that because they were wealthy businesswomen, Eumachia, Lydia, and Julia Felix would be considered upper-class, but this is not the case. Only legitimate birth into an aristocratic family made one a member of the elite. In our example, only Eumachia qualifies. Julia Felix was the freeborn illegitimate child of an elite father. It is unlikely that Lydia came from an elite family. The quality of purple dye depended upon whether it originated from the rare murex shellfish (most expensive) or from less expensive but plentiful plant sources. The manufacturing of dyed clothing involved the use of urine and was a difficult, smelly process. Elite families would probably avoid such an enterprise.

While neither Julia Felix nor Lydia were among the elite, they were probably of higher status than many freedmen, or even freeborn men from the trades who were their clients.[52] Status could be achieved in a number of ways, including acquisition of greater wealth and through public and personal patronage. No reconstruction of the lives of early Christian women is possible without considering the complex interplay of Greco-Roman cultural constructs such as social location and status, honor and shame, gendered public/private space, and patronage networks. It is to these concepts that we now turn.

---

50. *CIL* 4.1136, as cited by Osiek and Balch, *Families*, 27.
51. Osiek and Balch, *Families*, 28.
52. Ibid., 93.

SOCIAL LOCATION AND STATUS

Romans were obsessed with status. Whether one was a member of the emperor's household, a freeborn craftsperson, or a slave managing her owner's business, status could be more influential than class (except for aristocratic elites).[53] The aristocratic class included military and religious elites of the senatorial and equestrian orders, the emperor and his entourage, and highborn persons from the provinces such as *decurians* (taxation managers) and aristocratic rulers such as the Herodian family in Palestine. All political power was concentrated in this elite group, who accounted for only 3 percent of the population. Aristocrats owned most of the land and divided their time between overseeing work on their rural estates and influencing politics in the city. They were served by a small class of bureaucrats and religious functionaries, "whose positions depended directly on the elites but who profited socially and economically by their status."[54] In the Roman Empire, such functionaries were often slaves and freed persons from aristocratic households, including that of the emperor.

Ninety percent of people in the empire were rural peasants like Jesus of Nazareth and his family. They worked the land and "supported small peasant villages [that] ultimately bore the crushing economic burden of taxation, which forced them to give up the fruit of their labors to support the luxuries, military campaigns, and religious pomp of the urban wealthy."[55] Just 7 percent of the population lived in cities where a merchant class resided to cater to the elites. In Galilee, Sepphoris had eight to ten thousand inhabitants, who were primarily wealthy Jews. They were probably connected to the Herodian client kings who supervised the two main empire-wide priorities: taxation and the *Pax Romana*.[56]

What was the social location and status of early Christians in general, and Christian women in particular? Wayne Meeks's study of eighty Christian names found in Paul's undisputed letters and Acts demonstrates that Christians clustered in urban communities

53. Ibid.
54. Ibid., 37.
55. Ibid.
56. Johnson, *Truly Our Sister*, 154–55.

and were sociologically diverse.[57] Early Christian networks included heads of households, slaves, freeborn persons, slave owners, freed persons, artisans, small-scale traders, the poor, and the financially well off. Meeks believes that while they ranked low in Greco-Roman indicators of prestige—such as birth, citizenship, or membership in Roman class *ordines* (i.e., senatorial, equestrian, etc.)—their actual wealth gave them a certain prestige that resulted in "status inconsistency."[58] In other words, although they had little ability to influence elite-controlled political systems, their financial resources gave them significant influence within their social networks. Particularly noteworthy for our purposes is Ross Kraemer's analysis of the status of women in these first-century communities. Using Meeks's data, Kraemer finds it significant that very few Christian names have paternal identification "in a culture that routinely identifies free person by the names of their fathers."[59] Slaves and freed persons obviously had biological fathers but not legal ones. They were in hierarchical relationships to their masters or, after manumission, with their former owners, who had become their patrons. After pointing to the scant evidence that any of the sixteen named women in Meeks's sample were married,[60] Kraemer theorizes:

> For many of the women and men in our Pauline sample, then, the absence of paternal identification or evidence for spouses may be related to their status as slaves and freedpersons. For the women explicitly

57. Paul's undisputed letters include 1 Thessalonians, 1 Corinthians, 2 Corinthians, Galatians, Philippians, Philemon, and Romans. Fifty percent of scholars do not believe Paul actually wrote 2 Thessalonians and Colossians. Eighty percent do not believe Paul wrote Ephesians, the Pastoral Epistles, 1 Timothy, 2 Timothy, and Titus. The Pastoral Epistles appear to have been written much later by scribes anxious to claim Paul's authority for evolving church policies. Father Felix Just, SJ, supplies a useful reminder: "Judging a particular letter to be pseudepigraphic does not mean that it is any less valuable than the other letters, but only that it was written later by someone other than Paul. All thirteen of the letters attributed to Paul are still considered 'canonical'; all of them are still part of the Holy Bible and foundational for the Christian Church. Distinguishing the letters based on actual authorship, however, allows scholars to see more clearly the development of early Christian theology and practice." See Felix Just, "The Deutero-Pauline Letters," Catholic Resources for Bible, Liturgy, Art, and Theology, February 17, 2012, http://tinyurl.com/yc5x5fce.

58. Wayne Meeks, *The First Urban Christians: The Social World of the Apostle Paul* (New Haven: Yale University Press, 1983), 57, as cited by Kraemer, *Her Share*, 135.

59. Kraemer, *Her Share*, 137.

60. Kraemer cautions that we should not infer that this is an accurate representation of the proportion of women to men in the early communities since women are notoriously underrepresented in historical sources.

identified as householders such as Nympha of Laodicea (Col 4:3), Lydia of Thyatira, residing at Philippi, and Phoebe of Cenchreae, the failure to mention spouses may be more telling, and may point either to their status as widows or to divorce, whether instigated before or after their entrance into a Christian community.[61]

ABOUT SLAVERY

The ancient world took slavery for granted and could not function without it. One became a slave in four ways: by being born to an enslaved woman, by being a member of a conquered people, by being abandoned (exposed) and then claimed by a master, or by selling oneself into slavery to pay off debts. Slaves were private property and had neither legal rights nor honor. Their owners had absolute control over their bodies, including the legal right to torture and kill them. It was a cultural given that the male head of household could and did sleep with whomever he chose. Both female and male slaves were expected to be sexually available to their owners. This was not considered dishonorable because by definition they had no right to free choice and were therefore incapable of honor or dishonor. If a matron had sex with her male slave, however, she could be divorced for adultery, although such liaisons often occurred without consequence.

A female slave was especially vulnerable because she risked pregnancy and the hazards of childbirth. Her baby did not belong to her but to her owner, presuming he or she accepted it. Slave owners could and did expose/abandon babies who would die unless someone claimed them to feed and raise. If the claimed child was female, she was often doomed to life in a brothel so as to enrich her owner after he raised her. There was little attempt to keep a slave mother and her baby together. The baby was handed off to a wet nurse so the mother would more quickly conceive again or, if a prostitute, return to work.[62] Exposed female infants were frequently claimed because their potential offspring would add more slaves to the household. There is evidence from Egyptian sales records of the first two

---

61. Kraemer, *Her Share*, 138.
62. Osiek and MacDonald, *A Woman's Place*, 99–100.

centuries BCE that female slaves of childbearing years brought higher prices than male slaves for this very reason.[63] Citing Philo's account that babies were sometimes raised by "the kindness of strangers,"[64] Osiek and MacDonald believe that members of house churches may have rescued abandoned infants and adopted them as part of the community.[65] Again and again, early Christian leaders write about caring for "the widows and the orphans." In a letter to the emperor Hadrian, a second-century Christian apologist, Aristides, provides a touching picture of how early Christian communities cared for one another:

> Further, if one or other of them have bondmen and bondwomen or children, through love towards them they persuade them to become Christians, and when they have done so, they call them brethren without distinction. . . . Falsehood is not found among them; and they love one another, and from widows they do not turn away their esteem; and they deliver the orphan from him who treats him harshly. . . . And whenever one of their poor passes from the world, each one of them according to his ability gives heed to him and carefully sees to his burial. And if they hear that one of their number is imprisoned or afflicted on account of the name of their Messiah, all of them anxiously minister to his necessity, and if it is possible to redeem him they set him free. And if there is among them any that is poor and needy, and if they have no spare food, they fast two or three days in order to supply to the needy their lack of food.[66]

Jews and Christians also owned slaves and most households had at least one female slave.[67] How slaves were treated depended on the temperament of their owner and their value to the prosperous functioning of the estate. As counterintuitive as it seems, there were some advantages to being a slave. They were given food and clothing, often learned a trade, and could expect to be freed after thirty years if born into the household—earlier if contractually enslaved to pay off a debt. Freed persons were expected to continue providing services to their former master, who automatically became their patron and assumed responsibility for their burial. Some slaves could expect later

---

63. Ibid., 99.
64. Ibid., 66.
65. Ibid.
66. Aristides, *Apology* 15.7–9 (D. M. Kay [Early Christian Writings, http://tinyurl.com/y8w4qy9f]).
67. Corley, *Private Women, Public Meals*, 15.

social advancement if they received their patron's name and citizen-ship rights upon manumission.[68] Slaves who managed the financial affairs of wealthy owners could themselves be patrons to poorer freed or freeborn clients. While legally forbidden to own anything, slaves could control significant financial resources and property set apart for them by the head of household. These resources were used to run businesses that expanded the family's wealth.[69]

There is interesting literary evidence from the first letter of Clement that some first-century Christians in Rome sold themselves into slavery on behalf of the community: "We know that many among ourselves have delivered themselves to bondage, that they might ransom others. Many have sold themselves to slavery, and receiving the price paid for themselves have fed others" (1 Clem. 55.2).[70] Both 1 Clement and Aristides provide evidence that early Roman Christians were both quite poor and highly committed to one another. Peter Lampe believes it exemplifies

> how very successful Christianity was in attaining some solidarity and integration within the lower strata of society. . . . The lower strata in large measure lacked collective consciousness as well as supraregional cohesion. Christianity here provided a socially integrating contribution to society at large, which must not be undervalued.[71]

HONOR/SHAME—PUBLIC/PRIVATE SPACES

In the Greco-Roman world, as in some parts of the world today, a man's honor consisted in defending the male members of his kin-ship group against threats from outsiders. Every public interaction between men of different kinship groups was a battle for honor. Each man was expected to give absolute loyalty and deference to the males who outranked him in the patriarchal family system. A woman's honor in this system consisted solely in guarding her sexual purity: "Because they ultimately have the power that provides legitimate

---

68. Peter Lampe, *From Paul to Valentinus: Christians in Rome in the First Two Centuries* (Minneapolis: Fortress Press, 2003), 85.

69. Osiek and Balch, *Families*, 77.

70. Lampe, *From Paul to Valentinus*, 85.

71. Ibid., 86.

offspring, they must be protected from outsider males and therefore controlled. . . . The surest way for a male to dishonor an individual male or family is to seduce or rape its women, for this demonstrates that the males lack the power to protect their vulnerable members."[72] Honor for women as defined by men, then, depended on sexual propriety and marital and virginal chastity.

A different honor code prevailed, however, when women related exclusively to women. Here, female honor is defined more positively as valuing friendship, honesty, confidence, and industry.[73] Honor and shame for a female slave and/or a freedwoman functioned quite differently. As we have seen in the slave system, safeguards to protect women did not apply because by definition slaves had no honor and could never acquire honor. They existed outside the honor system of Greco-Roman society. Thus, "[the female slave's] honor cannot be violated because it does not exist, though the property rights of her owner over her can be infringed upon in the case of sexual violation, injury, or death by another who does not hold such property rights. No legal recognition is granted to the sexual privacy of the female slave."[74]

Many women born into slavery eventually earned enough money to purchase their freedom. Since freedwomen were once sexually available, their public respectability would be forever tarnished even though many acquired significant status as wealthy businesswomen and patrons. While freed persons tended to mimic elite values and practices, freedwomen were not held to the same standard as matrons. This was due in part to a tendency to stereotype them as sexually promiscuous. Some freedwomen had earned their freedom by prostitution and then continued as brothel madams or courtesans after manumission.[75] Numerous freedwomen eventually married their former master or became his concubine. Kathleen E. Corley believes freedwomen "probably did exercise more freedom of movement in

---

72. Osiek and Balch, *Families*, 39.

73. Ibid., 40.

74. Osiek and MacDonald, *A Woman's Place*, 97.

75. Corley, *Private Women, Public Meals*, 13. Corley cites many experts including R. H. Barrow, *Slavery and the Roman Empire* (New York: Barnes & Noble, 1928); and Orlando Patterson, *Slavery and Social Death: A Comparative Study* (Cambridge, MA: Harvard University Press, 1982). See her excellent book for comprehensive treatment.

public places, their former slave status affording them a certain level of freedom."[76]

Another important expectation affecting women in Greco-Roman culture was the notion of gendered public and private spaces. The first-century Jewish philosopher Philo describes this elite male ideal:

> Marketplaces and council-halls and law-courts and gatherings and meetings where a large number of people are assembled, and open-air life with full scope for discussion and action—all these are suitable to men both in war and peace. The women are best suited to the indoor life which never strays from the house, within which the middle door is taken by the maidens as their boundary, and the out door by those who have reached full womanhood.[77]

Philo's description of the mostly Eastern Mediterranean practice of confining elite women away from public view has been described as "pretty much a male fantasy" at the time it was written.[78] Romans, on the other hand, prided themselves on their more open practices. Around 35 BCE, the Roman biographer Cornelius Nepos writes:

> Many actions are seemly according to our code, which the Greeks look upon as shameful. For instance what Roman would blush to take his wife to a dinner party? What matron does not frequent the front rooms of her dwelling and show herself in public? But it is very different in Greece; for there a woman is not admitted to a dinner party unless relatives only are present, and she keeps to the more retired part of the house called "the woman's apartment," to which no man has access who is not near of kin.[79]

Though defined differently in different locales, identification of men with the public arena and women with the private or domestic domain was widespread throughout the empire.[80]

Dichotomies of public/private space could also be interpreted differently depending on social class. Freedwomen and slaves commonly engaged in public business. Another custom from antiquity

---

76. Corley, *Private Women, Public Meals*, 13.

77. Philo, *Spec.* 3.169 (Colson, LCL), as cited by Osiek and Balch, *Families*, 43.

78. Osiek and MacDonald, *A Woman's Place*, 8.

79. Cornelius Nepos, *praef.* 6–7 (Rolfe, LCL), cited by Corley, *Private Women, Public Meals*, 29.

80. Osiek and Balch, *Families*, 44.

arising from the public/private–honor/shame dichotomies is that respectable women did not leave the household unescorted. While women in classical Greek and Roman cultural milieus customarily wore veils in public, by the mid-first century this practice was less prevalent in the western empire.[81] In portraiture, however, women are frequently depicted lightly veiled so as to evoke an aura of respectability. Strict observance of these public/private–honor/shame norms meant that a respectable woman's name would not be spoken in public lest she appear to be beyond male control. This may be one explanation for the scarcity of named women in ancient texts. If a woman had to be named in public, she was usually described according to her relationship with her nearest male kin such as father, husband, son, or brother.[82]

Paradoxically, an abundance of archaeological evidence attests that "Roman aristocratic women were patrons of public associations, with their names inscribed and their dedicatory statues on display" in Pompeii, Corinth, and other sites in Asia Minor (modern day Turkey).[83] Publicly naming women was acceptable when it involved building temples or public buildings to benefit city dwellers. Paul's letters are another exception. They directly name female coworkers and benefactors without reference to their marital or family status. This points to their financial independence and, if Kraemer is correct, their nonelite social standing.[84]

CULTURAL NORMS IN NEW TESTAMENT WRITINGS

Awareness of the interplay of cultural norms can be helpful in interpreting early Christian writings. It also sheds light on male tension over female noncompliance with expected behaviors, which eventually led to attempts to suppress women exercising ecclesial authority. As Christianity gained traction among people of higher social standing, some biblical texts, such as 1 Timothy 2:11–15, forbade women

---

81. Osiek and MacDonald, *A Woman's Place*, 8.
82. Ibid.
83. Ibid. See also Osiek and Balch, *Families*, 50–52, for comprehensive listing.
84. For example, in Romans 16 we find Phoebe, Mary, Tryphaena, Tryphosa, Persis, and Julia. Likewise, Phil 4:2 names Euodia and Syntyche without referencing male kin.

to teach men and demanded that they keep silent at worship. The very existence of this command tells us that women must have been teaching men and speaking at Christian worship or there would have been no need for a rebuke. Most biblical scholars believe the Pastoral Epistles (Timothy and Titus) were written not by Paul but by a later author.[85] Far from silencing women, Paul's undisputed letters presume they will speak and prophesy in the assembly (1 Cor 11:5). While it is true that 1 Corinthians 14:33b–36 mimics Timothy's command to be silent, there is strong textual and manuscript evidence that this segment was inserted by a later scribe, perhaps striving to make Paul's genuine letter consistent with 1 Timothy 2:11–15.[86] According to Marcus Borg and John Dominic Crossan:

> The best explanation for 14:33b–36 is that a scribe had just copied out 14:33a, which states, "God is a God not of disorder but of peace," and, considering female teachers an example of such disorder, added this summary of 1 Timothy 2:8–15 in the margin of the manuscript at this point. Thence it was later inserted into the text at different places—after 14:33a or 14:40 by subsequent copyists.[87]

The male author of Timothy expects women to conform to elite norms of public behavior by being silent at community worship. Another possibility is that he did not like or agree with the way women prophets and teachers were interpreting the gospel.

Other biblical texts contemporaneous with the Pastorals (ca. 90–100 CE) have a very different take on female leadership and the message of Jesus. One of these is the Gospel of John. According to Elisabeth Schüssler Fiorenza, "The discipleship and leadership of the Johannine community is inclusive of women and men."[88] The story of the Samaritan woman (John 4) disregards cultural norms about female propriety. Instead, the Johannine author highlights Jesus's choice of the last and least for proclaiming good news. Noting that

---

85. Robert A. Wild, "The Pastoral Letters," in *The New Jerome Biblical Commentary*, ed. Raymond E. Brown, Joseph A. Fitzmyer, and Roland E. Murphy (Englewood Cliffs, NJ: Prentice Hall, 1990), 892.

86. Marcus J. Borg and John Dominic Crossan, *The First Paul: Reclaiming the Radical Visionary Behind the Church's Conservative Icon* (New York: HarperCollins, 2009), 56–57.

87. Ibid., 57.

88. Schüssler Fiorenza, *In Memory of Her*, 326.

exegetes such as Rudolf Bultmann and Raymond Brown agree that John's community had many Samaritan converts, Schüssler Fiorenza writes, "The dramatic dialogue [between the Samaritan woman and Jesus] is probably based on a missionary tradition that ascribed a primary role to a woman missionary in the conversion of the Samaritans."[89] Jerome H. Neyrey's analysis spells out in detail just how unconcerned John's community was about female propriety: "In John 4, all social taboos customarily separating males and females into separate worlds are systematically recognized, but broken and transformed. This upsetting of cultural taboos, moreover, is conscious and intentional; it constitutes an essential part of the author's communication."[90]

What are the social taboos that are "broken and transformed" by the text? First, a solitary Samaritan woman approaches Jesus, a man outside of her kinship circle, at a public well at the wrong time of day. Since village women normally drew water only at dawn and dusk, a solitary woman appearing alone at noon would have been considered improper. Jesus speaks to her and a lengthy conversation ensues. The woman remarks on Jesus's impropriety since Jews disliked and shunned Samaritans and it was considered inappropriate for men to speak to unknown women in public. Second, the narrator portrays the woman as having a checkered marital history. While scholars have offered various historical and symbolic interpretations of this puzzling text, there is as yet no consensus.[91] Yet, since women were rarely permitted to initiate divorce in Palestinian cultures, the woman's former husbands must have either died or divorced her. This would have been disastrous in a culture in which women relied on the patriarchal household for sustenance. Since she is now with someone who is not her husband, she is living as an adulteress or a concubine, perhaps simply to survive.[92] If she were a freedwoman and

89. Ibid., 327.

90. Jerome H. Neyrey, "What's Wrong with This Picture? John 4, Cultural Stereotypes of Women, and Public and Private Speech," in *A Feminist Companion to John*, vol. 1, ed. Amy-Jill Levine with Marianne Blickenstaff (Cleveland, OH: Pilgrim, 2003), 100.

91. Ibid., 98–99.

92. Osiek and MacDonald (*A Woman's Place*, 23) cite evidence that, "on a practical level concubinage sometimes functioned as the equivalent of marriage, was recognized in the law code as a position similar to that of a legal wife, and could be public and honorable—though it could potentially quickly be rendered dishonorable upon the discovery of the woman's adherence to

her partner freeborn, concubinage would have been her only option since legal marriage was not permitted between people of differing social status.[93] Third, when Jesus asks the woman to call her husband, Neyrey says, "[she] went into the village marketplace where all the men are gathered. The narrative does not say 'marketplace,' but from our knowledge of that culture, we would be culturally accurate in imagining males gathered together in an open-air space, such as a marketplace."[94]

The message is clear. The Samaritan woman is as far removed from the proper *matrona* ideal of Greco-Roman culture as anyone could imagine. And yet, she exhibits significant theological acumen, sparring with Jesus over where true worship is found. Unlike the respected rabbi Nicodemus, who meets secretly with Jesus at night and departs still doubting, the Samaritan woman meets him in broad daylight and departs a true believer. The Johannine author portrays her as the privileged recipient of Jesus's self-revelation as "Messiah" and the great "I Am," hearkening back to Moses and pointing to Jesus's oneness with the divine. On her word, "Many of the Samaritans of that town began to believe in him" (John 4:39). For the Johannine community, the Samaritan woman represents the consummate "outsider" who, after her transformative encounter with Jesus, becomes not only an "insider" but also a leader, publicly proclaiming Jesus the Messiah to both men and women via informal village communication channels. Along the way, the narrative deliberately highlights and then discounts stereotypical female behaviors to which she does not conform. Yet her nonconformity presents no obstacle to her acceptance and subsequent leadership in Jesus's kinship network. For Neyrey,

> Ultimately, [the Samaritan woman] represents inclusivity in the Christian group in a most radical way. The stereotype of gender expectations serves to portray her precisely as the quintessential deviant, the last and least person who would be expected to find favor with God (see 1 Cor.

what was considered a superstition, such as Christianity." See also Beryl Rawson, "Roman Concubinage and Other De Facto Marriages," *Transactions of the American Philological Association* 104 (1974): 288.

93. Given the Palestinian religious context, it seems clear she stood outside the socially acceptable marriage norms of her village however defined.

94. Neyrey, "What's Wrong," 111.

15.8–9). Her status transformation in 4.6–26 is basically that of a person moving from "not in the know" to "in the know" and from outsider to insider. . . . As we note "what's wrong with this picture," the Samaritan woman becomes that much stranger and that much more unlikely a candidate for inclusion. Then how much more extraordinary is she as an example of God's inclusivity and Jesus's reform of social conventions![95]

Recalling that the early church gathered in households and modeled itself after the private institution of the family, Neyrey believes the Johannine author intends that

> the meetings of Jesus and the woman (4.7–26) and the woman and the villagers (4.39–42) should ultimately be seen as the formation of fictive kinship groups, and so they are governed by the customs of the "private," not "public" world.[96]

While the author of John viewed household communities as private kinship networks, the author of 1 Timothy apparently imposes "public space" norms on such gatherings and demands that women be silent. Differing interpretations of public and private ecclesial space led to differing opinions about the propriety of female leadership, which would continue as a source of controversy for centuries to come.

PATRONAGE AND HOUSE CHURCHES IN THE GRECO-ROMAN WORLD

From the first century, we see a repeating pattern of prominent women exercising significant initiative and authority in the growth of Christianity. Women founded and led house-church communities (Lydia, Prisca, Nympha, Mary of Jerusalem, Tabitha); prophesied (Philip's daughters, Corinthian women); taught male evangelists (Prisca); functioned as apostles (Junia, Mary Magdalene), benefactors, and envoys (Phoebe); and probably led communities in Philippi as *episcopoi* and *diakonoi* (Euodia and Syntyche).[97] These women, along

95. Ibid., 124.

96. Ibid., 100.

97. It should be noted that *episcopoi* and *diakonoi* cannot simply be translated as "bishops" and "deacons" as we understand these church offices today. The words do, however, indicate a lead-

with many men, expanded access to the ubiquitous Greco-Roman social networking construct called patronage. Carolyn Osiek and Margaret Y. MacDonald have written extensively on women patrons in late antiquity.[98] Excavations of statuary at the ancient Roman town Herculaneum reveal that 40 percent of the dedicatory statues are of women. These were erected alongside statues honoring men without any discernible gender pattern.[99]

> In the Roman social system, as distinct from the older Greek ways, status took precedence over gender as a marker of prestige and power. A person of higher social status and access to power could function as a mediator and dispenser of favor regardless of sex, with the same expectations of reciprocity in terms of honor, praise, and loyalty on the part of clients.[100]

With many other scholars, Osiek and MacDonald understand patronage as foundational to Greco-Roman society and an important factor in the growth of Christianity. "The model of social networks based on informal and asymmetrical relationships for the exchange of goods and resources is the social reality underlying the relationships that created the early Christian communities."[101] In this system, honor accrues to a patron such as Phoebe, Lydia, or Nympha who provided hospitality, goods, and services to clients of lower social status, including many early Christians, perhaps even Paul himself.[102] In such a relationship, "the one who received had to recognize subordination. With honor came the expectation of authority. There is no

ership function of some kind. It may be more accurate to consider them overseers and envoys of their communities. Here are biblical citations for the women listed: Lydia (Acts 16:14–40), Prisca (Rom 16:3–5, and others), Nympha (Col 4:15), Mary of Jerusalem (Acts 12:12), Phoebe (Rom 16:1–2), Euodia and Syntyche (Phil 4:2–3), Mary of Magdala (John 20:1–18, and others), Junia (Rom 16:7).

98. For a comprehensive treatment of women's patronage in the Roman world, including names of both elite and nonelite (freedwomen) patrons, see Osiek and MacDonald, *A Woman's Place*, 199–203.

99. Ibid., 209.

100. Ibid.

101. Ibid., 210.

102. It is conceivable that Paul received personal patronage from members of the church at Philippi such as Lydia, Euodia, or Syntyche. Paul writes: "You Philippians indeed know that in the early days of the gospel, when I left Macedonia, no church shared with me in the matter of giving and receiving, except you alone. For even when I was in Thessalonica, you sent me help for my needs more than once" (Phil 4:15–16). However, most female patrons such as Phoebe and Prisca exercised a type of public patronage on behalf of the house churches.

evidence that in ordinary patronage relationships this was any different for women than for men."[103]

By the fourth century, patronal power would be absorbed into the hands of the bishop, yet "in early Christianity there was little difference between the patronage of men and women, but the patronage function was an essential ingredient in the life of house churches."[104] As we have seen, house churches were frequently located in the homes of women with status. Through the house church, early Christians gained access to social networks that brought them into contact with people from diverse social classes. When a female head of household, perhaps a wealthy widow or freed woman, converted to Christianity, Christian evangelists such as Prisca or Paul gained access not only to her domestic household but also to her patronage network. This meant that her slaves, freed persons, children, relatives, and patronal clients would often convert as well. Thus, when Paul converted Lydia, he automatically gained entry to a broad swath of social relationships and a potentially wide audience. Harry O. Maier summarizes:

> When New Testament authors send greetings, such as the salutation to Nympha "and the church at her house" (Col 4:15), to Prisca and Aquila and "the church in their house" (Rom 16:5) or from "Gaius, host to me and the whole church" (Rom 16:8) it is this hierarchically ordered social world of the household that we are to imagine.[105]

From these domestic communities, new Christians, especially Christian women, evangelized slaves, freed persons, stewards, and clients in other households. Thanks to this informal grassroots network, over the next three centuries Christianity spread rapidly, albeit not without resistance, throughout the Roman Empire. Of particular interest to this study is that many ancient churches and catacombs in Rome began as private house churches and cemeteries owned by women patrons. The catacombs of Priscilla, Domitilla, Commodilla, Lucina, and Balbina are named for women who provided

103. Ibid., 219.
104. Ibid.
105. Harry O. Maier, "Heresy, Households, and the Disciplining of Diversity," in *Late Ancient Christianity*, ed. Virginia Burrus (Minneapolis: Fortress Press, 2005), 215.

burial space for Christians who had no other final resting place. Other women's names associated with the catacombs are Thecla, Bassilla, Agnes, and Felicitas.[106] Peter Lampe lists twenty pre-Constantinian titular churches in Rome. Twelve are named for women.[107] Even though the origins of titular churches are now traceable only via local legend, Lampe finds convincing legal support for private ownership:

> The Christian use of the term "tituli" is often seen to originate in the pre-Constantine period when Christian communities assembled in private homes. . . . "Titulus" was a concept of property rights and indicated the legal basis for the ownership of material goods. . . . It fits this understanding of the term that the original names of the "tituli" were names not of saints but of private persons who had founded these title churches.[108]

There is good reason to surmise that over half of Rome's early house churches were founded and hosted by female patrons.

MORE ABOUT WOMEN HEADS OF HOUSE CHURCHES

What were house churches like? Much depended on whether the household was owned by a prosperous purple-dye merchant such as Lydia or rented by modest craftspeople such as the tentmakers Prisca and Aquila. Lydia must have lived in a relatively large dwelling, perhaps a *domus*, to accommodate her own household, Paul and Silas, and "the brothers and sisters who gathered there" (Acts 16). A *domus* was a freestanding building. It would have included one or more dining areas, called a *triclinium*, that opened onto an atrium or, in larger homes, a columned (peristyle) courtyard. Here, a much larger Christian group, perhaps as many as two hundred, could share in the eucharistic meal, reflect on Scripture, and listen to teachings from

---

106. Carolyn Osiek, "Roman and Christian Burial," in *Commemorating the Dead: Texts and Artifacts in Context; Studies of Roman, Jewish, and Christian Burials*, ed. Laurie Brink and Deborah Green (New York: de Gruyter, 2008), 255.

107. Lampe, *From Paul to Valentinus*, 360–61. In the following list by Lampe, the names in parentheses are post-fourth century: Aemilianae (SS. Quaturo Coronatorum), Anastasiae, Caeciliae, Crescentianae (S. Sixti via Appia [?]), Fasciolae (SS. Nerei et Achilei), Gai (S. Susannae), Lucinae (S. Laurentii in Lucina), Praxidis, Priscae, Pudentis (S. Pudentianae), Sabinae, Tigridae (S. Balbinae).

108. Ibid., 362.

Paul and/or to prophetic words from Euodia and Syntyche, the two prominent women leaders at Philippi that Paul calls his "coworkers" (Phil 4:2).[109] Most early house-church gatherings were probably much smaller, perhaps similar to those hosted by Prisca and Aquila. In Romans 16:3–5, Paul writes: "My greetings to Prisca and Aquila, my coworkers in Christ Jesus, who risked death to save my life. I am not the only one to owe them a debt of gratitude; all the churches among the Gentiles do as well. My greetings also to the church that meets at their house."

Prisca and Aquila were financially independent tentmakers who were deeply involved in the first-century expansion of the Jesus movement. They founded and directed house-church communities in three of the most important centers of early Christianity: Corinth, Ephesus, and Rome. They arrived in Corinth around 42 CE after the emperor Claudius expelled some Jewish Christ believers from Rome, probably owing to opposition from a prominent local synagogue that Claudius also closed. When Paul arrived in Corinth some nine years later, the couple's tent-making business was sufficiently established that they could offer Paul, who was also a tentmaker, both lodging and steady work. Even though Acts portrays Paul as founding most of the early communities in Greece and Asia Minor, Prisca and Aquila had evangelized many Corinthian converts before he arrived. They would do the same in Ephesus.[110]

The tent-making trade required more manual dexterity than brute strength, permitting time for conversation in a quiet atmosphere. House churches such as Prisca's provided a stable base of operations for evangelizing, worship, preaching, and eucharistic table sharing. Their home was probably a typical two-story apartment (*insula*), containing a lower-level workshop with a ladder connecting to the

---

109. Osiek and Balch speculate that as many as 180–500 people could have been accommodated in a large *domus* with a peristyle, although these are likely to have been gatherings of all the smaller churches in one city. They caution: "It is unwise to set a hard upper limit of 30–40 for the number of Christians who might celebrate the Lord's Supper in a Roman *triclinium* plus peristyle or in open gardens." Osiek and Balch, *Families*, 202–3.

110. Jerome Murphy-O'Connor, "Prisca and Aquila: Traveling Tentmakers and Church Builders," *Bible Review* 8, no. 6 (December 1992): 40–51, 62.

upper room where the family ate and slept. Jerome Murphy-O'Connor describes an early Christian gathering:[111]

> Such was the room in which Christians gathered with Prisca and Aquila to celebrate the Lord's Supper (1 Cor 11:17–34). It was not luxurious, but it was clean, and the leather and canvas stacked against the walls served as improvised couches. Others sat on the benches or stools. Children were ranged on the ladder. Depending on the size of the room the assembly numbered between 10 and 20 believers. . . . [In the summer] the shutters could not be left open without attracting the unwelcome attention of the street. The flickering flames of oil lamps intensified the heat of the airless crowded room. Such discomfort, however, mattered little to those whose sharing of bread and wine brought Christ into their midst.[112]

Prisca and Aquila's house church at Corinth was probably small since Paul soon moved to Titius Justus's home after resistance from synagogue leaders required him to find a new location to preach (Acts 18:5). Justus's prime location next to the synagogue was ideal for reaching Godfearers who were attracted to monotheism and Jewish ethical standards but not keen on circumcision.

Early evangelists like Paul in Corinth and Prisca and Aquila in Rome often ran afoul of synagogue leaders because numerous Godfearers became Christ believers. All told, Prisca and Aquila are named six times in the New Testament. Only twice is Aquila named first, once in the form of "Aquila and Priscilla" (Acts 18:2) and once as "Aquila and Prisca" (1 Cor 16:19). Priscilla is the diminutive of Prisca and is used consistently by the Lukan author of Acts. Paul's letters, on the other hand, always use the adult form that Murphy-O'Connor believes may reflect a more favorable attitude toward women. In the remaining four New Testament references, Prisca is named first, which is highly unusual. Since women were rarely named in ancient texts, let alone named before their husbands, Prisca is thought to have been the more important of the two. Since Acts 18:3 identifies her as a tentmaker who worked manually side by side with her husband, she does not meet secular criteria for prominence, having neither greater social status nor independent wealth. The only

111. Ibid., 49.
112. Ibid., 50.

remaining explanation is that she was considered more important because of her work in the church. "The public acknowledgement of Prisca's prominent role in the church, implicit in the reversal of the secular form of naming the husband before his wife underlines how radically egalitarian the Pauline communities were."[113]

This "radically egalitarian" quality is also seen in Romans 16:3 and 1 Corinthians 16:19 where Paul in both instances sends greetings to Prisca and Aquila "and the church at *their* house" (italics mine). In this patriarchal society, the house of a married couple would normally be identified as belonging to the male head of the family. Biblical scholar Florence M. Gillman believes the unusual use of the possessive plural "may hint at something about Paul's view of marriage partners as equals in Christ as well as about his perception of Prisca's importance as a leader in the Church."[114]

Figure 1.3. Late third-century sarcophagus relief of a Roman *symposia*, or meal scene, that is probably similar to early Christian eucharistic meals. On the left, a seated man reads from a scroll. Two female *orans* flank him, either one of whom could be prophesying. A partially clad philosopher is in the center, while diners are seated around a *stibadium* (couch used for dining). RS 1, no. 151. Photo © Vatican Museums, inv. 31526. All rights reserved.

Worship at house-church gatherings in the first century was modeled on the Greco-Roman symposium or banquet. At a typical symposium, the meal came first and entertainment followed. Usual forms of entertainment included the arts (music or theatrical) and/or discourse with philosophers with whom guests interacted in learned and lively discussion (see figure 1.3). Early Christians followed

113. Murphy-O'Connor, "Prisca and Aquila," 40–42.
114. Florence M. Gillman, *Women Who Knew Paul* (Collegeville, MN: Liturgical Press, 1992), 52.

this pattern, with the eucharistic meal being shared first, followed by reflection on Scripture, discussion, and prayer. In later centuries, as Sunday gatherings moved to larger spaces and the eucharistic ritual moved away from an actual meal setting, the order was reversed. A third-century house church at Dura-Europos in Syria shows signs of having been reconfigured from a private dwelling to a building capable of handling a larger assembly.[115]

Figure 1.4. A wall painting of women at the tomb adorns the baptistery of the third-century Christian house church originally located at Dura-Europos. It is either the earliest known painting of the women at the tomb or a depiction of the ten virgins awaiting the bridegroom (Matthew 25). Now housed at the Yale University Art Gallery in New Haven. Public domain. http://tinyurl.com/yanmmye3.

A similar process may have guided the reconfiguration of Rome's titular churches. The Dura-Europos structure is the earliest datable Christian house church.[116] Its baptistery contains paintings of at least

115. Osiek and Balch, *Families*, 211; and Osiek and MacDonald, *A Woman's Place*, 161.

116. Faith Steinberg, "Women and the Dura-Europos Synagogue Paintings," *Religion and the Arts* 10, no. 4 (2006): 471. The Yale University Art Gallery in New Haven houses the Christian baptistery murals and baptismal font. Nearly one hundred thousand artifacts from the Dura site—including items from a synagogue and a Mithraeum—are also at the Yale museum.

nine women: a woman drawing water from a well, the feet of five unknown women, and what is thought to be either a procession of the virgins awaiting the bridegroom or the earliest known painting of the women at the tomb (see figure 1.4).[117] Faith Steinberg suggests: "The prominence of these depictions may reflect the extent to which Christian women participated in the liturgies."[118] Given the preponderance of murals of women at Dura-Europos, it is tempting to speculate that the original dwelling was owned by a female patron, but there is no way of knowing for certain.

When worshipping at a house church, the head of the household, such as Prisca, Aquila, Lydia, Tabitha, or Titius Justus, would normally preside at the meal and offer the blessing over cup and bread. According to the Didache, a second-century liturgical manual, if an itinerant prophet or apostle were present, he or she would "conduct the sacred meal and Eucharistic thanksgiving 'in the Spirit'" as they saw fit.[119] New Testament women prophets who may have led such worship include Philip's four prophetic daughters who, according to the church historian Eusebius, evangelized much of Asia Minor (Acts 21:9). After the eucharistic meal, a lector read from the Scriptures and/or from letters by church leaders. The role of the reader (lector) was a specialized one, since it involved reading texts aloud with a certain performative emphasis.[120] After the readings, a teacher reflected aloud about the meaning of the texts for the spiritual edification of the assembly. Osiek and MacDonald carefully point out that while there was little concern about qualifications of the presider and leader of the ritual meals, "the same cannot be said for teachers. . . . Great care was given to the selection of persons for this leadership. . . . The two functions of presiding and teaching were seen as distinct, probably until some time in the second century."[121] Women have always been important teachers of other women. But, as we shall see, women teaching in the Christian assembly would become a source of controversy despite evidence that one woman—Prisca—had taught the

---

117. Michael Peppard, *The World's Oldest Church: Bible, Art, and Ritual at Dura-Duropos Syria (Synkrisis)* (New Haven: Yale University Press, 2016), see chapter 4.
118. Steinberg, "Women and the Dura-Europos," 471.
119. Schüssler Fiorenza, *In Memory of Her*, 298.
120. Osiek and MacDonald, *A Woman's Place*, 162.
121. Ibid.

prominent evangelist Apollos shortly after he arrived in Ephesus (Acts 18:24–28).

EDUCATION OF WOMEN AND GIRLS

Roman elite families valued education for both girls and boys, although the education of girls was oriented to providing skills for managing the domestic estate. Families who wanted their children to become fluent in both Greek and Latin often contracted with Greek-speaking wet nurses. Peasant children began working the soil as soon as they were strong enough. Some scholars believe all children learned the rudiments of how to read, write, and count.[122] Most of the population remained functionally illiterate, however, since the ability to read and write lengthy works "was a relatively rare skill in the Greco-Roman world, and was restricted largely to scribes and an intellectual elite."[123] Mothers were the primary caregivers and therefore educators for young children. Fathers of higher-status families assumed primary teaching duties for children between the ages of seven and sixteen, often hiring a tutor to help. In their midteens, boys from prominent families were formally educated in rhetoric, philosophy, geometry, music, and astronomy, either at special schools or with a philosopher or rhetorician at home.[124] Young women were usually tutored at home. Since there is good historical evidence that women participated in philosophical circles, Beryl Rawson suggests it is reasonable to "extrapolate backwards" and assume that philosophical education was available for some girls. Rawson points to Cornelia, the daughter of Metellus Scipio, whom Plutarch describes as "well versed in literature and in playing the lyre and in geometry, and she had been accustomed to listen to philosophical discourses with profit."[125]

---

122. Osiek and Balch, *Families*, 67.

123. John P. Meier, *A Marginal Jew: Rethinking the Historical Jesus*, vol. 1, *The Roots of the Problem and the Person* (New York: Doubleday, 1991), 255–56. Meier cites William V. Harris, *Ancient Literacy* (Cambridge, MA: Harvard University Press, 1989).

124. Meier, *A Marginal Jew*, 1:67.

125. Osiek and MacDonald, *A Woman's Place*, 86. See also Beryl Rawson, *Children and Childhood in Roman Italy* (Oxford: Oxford University Press, 2003), 155, as cited in Osiek and MacDonald, *A Woman's Place*, 86.

Figure 1.5. Public library at Ephesus. Photo by author.

From the second century onward, philosophical education became increasingly valued and available to anyone regardless of social origin. According to Peter Lampe, philosophers were seen as educators, advisors, and teachers of ethics. Their teaching was open to the public and many were missionaries and popular preachers. Anyone

—whether slave, freed person, or freeborn—could increase his or her status by studying as a philosopher.[126] Public instruction and public libraries flourished (see figure 1.5). It is reasonable to assume that female Christians had access to philosophical education. In a careful study of the "essentially reliable" *Acta Iustini* (Acts of Justin), Lampe points to a Christian woman, Charito, who, along with six male students, studied philosophy with Justin Martyr. She was beheaded with Justin and his other students in 165 CE after refusing to offer sacrifice in the imperial cult.[127]

RELIGION AND WOMEN'S PATRONAGE IN GRECO-ROMAN CITIES

Religious worship throughout the Greco-Roman world was polytheistic and diverse, the only commonality being the imperial cult in which everyone was expected to offer sacrifice to secure the well-being of the state. In addition to the imperial temple, each Roman city had its own pantheon of local gods and goddesses who were honored in a variety of ways, including animal sacrifice, participation in public feasts, theatrical performances, and processions. These functioned to build a sense of communal identity and to enhance belief in divine protection for the city. In Ephesus, processions honoring the hunter-goddess Artemis (Roman Diana) were held every two weeks. Pilgrims came from great distances to worship at her temple, which was regarded as one of the Seven Wonders of the World. Paul was forced to flee Ephesus after publicly proclaiming, "gods made with hands are not gods," because the Ephesian silversmiths rioted over fear of losing sales of their small silver statues of Artemis (Acts 19:26). The same god or goddess could be worshipped in different ways in different cities. In Athens, Athena was worshipped as the warrior god who protected the city, but in Ephesus, she was revered as a patron of the arts.[128] Aphrodite (Roman Venus) functioned as the "goddess of [illicit] love" in some cities but a city protector of legitimate marriage in others. In still other places, guilds of prostitutes honored Aphrodite

126. Lampe, *From Paul to Valentinus*, 280.
127. Ibid., 276–78.
128. LiDonnici, "Women's Religions," 84–85.

as their patron.[129] The empire was tolerant of diverse religious cults as long as they did not threaten public order. A person could and often did participate in many different religious cults at the same time.

During the early Christian period, most inhabitants of the empire saw their gods and goddesses as "wholly other" and unconcerned with their daily lives.

> One of the most central religious messages throughout Greco-Roman worship for both women and men, was this emphasis on the unbridgeable gap between humanity and divinity, and the foolishness—and danger—of forgetting this distance. . . . This sense of difference means that the gender of a deity is not often a good indicator of the gender of the worshippers or officiants, because, although sometimes a given believer may be unconsciously looking for identification with a god, at other times he or she may seek out a symbol that reflects this basic and unchangeable difference.[130]

Nearly all religions except Judaism and Christianity assumed that the universe was polytheistic and that the world was full of deities, some friendly and some not. People attributed military defeats and natural disasters to interference by an opposing god or punishment by a favored one. Sacrifice on behalf of the public good ensured the protection of one's city. What was good for the city was good for everyone. There was great prestige to be gained by patrons and benefactors, both women and men, who sponsored religious functions. It was their job to buy the animals for sacrifice, hire priests to slaughter them, and see to all the details involved in creating a spectacular, city-wide celebratory feast. The city named such patrons to public offices such as magistrate and honorary priest, usually for a year, and granted them the right to have dedicatory statues erected in their honor (see figure 1.6.)

129. Ibid., 82.
130. Ibid., 81.

Figure 1.6. Second-century marble statue of
Plancia Magna, who served as city magistrate in
the city of Perge in Asia Minor. Joshua
Clutterham/BiblePlaces.com.

There is abundant archaeological evidence that many women held
such public offices, particularly in Asia Minor (modern day Turkey).
During the second century CE, Plancia Magna was a city magistrate
and superintendent of the *palestra* (public training facility for athletes)

in the city of Perge in Asia Minor.[131] Tata of Aphrodisias, also in Asia Minor, held a number of titles, including a priestess of the imperial cult.[132] Julia Severa in Phrygia (western Asia Minor) was appointed to numerous city offices, including priesthood in the city of Acmonia, and donated money to the local synagogue.[133] Prominent female converts to Christianity, especially in Asia Minor, may well have expected to hold similar leadership roles in their new religion. Other patrons built temples, fountains, and sports arenas. Still others offered public feeding programs, often for poor children. In memory of her mother, Fabia Agrippina donated one million sesterces for a monthly meal for one hundred girls in Ostia.[134] Her deliberate attention to girls was probably meant to counterbalance officially sponsored feeding programs that favored boys.[135] Thus, although women could not vote or hold elected office (patronage offices were appointed), they could and did exercise significant political and religious influence.

While public worship of distant gods was deemed essential to securing the well-being of society, people had their own personal fears and sufferings. It is therefore unsurprising that "both women and men were on the lookout for new and effective deities, who cared about the personal events of human life and who would step in . . . to help or save their worshipers within the context of a random or fated universe."[136] Some cults addressed these needs, primarily through myths and stories that resonated with human concerns. The Egyptian goddess Isis, for example, was the most widely worshipped deity in the empire because her painful story was one to which people could relate and empathize. According to Plutarch's version of the myth, Isis was widowed after her brother-husband Osiris was nailed into a coffin and thrown into the Nile. The annual overflow of the Nile was attributed to the tears she shed searching for her dead husband. When Isis at last finds Osiris's sarcophagus, she is

131. Osiek and MacDonald, A Woman's Place, 205.

132. Ibid.

133. Ibid., 203.

134. According to graffiti signs found in Pompeii (first century CE), a loaf of bread cost one half of a sesterce, and a slave could subsist on it for one and a half days. See Lampe, From Paul to Valentinus, 193–94.

135. Osiek and MacDonald, A Woman's Place, 205.

136. Ibid., 83.

heartbroken to discover he had fathered a child with another woman. Isis's travails resonated strongly with female experiences involving the death of a spouse, child-rearing, and infidelity. Her iconographic representation holding her son, Horus, would later be adopted by Christians to depict Mary holding Jesus. A people used to worshipping God in female as well as male metaphor could not easily relinquish beloved female representations of the divine.

Every Greco-Roman city had a temple devoted to healing. The god Asclepios and his daughter Hygieia were petitioned to intervene and heal infertility or a chronic illness. One version of Asclepios's myth depicts him as a human doctor with great medical skill whom the gods eventually killed for restoring the dead to life. Asclepios eventually evolved into a compassionate god who continued to help people. Concern for personal and familial well-being in the midst of suffering and the hope of an afterlife explained in part why the Jesus movement was attractive to a polytheistic society. The lowly, suffering Christ who was eventually raised up resonated not only with their sufferings but also with the need for a powerful saving figure who promised life after death.

WHY THE JESUS MOVEMENT ATTRACTED WOMEN

Women and men in the early Jesus movement expected the world to end very soon. Christ would return in glory to inaugurate a new reign of God, a just social order, where the last would be first and the first last. Within this apocalyptic context, Kraemer notes: "The Jesus movement advocated a radical interim ethic that had far-reaching ramifications for social roles, including those associated with gender distinctions."[137] In the Synoptic Gospels, Jesus's followers are repeatedly asked to leave families, homes, and livelihoods to follow him (Matthew 19, 23–30). Likewise, Paul's mid-first-century letter to the Corinthians counseled celibacy over marriage because "the appointed time has grown short; from now on, let even those who have wives be as though they had none" (1 Cor 7:29). Many women and men would embrace Paul's admonition to celibacy in coming centuries.

---

137. Kraemer, *Her Share*, 138.

While a man's choice of celibacy was unusual in the Greco-Roman context, it would not have been regarded as socially disruptive. A young woman's decision not to marry but to embrace virginity, or a married woman's decision to live a celibate lifestyle, was not only against the Augustan marriage legislation but became a major challenge to the prerogatives and constraints of patriarchal marriage. Kraemer summarizes: "The negation of sexuality, marriage, and childbearing brought with it the possibility of expanded roles for women within the Jesus movement, including substantial participation in the public life of Christian communities. It also effectively freed at least some women from the control of husbands and fathers."[138]

Within the context of first-century Palestinian Judaism, Kraemer cautions against any notion that Jesus saved Jewish women from Judaism. Instead, she suggests,

> To understand why Jewish women joined the Jesus movement, we must look to the issues that engaged Jews of both genders of the first century (the oppressive presence of the Romans, the corruption of the Herodians, the purity and efficacy of the temple) and to the pressures on women, Jewish and otherwise, to conform to ancient understandings of gender. . . . There seems to be little reason to argue that the particular constructions of gender within Judaism led Jewish women to join the Jesus movement.[139]

Social stratification in early Christian communities also played a part in attracting people to the new movement. The first letter to the Corinthians was written in response to a delegation of "Chloe's people," who appealed to Paul to address various quarrels and divisions. Corinthian Christians were a motley crew composed of people of higher and lower social status. It is likely that Chloe was a female head of an extended household that included Christian slaves and freed persons. Chloe herself may or may not have been Christian, since household slaves and freed persons were at liberty to choose their own religious practices and "subordinate members of the household sometimes joined early Christian groups independently (and perhaps

138. Ibid., 139.
139. Kraemer, "Jewish Women," 46.

without the knowledge) of the heads of households (e.g. 1 Tim 6:1–3; 1 Pet 3:1–2)."[140]

Determination of status is a complex matter in which slaves or freed persons with independent wealth or access to the powerful could be of higher status than their social class would indicate. Margaret Y. MacDonald notes that Christianity was particularly attractive to people who fell into this ambiguous category:

> Scholars have suggested that individuals such as freed persons and women who displayed status inconsistency (indicators of higher status combined with features of lower status) were particularly attracted to Pauline Christianity with its paradoxical beliefs, such as the "crucified Messiah," which celebrated the ambiguities of their existence.[141]

The author of Acts writes that Paul found many converts among prominent women at Thessalonica (Acts 17:1–9), Beroea (17:10–15), and Athens (17:16–34). This text leads Osiek and MacDonald to observe: "The sympathy of powerful women seems to be one of the themes developed by the author of Acts in an effort to communicate the respectability and independence of early Christianity."[142]

140. Margaret Y. MacDonald, "Reading Real Women through the Undisputed Letters of Paul," in Kramer and D'Angelo, *Women and Christian Origins*, 200.

141. Ibid., 201. MacDonald cites Meeks, *First Urban Christians*, 51–73, 164–92.

142. Osiek and MacDonald, *A Woman's Place*, 235.

2.

Women and Early Christianity: Female Authority Opposed

EARLY CHRISTIAN WOMEN AND ECCLESIAL AUTHORITY

That women exercised authority in the first-century Christian churches is reflected in Paul's letters, Acts, and other early Christian writings. The seven undisputed letters of Paul are the earliest Christian manuscripts we have and constitute strong historical evidence for women's influence and authority in the early church. Of the twenty-eight individuals identified in chapter 16 of Paul's letter to the Romans, ten are women. They are, respectively, Phoebe, Prisca, Mary, Junia, Tryphaena, Tryphosa, Persis, Rufus's mother, Julia, and Nereus's sister. Peter Lampe deduces that women may have been more active than men in the first-century Roman church because Paul uses the verb "to work" (κοπιαω) four times, always in relationship to a woman but never in relationship to a man.[1] The four women so described are Mary, Persis, Tryphaena, and Tryphosa. Lampe notes that the Greek word "to work" (κοπιαω) is "a technical term in missionary language" and points to "Galatians 4:11 and 1

---

1. Lampe, *From Paul to Valentinus*, 166.

Cor 15:10 where the word is predicated of Paul himself."[2] Four other women of authority who are associated with Paul include Lydia (Acts 16:11–40), Euodia and Syntyche (Phil 4:2–3), and Nympha (Col 4:14–16). In addition to Prisca, Lydia, Euodia, and Syntyche, four more women must be considered: Phoebe, Junia, Nympha, and Tabitha.

Figure 2.1. Shops at Philippi. Lydia may have sold her purple dye goods near here. Photo by author.

PHOEBE

Paul had never visited the church of Rome when he wrote the letter to the Romans. To provide credibility for himself and his official envoy, Phoebe, he names all of the people in the Roman community who know him and can testify to his reputability. He begins his letter:

> I commend to you Phoebe our sister, who is a *diakonos* of the church at Cenchreae, that you may receive her in the Lord in a manner worthy of the holy ones, and help her in whatever she may need from you, for she has been a benefactor to many and to me as well. (Rom 16:1–2).

2. Ibid., 166n41.

Phoebe's title, *diakonos*, is commonly mistranslated as "deaconess," despite the masculine ending in Greek. There were fourth-century deaconesses, but their ministry was far more circumscribed than the first century *diakonos*. While the exact meaning of *diakonos* in the first-century church is unclear, it is significant that the title is the same one Paul uses for his own ministry (1 Cor 3:5; 2 Cor 6:4). We know this title was also used for male office holders in early second-century Christianity, and there is evidence to suggest there were women with similar roles. Some believe the two female slave *ministrae* tortured by Pliny the Younger in Asia Minor may have had roles similar to the *diakonoi*, but this is uncertain.[3]

The second-century letter of 1 Timothy 3:11 is also thought to refer to women deacons.[4] The *diakonos* office seems to have been an important position in the Pauline mission. Schüssler Fiorenza believes the evidence is such that "Phoebe is recommended as an official teacher and missionary in the church of Cenchreae."[5] Yet her other title is probably more important. She is called a benefactor (*prostatis*) to Paul "and many others." Phoebe was an independent woman of wealth who, like Mary Magdalene, Joanna, and Susanna before her, financially supported the missionary outreach of the early church. She is one of many female patrons whose support and leadership permitted Christianity to spread rapidly in the Hellenist world.

JUNIA

"Greet Andronicus and Junia, my relatives, who were in prison with me; they are prominent among the apostles, and they were in Christ before I was" (Rom 16:7). Junia and Andronicus are a missionary couple that Paul identifies as "prominent among the apostles." For centuries, Junia's name was translated in a masculine form, Junias, because transcribers could not believe a woman would bear the title

3. See Kevin Madigan and Carolyn Osiek, eds., *Ordained Women in the Early Church: A Documentary History* (Baltimore: Johns Hopkins University Press, 2005), 27. Noting that Pliny's letter says nothing about the women's function or status in their communities, the authors write: "It is probably best to conclude that *ministra* signifies a reasonably well defined and acknowledged role in the community and to recognize that we can say nothing very exact about it."

4. MacDonald, "Reading Real Women," 208.

5. Schüssler Fiorenza, *In Memory of Her*, 171.

apostle, even though virtually all early Christian writers, from Chrysostom to Origen to Peter Lombard, assumed that Junia was a woman apostle. Eldon Jay Epp's exhaustive textual analysis found no male name Junias exists in ancient sources, while the female Junia is common.[6] Paul tells us they are his relatives who were imprisoned with him, most likely because their itinerant missionary work led to the same persecution he frequently experienced.

NYMPHA

Another important female head of a house church named in the New Testament is Nympha: "Give my greetings to the brothers and sisters in Laodicea and to Nympha and the church in her house. And when this letter has been read among you, have it read also in the church of the Laodiceans." (Col 4:15–16). It is ironic that the deutero-Pauline author of Colossians acknowledges Nympha as leading a house church, since a main point of the letter is to impose Greco-Roman hierarchical order and subordination in Christian households. As a leader of a house church, Nympha ministered to the church at Laodicea. Two centuries later, a council at Laodicea forbad women leaders to enter the sanctuary or be installed in the church.[7] According to Ute Eisen: "We must presume that these women both led the assembly and presided at the Eucharist."[8] Is it possible that these fourth-century women were ministerial descendants of Nympha?

WIDOWS AND SECOND-CENTURY WOMEN WHO EXERCISED AUTHORITY

TABITHA

Widows played an important role in early church expansion. They supported the church's mission as patrons and converted others to the Jesus movement. The support of wealthy widows for poorer wid-

6. Eldon Jay Epp, *Junia: The First Woman Apostle* (Minneapolis: Fortress Press, 2005).
7. Eisen, *Women Officeholders*, 143.
8. Ibid., 122.

ows and orphans was a powerful evangelizing witness in a culture that regularly exposed unwanted babies to die. In Acts 9:36–43, we read of Tabitha, "a disciple" who led a house church in Joppa, just thirty miles northwest of Jerusalem. She fell ill and died, leaving "all the widows . . . weeping and showing tunics and other clothing she had made for them" (Acts 9:39). Luke shows Peter hastening to Joppa where, after her prays over her, Tabitha is raised from the dead. Because she is the only woman given the grammatically feminine title of "disciple" (*mathetria*) in the entire New Testament, some commentators suggest Tabitha was one of the women in Jesus's Galilean discipleship. The masculine form, *mathetes*, "is a term chosen by evangelists to describe followers of Jesus including the Twelve."[9] Peter may have known her well.[10] Since no male relative is anywhere in evidence, Tabitha may have been a widow herself. Bonnie Thurston suggests she was a leader of a congregation of widows at Joppa and a foremother of the "order of widows" prominent in the church into the third century.[11]

GRAPTE

In the second century, the Roman author of Shepherd of Hermas had a vision in which he was told to write "two little books and send one to Grapte and one to Clement." Grapte must "instruct the widows and the orphans," and Clement is to send the other book "to all the foreign cities." Hermas is also asked to read the book "to this city [Rome] along with the elders that preside over the Church." Clement is remembered in church history as a leader and communicator for the other house church leaders of Rome. Since Rome did not embrace the monarchical episcopacy as quickly as other urban communities, Clement's letter was sent to Corinth on behalf of all the house churches of Rome, not on his own behalf. The Roman church was led by a "plurality of presbyters" during this time, not a

9. Bonnie Thurston, *Women in the New Testament: Questions and Commentary* (New York: Crossroad, 1998), 120.
10. Ibid., 121.
11. Ibid., 122.

monarchical bishop.[12] It is notable that Shepherd of Hermas sharply reprimands Rome's *diakonoi* who "despoil the living of widows and orphans," in contrast to Grapte who cares for and ministers to them. As Lampe sees it, Grapte "was entrusted with this work by all the communities of Rome."[13]

Both Grapte and Clement are identified as leaders whose responsibilities involve all the house church communities at Rome. While Clement is remembered in church history, Grapte is not. Many early writings attest that care of widows and orphans was an ethical priority for early Christians. What is less obvious is that this ministry was often, if not usually, carried out by women. A pattern emerges in which we find wealthier widows caring for other widows and, like Tabitha, welcoming them into their households. This pattern persists well into the fifth century, as early church orders attest.[14] These communities of widows, including the "widows called virgins"—named by Ignatius of Antioch in the second-century *To the Smyrnaeans*—became centers of evangelization and hubs of female leadership.

TAVIA, ALCE, THE "ELECT LADY," AND OTHER WOMEN LEADERS IN ASIA MINOR

Ignatius of Antioch greets several female heads of house churches by name in his letters to the churches of Asia Minor. In addition to the "virgins called widows" and "households of brothers with their wives," he singles out "Tavia and her household" and Alce "who means a great deal to me" in *To the Smyrnaeans* (13.1). In *To Polycarp*, Ignatius again greets "Alce, my dearly beloved" and the "wife of Epitropus with all her house and her children" (8.3). Since Epitropus is not greeted directly, it is likely that either she is widowed or Epitropus is not Christian.[15] The second Epistle of John in the New

---

12. Lampe, *From Paul to Valentinus*, 397–407.

13. Ibid., 401.

14. See Roger Gryson, *The Ministry of Women in the Early Church* (Collegeville, MN: Liturgical Press, 1976); and Francine Cardman, "Women, Ministry, and Church Order in Early Christianity," in Kraemer and D'Angelo, *Women and Christian Origins*, 300–322.

15. Schüssler Fiorenza, *In Memory of Her*, 247–48.

Testament is addressed to "the elect lady" and her "elect sister" in Asia Minor. Schüssler Fiorenza disputes the theory that the female names are symbolic for churches in Asia Minor:

> These expressions are best understood as honorifics for the women leaders of house churches, since *kyria* or *domina* is a familiar title for the materfamilias and "sister" is used as a missionary title by Paul. . . . Since 3 John is also addressed to the head of a house church, nothing prevents us from assuming the same for 2 John.[16]

The "elect women" of John's Epistle, Alce, Tavia, the "virgins called widows," and Epitropus's wife are just a few of the highly influential women who exercised authority in Asia Minor in the second century.[17]

ATTEMPTS TO CURTAIL THE FEMALE EXERCISE OF AUTHORITY

COLOSSIANS AND EPHESIANS

Both of these epistles from the canonical Christian Scriptures are considered "deutero-Pauline" because a majority of scholars believe they were written not by Paul but by later interpreters of his teachings. Nympha, the head of a house church in Laodicea, is the only woman named in either text. These two letters contain what biblical scholars call "household codes," which were meant to advise on appropriate behavior, particularly that of women, children, and slaves. Even though Paul's letter to the Galatians celebrates a new equality ("there is no longer Jew or Greek, slave or free, male and female"), the household codes view a woman's submission to her spouse as ideal behavior (Col 3:18; Eph 5:22).

But why? Could it be because early Christian ideals of equality in

---

16. Ibid., 248.

17. Robert M. Grant, "The Social Setting of Second-Century Christianity," in *The Shaping of Christianity in the Second and Third Centuries*, ed. E. P. Sanders, vol. 1 of *Jewish and Christian Self-Definition* (London: SCM, 1980) 16–29, as cited by Schüssler Fiorenza, *In Memory of Her*, 248.

Christ were playing themselves out in the actual behavior of Christians, including Christian women? MacDonald writes:

> It has frequently been suggested that the greater correspondence between the ethical exhortations concerning household relations and the ethic of Greco-Roman society that emerges in deutero-Pauline literature [Colossians, Ephesians, 1 and 2 Timothy, and Titus] was the result of an attempt to offer an apologetic response to those who critiqued Christians for the effect they had on the household and on the behavior of women.[18]

Women preaching and evangelizing, slaves and freed persons converting their counterparts in other households, Christian rituals conducted in private, domestic space—all of these behaviors attracted censure from the larger society. As a result, early churchmen sought to quell criticism by controlling the behavior of Christian households, and particularly the behavior of women. We shall see this pattern repeat itself many times over the next three centuries.

PASTORAL EPISTLES (1 AND 2 TIMOTHY, TITUS)

"Let a woman learn in silence with full submission. I permit no woman to teach or to have authority over a man; she is to keep silent" (1 Tim 2:11–12). This injunction from 1 Timothy is the most widely quoted justification for restricting women's leadership in the early church. Some denominations cite it even to this day in an attempt to silence Christian women. The letters of Timothy and Titus have been called the Pastoral Epistles because they are concerned with governing the life of the existing church "flock." Scholars date the Pastorals to the early or mid-second century and believe they originated in the Aegean area of Asia Minor, perhaps near Ephesus. Most agree they were written not by Paul but by churchmen who viewed themselves as interpreters of his teachings.[19] For MacDonald:

---

18. MacDonald, "Reading Real Women," 246.

19. Robert A. Wild, "The Pastoral Letters," in *The New Jerome Biblical Commentary*, ed. Raymond E. Brown, Joseph A. Fitzmyer, and Roland E. Murphy (Englewood Cliffs, NJ: Prentice Hall, 1990), 892–93.

One of the major priorities of the Pastoral Epistles is the management of women's behavior. In general, the Pastoral Epistles offer abundant material for illustrating that New Testament texts should be read with an understanding of the cultural values of Greco-Roman society; they reflect common stereotypes about the nature of the female character, such as the tendency for women to gossip (1 Tim 5:13) or their inclination for being easily duped (2 Tim 3:6).[20]

It is apparent that 1 Timothy 5:3–16 is much concerned with controlling the behavior of widows, particularly young widows. Contrary to Paul's recommendation of celibacy for widowed men and women (1 Corinthians 7), young widows are to "marry, bear children, and manage their household so as to give the adversary no occasion to revile us. For some have already turned away to follow Satan" (1 Tim 5:14–15). Enrolled widows were expected to observe celibacy, but the author of 1 Timothy does not encourage this for young widows because "when their sensual desires alienate them from Christ, they want to marry, and so they incur condemnation for having violated their first pledge. Besides that, they learn to be idle, gadding about from house to house; and they are not merely idle but also gossips and busybodies saying what they should not say" (1 Tim 5:11–13). Timothy's negative description of women "gadding about" is polemical and mimics stereotypes from Greco-Roman culture. The text instructs the community to enroll only "real widows," that is, women past the age of sixty who have married only once and have no children or relatives to care for them. Further, they are to have "shown hospitality, washed the saints' feet, helped the afflicted and devoted [themselves] to doing good in every way."

Using a skewed interpretation of Genesis, 1 Timothy subjects women to the authority of men: "For Adam was formed first, then Eve; and Adam was not deceived, but the woman was deceived and became a transgressor. Yet she will be saved through childbearing provided they continue in faith and love and holiness, with modesty" (1 Tim 2:13–15). This extreme—indeed doctrinally incorrect—statement is contrary to Paul's teaching that belief in Christ is the way to salvation, not childbearing. The self-evident strength of 1 Timothy's attempt to control female behavior prompts MacDonald to surmise:

20. MacDonald, "Reading Real Women," 246.

The activity of the widows is apparently understood by the author of the Pastoral Epistles as one of the reasons why the community has been experiencing slander. The desire of the young women to remain unmarried, and their active movements from house to house have apparently contributed to the community being viewed as suspicious. As the early Christian groups moved into the second century CE, hostile reactions of outsiders increasingly tended to ignite into physical violence.[21]

CHANGING ROLES OF WOMEN AND THREATS OF VIOLENCE

The early Jesus movement's wholehearted embrace of a more inclusive social ethos particularly with regard to the leadership of women—even slave women, such as the female *ministrae* attested by Pliny the Younger—was shocking to many in the Greco-Roman culture. As the movement grew in influence, it attracted censure from opponents who lodged accusations of treason with local authorities. When Christian women and men refused official demands to sacrifice to the emperor, death inevitably followed. Most persecutions were local outbreaks instigated by citizens who opposed the new religion. Empire-wide persecution was rare.

Since family stability equated to stability of the empire, a religious sect that tolerated a woman's refusal to marry because of a commitment to virginity, or worse, a married woman's embrace of celibacy, was seen as a threat to the public order. One prominent early critic was Celsus, for whom "the Christian family is at the very heart of the growth of a troublesome new movement."[22] In Celsus's view, Christians encouraged insubordination and convinced the "foolish, dishonorable and stupid and slaves, women and little children," not "to pay any attention to their father and school teachers" and "leave father and their school masters, and go along with the women and little children who are play fellows to the wooldresser's shop, or the cobblers' or the washer woman's shop."[23] Celsus's critique coincides with evidence from Christian texts that the early Jesus movement

21. Ibid., 248.
22. Osiek and MacDonald, *A Woman's Place*, 221.
23. Origen, *Against Celsus* 3.55 (Henry Chadwick, *Origen: Contra Celsum* [Cambridge: Cambridge University Press, 1953]), as cited in Osiek and MacDonald, *A Woman's Place*, 222.

expanded through house churches and small business networks such as those of Lydia, Prisca, Grapte, and Paul. Evangelization was conducted person-to-person, house-to-house by women who reached out to other women, children, freed persons, and slaves. Women's quiet exercise of authority in the context of everyday domestic life is one oft-unheralded key to Christianity's rapid expansion.

Elite women were also attracted to the new movement. The Roman matron in Justin Martyr's *Apology* exemplifies the dangerous dynamic that could result when a higher-status woman became a Christ believer but her husband did not.[24] Justin describes a matron who lived a sexually licentious and drunken lifestyle alongside her husband until she "came to the knowledge of the teachings of Christ." After trying and failing to persuade her husband to change his ways, she wants to divorce him, "considering it wicked to live any longer as a wife with a husband who sought in every way means of indulging in pleasure contrary to the law of nature, and in violation of what is right." Her Christian friends dissuaded her for a time. But when her husband "conducted himself worse than ever," the matron decides that she can no longer share the same bed and gives him a bill of divorce. Enraged, her husband denounces her as a Christian to the authorities and a trial is set. She asks the judge to postpone her trial until she can put her financial affairs in order and he grants her request. (That she has finances to put in order indicates she is a wealthy woman of status.) Frustrated, the husband denounces the matron's Christian teacher, Ptolemaeus, who is summarily thrown into prison, tormented, and eventually executed along with two Christian spectators who publicly protested his unjust treatment.

Justin's text never names the woman herself nor mentions what happens to her. Lampe suggests she may have been a woman of high status named Flora, "to whom a Valentinian Roman teacher wrote a letter: the letter of Ptolemaeus, which Epiphanius preserved in his 'medicine chest, against heretics' (*Panarion Haer.* 33.3–7)."[25] Justin's description of what happened to Ptolemaeus and his companions is

24. Justin Martyr, *Second Apology* 2 (Roberts-Donaldson, *Ante-Nicene Fathers*, vol. 1 [Buffalo, NY: Christian Literature, 1886], reprinted on Early Christian Writings, http://tinyurl.com/yd6ese5f).

25. Lampe, *From Paul to Valentinus*, 239.

one of the first authentic Roman martyrdom accounts in existence.[26] The story of the Roman matron exemplifies the threats faced by the early communities when women converted and sought to live their new faith with integrity in a culture that saw the patriarchal household and patriarchal marriage as central to its identity.

APOCRYPHAL ACTS OF THE APOSTLES— ACTS OF THECLA

An all but invisible chapter in the history of women in the early church can be recovered from the apocryphal Acts of the Apostles. Written from the mid-second to early third centuries, these popular stories were told and retold in the Hellenistic communities of the eastern Mediterranean. Although five of the six "Acts" are named for male apostles, (Thomas, Peter, Paul, John, and Andrew) all of the texts (including the Acts of Xanthippe, a woman) feature female protagonists whose decision to embrace the celibate lifestyle recommended by Paul leads to persecution and upheaval. Steven L. Davies believes "these Acts may have come from a community of women grappling with the demands of male authorities who are armed with presumed Pauline quotations that they keep silent."[27] Contemporary scholarship makes a persuasive case that the apocryphal Acts originated in female oral traditions in Asia Minor and Greece.[28] By comparing aspects of the stories with historical evidence from the same time period, it is possible to recover something of the history of actual women behind these traditions. Virginia Burrus explains:

> If we know from Pliny's letter to Trajan that persecutions of Christians in second-century Asia Minor were initiated not by the Romans but by the local communities, then we have some grounds for believing that the chastity stories' presentation of the initiation of persecution of Christians by families and local communities is historically accurate.[29]

26. Ibid., 238.

27. Stevan L. Davies, *The Revolt of the Widows: The Social World of the Apocryphal Acts* (London: Feffer & Simons, 1980), 66.

28. Burrus, *Chastity as Autonomy*; Dennis Ronald McDonald, *The Legend and the Apostle: The Battle for Paul in Story and Canon* (Philadelphia: Westminster, 1983).

29. Burrus, *Chastity as Autonomy*, 81. Burrus cites Pliny, *Letter to Trajan X*: "An anonymous document was published containing the names of many persons. . . . I judged it all the more

It is interesting that the female heroines of the apocryphal Acts are all women of high status. While this could be due to the tendency of folktales to exaggerate, there is good reason to surmise an underlying historical kernel, since "by the late second century, Christianity had begun to reach the upper levels of Greco-Roman society, and there its greatest and earliest success seems to have been among women."[30] The stories were shaped by the female tellers' "concern to legitimate their [celibate] lifestyle and beliefs and by their need to break away psychologically from their dependence on their husbands and families."[31] Burrus suggests the conversion stories introduced a new lifestyle in which celibate women created "an alternative society based on abolishing traditional social relationships including sex roles and class distinctions."[32] In such a society, perpetual virginity was a positive alternative to mandatory marriage into a patriarchal system. Freely chosen celibacy could be a healthy response to spousal oppression and/or the subjugation of women.[33] Although the apocryphal Acts are thought to derive from female oral traditions, five of the six Acts are named for men. This is probably because female authorship was not accepted by the culture, and a woman had "few alternatives other than to attribute her ideas to an absent man."[34]

Dennis R. McDonald and others convincingly argue that the Pastoral Epistles were written in response to the wildly popular Acts of Paul and Thecla, one of the apocryphal Acts that was widely accepted by the early church well into the fifth century.[35] According to Sheila E. McGinn, the Acts of Thecla originally circulated as a woman's oral tradition but was later "domesticated" by a male author from the mainline church of Asia Minor who sought to give Paul more prominence, thereby transforming it to the Acts of Paul and Thecla.

necessary to find out what the truth was by torturing two female slaves who were called *ministrae*. But I discovered nothing else."

30. Burrus, *Chastity as Autonomy*, 100.
31. Ibid., 108.
32. Ibid., 116.
33. Ibid.
34. Davies, *Revolt of the Widows*, 105.
35. See McDonald, *Legend and the Apostle*; and Sheila E. McGinn, "The Acts of Thecla," in *Searching the Scriptures*, ed. Elisabeth Schüssler Fiorenza (New York: Crossroad, 1994), 800–828.

Figure 2.2. Sixth-century fresco of Thecla at her window (left), Paul (center), and Thecla's mother, Theokleia, (right). Theokleia is commonly mistaken for Thecla in this fresco, but the Greek inscription is clear. This depicts the scene from the Acts of Thecla in which Theokleia complains that her daughter does nothing but sit at the window listening to the preaching of Paul. Photo courtesy of Ephesus Foundation.

In the second and third centuries, "magic and miracle, dismissed today as superstition, were taken to be a part of reality."[36] Illness and misfortune were commonly attributed to the work of malign spirits, and being afflicted with such a "demon" did not necessarily imply moral failure or sin. Early church writers such as Justin Martyr and Tertullian wrote at length that Christians' charismatic preaching power was more effective than pagan magic. Christian prayer, says Tertullian, can "extort the rains of heaven, recall the souls of the departed from the very path of death, transform the weak, restore the sick, purge the possessed, open prison bars, loose the bonds of the innocent."[37] Like all of the apocryphal Acts, the Acts of Thecla is steeped in these early understandings of miracle and charismatic power.

As the story goes, after being inspired by the teaching of Paul, our

36. Davies, *Revolt of the Widows*, 17.
37. Tertullian, *De oratione* 29, as cited by Davies, *Revolt of the Widows*, 21.

heroine Thecla breaks her engagement, takes a vow of chastity, and risks her life preaching Christianity (see figure 2.2). She is twice condemned to death but miraculously escapes: when Thecla is exposed to wild beasts, a female lioness dies protecting her from the other beasts. Thecla then baptizes herself "in the name of Jesus Christ," whereupon a flash of lightning and a cloud of fire signal divine approbation. Before freeing her, the governor asks why she has not been harmed. Thecla proclaims the power of Christ as "the city shakes" with the shouted acclamations of women praising God. McGinn spells out what this folktale might have meant to the women who loved and retold the story:

> It is not simply the loud noise that "shakes the city," but the content of the acclamation: God protects and delivers a woman who opposes the sex-role definitions of the city, showing God's power over the culture as a whole. Female chastity and divine power are victorious over male law and aggression.[38]

Thecla seeks out Paul, who finally recognizes her prophetic gift and commissions her to "go and teach the word of God." She does exactly that and, after other adventures, is last seen in Seleucia, where "she enlightened many with the word of God."[39]

Pointing to a contemporaneous Greek legend about Hagnodice, who was allegedly the first female Greek physician, McDonald suggests: "Apparently the [Hagnodice] story was told to legitimate the existence of women in that profession, just as the story of Thecla was used to support a role for women in teaching and baptizing."[40] McDonald makes a good case that behind the legend there existed a historical Thecla. All first-millennium authors presumed her existence and revered her as a saint, some calling her a protomartyr and apostle. Further, Francine Cardman believes "it is likely that Thecla represents . . . many women of the first and early second centuries who publicly preached and baptized, claiming the authority of Paul for their ministries."[41] She notes that Tertullian's early third-cen-

38. McGinn, "Acts of Thecla," 818.

39. Acts of Paul and Thecla 2.43 (M. R. James, *The Apocryphal New Testament* [Oxford: Clarendon, 1924], reprinted on Early Christian Writings, http://tinyurl.com/ydeofur4).

40. McDonald, *Legend and the Apostle*, 19.

41. Cardman, "Women, Ministry," 302.

tury *On Baptism* rejects the claim of a woman (she unfortunately goes unnamed) who was teaching and baptizing. Tertullian denounces "certain Acts of Paul . . . [that] claim the example of Thecla for allowing women to teach and baptize." He quotes 1 Corinthians 14:35 and asks: "How could we believe that Paul should give a female power to teach and to baptize, when he did not allow a woman even to learn by her own right?"[42]

Many scholars doubt Paul's authorship of 1 Corinthians 14:35 since it is not consistent with Paul's presumption that Corinthian women prophets will pray and prophesy in the assembly (1 Cor 11:5). As is often the case in ancient writings, the more male church writers rail against any given female ministerial behavior, the more likely it is that such behavior was having an impact. For Cardman: "The continuing memory of Thecla challenged the developing structures of ministry in the churches. It is not difficult to imagine women telling and retelling the story of Thecla to authorize their own ministries."[43]

PROPHECY AND THE MONARCHICAL EPISCOPACY

Prophecy was an important and valued leadership role in the early church. Paul tells us that prophets are second only to apostles in the exercise of spiritual leadership:

> Now you are Christ's body, and individually parts of it. Some people God has designated in the church to be, first, apostles; second, prophets; third, teachers; then, mighty deeds; then, gifts of healing, assistance, administration, and varieties of tongues (1 Cor 12:27–28).

There were many female prophets in early Christianity. Paul instructs the women prophets at Corinth to cover their heads while prophesying, perhaps to differentiate their ministry from female prophets in other cults. (Note that he does not tell them to be silent and stop prophesying.) Luke's Gospel shows us the prophet Anna, who recognizes the infant Jesus as the redeemer of Israel, and Elizabeth, who prophesies to Mary about her unborn child. In the book of

42. Tertullian, *On Baptism* 17 (Ernest Evans, *Tertullian's Homily on Baptism* [London: SPCK, 1964]), as cited by Cardman, "Women, Ministry," 302.
43. Ibid.

Acts, we learn about Philip's four prophetic daughters (Acts 21:9). The fourth-century church historian Eusebius attributes the apostolic origins of the provincial churches in Asia Minor to their ministry, thereby acknowledging that at least some women were transmitters of apostolic tradition. The Didache, an early worship manual, names prophets as leaders of eucharistic celebrations.[44] As we have seen, these were often held in the homes of prominent women.

Prophetic women played important roles in guiding and building up the earliest church communities, often through inspired proclamations in liturgy. As seen in the book of Acts, Paul's letters to Corinth and Thessalonica, and the apocryphal Acts of Paul and Thecla, Christian prophecy was common throughout the Mediterranean world.[45] Didache 11.8 names an important criterion for judging true prophecy: "But not everyone who speaks in the Spirit is a prophet, except the one who has the behavior of the Lord." In other words, prophets must practice what they preach. The text notes that false prophets will stay too long in one place or ask for money.

Montanism was one of many prophetic movements in the early church. Founded by the prophet Montanus in what is now west central Turkey, the sect included two influential female prophets, Priscilla and Maximilla. Montanism was later deemed heretical by the mainstream church, though some scholars doubt that orthodoxy was the real issue. The prominence of women leaders and "competition between radically different church structures" were more likely sources of heresy accusations.[46] According to Schüssler Fiorenza: "The Montanists, as well as many other church groups, stressed the authority of the Spirit, that is, the authority of the prophets or ascetics, over against the authority of the non-charismatic local officers."[47] Ammia is another prophetic Montanist woman who lived in Asia Minor at the end of the second century. Eusebius claims her as part of the mainstream orthodox church and includes her in a succession list of recognized prophets: Agabus, Judas, Silas, the daughters of

---

44. Schüssler Fiorenza, *In Memory of Her*, 298.
45. Ibid., 297.
46. Ibid., 302; and Kraemer, *Her Share of the Blessings*, 157, 195.
47. Schüssler Fiorenza, *In Memory of Her*, 303; and Kraemer, *Her Share of the Blessings*, 157–58.

Philip, and "Ammia in Philadelphia."[48] Other female prophets named in the apocryphal Acts of Paul include Theonoe, Stratonike, Eubulla, Phila, Artemilla, Nympha, and Myra, who tells Paul not to lose heart because his enforced exile "will save many in Rome and will nourish many with the word."[49] Whether these names are actually historical women may not be as important as the fact that, like Thecla, they represent the many female prophets ministering in Asia Minor.

As Paul's first letter to the Corinthians and John's Gospel attest, all Christians receive the Holy Spirit and, at least in principle, "have equal access to authority, leadership, and power."[50] Since all Christians were spirit-filled, Schüssler Fiorenza suggests that communal worship in the early Jesus movement may have been characterized by rotating leadership: "This practice . . . would explain why the New Testament never identifies a presider or leader at the eucharist, and why non-canonical writings understand the prophet as such a eucharistic leader."[51]

In the second and third centuries, hierarchical governance, led by a monarchical episcopacy, gradually replaced early Christian prophecy movements. In the first century, prophets and apostles such as Paul, Prisca, Aquila, Junia, and Andronicus travelled from place to place to establish and build up nascent Christ-believing communities. Local leaders such as the *episcopoi, presbyteroi*, and *diakonoi* remained stationary and eventually acquired more authority than itinerant prophets, apostles, and teachers.[52] Some second-century bishops, such as Polycarp of Smyrna, Papias of Asia Minor, and Melito of Sardis, were also gifted with prophetic revelations. Gradually the function of prophecy was claimed by monarchical bishops to strengthen their authority. Soon, the bishops' authority replaced that of prophets, until "only the official hierarchy could speak 'with God's own voice.'"[53]

48. Schüssler Fiorenza, *In Memory of Her*, 300.
49. Ibid.
50. Ibid., 286.
51. Ibid., 299.
52. These are Greek titles that translate into English as bishops, priests, and deacons, respectively. However, as used in the first century, these titles are not synonymous for the offices of bishop, priest, and deacon as understood today.
53. Schüssler Fiorenza, *In Memory of Her*, 302. Gail Corrington Streete ("Women as Sources of Redemption and Knowledge in Early Christian Traditions," in Kraemer and D'Angelo, *Women and Christian Origins*, 345) sums it up well: "These two opposing strains to Christianity

CHURCH ORDERS AND OFFICIAL ROLES FOR WOMEN

From the third to the fifth centuries, early church documents, known as church orders, sought to establish lines of authority for church governance. Each appealed to the authority of the apostles as a means of bolstering their credibility, though by the third century this was clearly a rhetorical device rather than grounded in historically retrievable linkages.[54]

For our purposes, it is important to note that early church orders appealed to the authority of the apostles rather than to the genuine letters of Paul, whose memory was evoked in the Acts of Paul and Thecla. Scholars have long been aware that early church orders are not only descriptive of early communities but prescriptive insofar as they tell us what church leaders wanted to see in governance as opposed to what was actually happening. When church orders repeatedly prohibit women from teaching and baptizing, they illuminate the reality that women were doing both and the practice was probably widespread. Significant documents in this context include *Apostolic Tradition, Didascalia Apostolorum, Apostolic Constitutions*, and *Testamentum Domini*. These texts disclose how much time and energy was spent trying to control the behavior of independent Christian women, especially widows. They attest that from the third to the fifth centuries, older women (over age fifty to sixty) whose husbands had died were formally enrolled or appointed to the office of widow in both the Eastern and Western church. Some were enrolled to receive subsistence support from the community while others were appointed for specific church duties.

While the third-century *Apostolic Tradition* (Rome?) specifically instructs church leaders not to ordain widows, the late fourth-century

in the second to the fourth centuries (the New Prophecy and its followers and those bishops and their followers who called themselves orthodox) both claimed scriptural warrant for their beliefs. The first held that scriptural precedent validates both the charismatic gift of prophecy and clerical leadership for women, while the other found scriptural counter-examples to close both prophetic and institutional power to women. The latter voice was the one that prevailed."

54. See William A. Jurgens, *The Faith of the Early Fathers*, 3 vols. (Collegeville, MN: Liturgical Press, 1970–79), 2:127: "The [*Apostolic Constitutions*] pretends to be of Apostolic origin, written out and sent around to all bishops and priests by St. Clement of Rome. In that respect it is a forgery of the grosser and more impious sort. Here the use of Clement's name is not merely a congenial literary device. It was done with deliberate intent to deceive."

Testamentum Domini (Syria, Asia Minor, or Egypt) devotes a whole chapter to ordained widows, includes them in the hierarchy of the church, and attests that their ordination is the same as that of other major clerics.[55] A diversity of views clearly existed (perhaps reflecting differences in Eastern and Western customs) as to what ministerial roles official widows had. As these texts prescribe, the responsibilities of both enrolled and ordained widows were prayer, petition, theological instruction, and the anointing of women at baptism. The *Testamentum Domini* also mentions that widows examined ("tested") deaconesses. Other duties included visiting and caring for the sick and receiving offerings.

The analyses that follow, however, suggest that the ministry of widows may well have been broader than these early documents indicate. Epigraphical evidence for the order of widows is found in Italy in the catacomb of Priscilla, where we find this second-century inscription: "The widow Flavia Arcas, who lived eighty-five years. Flavia Theophila, her daughter, erected (this epitaph) to the sweetest of mothers." Other widows identified from their tombstones were Regina, whose daughter commemorates her in the Rome cemetery of St. Saturninus, and Laurentia, the mother of Pope Damasus (366–384). We know that women were enrolled as widows because the title χηρα (widow) was engraved on their tombstones. Inscriptions from this period did not use the term widow for women whose husbands had predeceased them.[56]

APOSTOLIC TRADITION

Between 210 and 220, Hippolytus of Rome is believed to have written the *Apostolic Tradition*, a composite document that sought to regulate liturgy and the hierarchical organization of church ministries.[57] Recent scholars question the origins and dating of this document, though not the historical figure of Hippolytus of Rome. The treatise

---

55. Madigan and Osiek, *Ordained Women*, 153–54.

56. Eisen, *Women Officeholders*, 144.

57. Jurgens, *Faith of the Early Fathers*, 1:166. The *Apostolic Tradition* also contains an early eucharistic prayer that was reinstated as Eucharistic Prayer II in the Catholic Mass after the document's discovery in the early twentieth century.

may have emerged at a time when the church of Rome was arguing whether Christians who sinned after baptism could be reconciled to the community, the nature of the divinity of Christ, and whether it was proper to recognize unions between upper-class women and men of lower status. Callixtus, a Roman deacon who would later become bishop of Rome, differed from Hippolytus on these issues, believing in forgiveness and the propriety of marital unions between unequal partners. Widows and other women of means had considerable influence in the Rome of Hippolytus's day.

Wealthy, socially elite women were having difficulty finding Christian husbands since most men of their social class persisted in their non-Christian beliefs and it was illegal for a high-status woman to marry a male slave or freedman. Although she could legally marry a socially inferior freeborn man, she would simultaneously lose her *clarissima* (noblewoman) status and all the rights that adhered to it. Rather than marry a non-Christian man of equal status, many wealthy Christian women chose to live in permanent concubinage with lower-status Christian men. According to Lampe, this arrangement, "received the blessings of Callistus. . . . In this way he prevented two things: mixed marriages with pagans and the social decline of Christian women. Both were in the interests of the community."[58] After Callixtus was elected bishop of Rome, Hippolytus refused to remain in communion with the larger church.[59] The *Apostolic Tradition* details the selection, ordination, and duties of the clergy, including ordination prayers for each office. It creates a definite ranked order among ministers, with presbyters being subject to bishops, deacons subject to presbyters, and subdeacons subject to deacons. Cardman suggests this hierarchy was emphasized because Hippolytus was himself a presbyter and wanted to be clear about Callixtus's lowly status as a deacon.[60]

While the *Apostolic Tradition* identifies appointed widows as clergy, it sharply delineates between offices that require ordination (bishop, priest, deacon) and those that require only acknowledgement (widows and virgins). This directive effectively marginalizes women's

58. Lampe, *From Paul to Valentinus*, 121.
59. Henry Chadwick, *The Early Church* (London: Penguin, 1967), 88.
60. Cardman, "Women, Ministry," 306.

ministries and restricts their opportunities for leadership. For the first time, priestly ordination rituals and prayers are prescribed: "When a presbyter is to be ordained, the bishop shall impose his hand upon his head, while the presbyters touch the one to be ordained." But, when it comes to the order of widows, the *Apostolic Tradition* three times repeats a directive that widows are not to be ordained but only appointed:

> When a widow is to be appointed, she is not to be ordained, but is designated by being named such. . . . A widow is appointed by words alone, and is then associated with the other widows. Hands are not imposed upon her, because she does not offer the oblation and she does not conduct the Liturgy. Ordination is for the clergy because of the Liturgy; but a widow is appointed for prayer, and prayer is the duty of all.[61]

The text advances a circular argument for excluding women: "Women do not perform liturgical ministry because they are not ordained; therefore they do not need to be ordained (indeed, may not be) since ordination is for liturgical ministry, which they do not do."[62] According to Cardman:

> The widows described here are recognizable descendants of those in the Pastoral Epistles and seem to be a source of difficulty for some of the clergy in Rome. . . . The adamant reiteration signals the importance of the issue for Hippolytus, as well as the likelihood that widows were being ordained in the Roman church at the time, a practice that he was determined to halt?[63]

Interesting exceptions are confessors who have "been in chains for the name of the Lord." If a Christian is jailed or tortured but not executed for following Christ, he (or she?) is regarded as already having the "honor of the presbyterate by the fact of his confession" of faith.[64] One wonders if such a rule would have applied to women confessors, since many women were also imprisoned and tortured. The *Apostolic Tradition* was not particularly influential in the Western

---

61. Jurgens, *Faith of the Early Fathers*, 1:169.
62. Cardman, "Women, Ministry," 307.
63. Ibid.
64. Jurgens, *Faith of the Early Fathers*, 1:168.

church,[65] probably owing, at least in part, to the political circumstances under which it was created. If Hippolytus is the author, his opposition to church approval for the marriages of wealthy Christian women to Christian men of lower rank may have made his teachings unpalatable to those outside his own community. It is another irony of church history that the writings of a man who publicly opposed the bishop of Rome should later be held up as a model of "apostolic authority."

DIDASCALIA APOSTOLORUM
(TEACHINGS OF THE APOSTLES)

The *Didascalia* reflects the pastoral situation of some church communities in Syria and Palestine in the late third century. It concerns itself with the conduct of the laity, the need to observe important doctrinal and disciplinary precepts and avoid heresy, and the organization of ministry and leadership in the church. Urging a ministry organized around the local bishop, it enumerates the requirements for bishops in considerable depth, emphasizing their authority over the other ministers and the laity and delineating the duties of deacons and deaconesses. It has relatively little to say about presbyters, perhaps implying that their role was as yet undefined.[66]

The *Didascalia* pays an extraordinary amount of attention to the conduct of widows, making a pointed contrast between "good" and "bad" widows. Among the worst faults of the widows is that they "run about asking questions"[67] and they "wish to be wiser and to know better, not only than the men, but even than the presbyters and the bishops."[68] They are instructed to "have no other care save to be praying for those who give, and for the whole church" and are forbidden to receive donations without permission.[69] This directive

65. Cardman, "Women, Ministry," 308.
66. Ibid.; I am indebted to Francine Cardman's helpful summary of the scope of the *Didascalia* throughout this essay.
67. *Didascalia Apostolorum* 15.3.10 (R. Hugh Connolly [Oxford: Clarendon Press, 1929], reprinted on Early Christian Writings, http://tinyurl.com/ydefsawf; all translations taken from here).
68. Ibid., 15.3.8.
69. Ibid., 15.3.5.

effectively "prevents them from establishing close relationships with benefactors [and] . . . deprives the widows of the power implicit in providing the donor the opportunity to exercise charity."[70] Cardman summarizes: "Circumscribing the widows' role in this way ensures that the bishop will retain control over the system of donations and distribution and thus over both benefactors and beneficiaries."[71] Significantly, whenever the needy are invited to a supper, the *Didascalia* describes a top-down distribution system for those in church orders, and widows are at the bottom of the food chain:

> But how much (soever) is given to one of the widows, let the double be given to each of the deacons in honour of Christ, (but) twice twofold to the leader for the glory of the Almighty. But if anyone wish to honour the presbyters also, let him give them a double (portion), as to the deacons; for they ought to be honoured as the Apostles, and as the counsellors of the bishop, and as the crown of the Church; for they are the moderators and councillors of the Church.[72]

Widows are enjoined to silence and forbidden to teach, baptize, fast with, pray over, or lay hands on anyone without being commanded to do so by the bishop or the deacon. The repeated and insistent proscriptions of women baptizing and teaching tell us that they were doing both. To justify the prohibition, the document argues that Jesus was baptized by John, not by his mother,[73] and that he did not commission the women disciples to teach:

> It is neither right nor necessary therefore that women should be teachers, and especially concerning the name of Christ and the redemption of His passion. For you have not been appointed to this, O women, and especially widows, that you should teach. . . . For if it were required that women should teach, our Master Himself would have commanded these to give instruction with us.[74]

Instead, the *Didascalia* instructs, "But let a widow know that she is the altar of God; and let her sit ever at home, and not stray or run

70. Cardman, "Women, Ministry," 310.
71. Ibid., 311.
72. *Didascalia Apostolorum* 15.2.27.
73. Ibid., 15.3.9.
74. Ibid., 15.3.6. See also Cardman, "Women, Ministry," 310.

about among the houses of the faithful to receive. For the altar of God never strays or runs about anywhere, but is fixed in one place."[75] Still, says Cardman: "The reality of church life, however, did not conform to the *Didascalia*'s orderly vision. Nowhere is it less accurate than with regard to widows. Despite the efforts of the Pastoral Epistles to restrain them, the widows remained a disruptive force in the evolution of ministerial structures."[76] The *Didascalia*'s dramatic effort to prevent widows from teaching and baptizing while restricting their access to grateful, wealthy benefactors suggests they were active and successful evangelists. While sharply criticizing uppity widows, the *Didascalia* approves the public ministry of female deacons, who were more subject to hierarchical control and who may have been enlisted to counter the widows' influence. Female deacons were forbidden to baptize but permitted to teach women, visit them when ill, and anoint their bodies at baptism.

APOSTOLIC CONSTITUTIONS

The *Apostolic Constitutions*, an eight-volume work, originated in Syria in the late fourth century. It compiles and enlarges upon several earlier works including the Didache, the *Apostolic Tradition*, and the *Didascalia*, while adding some new material of its own.[77] The first six books reprise and revise the *Didascalia*, updating it to reflect church orders in Syria. It vehemently addresses the intransigence of women continuing to preach and baptize. The document amplifies the *Didascalia*'s hierarchical divine order for the post-Constantinian church, instructing Christians to honor the bishop who "sits for you in the place of God Almighty." The male deacon is likened to Christ, the male presbyter represents the apostles, and the female deacon is likened to the Holy Spirit.[78] Widows are notably absent. One should not, however, surmise that women deacons escaped subordinate status by being likened to a type of Holy Spirit. The

75. *Didascalia Apostolorum* 15.3.6.
76. Cardman, "Women, Ministry," 310.
77. Jurgens, *Faith of the Early Fathers*, 2:128.
78. *Didascalia Apostolorum* 15.2.26.

Apostolic Constitutions clarify that she is to do nothing on her own authority: "Let also the deaconess be honoured by you in the place of the Holy Ghost, and not do or say anything without the deacon; as neither does the Comforter say or do anything of Himself, but gives glory to Christ by waiting for His pleasure."[79] The *Constitutions* also rule that no woman was to visit a bishop or a deacon without a deaconess along. One wonders what underlying issues might have prompted this decree. Sexual abuse cannot be ruled out. Book 8 calls for suspension of bishops, presbyters, and deacons who are guilty of fornication and for anyone who "offered violence to a virgin not betrothed, and keeps her."[80] The *Apostolic Constitutions* omits the *Didascalia*'s inadvertent admission that widows were laying on hands in what today is known as the sacrament of the sick. Gryson concludes: "By dropping the reference to their power of blessing, and by refusing to mention them after the bishop, presbyter, and deacon, the Constitutions actually strip the widow of everything which suggested the idea of an ecclesiastical function in the *Didascalia*."[81] Like the *Didascalia*, the *Apostolic Constitutions* forbids a woman to teach in church or baptize—enjoining her

> to own herself to be the "altar of God," and let her sit in her house, and not enter into the houses of the faithful, under any pretense, to receive anything; for the altar of God never runs about, but is fixed in one place. Let, therefore, the virgin and the widow be such as do not run about, or wander to the houses of those who are alien from the faith.[82]

These repeated injunctions attest that by the late fourth century, women were still baptizing, teaching, and evangelizing, as they had been doing since the second century. The increased vehemence of

---

79. *Apostolic Constitutions* 2.4.26 (James Donaldson, *Ante-Nicene Fathers*, vol. 7 [Buffalo, NY: Christian Literature, 1886], rev. and ed. Kevin Knight for New Advent, http://tinyurl.com/y96at8mb; all translations taken from here).

80. *Apostolic Constitutions* 8.5.47.25 (italics original): "Let a bishop, or presbyter, or deacon who is taken in fornication, or perjury, or stealing, be deprived, *but not suspended; for the Scripture says: 'You shall not avenge twice for the same crime by affliction'.*" Ibid., 8.5.47.67: "If any one has offered violence to a virgin not betrothed, and keeps her, let him be suspended. But it is not lawful for him to take another to wife; but he must retain her whom he has chosen, although she be poor."

81. Gryson, *Ministry of Women*, 59.

82. *Apostolic Constitutions* 3.1.6.

the prohibition suggests women's exercise of ministerial authority
had continued unabated and was probably quite common:

> Now, as to women's baptizing we let you know that there is no small
> peril to those that undertake it. Therefore, we do not advise you to it;
> for it is dangerous, or rather wicked and impious. . . . For the principal
> part of the woman is the man, as being her head. But if in the forego-
> ing constitutions we have not permitted them to teach, how will anyone
> allow them, contrary to nature, to perform the office of a priest?[83]

The author of *Apostolic Constitutions* understands the ministry of baptism as exclusive to a priesthood to which a woman could never aspire
because of her supposedly subordinate nature in the order of creation. Like the *Didascalia*, *Constitutions* restricts widows' contact with
benefactors. Osiek and MacDonald see such attempts as "a conscious
attempt on the part of church authority to control women's patronage as well as men's and to break the network of personal patronage
that had been the backbone of social relationships."[84]

Yet, female patronage power did not disappear. Women patrons
provided burial spaces for poor Christians into the fourth century,
and wealthy widows such as Olympias commanded considerable
respect as major benefactors to the church. But in the meantime, the
widows of the *Apostolic Constitutions* were placed at the bottom of
the pecking order. Adding insult to injury, they were now subject to
women deacons, with appropriate punishments if they did not
comply:

> The widows therefore ought to be grave, obedient to their bishops, and
> their presbyters, and their deacons, and besides these to the deaconesses,
> with piety, reverence, and fear; not usurping authority, nor desiring to
> do anything beyond the constitution without the consent of the deacon:
> as, suppose, the going to anyone to eat or drink with him, or to receive
> anything from anybody. But if without direction she does any one of
> these things, let her be punished with fasting, or else let her be separated
> on account of her rashness.[85]

Though placed ahead of the widows, ministerial responsibilities for

83. Ibid., 3.1.9.
84. Osiek and MacDonald, *A Woman's Place*, 218.
85. *Apostolic Constitutions* 3.1.

female deacons are more restricted than in the *Didascalia*. They have now been reduced to doorkeepers and assisting presbyters at female baptism: "A deaconess does not bless, nor perform anything belonging to the office of presbyters or deacons, but only is to keep the doors, and to minister to the presbyters in the baptizing of women, on account of decency."[86]

TESTAMENTUM DOMINI

In marked contrast to other church orders, the *Testamentum Domini* not only ordains widows but shows them seated alongside the bishop at liturgy, in a more prominent place than presbyters and deacons: "Let the position of the bishop be near to the place that is called the front stage. Likewise, let the place of the widows, who are said to have precedence in sitting, be in the same place."[87] Though dating and authorship are uncertain, scholars estimate the original text was written in Greek sometime in the late fourth or early fifth century in Syria, Egypt, or Asia Minor, with Asia Minor thought to be most likely.[88] In this church order, female deacons have a minimal role, limited to greeting and overseeing female churchgoers as they enter the assembly. Still, during the Eucharist, widows and deaconesses are both named among those who celebrate the sacred rites behind the veil, as was customary in the East. Female presbyters (elders) are also named as members of the clergy, though they do not exercise liturgical leadership and their primary function seems to have been prayer. Widows, rather than female deacons, have a prominent role to play during female baptism: "Let the women [to be baptized] be anointed by the widows who sit in front, while the presbyter recites over them the formula. And also at the baptism let those widows receive the woman wrapped in a veil while the bishop offers the formulas of profession; and again while he offers the formulas of renunciation."[89]

The *Testamentum Domini* makes it plain that ordained widows

---

86. Ibid., 8.2.28.
87. *Testamentum Domini* 1.19, as cited in Madigan and Osiek, *Ordained Women*, 150.
88. Madigan and Osiek, *Ordained Women*, 150.
89. *Testamentum Domini* 2.8, as cited in Madigan and Osiek, *Ordained Women*, 153.

exercised wide-ranging pastoral responsibilities for ministering to other women. They taught female catechumens, visited sick women, instructed the ignorant and encouraged women pursuing a celibate spiritual path. Gryson writes, "She is not a subordinate minister, not just an assistant; on the contrary, she has a pastoral responsibility, being especially charged with the care of souls."[90] But first and foremost, widows in the *Testamentum Domini* were honored for their ascetic lives of contemplation and prayer and "persevering at the altar night and day."[91] The admonition for widows to "be silent in Church and assiduous in prayer" is slipped in between their duties of admonishing "those saying superfluous and vain things" and visiting sick women on Sundays "taking with her one or two deacons to help them."[92]

One wonders why two deacons needed to accompany her. It may have been for propriety's sake or to ensure that she did not accept gifts without supervision. Unlike earlier church orders, there are no heated chastisements for baptizing, teaching, accepting benefactions, or moving from house to house. Instead, as previously enjoined by the *Apostolic Constitutions*, the widows of the *Testamentum Domini* are praised for their stable, silent, ascetic lives oriented around "the altar of God [that] never runs about, but is fixed in one place."[93] While the *Testamentum Domini* demonstrates that at least some churchmen in Asia Minor had succeeded in taming the daughters of Thecla, other contemporaneous writings paint a different picture. A late fourth-century manuscript, *The Anonymous Dialogue Between a Montanist and an Orthodox*, not only forbids women to speak in the churches but also prohibits them from writing books. "But we do not permit women to speak in the assemblies, nor to have authority over men, to the point of writing books in their own name."[94] While female authors were apparently considered heretical by the "Orthodox," women teaching in church still attracted heated opposition.

90. Gryson, *Ministry of Women*, 68.
91. *Testamentum Domini* 1.40, as cited in Madigan and Osiek, *Ordained Women*, 153.
92. Madigan and Osiek, *Ordained Women*, 154.
93. *Apostolic Constitutions* 3.1.6.
94. Gryson, *Ministry of Women*, 76.

This means, of course, that women were doing that very thing or there would have been no need for a rule.

In the late fourth century, John Chrysostom distinguishes between women teaching in public and in private, the former forbidden and the latter permissible. Still, he inveighs against women who "endeavor to thrust themselves into [the sanctuary]" even though the divine law has excluded them: "For the blessed Paul did not suffer them even to speak in the church. But I have heard some say that they have obtained such a large privilege of free speech as even to rebuke the prelates of the Churches, and censure them more severely than masters do their own domestics."[95] Gryson concludes: "Not only, therefore, are women not admitted into the sanctuary, but they are not supposed to interfere in any way in ecclesiastical affairs."[96] From the early second to the fifth century, churchmen repeatedly invoke 1 Timothy 2:12 when they prohibit women from teaching, baptizing, or exercising authority in the church. That these mandates continue for four centuries suggests not only that women continued to exercise ministerial authority but that the issue of women's leadership was no more settled in the early church than it is in some Christian denominations today.

WOMEN DEACONS

Although male church leaders sought to curtail the wide-ranging ministry of widows, there is ample literary and archaeological evidence for ordained female deacons. Many scholars, however, suggest that ordaining female deacons allowed male leaders to control what public ministries women could and could not perform.[97] The earliest references to deacons in the New Testament are found in Paul's letters. According to Osiek, the opening lines of Paul's letter to the Philippians "contain a reference found nowhere else in the greetings of his letters: he and Timothy greet not only the holy ones or saints in Philippi, but add a greeting to their *episcopoi* and *diakonoi*."[98] The

---

95. John Chrysostom, *On the Priesthood* 3.9, as cited by Gryson, *Ministry of Women*, 84.
96. Gryson, *Ministry of Women*, 85.
97. Cardman, "Women, Ministry," 310–11.
98. Carolyn Osiek, *Women in the Ministry of Paul* (Cleveland: FutureChurch, 2010).

Greek word *episcopos* (overseer) does not yet mean what later came to be the office of bishop but "is more likely a reference to the leaders of house churches, groupings of believers that met in private houses for worship and other means of nurturing their faith life."[99] The term *diakonoi* is "a general word for official representatives, ministers, attendants, and agents. Here it refers to a designated group of persons who provide some kind of assistance in the community."[100] As we have seen, there is good reason to believe that two women, Euodia and Syntyche, were among the *episcopoi* and *diakonoi* at Philippi (Phil 4:2).

Thanks to the work of scholars such as Osiek, Macy, and others, we now know that titles for church officials—such as bishop, priest, and deacon—in the first millennium are not equivalent to the meaning of these titles today. For example, in some third and fourth century communities, deacons served as important administrators of church properties whose authority was second only to that of the bishop.[101] By the twelfth century, the separate ministry of deacon was subsumed into the priesthood, becoming a preliminary step to ordination. Only at the second Vatican Council did the separate ministry of permanent deacons reemerge. Women deacons are specifically identified in two places in the New Testament: Romans 16 and 1 Timothy 3:11. In the first two verses of Romans 16, Paul writes:

> I commend to you our sister Phoebe, a deacon [*diakonos*] of the church in Cenchreae. I ask you to receive her in the Lord in a way worthy of his people and to give her any help she may need from you, for she has been the benefactor [*prostatis*] of many people, including me.

In the first century, the use of the masculine singular title *diakonos* for a female leader does not have the specificity of meaning that it acquired in later centuries. Therefore, it can be translated as either minister or deacon, but not deaconess, since this title did not emerge until later. The title *diakonos* is thought to connote an official leadership function such as minister, attendant, or envoy. The latter is

---

99. Ibid.
100. Ibid.
101. John Wijngaards, *Women Deacons in the Early Church: Historical Texts and Contemporary Debates* (New York: Crossroad, 2006), 12.

the likely meaning in the letter to the Romans since most scholars believe Paul's recommendation of Phoebe to the Christians in Rome indicates that she is the carrier of his letter to that community. However, Phoebe's other title, "benefactor" or patron (*prostatis*), is probably more significant since it reveals that she is among the many wealthy women patrons who hosted house churches and provided financially for Paul and other evangelists in the burgeoning Christian missionary movement. Phoebe's important leadership in the early church is inexplicably deleted from the lectionary when the Romans 16 text is read on week thirty-one, year one.

The first letter of Timothy describes qualifications for *diakonoi*, concluding with what is probably a reference to women deacons.

> In the same way, [male] deacons (*diakonoi*) are to be worthy of respect, sincere, not indulging in much wine, and not pursuing dishonest gain. They must keep hold of the deep truths of the faith with a clear conscience. They must first be tested; and then if there is nothing against them, let them serve as deacons. In the same way, the women are to be worthy of respect, not malicious talkers but temperate and trustworthy in everything (1 Tim 3:8–11).

While it is possible that the wives of deacons are meant, it is likely that the text refers to women deacons ministering in Timothy's community. John Chrysostom, Theodoret of Cyrrhus, and Theodore of Mopsuestia are three early commentators who understood the text to refer to female deacons.[102]

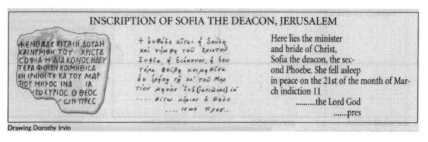

INSCRIPTION OF SOFIA THE DEACON, JERUSALEM

Here lies the minister and bride of Christ, Sofia the deacon, the second Phoebe. She fell asleep in peace on the 21st of the month of March indiction 11 ....the Lord God ......pres

Drawing Dorothy Irvin

Figure 2.3. A reproduction by Dr. Dorothy Irvin of an inscription found on the Mount of Olives in Israel that dates to the fourth or fifth century. Used with permission.

102. Madigan and Osiek, *Ordained Women*, 18–20.

WOMEN DEACONS IN THE EAST

The office of female deacon or deaconess was more prevalent in the East than the West. We first see the Greek title *diakonos* with a masculine grammatical ending given to the Phoebe in Romans 16. It has been falsely assumed that *diakonos* was replaced with the feminine deaconess (*diakonissa*) by the third century. However, *diakonos* and *diakonissa* are both used for women deacons in literary sources and archaeological inscriptions until the sixth century.[103] For example, a fourth century tombstone on the Mount of Olives has a Greek inscription that reads: "Here lies the minister and bride of Christ, Sofia the Deacon, a second Phoebe. She fell asleep in peace on the 21st of the month of March . . ." (see figure 2.3). It is notable that for both Phoebe in the first century and Sofia in the fourth, the title *diakonos* with a Greek masculine ending is used. The Christian community in Jerusalem apparently understood Sofia's ministry to be part of a three-hundred-year-old tradition dating back to the Phoebe of Romans 16. Madigan and Osiek surmise that "Phoebe and other unnamed women deacons like her in the first and perhaps second century belonged to an office or function that was not distinguished by sex."[104] Phoebe's first-century leadership probably bore little resemblance to those of later deaconesses. The *Didascalia Apostolorum* goes to great lengths to restrict the role of widows, while approving the public ministry of female deacons, allowing them to teach and anoint but not to baptize. The *Apostolic Constitutions* further restricts the ministry of women deacons by forbidding them to teach. Since church rules (canons) are often prescriptive as well as descriptive, literary and archaeological data often provide evidence for more expanded roles for women than one would expect. For example, Olympias, Dionysia, and other women deacons assisted in the liturgy, financially supported and advised male church leaders, served the poor, and, most often, taught women and anointed them at the time of their baptism. There is ample archaeological evidence

---

103. Ibid., 3.
104. Madigan and Osiek, *Ordained Women*, 5.

of other female deacons who ministered from the first to the sixth centuries in Palestine, Asia Minor, Greece, and Macedonia.[105]

WOMEN DEACONS IN THE WEST

The literary and archaeological evidence for female deacons in the West does not appear until the fifth century, when texts proscribing women presbyters also appear. Western conciliar documents plainly indicate the displeasure of churchmen over women's ordination to the diaconate or any other office. Canon 26 of the Council of Orange, held in November 441, forbade the ordination of female deacons. In 517, the Council of Epaon abolished "the consecration of widows who are called women deacons."[106] However, texts written by male church authorities are one thing and the actual ministry of women is quite another. Literary references to women deacons in the West, while not abundant, are definitely present over a seven-century period. They are found in wills, letters, and chronicles of women deacons. For example, Remigius, the bishop of Reims (433–533), left a will bequeathing part of a vineyard to "my blessed daughter, Helaria the deaconess," well after the Council of Epaon forbade such a ministry.[107] In the mid-sixth century, the Frankish queen Radegund was ordained a deacon by Bishop Medard, a bishop of Noyons and Tournai. Other women deacons in the West known to us by tombstone inscriptions include Anna, a sixth-century woman deacon from Rome; Theodora, a female deacon from Gaul buried in 539; and Ausonia, a sixth-century woman deacon from Dalmatia. In 753, the archbishop of Ravenna, Sergius, "consecrated his wife, Euphemia, a deacon (*diaconissa*)." And in 799, Pope Leo III was greeted by the entire population of Rome including "holy women, women deacons (*diaconissae*) and the most notable matrons" upon his return to that city.[108]

Abbesses in the Western church were sometimes deacons as well.

---

105. See Eisen, *Women Officeholders*.
106. Ibid., 145–46.
107. Gary Macy, "Women Deacons: History," in *Women Deacons, Past, Present, Future*, by Gary Macy, William T. Ditewig, and Phyllis Zagano (New York: Paulist, 2011), 13.
108. Ibid., 17.

Some commentators on canon law in the ninth and tenth centuries simply assumed that abbesses were deacons.[109] Despite persistent early efforts to suppress women deacons in the West, Pope Benedict VIII wrote a letter in 1017 conferring on the bishop of Porto in Portugal "in perpetuity every episcopal ordination not only of presbyters but also of deacons or deaconesses (*diaconibus vel diaconissis*) or subdeacons."[110] This privilege was continued by subsequent popes up to the time of Bishop Ottone, the bishop of Lucca in Italy (1139–46). Abelard and Heloise—twelfth-century theologians—both referred to Heloise as a deacon.[111]

ORDINATION RITES FOR WOMEN DEACONS

For centuries, scholars have agreed that the earliest Eastern ritual used to ordain female deacons is the same one used for male deacons. Jean Morin, a seventeenth-century liturgical expert, catalogued a large collection of ordination rites in Greek, Latin, and Syriac:

> Three of the most ancient Greek rituals, uniformly one in agreement, hand down to us the ordination of women deacons, administered by almost the same rite and words by which deacons [were ordained]. Both are called ordination [χειρτονια, χειροθεσια]. Both are celebrated at the altar by the bishop, and in the same liturgical space. Hands are placed on both while the bishop offers prayers. The stole is placed on the neck of both, both the ordained man and the ordained woman communicated, the chalice full of the blood of Christ placed in the hands of both so they may taste of it.[112]

The bishop ordained a female deacon in the presence of the "presbyter, the deacons and the deaconesses" and the *Apostolic Constitutions* contains a fourth-century ordination prayer that reads:

> O, Eternal God, Father of our Lord Jesus Christ, creator of man and of woman, you who have filled with your Spirit Miriam and Deborah, Anna and Huldah; you who have not deemed it unworthy that your only begotten Son be born of a woman; you who instituted women as

109. Ibid., 29.
110. Ibid., 17.
111. Ibid., 29.
112. Ibid., 19.

guardians of the holy parts of the tent of the covenant and of the temple; You, even now, look upon this [female] servant of yours elected to the diaconate; grant her the Holy Spirit and purify her from all sins of the flesh and of the spirit: so that she might fulfill the task entrusted to her for your glory and for the glory of your Christ, with whom and with the Holy Spirit, glory and adoration be to you and forever and ever.[113]

It is significant that the phrase "cleanse her from all sins of flesh and spirit" does not appear in ordination prayers for male clergy. Cardman comments: "Uncleanness of flesh or spirit is thus a peculiarly female liability. It can be overcome to some degree by the gift of the Holy Spirit in ordination, but must be kept under control by the deaconess's obedience to the bishop and other clergy who have authority over her."[114]

The earliest ordination ritual in the West is found in an eighth-century liturgical book by Bishop Egbert of York. It contains a single prayer used for ordaining either a male or female deacon. The prayer reads:

Give heed, Lord, to our prayers and upon this your servant send forth that spirit of your blessing in order that, enriched by heavenly gifts, he [or she] might be able to obtain grace through your majesty and by living well offer an example to others.[115]

Other rituals for the ordination of female deacons appear in ninth- tenth-, and twelfth-century sacramentaries and pontificals. By the thirteenth century, the ordination rites for women deacons were eliminated from the Roman pontifical and do not appear again.

In the twentieth century, protestant denominations began ordaining women to the diaconate and to the priesthood, but in the Roman Catholic Church women's ordination is not permitted. In 1974, Cipriano Vagaggini, OSB, Cam., (1909–99) published a fifteen-thousand-word document about the possibility of ordaining women to the diaconate. Vagaggini was a member of the Vatican's International Theological Commission (ITC) at the time and Pope Paul VI reportedly requested his research. At issue was whether or not

---

113. Cipriano Vagaggini, *Ordination of Women to the Diaconate in the Eastern Churches*, ed. Phyllis Zagano (Collegeville, MN: Liturgical Press, 2013), 36.
114. Cardman, "Women, Ministry," 317.
115. Macy, "Women Deacons," 20.

female diaconal ordinations were the same as male diaconal ordinations. At the study's conclusion, Cipriano Vagaggini responded in the affirmative:

> It seems to me certain that in the history of the undivided church the Byzantine tradition maintained by nature and dignity the ordination of deaconesses belonged to the group of bishops, presbyters, and deacons and not to the group of lectors and subdeacons. . . . Theologically, in virtue of the use of the Byzantine Church, it appears that women can receive diaconal ordination, which, by nature and dignity is equated to the ordination of the deacons.[116]

In 1987, Vagaggini was asked to prepare a presentation on his work to the Vatican's Synod on the Laity; however, there was no mention of his work in the final synod document, *Christifidelis laici* (1988). In 2002, the ITC issued a study document advising that "the question of including women in the restored diaconate is something that the church's 'ministry of discernment' should decide."[117] At this writing, the vigorous discussion about the place of women in the Roman Catholic Church, and especially within ordained ministry, continues unabated. Citing the need to follow their consciences and the call of God, nearly two hundred Catholic women have accepted excommunication by being ordained outside the official canons of the church, first to the diaconate and then to the priesthood. Both Pope Benedict and Pope Francis have frequently spoken about the necessity of giving women more space in the church. Yet what that "space" might be remains obscure.

THE DECLINE OF FEMALE DEACONS

By the twelfth century, women deacons had become very rare, though they persist in some Eastern rites into the modern period.[118] A twelfth-century Greek canonist, Theodore Balsamon, wrote: "In times past, orders of deaconesses were recognized and they had access

---

116. Vagaggini, *Ordination of Women*, 61.

117. Phyllis Zagano, introduction to Vagaggini, *Ordination of Women*, 10.

118. Phyllis Zagano, "It's Time: The Case for Women Deacons," *Commonweal* 139, no. 22 (December 12, 2012): 8–9.

to the sanctuary, but the monthly affliction banished them."[119] In the fourteenth century, another Eastern canonist, Matthew Blastares, acknowledged that while women deacons had existed, they were later forbidden "because of the monthly flow that cannot be controlled."[120] In the West, even though Pope Gregory I (590–604) said that menstruation should not be an obstacle to women attending church, the purity rules eventually prevailed. In the end, women deacons would be banned at least partly because of their normal biological functions.

Another significant event leading to the demise of women deacons in the West came in the mid-twelfth century when the definition of ordination underwent a dramatic shift. In the first millennium, a Christian was ordained, consecrated, or blessed to perform a specific job or ministry needed by the community. Gary Macy writes:

> Ordination did not give a person, for instance, the irrevocable and portable power of consecrating the bread and wine, or of leading the liturgy; rather, a particular community charged a person or persons to play a leadership role within that community (and only within that community) and that person or persons would lead the liturgy because of the leadership role they played within the community.[121]

In the twelfth century, the definition of ordination came to signify that recipients were given an indelible character marking them as different from other Christians. Now the priest and only the priest received the power to consecrate bread and wine. Further, the indelible character and power to consecrate was portable and could be exercised anywhere, in any community. Ordination now authorized only ministries that related to service at the altar, so only the orders of priest, deacon, and subdeacon were recognized. Finally, "all of the other earlier orders were no longer considered to be orders at all."[122]

A highly influential late twelfth-century Western canonist, Huguccio of Bologna, wrote that even if a woman were to be ordained it would not "take" because of "the law of the church and

---

119. Macy, "Women Deacons," 31.
120. Ibid.
121. Ibid., 33.
122. Ibid., 34.

sex."[123] In other words, the fact of being biologically female prevented women from being ordained, and what is more, because they were biologically female, they never could have been truly ordained in the first place. Therefore, all past female ordinations were not ordinations at all, at least according to the new understanding of ordination. Given that male ordinations in previous centuries also entailed a different understanding of the meaning of orders, one could argue that those male ordinations did not "take" either, a point that seems to have escaped our esteemed canonists.

By the early thirteenth century, the ancient tradition of women deacons had been defined out of existence in the West. One wonders if it is more than mere coincidence that as women deacons were being extinguished, a new movement of ministerial women was coming to birth. These were independent female communities, known as Beguines, that operated outside the control of male church leaders. The Beguines served as prototypes (although not without persecution) to the later meteoric rise of women's apostolic religious communities. Like their foremothers (and still today), these women religious attracted the ire of clerics, perhaps because their advocacy for the marginalized often unsettled the status quo.

EVIDENCE FOR WOMEN PRESBYTERS

Formerly, archaeologists and other scholars interpreted inscriptions of female deacons, priests, and bishops exclusively as the wives of these officeholders, rather than a female holding the office. The title *presbytera* was also thought to indicate an elderly or senior woman rather than a female priest. Recent scholarship is more nuanced, acknowledging that in some contexts, such as 1 Timothy 5:1–2, the terms *presbyteroi* and *presbytera* refer to elderly male and female persons, while the *presbyteroi* of 1 Timothy 5:17 probably refer to an authoritative position.[124] Even though *presbytera* can sometimes mean the wife of a male presbyter, the title was also used for women who were neither elderly nor the wives of priests.

123. Ibid., 36.
124. Madigan and Osiek, *Ordained Women*, 163.

Madigan and Osiek find that "while synods and councils, both East and West, repeatedly condemned the practice of women presbyters, the epigraphical and literary evidence suggests their ongoing existence, even if in small numbers."[125] Dorothy Irvin explains:

> The word presbytera is not the word that was used for a woman priest of any Greek or Roman religious cult. Presbyter, a Greek word meaning "elder" was one of the New Testament designations of ministry that became normative, together with deacon and bishop. In the Latin-speaking areas of the early Church, a feminine ending was added to form the title of women holding this office.[126]

In English, the word was shortened to "prester" and eventually to "priest."[127] Ute Eisen's careful study of tombstone inscriptions and literary attestations found that women with titles such as *presbytera, presbytides,* and *presbiterissa* functioned in both the Eastern and Western churches from the second to the ninth centuries.[128]

EXAMPLES OF WOMEN WITH PRESBYTERAL TITLES IN THE EAST

Ammion the Presbyter, Epikto the *Presbytis*, Artemidora the Presbyter: these epigraphic titles for women leaders date from the second to the fourth century. They were found in Asia Minor, Greece, and Egypt respectively. Artemidora's inscription was actually a label for her mummy: "(Mummy of) the presbyter Artemidora, the daughter of Mikkalos (and the) mother Paniskiaina. She has fallen asleep in the Lord."[129] In addition to tombstone evidence, Eisen cites contemporaneous literary sources including Epiphanius's *Panarion against Eighty Heresies* (ca. 374–77) and Canon 11 of the Synod of Laodicea (ca. 341–81). Both documents provide historic evidence that the practice of women ministering "at the altar" was widespread enough to attract

---

125. Ibid.
126. Dorothy Irvin, "The Archaeology of Women's Traditional Ministries in the Church 100 to 820 AD," in *Calendar 2003* (St. Paul, MN: Self-published, 2003).
127. Ibid.
128. Eisen, *Women Officeholders,* 116–34.
129. Ibid., 126.

censure, and that the suppression of their ministry was based on the belief that women are subordinate to men.

Epiphanius sought to demonstrate women's inferiority by citing Scripture selectively (Gen 3:16; 1 Cor 11:8; and 1 Tim 2:12–15) while dismissing other Scriptures (Gal 3:28 and Gen 1:27) that point to female equality. Epiphanius wrote especially against groups that ordained women as priests and bishops (Quintillianists, Pepuzians, Priscillianists) and linked them with the Montanists who were eventually deemed schismatic. This condemnation may have led to the erroneous conclusion that only schismatic groups permitted female clergy. But the Synod of Laodicea attests that ordained women presbyters, called *presbytides*, acted as presidents of their congregations. Canon 11 from the synod forbids such women presiders to be installed in the church. Says Eisen: "In light of their location . . . within the higher clergy we must presume that these women both led the assembly and presided at the Eucharist."[130] Canon 44 of the synod also forbade women to enter the sanctuary. Eisen concludes: "We thus find that until some time in the fourth century there were women presbyters . . . active in the Church in Asia Minor. They were found not only in schismatic groups, as Epiphanius tried to show, but also in the Great Church, as attested by Canon 11 of the Synod of Laodicea."[131]

EXAMPLES OF WOMEN WITH PRESBYTERAL TITLES IN THE WEST

Kale, *presbytera*; Leta the *Presbytera*; and Flavia Vitalia, the holy presbyter: these three inscriptions were found in Sicily, Italy, and Yugoslavia respectively and date to the fourth and fifth centuries. Leta and Kale may have been among the women priests to whom Pope Gelasius I objected in his letter to bishops in southern Italy and Sicily (ca. 494 CE):

Nevertheless we have heard to our annoyance that divine affairs have come to such a low state that women are encouraged to officiate at the

130. Eisen, *Women Officeholders*, 122.
131. Ibid., 123.

sacred altars and to take part in all matters imputed to the offices of the male sex to which they do not belong.[132]

Gelasius's objections notwithstanding, the inscriptions point to the reality that a number of Italian and Sicilian communities valued their female presbyteral leaders. Flavia Vitalia is described as a *matrona*, indicating a married freeborn woman described as "holy" (see chapter 4).

CONCLUSION

Early Christian evangelists, both male and female, spread the gospel message primarily in urban settings of the Roman Empire such as Antioch, Ephesus, Philippi, Carthage, Corinth, Alexandria, and Athens. These cultural settings were far removed from the agrarian roots of the Galilean Jesus movement whose subsistence communities valued and integrated women's work in the struggle to survive. As the Jesus movement spread, it attracted diverse social cohorts, including slaves, freed women and men, and the freeborn poor, as well as many high-status women and a few high-status men. Elite women and higher-status freeborn and freedwomen from the artisan and small business classes were especially attracted to the new movement. Paul's affirmation of celibacy in light of his expectation of an imminent *parousia* would, in later generations, came to be valued for its own sake—especially by women. Undoubtedly, many women pursued a celibate path out of spiritual devotion; however, freedom from the demands of patriarchal marriage and the household-code ideal of wifely subordination seems to have been an added inducement. Christian virgins sought to forego marriage altogether, younger and older widows chose not to remarry, and some women chose to divorce their nonbelieving spouses, often because of the double standard that existed over sexual fidelity. Such decisions were a constant source of tension between early Christian communities and the broader Roman culture, and would have far-reaching conse-

132. Ibid., 129.

quences over many centuries. They would also transform patriarchal marriage.

In the early Jesus movement, women exercised significant ecclesial authority as patrons, itinerant prophets, evangelists, apostles, teachers, and missionaries. They founded and presided over house church worship in most urban centers and held titles such as *diakonoi* and probably *episcopoi* as these roles were understood in the first century. Yet, the public leadership of women was unsettling to the mainstream culture. Based as they were on gendered understandings of public and domestic space, hierarchical Greco-Roman household codes eventually became normative—not only in families but also in church structures. As hope for the parousia dimmed, more and more Christian communities sought some level of accommodation with and integration into the dominant culture. This resulted in an ever-increasing resistance to the leadership of women. From the early second century to the early fifth century, male church leaders repeatedly cited 1 Timothy's admonishment "Women are to be silent in the churches" as justification for curtailing women's exercise of ecclesial authority. Yet, women persisted in teaching, evangelizing, baptizing, and presiding at eucharistic meals despite official sanctions.

One could ask whether, in the final analysis, the initiative of Christian women made any difference. I submit there is ample evidence that it did. There are at least three significant differences between first- and fourth-century societies that can be attributed to the influence and authority exercised by Christian women. First, by the fourth century it had become both possible and socially acceptable for women to forego marriage. The freedom to choose a life of celibacy effectively dismantled one pillar of patriarchy—mandatory marriage. While forgoing the pleasures of intercourse and children may seem to our contemporary era a high price to pay, it is likely that women in late antiquity viewed this choice quite differently. No longer could they be forced into unwanted, loveless unions with older men who were free to couple with whomever they chose regardless of health risks. The continued ability of unmarried women to control their own finances (often generously shared with the church) made it possible to live an independent life free of the demands of patriarchal marriage. Joining a communal network of spiritually minded, often highly educated female virgins and widows may have also been attractive.

A second difference is that Christian widows and virgins rescued, socialized, baptized, and educated thousands of orphans who would otherwise have died of exposure or, in the case of baby girls, been doomed to lives of prostitution. In 374, Emperor Valentinian made the exposure of infants a capital crime.[133] Even though offenders were rarely prosecuted, this heinous practice was no longer socially sanctioned.[134] Christian values held by both women and men had significant societal impact. The implementation of those values when it came to children, however, was in the hands of women.

On February 14, 2007, Pope Benedict XVI made the rather remarkable statement that in the early Christian communities, "The female presence was anything but secondary."[135] This observation from, arguably, the most erudite of contemporary popes, is another way of saying that the ecclesial influence of early Christian women was either primary or equal to that of Christian men. The third and most significant difference made by women in the early church is the transformation of Roman society from a predominantly non-Christian to a predominantly Christian culture. While much necessary scholarly ink has been spilled tracking the decline of women's public leadership authority in early Christianity, what is easily overlooked is that Christianity's rapid expansion is largely due to the domestic networking and evangelizing efforts of women. Osiek and MacDonald cite several contemporary scholars in support of this realization:

> In his magisterial study *Pagans and Christians*, Robin Lane Fox has written that "Christian women [were] prominent in the churches' membership and recognized to be so by Christians and pagans," and he recalls the claims of Adolf von Harnack about women playing "a leading role in the spread of this religion." More recently, the involvement of

133. Osiek and Balch, *Families*, 66.

134. See Samuel X. Radbill, "A History of Child Abuse and Infanticide," in *Violence in the Family*, ed. Suzanne K. Steinmetz and Murray A. Straus (New York: Dodd, Mead, 1974), 173–79.

135. "Pope: History of Christianity Would Be Very Different without Women," *Asia News*, February 14, 2007, http://tinyurl.com/yb2v3e6s.

women has been central to Rodney Stark's thesis about the involvement of women in the rise of Christianity.[136]

Stark's 1996 book, *The Rise of Christianity*, uses methodologies gleaned from the social sciences to explore the rapid expansion of Christianity. Some of his findings resonate with what has been discussed in these first two chapters. Stark suggests that owing to Christian prohibitions against exposure, infanticide, and abortion, more Christian children than pagan were raised in the new religion. Concurring with feminist scholarship, he finds that "Christian women enjoyed substantially higher status within the Christian subcultures than pagan women did in the world at large . . . [and that] women also filled leadership positions."[137] Elizabeth Castelli and Michelle Renee Salzman dispute Stark's argument that there were more Christian women than Christian men, that Christian women enjoyed higher status within their subculture than their pagan sisters did within Roman society, and that exogamous marriages (i.e., to pagan men) led to higher rates of conversion.[138] Significantly, Brent D. Shaw's study of Christian funerary inscriptions in Rome with date of death included found essentially equal proportions of male (n=1918) and female inscriptions (n=1815).[139] Although Shaw's findings apply only to Rome, they undercut Stark's hypothesis that there were substantially more Christian women than Christian men throughout the Roman empire. Still, I believe Stark is probably correct that in at least some communities, Christian women enjoyed higher status within their own subcultures than non-Christian women did within theirs. While most Christian women were not of a higher *class* than their non-Christian counterparts, it is important to distinguish between *class* and *status*. Aristocratic women (whether pagan or Christian)

136. Osiek and MacDonald, *A Woman's Place*, 223.

137. Rodney Stark, *The Rise of Christianity: How the Obscure Jesus Movement Became the Dominant Religious Force in the Western World* (San Francisco: HarperCollins, 1996), 128.

138. See Elizabeth Castelli, "Gender, Theory and the Rise of Christianity: A Response to Rodney Stark," *Journal of Early Christian Studies* 6, no. 2 (1998): 227–57; and Michelle Renee Salzman, "Aristocratic Women: Conductors of Christianity in the Fourth Century," *Helios* 16, no. 2 (1989): 207–20. Both Castelli and Salzman argue convincingly against Stark's contention that there were more Christian women than Christian men and that exogamous marriages (i.e., to non-Christian men) led to higher rates of conversion.

139. Brent D. Shaw, "Seasons of Death: Aspects of Mortality in Imperial Rome," *The Journal of Roman Studies* 86 (1996): 107.

had both high class and high status but enjoyed less public independence than lower-class Christian women (whether freed or freeborn), who were able to move independently about in public, engage in commercial ventures, and accumulate wealth. Within their Christian social networks, these lower-class Christian women had money, high status, and freedom of movement. As we have seen, each of these contributed to the rapid expansion of early Christianity. Osiek and MacDonald correctly conclude: "Stark is clearly drawing on a particular sociological notion of conversion that focuses on the use of available social 'networks' in contributing to the expansion of the group. The network in question in this case is the extended household of antiquity."[140] For over four centuries, women's missionary authority and leadership to and within these extended households attracted both praise and blame. It would also change the face of the Roman Empire.

Peter Lampe's exhaustive work *From Paul to Valentinus* identifies a preponderance of high-ranking women in the Roman church, including businesswomen and members of the nobility. In third- and fourth-century Rome, he finds "most Christian aristocrats were women" even though most Christians were of lower status. Even after Constantine legalized Christianity, Roman aristocratic families were "the last bastion of paganism."[141] Lampe points to two late fourth-century scions of the noble Ceionii family, Ceionius Rufius Albinus and Publilius Ceionius Caecina Albinus. Both held high political offices—the former as prefect of Rome and the latter as governor of Numidia. The brothers each married Christian women but remained pagan themselves. The daughters and granddaughters of these unions were raised as devout Christians and they married other Christians. The sons, however, remained pagan until being baptized on their deathbeds. Lampe concludes:

---

140. Osiek and MacDonald, *A Woman's Place*, 223–24.
141. Lampe, *From Paul to Valentinus*, 149.

The men of the family preserved the pagan family tradition even after the official suppression of paganism, while the women gave the family the necessary Christian appearance. This example also shows that, still in the fourth century, the road to Christianization led through the female members of the family.[142]

142. Ibid., 150.

3.

Interpreting Early Christian Art

Studying early Christian art is a fascinating way to appreciate the cultural and political challenges facing early Christians. Tracing the trajectories of these simple, beautiful, and evocative images can provide believers with a precious view of the newborn faith within which their Christian ancestors lived and died. The images also help us uncover clues about early Christian women. This chapter provides a broad overview of methods used by art historians to analyze early Christian art as well as the interpretive challenges of relating it to the history of early Christian women. Before engaging in an in-depth discussion of early Christian art, a brief discussion of the role of art in antique religion may be in order.

Most inhabitants of the Roman Empire were illiterate, so an important way of communicating was via images. People learned about the emperor through his image on coins and via paintings and statues that were erected in the imperial temples and other public spaces in cities throughout the Mediterranean world. They came to know their gods and goddesses through carefully sculpted and individualized statues depicting them. Polytheism did not include written scriptures or hierarchical leadership such as we find in late antique Christianity. Instead, it was characterized by myriad local cults, each with its own set of myths and rites administered by local communities and led by a priesthood that was usually hereditary.[1] As Jaś Elsner sees it, "Images and myths provided the main forms of 'theology' in the ancient world—giving worshippers the means to recognize and think about their gods." In general, the diverse religions of the empire were pluralistic and tolerant so long as the imperial cult was duly honored. It was one's civic duty to offer sacrifice at the numerous imperial temples spread throughout the empire to protect the Roman way of life through venerating the emperor and his family.[2] With the coming of Christianity, "the role of art in religion changed, though it did not lose its central importance. The Christian God, unlike His pagan predecessors, was known not through graven images but through sacred scripture."[3] Since Scripture scrolls and codices were available only to a literate few, it became necessary to teach about the sacred texts via homilies preached to local congregations and through images that would be seen directly by worshippers.

Chronologically, there is little evidence of identifiably Christian art until the late second or early third century. Several theories have been proposed about why it took so long to appear. One is that early Christians avoided making artistic representations of their faith because of the influence of earlier Jewish culture, which did not permit graven images, seeing this practice as a form of idolatry. While this belief may have been a factor in some early communities, the explanation is inadequate. After the first century, most Christians were not Jews. Additionally, the discovery of elaborate Jewish artwork at an excavated synagogue at Dura-Europos proves that at least some Jewish communities had no problem representing their religious history and beliefs with artistic imagery.[4] Other scholars suggest that first- and early second-century Christians were struggling to survive and had neither the leisure time nor the financial resources to create religious works of art. Historians believe the earliest Christians began adapting images from the surrounding Hellenistic culture to visually express their faith. An early letter of Clement of Alexandria (ca. 150–215) supports this theory. Clement describes

1. Jaś Elsner, *Imperial Rome and Christian Triumph* (New York: Oxford University Press, 1998), 12.
2. Ibid.
3. Ibid., 12–13.
4. Steinberg, "Women."

how Christians should make appropriate use of common items such as seal rings found in the Greco-Roman culture:

> And let our seals be either a dove, or a fish, or a ship running with a fair wind, or a musical lyre, which Polycrates used, or a ship's anchor, which Seleucus had engraved; and if the seal is a fisherman, it will recall the apostle, and the children drawn out of the water. For we are not to depict the faces of idols, we who are prohibited from attaching ourselves to them, nor a sword, nor a bow, since we follow peace, nor drinking cups since we are temperate.[5]

In *Understanding Early Christian Art*, Robin Jensen identifies four groupings of early Christian images:

1. Borrowings from the Greco-Roman religious world that were adapted to serve Christian teachings

2. Religiously neutral images based on traditional decorative motifs, but that may have been given particular Christian symbolic significance

3. Narrative-based images drawn from favorite stories from the Hebrew and Christian Scriptures

4. Portraits of Christ and the saints[6]

She divides early Christian art into two major chronological periods and describes distinctive themes and motifs from each period. The pre-Constantinian period dates from the second century to the first quarter of the fourth century, and the post-Constantinian period extends from the second quarter of the fourth century to the sixth century.

---

5. Clement of Alexandria, *Paedagogus* 3.59.2–60.1, as quoted in Jeffrey Spier, *Picturing the Bible: The Earliest Christian Art* (Fort Worth, TX: Kimble Art Museum, 2007), 5.
6. Jensen, *Understanding Early Christian Art*, 10.

Figure 3.1. This is one of the earliest Christian images. It is a marble sculpture of Jonah being cast out of the sea monster and was found in the tomb of a married couple. 280–90 CE. © The Cleveland Museum of Art.

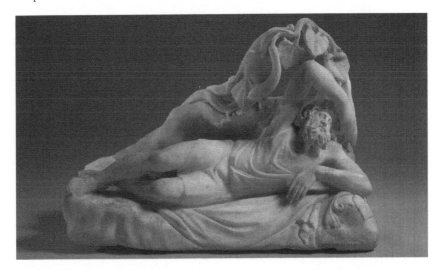

Figure 3.2. Marble depicting Jonah under the gourd plant. 280–90 CE. © The Cleveland Museum of Art.

PRE-CONSTANTINIAN PERIOD
(SECOND CENTURY TO 325 CE)

Most of the art of this period encompasses images from the first three groupings previously listed and detailed below.[7]

BORROWINGS FROM GRECO-ROMAN
RELIGIOUS WORLD

Jensen's examples of artistic motifs from the first grouping adapted from Roman culture include fishermen, philosophers, a praying person (*orans*), a shepherd with a sheep on his shoulders, meal scenes, and scenes including grapes or wheat representing the harvest. In the early Christian funerary context, these motifs from Greco-Roman art were adopted to symbolically represent biblical themes.

DECORATIVE SYMBOLIC IMAGES

Decorative symbolic images are believed to be early Christian when found in proximity to explicitly scriptural subjects. In the following listing, the Christian symbolic meaning is listed in parentheses: doves (peace), peacocks (paradise), twining vines and grapes (paradise, Eucharist), fish (Christ or Christians), boats (the church or fishers of men), lambs (Christians), and palm trees (resurrection, sacraments, etc.). About such decorative images, Jensen warns, "Their pagan roots or parallels are undeniable, and their decorative aspects suggest caution against over interpretation. One person's meaningful symbol may be another's lovely decoration, and nothing more than that."[8] That said, some images seem to have become specifically identified as Christian symbols. An anchor with two fish came to represent Christ and two Christians. A dove with an olive branch in its beak represents peace. Some images in this second grouping (birds, cherubs, flowers, fruit, urns, garlands, etc.) are purely decorative. Jensen reminds us that early Christians were people of their culture: "Both Christian

7. Ibid., 9, 13.
8. Ibid., 17.

and pagan tomb decoration might include geometric designs, masks, grapevines, urns, floral garlands, birds and images of a shepherd with one or two of his flock."[9]

NARRATIVE, BIBLICALLY BASED IMAGES

The third grouping is the most obviously Christian because it contains images from both Hebrew and Christian writings, which Jensen describes as "biblically based," although technically the Christian bible wasn't nearing its final form until the late fourth century.[10] By this time, most early Christian funerary art had already been created. In this category, we find images such as Jonah (figures 3.1 and 3.2), Noah in the ark, Daniel with the lions, Moses striking the rock, Susanna, and Peter baptizing his jailors, as well as images of the baptism of Jesus, the healing of the paralytic, the hemorrhaging woman, multiplication of the loaves, the raising of Lazarus, the wedding feast at Cana, and others. Scholars believe that certain stories from the Hebrew Scriptures (Noah, Daniel, Isaac) were used because they were especially meaningful to early Christians who experienced persecution under Nero, Decius, Diocletian, and other emperors from the mid-first to early fourth century. Hence, themes of deliverance and protection (Noah, Daniel, Susanna) were common alongside those evoking resurrection (Jonah, the raising of Jairus's daughter, the raising of Lazarus).

9. Ibid., 19.

10. Raymond E. Brown and Raymond F. Collins, "Canonicity," in *The New Jerome Biblical Commentary*, ed. Raymond E. Brown, Joseph A. Fitzmyer, and Roland E. Murphy (Englewood Cliffs, NJ: Prentice Hall, 1990), 1036.

FREQUENCY OF BIBLICAL IMAGES

Table 3.1 Scenes from Hebrew Scriptures on Third- to Sixth-Century Christian Sarcophagi

Hebrew Scriptures[11]	Incidence	Pre-325/ 333 CE[12]	Post 325/ 333 CE[13]	Uncertain
Jonah	73	52 (37/15)	16	5
Moses: Sacrifice of Isaac	67	28 (15/13)	38	1
Daniel and Lions	55	21 (10/11)	33	1
Adam and Eve: Work (9), Fall (43)	52	21 (13/8)	27	4
Moses: Receives Law	43	12 (4/8)	28	3
Three in Fiery Furnace	27	13 (5/8)	12	2
Noah	25	16 (11/5)	7	2
Daniel Kills Babylonian Dragon	21	2 (0/2)	19	0
Moses/Miriam at Reed Sea (17 with Miriam)	20	2 (0/2)	18	0
Cain and Abel	15	1 (1/0)	14	0
Susanna	12	3 (1/2)	8	1
Three before Nebuchadnezzar	12	6 (4/2)	6	0
Moses Burning Bush "Sandal Scene"	11	4 (1/3)	6	1
Moses: Water from Rock	9	2 (2/0)	6	1
Ezekiel Raising Dry Bones	8	6 (1/5)	2	0
Job	7	0	7	0
"Quail" Scene in Desert	6	2 (0/2)	4	0
Total	**463**	**191** (105/86)	**251**	**21**

11. Scenes occurring fewer than four times were not included.

12. Includes "first quarter of the fourth century" and earlier and "first third of the fourth century" descriptors from RS volumes.

13. Includes "second quarter of the fourth century" and later, per descriptors in RS volumes.

Table 3.2 Scenes from the Christian Scriptures on
Third- to Fifth-Century Christian Sarcophagi

Christian Scenes[14]	Incidence	Pre-325/333 CE[15]	Post 325/ 333 CE[16]	Uncertain
Multiplication of Loaves and Fish	109	43 (17/26)	61	5
Healing of Blind Man	102	32 (13/19)	66	4
Peter Baptizes Jailers	96	46 (21/25)	47	3
Wedding at Cana	77	39 (29/10)	36	2
Raising of Lazarus	76	42 (23/19)	30	4
Peter Betrays Christ (Includes Rooster Scene)	75	25 (9/16)	49	1
Arrest of Peter	68	33 (9/24)	34	1
Healing of Woman with Hemorrhage	57	13 (3/10)	42	2
Visit of Magi	51	20 (11/9)	28	3
Healing of Paralytic (Bethsaida not included)	49	22 (9/13)	26	1
Peter "traditio legis," "commissioning" (no rooster), and "receives keys"	37	2 (1/1)	35	0
Healing of Son of Widow of Nain	25	9 (5/4)	15	1
Entry into Jerusalem	24	8 (2/6)	16	0
Pilate Handwashing / Jesus before Pilate	24	0	23	1
Nativity	14	4 (0/4)	10	0
Plea of Canaanite Woman	14	1 (1/0)	13	0
Samaritan Woman	12	0	12	0

14. Scenes occurring fewer than four times were not included.
15. Includes "first quarter of the fourth century" and earlier and "first third of the fourth century," per descriptors from RS volumes.
16. Includes "second quarter of the fourth century" and later, per descriptors in RS volumes.

Baptism of Jesus by John	10	5 (3/2)	5	0
Paul Arrested	10	1 (0/1)	9	0
Martyrdom of Paul	10	0	10	0
Centurion from Capernaum	9	0	9	0
Peter Reading Scene before Arrest	9	1 (1/0)	8	0
Peter Martyred	9	0	9	0
Healing of Jairus's Daughter	7	6 (4/2)	1	0
"Raising Dead"	7	2 (1/1)	5	0
Women at the Tomb	7	0	7	0
Judas Kiss	6	0	6	0
Healing of Paralytic at Bethsaida	5	0	5	0
Healing "Miracle" Scene	5	0	4	1
Zacchaeus	4	0	4	0
Arrest of Christ	4	1(0/1)	3	0
Tabitha	4	0	3	1
Traditio Legis (Paul)	4	0	4	0
Totals	**1020**	**355 (162/193)**	**635**	**30**

In *Understanding Early Christian Art*, Jensen undertakes the hazardous enterprise of gauging the popularity of biblical scenes in pre-Constantinian Christian iconography. Her counts are estimates from scholarly lists of sarcophagus carvings and catacomb frescos.[17] Jensen finds a predominance of scenes from the Hebrew Scriptures on pre-Constantinian sarcophagi: "In fact, Old Testament subjects occur as

17. Ibid., 69; see n. 6 wherein Jensen writes that she bases her estimates "on the identifications of J. Wilpert, *Die Malereien der Katakomben Roms* (Frieburg i. Beiesgau: Herdersch Verlag, 1903); F. Deichmann, G. Bovini, and H. Brandenburg, *Repertorium der Christlich-Antiken Sarkophage* (Wiesbaden: Steiner, 1967); and the tabulations of T. Klauser, "Studien zur Enstehungsgeschichte der christlichen Kunst," *JAC* 4 (1961): 128–45; P. Styger, Die altchristliche Grabeskunst, 6–8; and the most helpful enumeration by Snyder, *Ante Pacem*, 43."

much as four times more often than New Testament themes in the Christian art of the second through fourth century."[18]

Jensen's estimates were not confirmed by my own study of 558 third to fifth-century sarcophagus artifacts identified as "Christian" (see chapters 6 and 7 and table 6.2). Biblical scenes identified on these Christian tombs were recorded in a database and tabulated (see tables 3.1 and 3.2). This tabulation did not find a predominance of scenes from the Hebrew Scriptures, at least on sarcophagi, in the pre-Constantinian period (see table 3.3). The opposite was true, since scenes from Christian texts predominate. Of the 267 scenes from the Hebrew and Christian Scriptures on Christian sarcophagi dating to before 325 CE, 162—or 60.6 percent—were from Christian texts. If one adds the tombs categorized as "first third of the fourth century" (to 333 CE), 65 percent were scenes from Christian texts.

Table 3.3 Christian Sarcophagi Scripture Scene Distribution by Type and Date

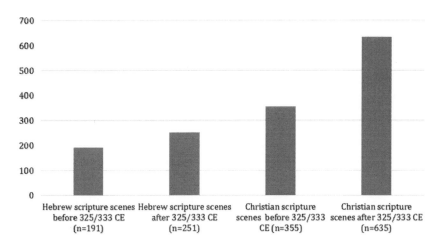

*Numbers exclude Hebrew and Christian Scripture scenes on sarcophagi with uncertain dates (see tables 3.1 and 3.2).

18. Jensen, *Understanding Early Christian Art*, 68–69.

With regard to the popularity of biblical scenes, this present study also had substantially different findings than Jensen, with the exception of the Jonah motif. Of subjects from the Hebrew Scriptures, Jensen identified Jonah as the overwhelming favorite with slightly under one hundred figures found on both catacomb frescos and sarcophagi art. My tabulations are consistent, with Jonah motifs (n=52) topping the popularity chart for Hebrew Scripture sarcophagus figures. But they do not confirm Jensen's other findings: that the story of Noah is a distant second with "a dozen or fewer images," followed by Moses striking the rock in the wilderness, or that Adam and Eve, Abraham offering Isaac, and Daniel in the lions' den each had less than ten examples. The sacrifice of Isaac (n=28), Daniel and the lions (n=21), and Adam and Eve (n=21) were all more popular than Noah configurations (n=16)—at least on Christian sarcophagi—in the pre-Constantinian period (see table 3.1). Moses striking a rock occurred just twice on Christian sarcophagi in the early period. Regarding scenes from Christian texts, Jensen found the baptism of Jesus and the raising of Lazarus to have only around six representations, while "the woman at the well, the healing of the paralytic, and the multiplication of the loaves and fishes are known in two or three versions."[19] A cursory examination of table 3.2 reveals substantially more occurrences of each of these scenes on sarcophagi in the pre-Constantinian period, with the exception of the woman/Samaritan woman at the well, which did not occur at all. (It occurred in catacomb frescos at that time however). Especially notable is the scene of Peter baptizing his jailors, which is the most popular Christian sarcophagus motif in the pre-Constantinian period (n=46). This is followed by the multiplication of the loaves (n=43), the raising of Lazarus (n=42), the wedding at Cana (n=39), and the healing of the blind man (n=32). The difference in these new findings compared to Jensen is probably explained by the fact that new catacomb frescos and sarcophagi are being discovered all the time. Also, volumes detailing Christian (or presumed Christian) sarcophagi may not have been available at the time Jensen reviewed her lists.[20] I discuss findings

19. Ibid., 69.
20. My findings are based an analysis of 2119 artifacts from three volumes of images and descriptions of all publicly available Christian, or possibly Christian sarcophagi: Friedrich W.

about biblical motifs here because in *Understanding Early Christian Art*, Jensen explores several theories that "tried to account for the prevalence of Old Testament subjects."[21] Since Hebrew Bible subjects are not more prevalent—at least on early Christian sarcophagi as originally surmised—this seems an important excursus.

POST-CONSTANTINIAN (325–525 CE)

After Constantine issued a decree of religious tolerance (313) followed by Theodosius's declaration of Christianity as the official religion of the empire (381), explicitly Christian subjects increased in all of Jensen's first three categories, but most dramatically in the third: scriptural events from the life of Christ (birth, trial before Pilate). There is a significant increase in theological and dogmatic images, including representations of Christ as lawgiver and king of heaven. The latter are consonant with developments in theology and dogma from the Council of Nicaea (325) onward, which proclaimed that Christ was divine as well as human and saw further developments in the doctrine of the Trinity.[22] It was not until the post-Constantinian period that we find artistic representations of the cross, probably because Christians no longer feared the shame associated with this gruesome form of capital punishment. Also at this time we see a gradual decline in the use of earlier iconic representations of the good shepherd (a motif borrowed directly from Greco-Roman art), Noah, Jonah, and the *orans*. Now, we find a greater prevalence of obviously "Christian" portrayals such as images of Christ and the saints, especially Peter and Paul.

Jensen's description of the relationship between early Christian art and history is a suitable summary of this segment:

Deichmann, Giuseppe Bovini, and Hugo Brandenburg, eds., *Rom und Ostia*, Repertorium Der Christlich-Antiken Sarkophage 1 (Wiesbaden: Franz Steiner, 1967), hereafter RS 1; Jutta Dresken-Weiland, ed., *Italien: mit einem nachtrag; Rom und Ostia, Dalmatien, Museen der Welt*, Repertorium Der Christlich-Antiken Sarkophage 2 (Mainz am Rhein: Philipp von Zabern, 1998), hereafter RS 2; Brigitte Christern-Briesenick, ed., *Frankreich, Algerien, Tunesien*, Repertorium Der Christlich-Antiken Sarkophage 3 (Mainz am Rhein: Philipp von Zabern, 2003), hereafter RS 3. The most recent volume was published after Jensen's book was published. All reference markers are to image numbers and not page numbers.

21. Jensen, *Understanding Early Christian Art*, 69.
22. Ibid., 20.

The art of the third and fourth centuries both reflects and parallels the change of fortunes both of Christians and of the institutional church over time. The Christian religion, although certainly focused on divine laws, transcendent issues, and other-worldly expectations, was lived out amidst and in reaction to political and cultural circumstances. . . . Similarly Christian art developed in and responded to particular social shifts and historical events. And even while it must bear evidence to its circumstances, as a product of a living religious community, visual art was also affected and shaped by contemporary theological debates, methods of scripture interpretation, and liturgical practices. In other words, Christian art evolved in an integrated environment and evolved in relation to external historical pressures as well as internal theological events.[23]

ART AND ARCHAEOLOGY AS SOURCES OF INFORMATION ABOUT EARLY CHRISTIAN WOMEN

Because most of history relies heavily on literary records authored by men, discovering reliable historical data about women's lives is an adventure fraught with complexity. This search is further complicated by the fact that later Christianity relied heavily, if not exclusively, on the written word as a primary means of understanding its history. Information about the early church to be gleaned from visual artifacts (frescos, paintings, sarcophagi friezes) and material artifacts (jewelry, clothing, household items) has been left almost exclusively to art historians and archaeologists.[24] Some historians of religion, such as Margaret Miles, argue that greater study of visual imagery and material artifacts could lead to increased understanding of a broader spectrum of the community being studied.[25] While literary sources normally connect historians with educated people from the upper classes, visual images and artifacts can provide a window into the world of the common people, who in fact always constitute the majority. While many visual images and artifacts do relate to the common people, others—particularly those in catacomb

23. Ibid., 26.

24. Janet Tulloch, "Art and Archaeology as an Historical Resource for the Study of Women in Early Christianity: An Approach for Analyzing Visual Data," *Feminist Theology* 12, no. 3 (2004): 278.

25. Margaret R. Miles, *Image as Insight: Visual Understanding in Western Christianity and Secular Culture* (Boston: Beacon, 1985), 29–30, quoted in Tulloch "Art and Archaeology," 278.

frescos and sarcophagi friezes—belong to individuals with greater financial resources. For example, the famous fresco of Veneranda and Petronella (figure 4.9) was found in the catacombs of Domitilla and the *Velata* fresco (figure 4.6) in the catacombs of Priscilla. Both catacombs are believed to have been donated by female patrons, Domitilla and Priscilla. Even though there were many female patrons in the early church—such as Mary of Magdala, Phoebe, Lydia, Domitilla, Paula, Olympias, and others—their presence is barely discernable in the literary sources. It did not take feminist scholars long to recognize that visual imagery and artifacts could provide information about prominent women in the early church either not available or sometimes distorted in the written history. Unfortunately, according to historian Robin Jensen, there is a "subtle but definite disparagement of images by many of those who come at history through texts. This disparagement may have a philosophical or even theological basis, or it may be nearly unconscious."[26]

INTERPRETIVE ISSUES

Janet Tulloch notes that while textual research and art historical research each have their own intellectual integrity and modes of inquiry, "the potential for knowledge of early Christian women through art and archaeology is too extensive to be foreclosed by earlier misunderstandings of the data."[27] She identifies commonalities between the study of visual data and the study of literary texts: "Both are representations of something that happened or existed beyond the page/visual frame. Both are subject to some degree to the understanding the author/artist imposed on his/her subject matter. Both documents are at the same time interpretations of something else (story, idea, event) as well as 'original' products (in the sense that primary sources are unique in some way)."[28] Tulloch delineates the difficulties for scholars seeking historical data about early Christian women through the visual and material arts. One difficulty is "an interpretive standard for identifying human figures as 'Christian,' which does

26. Jensen, *Understanding Early Christian Art*, 2.
27. Tulloch, "Art and Archaeology," 280.
28. Ibid., 283.

not recognize the potential for non-biblical figures to be representations of authentic early Christian people."[29] She points to the ubiquitous *orans* (praying) figure. While both male and female figures
are depicted in this prayer position, nearly all of the *orans* figures in
the Christian catacombs of Rome are female.[30] Likewise, this study
found the vast majority of *orans* figures on Christian sarcophagi are
female (see table 6.5). Rather than postulating that the female figure could represent a real historical woman, nineteenth- and twentieth-century scholars interpreted the female *orans* symbolically. The
figure was thought to be either a symbol of the soul in glory now
offering intercessory prayers for the living, or interpreted even more
abstractly, as a symbol of the church. If these rules are used, such a
female figure could not be construed to represent an early Christian
woman offering prayers on behalf of her community, nor could the
figure be a depiction of a female saint, lost to historical memory but
beloved by her circle of believers.[31] Since virtually all Greco-Roman
orans figures are female, it is easy to understand the early tendency to
view Christian *orans* figures symbolically. Yet, Tulloch makes a good
case that this very preponderance can obscure the possibility that not
all figures are symbolic. For example, the well-known *orans* figure in
the *Velata* chapel at the catacombs of Priscilla is so distinctive that it
is very open to other interpretations, the foremost being that it is an
actual portrait of the deceased (see figure 4.6). As we shall see in chapter 6, most *orans* figures on Christian sarcophagi were not symbolic
but self-representations of the deceased.

Another difficulty is an "ideology of gender" identified by Elizabeth Clark. She demonstrated that "the history of women in early
Christianity has been flattened to the myth of woman."[32] According
to Clark, gender ideology can be seen in the "Church Fathers' exhor-
tations to and chastisement of women, based on nostalgia for the
ideals of female behavior in an earlier era rather than on the laws

29. Ibid., 285.
30. Ibid., 286; see n. 15: "Up to 153 examples of this representation had been found in the
catacombs."
31. Ibid., 286–88.
32. Elizabeth A. Clark, "Ideology, History and the Construction of Woman in Late Ancient
Christianity," *Journal of Early Christian Studies* 2, no. 2 (1994): 170, as cited in Tulloch, "Art and
Archaeology," 288.

and customs pertaining to women in their own day."[33] Such an ideology obscures the particularity of any given historical woman in favor of an idealized feminine construct. James Arlandson upholds Clark's observation when he found that women of prominence were "known only through inscriptional and numismatic (coin) evidence, which almost always contradicts the literary and philosophical writings about women."[34] Tulloch sees a similar gender ideology at work in nineteenth- and twentieth-century scholarly interpretations of early Christian visual images where nonbiblical female figures in early Christian sites are viewed as either symbols or signs, and rarely as actual historical women.

Figure 3.3. Catacomb of Callixtus, Chapel of the Sacraments A3, Back Wall. Funerary banquet on right with seven male figures and eight baskets. Note female figure praying on left. Photo: Pontifical Commission of Sacred Archaeology.

CONTEMPORARY INTERPRETIVE TRENDS

With the notable exception of Stine Birk's recent work on visualizing gender (see chapter 6), recent scholarship (late twentieth to early twenty-first century) has tended to downplay gender in interpreting the female *orans* figure, emphasizing the meaning of the posture instead. While some have acknowledged that some *orans* figures are portraits of the deceased, others interpret these figures as the souls of the deceased.[35] Other contemporary interpreters simply avoid

33. Clark, "Ideology," 161, as cited in Tulloch, "Art and Archaeology," 289.
34. James Malcolm Arlandson, *Women, Class and Society in Early Christianity: Models from Luke-Acts* (Peabody, MA: Hendrickson, 1997), 35, as cited in Tulloch, "Art and Archaeology," 288.
35. Jutta Dresken-Weiland, *Bild, Grab und Wort. Untersuchungen zu Jenseitsvorstellungen von Christen des 3. Und 4. Jahrhunderts* (Regensburg: Schnell & Steiner, 2010), 38–76, cited in Stine

dealing with enigmatic female images altogether. Tulloch points to an interesting contemporary analysis of a painting in the catacomb of Callixtus in which a small male and female figure are depicted on either side of a tripod table with food on it (figure 3.3). The male figure extends his hand over the food while the female figure raises her hands in prayer. The scholarly discussion focuses on the furniture (is it a secular table or a cultic table?) and not on the meaning of either figure. Says Tulloch: "An absence of commentary on the female figure is particularly remarkable in light of early Christian proscriptions of women in leadership roles. Given her close proximity to the table, the female figure is clearly a co-participant in the portrayed actions."[36] Birk's detailed study of non-Christian portrait sarcophagi includes an analysis of transitional figures such as the *orans* that originated from a conflation of motifs in Greco-Roman iconography and became hugely popular on early Christian sarcophagi. Birk does not interpret all Christian female *orans* figures as souls of the departed. Rather, in addition to connoting values of fidelity and piety, she views them as "learned women." She points to the Christian *orans*'s iconic resonance with non-Christian portrayals of departed women who hold scrolls or musical instruments while dressed as philosophers or muses respectively.[37]

ANALYZING VISUAL DATA

Important differences between twenty-first-century art and early Christian art should be understood before attempting any analysis. Tulloch believes earlier scholarship "overlooked the degree to which early Christian art is aural in its representation."[38] Early Christianity did not emerge in a milieu that included email, social media, or television. Virtually all communication was face-to-face, whether

Birk, *Depicting the Dead: Self-Representation and Commemoration on Roman Sarcophagi with Portraits* (Aarhus, DNK: Aarhus University Press, 2013), 89–90.

36. Tulloch, "Art and Archaeology," 291. For a more recent discussion that identifies these figures as children, see Janet Tulloch, "Visual Representations of Children and Ritual in the Early Roman Empire," *Studies in Religion/Sciences Religieuses* 41, no. 3 (2012): 408–38, esp. 425–27, figs. 1.10–11.

37. Birk, *Depicting the Dead*, 89–90.

38. Tulloch, "Art and Archaeology," 294.

individually or listening to an orator in a crowd. Tulloch points to the hundreds of inscriptions on every day tableware, such as cups and wine containers that contain snippets of conversation about drinking. Some inscriptions are examples of conversations between the host and the guest: *MISCE Vivas* (Guest: *MISCE* [Give me mixed wine]; Host: *Vivas* [Cheers *or* May You Live]).[39] Early Christian art was an important means of discourse within the society in which it was situated. Tulloch writes,

> Ancient art was received within a cultural atmosphere of conviviality. Art understood as social discourse, whether sacred or secular, would have drawn the viewer in as a participant much the same way someone who overhears an interesting comment is drawn into a conversation.[40]

She argues that archaeological and visual remains should be understood within a cultural milieu wherein oral, rather than written, communications were the predominant means of discourse. Therefore, "scholars need to think in terms of replacing Christian artifacts back into their various contexts: social, cultural and physical (i.e. archaeological) for the purpose of adequate comprehension and explanation."[41]

Since artists of late antiquity used visual data to represent the spoken word, Tulloch believes historians should think of scenes of ongoing action as social communications. Because antique art was rhetorical, events were often represented as "registers," with one line of figures above another, often organized chronologically to tell a story scene by scene. Such registers can be seen in sarcophagi friezes. Catacomb artists did not yet have the tools of perspective developed in the Renaissance. To transform speech and action into a single two-dimensional image would have been impossible.[42] Tulloch identifies fifteen questions that can help historians determine "the lines of communication, status, function and inter-relationships between figures in art."[43] I list them in table 3.4 in the interest of understanding how

39. Ibid., 295.
40. Ibid., 298.
41. Ibid., 296.
42. Ibid., 266–97.
43. Ibid., 297.

art experts analyze images and to aid the reader wishing to reflect on the many images presented in this book.

Table 3.4: Questions that Help Historians Interpret Early Christian Art

- At what or at whom do the figures look?
- Is each figure looking at the same thing?
- Do any of the figures look at the viewer?
- What sort of hand gestures are the figures making?
- Do the figures hold anything? What is it?
- Are there inscriptions in or near the scene?
- How are the words used? Are they descriptive text or speech?
- If speech, who does the speaking?
- Are there mythological figures present? If so, who? Or what?
- What time of day is it? How is time represented?
- Are the figures standing? Sitting? Reclining?
- How is motion represented? What does the movement (image-action) tell us?
- What is the relationship between the movement (image-action) and the inscriptions (speech-action)?
- Does the speech happen before, during, or after the image-action?
- How is the status of individuals represented in the image?[44]

Robin Jensen identifies four important keys to "discovering clues to the symbolic message of a tomb's overall decoration, as well as to the possible meaning of any single subject."[45]

---

44. Janet H. Tulloch, "Art and Archaeology as an Historical Resource for the Study of Women in Early Christianity: An Approach for Analyzing Visual Data," *Feminist Theology* 12, no. 3 (2004): 297.

45. Jensen, *Understanding Early Christian Art*, 68.

- Frequency and repetition of certain figures
- The details or peculiarities of their composition
- Compositional patterns (e.g., regular proximity or juxtaposition to other subjects)
- Physical setting

Jensen emphasizes the need for familiarity with Christian textual documents to interpret what meaning the images might have had for early Christians. She cautions:

> By themselves, the images are still ambiguous and non-self-interpreting. The keys to their significance will continue to depend on the clues we find in the written documents, including theological treatises, liturgies, homilies and exegetical works. The most relevant documents will interpret the biblical stories [in funerary art] as allegories, typologies, or moral figures that give the "hidden" meaning or significance behind the narrative.[46]

She makes a strong argument for viewing early Christian art in conjunction with contemporary documents from the early Christian writers, mostly the second- and early third-century fathers of the church such as Clement of Alexandria, Hippolytus of Rome, Irenaeus of Lyons, Origen, and Tertullian of Carthage. She acknowledges that while early art historians were overreliant on the early texts for dating and interpretation, text historians tended to discount the historical value of early art, viewing it as merely illustrative. Apparently, in partial reaction to overreliance on erroneous text-derived meanings and dates postulated by their forbears, some contemporary art historians have sought "an almost radical disjunction," according to Jensen, of art from text. The difficulty with this presentation, she argues, is that "one of the dimensions of historical perspective was lost along with a key tool for interpretation—the literature of the community."[47]

Jensen is undoubtedly correct that all available textual documents should be explored in efforts to understand early Christian art. Such a methodology is sound so long as one remembers that early writings

46. Ibid.
47. Ibid., 29.

by church fathers were frequently prescriptive and not necessarily descriptive. That is, they may paint an idealized picture rather than what is actually transpiring in early communities. For example, when churchmen repeatedly prohibit women from teaching and baptizing, they illuminate the reality that women were regularly doing both or there would have been no need for repeated prohibitions. It is also important to recognize that some community members, such as women, the poor, and other marginalized people, were underrepresented or absent from the literary record. In particular, women's stories and experiences were viewed through an androcentric lens. It is nothing short of paradoxical that we know of women's exercise of authority in early Christianity primarily through the written documents of male leaders who were often trying to discourage female leadership. This is not to say that women, especially women of means, would not have commissioned religious art that incorporated the theological and scriptural motifs present in contemporaneous texts written by men. It is to say that while written documents may supply clues to the "hidden" meaning celebrated by male church fathers, there may also be clues specific to the experiences of women reflected in art and archaeology that do not appear in the literary text. Even so, careful study of contemporaneous writings is indispensable to uncovering early Christian history, especially as it relates to early Christian art. Retrieving possible "meaning clues" about the experience of influential early Christian women is a main objective of this exploration and both literary and archaeological data are important pieces of the puzzle (see chapter 8).

Another important factor in analyzing early Christian art is determining if the presence of written speech is taking place in "ordinary" or "mythical" time.[48] Scholars of classical narrative art suggest there are at least three modes of time that can be applied to an image with inscribed speech: (1) speech that occurs before the image-action of the scene, (2) speech occurring at the same time as the image-action, and (3) speech occurring after the image-action of the scene. "Ordinary time" usually means that when the image was created, all the figures are portrayed as if they are alive and acting at the same time.

48. Tulloch, "Art and Archaeology," 298.

"Mythical time" does not follow such a sequence. As is often seen in catacomb art, a deceased figure may be depicted as speaking to a living figure within the image frame or to an actual living person viewing the image and outside the frame.[49]

The notion of *visual performance* is one last concept that may aid our effort to discover the history of early Christian women via representation in art and archaeology. In this theoretical framework, "Art or artifacts are understood to perform meaning(s) not simply embed them."[50]

Like their non-Christian contemporaries, early Christians would have interacted with catacomb or sarcophagus images within a liminal ritual space. From this sacred space, they communed with the departed and with other sacred figures through the meaning evoked or "performed" by the image-action. As we shall see, many of these images were those of ecclesial women exhorting us to live lives worthy of the Christ in whom they believed and to whom they witness from beyond the grave.

49. Ibid.
50. Ibid.; see n. 47, which refers to Mieke Bal, *Reading Rembrandt: Beyond the Word-Image Opposition* (Cambridge: Cambridge University Press, 1992), 270–71.

4.

Women in Catacomb Frescos and Inscriptions

THE CATACOMBS OF PRISCILLA

The earliest frescos depicting Christian women are found at the catacombs of Priscilla, at 430 Via Salaria, an ancient thoroughfare that antedates the foundation of Rome. Scholars originally thought the oldest structures in the catacomb—the so-called Greek Chapel and cryptoporticus—were substructures of a suburban Roman villa, "perhaps a sort of underground dining room" that the family used to escape Rome's oppressive heat."[1] But, this theory was discarded in the 1960s when a Vatican engineer, Francesco Tolotti, found the original structures to be funerary chapels built for a wealthy Roman family, the Acilii Glabriones.[2] Christian inscriptions dating to the second century have been found at the Priscilla catacombs, although the Christian frescos in the Greek Chapel and *Velata* cubiculum date to the mid-third century. From this time, Christian believers apparently gathered to pray and to remember departed loved ones in the Greek Chapel.[3] And still today, pilgrims frequently celebrate Mass and/or

1. Nicola Denzey, *The Bone Gatherers: The Lost Worlds of Early Christian Women* (Boston: Beacon, 2007), 101.
2. Ibid., 120.
3. For dating of Christian frescos, see Barbara Borg, *Crisis and Ambition: Tombs and Burial Customs in Third-Century CE Rome* (Oxford: Oxford University Press, 2013), 252–57. For dat-

pray in the spacious cryptoporticus (figure 4.1). The catacombs of Priscilla, Callixtus, and Praetextatus each contain the earliest examples of Christian frescos yet found. But only the Priscilla site contains extensive frescos relating to women.[4]

Figure 4.1. Prayer service in the cryptoporticus of the catacombs of Priscilla. March 2014. Courtesy of Rebecca Parrish, Interchange Productions.

Priscilla was a wealthy woman patron of the senatorial Acilii family who probably donated the burial site. Her family name is inscribed in a small room (hypogeum) on the first level. During the fourth century, burials expanded dramatically to accommodate the ever-growing cult of the martyrs. Before the time of Constantine, the Priscilla catacombs are estimated to have contained 3500 underground burial spaces, but thousands more were added as the cult of the martyrs

ing of the earliest Christian inscriptions at the Priscilla catacombs, see Eisen, *Women Officeholders*, 143–44.

4. B. Borg, *Crisis and Ambition*, 257–59. The earliest frescos (third century) found at the catacombs of Callixtus include just one female biblical scene, the Samaritan woman, although a male and female *orans* are found on the rear wall of A4. Both third-century meal scenes at this catacomb appear to include only short-haired male figures, although the meal scene on the rear wall of cubiculum A3 is flanked on the left by a female *orans* and a male figure who has hands extended over fish and bread on a tripod. This image has in the past been interpreted as confecting the Eucharist. Two of the four preserved third-century frescos at the catacombs of Praetextatus are female biblical scenes—the Samaritan woman and the woman with the flow of blood.

expanded after the Edict of Milan.[5] Medieval guidebooks state six popes and more than three hundred named and unnamed martyrs were buried there, as well as the legendary Christian women, Pudenziana, Praxedis, and even the New Testament Prisca.[6] These guides are not necessarily historically accurate because they tell us only what the church of the Middle Ages wanted published. As Nicola Denzey notes, "Ancient history is murky, and all we know for sure is that a number of historical and legendary Priscillas were eventually combined in pious memory into the one figure of Saint Priscilla (or Saint Prisca)."[7] Still, it is plausible that the Priscilla for whom the burial complex was named is our Roman noblewoman from the Acilii family because her gravestone has been found there.[8] Priscilla was a common name, however, and there were others who came to be associated with the complex. One is a wealthy patron, Prisca, who probably opened her home for early Christian worship since she is associated with the Aventine Hill titular church of Santa Prisca. Another is a thirteen-year-old girl named Prisca who legend tells us was beheaded for refusing to renounce Christ. Her remains were later recovered by Pope Eutychianus (275–283 CE) and brought to the church of St. Prisca on the Aventine. An early twentieth-century professor of archaeology at the University of Rome, Orazio Marucchi, reports that the bones of Paul's missionary coworkers, Prisca and Aquila, were interred at the Priscilla catacomb until the ninth century when Pope Leo IV found and apparently moved them to a site that is now lost.[9]

There is precedent for venerating first-century leaders such as Prisca. The famous third-century historian, Eusebius, attests to the existence of *tropaia* (monuments) in Rome commemorating both Peter and Paul. In the mid-third-century, a legendary Christian woman, Lucina, apparently begged Pope Cornelius to exhume their

5. John Bodel, "From Columbaria to Catacombs," in Brink and Green, *Commemorating the Dead*, 238.

6. Fabrizio Mancinelli, *Guide to the Catacombs of Rome* (Firenze: Scala, 2007), 53.

7. Denzey, *Bone Gatherers*, 121.

8. Priscilla is a nickname for Prisca. Carolyn Osiek (email to author, November 23, 2016) believes there was probably a Prisca/Priscilla in the Acilii family in every generation.

9. Orazio Marucchi, *Manual of Christian Archaeology*, trans. Hubert Vecchierello (Patterson, NJ: St. Anthony Guild Press, 1935), 88, 178.

bones and place them closer to the holy sites of their martyrdoms. Lucina is one of many bone gatherers who appear in early church histories. They are always women.[10] The *Liber Pontificalis*, a listing of popes also dating from the third century, states that Cornelius agreed and moved Peter's bones to Vatican hill.[11] Lucina is said to have buried Paul's relics on her own property along the Via Ostiense, close to the traditional site where Paul was beheaded, now known as the church of St. Paul Outside-the-Walls.[12] Contemporary excavations at St. Peter's Basilica have uncovered a mid-second-century gravesite with Greek graffiti reading "Peter is here."[13] Recent excavations at St. Paul's have uncovered an ancient fourth-century sarcophagus with the Latin inscription: *Paulus Apostolus Mart* (To Apostle Paul, martyr).[14]

Given the evidence for early veneration of Peter and Paul, it is possible that Prisca, who with her husband, Aquila, founded house churches in Corinth, Ephesus, and Rome, was originally buried and venerated at the catacombs of Priscilla.[15] Theologian and early Christian archaeologist Jerome Murphy O'Connor postulates that Prisca and Aquila were freed slaves from the Acilii family on whose grounds the catacombs are located. Prisca, Priscilla, and Aquila (a variant of Acilius) were common Acilian family names. After being freed by Roman citizens, the slaves themselves could become Roman citizens, typically taking the names of their former owners.[16] Paul calls the couple his "coworkers in Christ," saying, "all the churches of the Gentiles" owe them thanks (Rom 16:3–5), and he greets "the church in their house" in Rome. With Paul, Prisca and Aquila could be called "Apostles to the Gentiles."

10. Denzey, *Bone Gatherers*, xii.

11. *Liber Pontificalis* 1.66–67.

12. Denzey, *Bone Gatherers*, xii.

13. "Historical Notes about St. Peter's Tomb," Society of Saint Pius X, http://tinyurl.com/yawyatqj.

14. Vatican, "The Basilica: The Tomb of the Apostle," The Papal Basilica: St. Paul Outside-the-Walls, http://tinyurl.com/ydewucce.

15. Denzey, *Bone Gatherers*, 121–24.

16. Murphy-O'Connor, "Prisca and Aquila."

Figure 4.2. Late third-century "*Fractio Panis*" fresco in the Greek Chapel. Recent scholarship interprets this as a female Christian funerary banquet led by a female host (possibly the middle figure). Some scholars suggest the seven baskets represent the miracle of the multiplication of the loaves, metaphorically evoking the Christian Eucharist (Mark 8:1–9; Matt 15:32–39). Photo by Eric Vandeville/akg-images.

Since she is mentioned before Aquila four of the six times the couple is mentioned in the Christian Scriptures, scholars suggest Prisca was the more prominent of the duo.[17] There are, therefore, good textual reasons from Paul's actual letter to the Romans to associate the couple with the church at Rome.[18] Prisca's burial site would have had great significance for the third-century Christian women who prayed in the beautifully decorated Greek chapel that Denzey theorizes may have originally contained an ossuary with her remains.[19]

THE "GREEK CHAPEL"

The so-called Greek chapel (named because of Greek inscriptions near the entry) has many frescos of women and female biblical figures. Perhaps the most famous is a meal scene, the *Fractio Panis* (bread breaking), so named because Rev. Josef Wilpert, the Catholic archaeologist who found it in 1894, believed it portrayed an early Christian Eucharist (figure 4.2). Today, with the discovery of many similar funerary meal scenes in both non-Christian and Christian frescos, most scholars, including Catholic ones, believe the image depicts

17. Ibid.
18. The couple is in Ephesus the last time they are mentioned in the Christian Scriptures (2 Tim 4:19). If this is historically reliable, one could wonder if they died there rather than in Rome. The question is probably moot, however, since most scholars believe 1 and 2 Timothy were written after Paul's death and not by Paul himself.
19. Denzey, *Bone Gatherers*, 121–24.

early Christians following the long established Roman custom of celebrating a funerary meal.[20] Romans invited family and friends to celebrate such meals on the day of the burial and on the ninth day following the funeral, which ended the period of official mourning. Similar funerary meals could be held forty days after death, and then annually on the deceased's birthday, as well as during the mid-February *parentalia* that honored ancestors.[21] To prove whether women presided over eucharistic meals, opponents and proponents of women's priestly ordination in the Catholic Church have long argued that the seated figures in this scene are either all men or all women.[22] But according to Robin Jensen, "This banquet motif appears on both pagan and Christian sarcophagi, as well as painted on walls of pagan and Christian hypogea [small rooms] in the Roman catacombs. In both pagan and Christian examples the assembly consists of seven (but sometimes five or twelve) diners reclining around a table set with wine, bread and fish."[23] As Jensen sees it, the obvious parallels to non-Christian funerary meal scenes make it more likely that the early Christian images "are scenes of actual funeral banquets."[24]

20. Robin Margaret Jensen, "Dining with the Dead: From the Mensa to the Altar in Christian Late Antiquity," in Brink and Green, *Commemorating the Dead*, 123. See also the excellent discussion in B. Borg, *Crisis and Ambition*, 256–57.

21. Jensen, "Dining with the Dead," 118.

22. Women patrons who opened their homes to early Christian communities probably did preside at eucharistic meals where it would have been culturally inconceivable for the host not to preside in their home. See chapter 1. Inscriptions for female presbyters and the numerous proscriptions of "women at the altar" found in literary records—such as the letter from Pope Gelasius in the fifth century or the fourth-century Synod of Laodicea—supply persuasive evidence that some women in the early church held titles and liturgical roles similar to those held by men. Third- and fourth-century Christian art alone, however, does not provide definitive evidence for either female presbyters or male presbyters.

23. Jensen, "Dining with the Dead," 111.

24. Ibid., 123.

Figure 4.3. Third-century fresco from the catacombs of Callixtus that probably represents a funerary meal with possible eucharistic connotations (seven baskets). Photo: Pontifical Commission of Sacred Archaeology.

Figure 4.4. Detail from late third- or early fourth-century Christian funerary meal from room 45 at catacombs of Pietrus and Marcellinus. Rare portrayal of a family with children. Note the female on the left who is proposing a toast to Agape (love). The large rectangular area is a loculus grave. Photo: André Held/akg-images.

It is possible to argue that some third-century Christians may have conducted eucharistic celebrations at their funerary meals because there is material and literary evidence from the fourth century attesting to the practice. In the later fourth century, large and small structures were built adjoining gravesites to accommodate both public and private funerary meals. Many were equipped with altars: "The presence of an altar in the large hall as well as one inside the small shrine enclosure indicates that a Eucharist could be held either place, perhaps moved to the hall when the size of the gathering required a large space."[25] Eventually, funeral rites with a eucharistic celebration were moved inside of churches, but only after strenuous efforts by churchmen to deter gravesite eucharistic celebrations.[26]

From an artistic perspective, the iconography of the *Fractio Panis* fresco and that of another meal scene in the catacombs of Callixtus (figure 4.3) seem subdued and almost reverential compared to the obvious toasting and revelry found in other funerary meal scenes (figure 4.4). Both include seven figures with seven baskets filled with more bread than could ever be consumed by the diners. While the present scholarly consensus is that these are funerary meals, whoever commissioned them may also have had something specifically Christian in mind. At minimum, these paintings evoke the miracle of the multiplication of the loaves (in which seven baskets were left over), perhaps witnessing to viewers the great abundance awaiting them in the final heavenly banquet (see Mark 8:1–9; Matt 15:32–39).

25. Ibid., 132. Also, according to Prudentius, a fourth-century Roman Christian poet, blessed bread was left on the stone *menza* beside the graves of the martyrs in Rome for pilgrims who lined up to take the eucharist at their tombs. *Liber Peristephanon* (Crowns of Martyrdom), book 11, "To Bishop Valerian on the Passion of the Most Blessed Martyr Hippolytus." I am indebted to Janet Tulloch for this reference.

26. Jensen, "Dining with the Dead," 132–35.

Figure 4.5. So-called Greek Chapel at the catacombs of Priscilla, with many early Christian frescos, especially of women, that date to the mid-third century. Note the bench for seating on the right side. Nicola Denzey suggests this may have been a special prayer space for early Christian women. Photo by Eric Vandeville/akg-images.

All but one of the figures at the *Fractio Panis* Christian funerary meal scene are probably female, judging from the clothing, jewelry, and the obviously veiled woman in the center.[27] This is significant. Nicola Denzey makes a persuasive case that the decoration of the Greek Chapel suggests it was a privileged space for female prayer and worship. In figure 4.5, the long bench along the right side would allow women to gather to pray, reflect, and remember their deceased loved ones. Denzey finds a "unifying theme" at the Greek Chapel in that many frescos are of female figures, emphasizing "the role of women in salvation history." She notes that while the scene of the raising of Lazarus has seventy-three surviving examples in catacomb art, only

27. See Tulloch's ("Visual Representations," 428–30, figs. 12a, 12b) discussion of the small figure on the left, whom she identifies as a youth. Carolyn Osiek ("Out of the Shadows" workshop, Xavier University, October 29, 2016) agrees that the figure on the far left is a child since it is unlikely that any adult would sit on or climb over the *stibadium* (couch) during a meal. The female to the right of the child could be his mother fixing him with a scolding eye while the attention of the other women is directed elsewhere.

the one in the Greek Chapel includes both Mary and Martha standing behind Jesus.[28]

Another fresco, traditionally identified as Daniel in the lion's den, does not correspond to formulaic depictions of Daniel. Denzey describes a lone figure wearing a floor-length garment standing before a cityscape. A barely discernible solo lion crouches to the figure's right. Any human with a lion would easily evoke Daniel iconography, which is how catacomb expert Josef Wilpert identified the fresco. But Denzey argues correctly that Daniel is always shown naked, not clothed, between two lions, not one. This figure wears a floor-length garment with hair carefully arranged in a bun. This is not Daniel but a female figure. A popular second-century story beloved of Christian women does fit the iconography of this scene: it is the story of Thecla from the apocryphal Acts of Paul and Thecla. Thecla's mother and fiancé, Thamyris, betray Thecla to the authorities to punish her for breaking her engagement and following Paul. She is condemned to be consumed by wild beasts, but a female lioness refuses to devour her. Instead, the lioness crouches submissively at Thecla's feet before rising up to defend her from the other beasts. As we saw in chapter 1, Thecla's story probably derives from actual women who were being criticized for evangelizing outside the home. Throughout the Mediterranean world, early Christian women invoked Thecla's name to validate their own ministries and celibate lifestyles. That the women of Rome knew her story is attested by several examples of Roman sarcophagus art on which Thecla appears.[29] If this early third-century tomb does venerate the bones of the New Testament Prisca, it is plausible that the story of another female disciple of Paul—Thecla—would also have been commemorated in the same way.

Lining the walls on either side of the sitting area in the Greek Chapel are large frescos traditionally identified as scenes from the Susanna cycle (see figure 4.5). One sidewall features a standing female *orans* usually interpreted as Susanna, who stands between three men. The two to her right are viewed as the corrupt elders who falsely accuse her and the figure on her left is thought to be Daniel, who

28. Denzey, *Bone Gatherers*, 105.
29. See RS 1, no. 832; RS 3, nos. 297.2 and 478.

defends her. Because the man on the left ("Daniel") is in front of a tomb or cave like structure, and the corrupt elders are paired together on the right rather than flanking Susanna as in most depictions, Denzey speculates the iconography could be from another biblical story, namely John 20, wherein Mary of Magdala first announces Jesus's resurrection.[30] Denzey also notes there is no tomb in Susanna's garden. She suggests the fresco may simultaneously represent two scenes from John 20:1–18: Mary's proclamation of the empty tomb to Peter and the Beloved Disciple (John 20:1–9), and Mary's solo experience of Jesus's risen presence after the two disciples returned home (John 20:10–18). There are difficulties with this interpretation. First, the iconography of the two men with outstretched arms—as if accusing or stoning the middle figure—fits better with the story of Susanna's corrupt elders than the two male disciples, who have no reason to attack Mary of Magdala. Second, viewing the fresco as a conflation of two texts is confusing. The prominent male figure outside the "tomb" or cave suggests that Mary and the two male disciples experienced Jesus as risen at the same time, which does not correspond to New Testament accounts. Another plausible interpretation is that Denzey's "tomb" could be viewed as the lion's den from the Daniel story, and this would favor a Susanna interpretation of the mysterious fresco.

The other large frescos along the sidewalls are equally puzzling. A male and female *orans* are depicted in front of yet another mysterious rocky structure, and a woman is shown between two men who each place one hand on her head. The former has been interpreted as Daniel and Susanna giving thanks to God in prayer and the latter as Susanna being accused by the corrupt elders. The text explicitly describes them as placing their hands on her head as they falsely accuse her (Sus 1:34).[31] Denzey suggests the latter scene could be a diaconal ordination for the woman who is commemorated by these frescos, but this is unlikely since no ordained female deacons are attested in the Western church until the fifth century.[32] Ultimately,

30. Denzey, *Bone Gatherers*, 108–13.
31. Kathryn A. Smith, "Inventing Marital Chastity: The Iconography of Susanna and the Elders in Early Christian Art," *Oxford Art Journal* 16, no. 1 (1993): 3-24, as cited by B. Borg, *Crisis and Ambition*, 255.
32. Madigan and Osiek, *Ordained Women*, 141.

any interpretation of the large frescos lining the sidewalls of the Greek Chapel is quite speculative since the iconography does not fit any known formula.[33] Yet, some inferences can be made. The first is that the frescos feature women as prominent figures. Second, the large size of the figures suggests these female depictions were important to whoever commissioned the tomb art. Last, the frescos were created in a ritual space that includes other paintings of women such as the *Fractio Panis*, the adoration of the magi, Thecla, Martha and Mary, and Susanna. Denzey sums it up well:

> However we interpret the Greek Chapel's extraordinary and unparalleled Susanna cycle, the room's focus on women's tales and sacred history seems to suggest that physical space in late ancient Christianity could be gendered—that space designed for women's use actually looked different from space used by men and women together. In the Greek Chapel, we may have one of our earliest examples of ancient Christian women's sacred space.[34]

Another interpretation offered by Carolyn Osiek is that so many women are depicted because a powerful female patron owned and was buried at the site and she decided what would be painted on the walls. In Osiek's view, the space was not necessarily reserved to women's use. Both scholars agree, however, that a woman or women probably made the decisions about which frescos would fill the space.[35]

33. Hanspeter Schlosser, "Die Daniel-Susanna-Erzählung in Bild und Literatur der christlichen Frühzeit," in *Tortulae: Studien zu altchristlichen und byzantinischen Monumenten*, ed. Walter Nikolaus Schumacher (Rome: Herder, 1966), 243–49, as cited in Denzey, *Bone Gatherers*, 108.

34. Denzey, *Bone Gatherers*, 113.

35. Carolyn Osiek, email to author, November 23, 2016.

Figure 4.6. Third-century fresco from the so-called *Velata* cubiculum at the catacombs of Priscilla. This portrait may signify that the deceased was an enrolled or ordained widow.

THE "*VELATA*" CUBICULUM

A late third-century fresco in the *Velata* (veiled woman) burial chamber contains several fascinating scenes that may provide a window into how one third-century Christian woman was remembered as a person of authority in the early church (figure 4.6). The fresco honors an unnamed woman who seems to appear in three separate scenes that have been variously interpreted.

Marucchi originally suggested that the scene on the left was a ceremony consecrating a virgin. This interpretation has since been discounted, in part because there are no contemporaneous descriptions of ordination/consecration ceremonies for virgins. Denzey, moreover, believes women in the order of virgins were not veiled at the time, judging from Tertullian's bitter complaints about virgins not wearing them.[36] Currently, catacomb guides describe this fresco as representing three scenes from the life of the deceased woman. The

36. Tertullian, *On the Veiling of Virgins* (S. Thelwall, *Ante-Nicene Fathers*, vol. 4 [Buffalo,

center figure is an *orans* figure meant to portray the deceased praying in paradise. The scene on the left of the *orans* is described as the scene of her marriage, and the scene on the right, say contemporary guides, represents the woman's life as a mother. There are problems with this interpretation. The foremost is that neither the clothing nor the postures in the left-hand scene are consistent with Roman wedding rituals. At both Roman and non-Christian weddings, the bride typically wore a yellow veil and the couple is shown together joining their right hands (see figure 7.6). There is no yellow veil visible in this fresco and neither is the couple holding hands.

Dorothy Irvin offers another interpretation. She suggests that the dalmatic (a robe with wide sleeves) worn by the female *orans* indicates that this is a woman deacon. That she also wears a veil on her head while praying evokes the office of prophet because Paul enjoined women to cover their heads while prophesying (1 Cor 11:1–13). For Irvin, the woman on the left is holding a Gospel scroll and clothed in a chasuble, a vestment worn only by a priest. Behind her sits a male bishop who is laying his right hand on her shoulder. According to Irvin, the female figure is being given a scroll and vestments to signify her priesthood. Irvin describes the male figure as a bishop because he is seated in a chair with a back. She argues that in the early church, only bishops sat on such a chair. It is from this tradition that we get the word "see" for a bishop's territory, from the Latin *sedis*, meaning seat. Irvin notes the male "bishop" figure also appears to be wearing a woolen cloak, or *pallium*, around his shoulders signifying his office. Irvin observes that the scene on the right seems to mirror the one on the left but now it is a woman seated in a high-backed chair wearing a robe like the bishop's. The woman also holds a baby. Irvin interprets this as

> Mary validating by her protective and watchful presence the ordination of women as deacons, priests and bishops. . . . Her portrait was included in this fresco with Christians of three centuries later because they believed she was still with them in Spirit, and because her example and

NY: Christian Literature, 1885] rev. and ed. Kevin Knight for New Advent, http://tinyurl.com/ydy9rhgs).

approval of women's Church leadership were accepted and important in the Church community.[37]

Janet Tulloch, a cultural historian in ancient religions and material culture, suggests that the fresco could represent a woman being commissioned for a special role in the church but believes it is impossible to say based solely on the painting.[38] She suggests there is a further complication in the detail of the praying figure's veil, which clearly resembles a Tallit, or Jewish prayer shawl. For Tulloch, a plausible interpretation of the entire wall that takes into account all of the visual evidence has yet to be achieved.

Denzey suggests that the images probably refer to a married woman because the seated female on the right holds a baby and has the same hairstyle as the unveiled woman on the left. Since the male background figure on the left is either a slave or an attendant, the woman was either divorced or her husband was not alive when the fresco was painted. Denzey finds his absence "telling" and consistent with many other Christian catacomb frescos where "precious few images exist of women with their husbands or with their children."[39] Despite writings by church fathers such as Tertullian that laud domestic harmony, "catacomb images, by contrast, rarely if ever emphasize devotion through domestic harmony. Instead, women are disproportionately represented as solitary figures, often in the *orans* pose that the *Velata* assumes in the central, dominant image on her grave."[40] Denzey emphasizes the significance of a woman bearing a scroll: "The *Velata* tells us not that she is married, but that *she can read*, and that her act of public reading was even endorsed by a bishop at a moment in her life she found significant enough to record on the walls of her grave."[41] But what exactly was that moment? Paul-Albert

37. Dorothy Irving, "The Archaeology of Women's Traditional Ministries in the Church 60–1500 AD," in *Calendar 2005* (St. Paul, MN: Self-published, 2005).

38. Janet Tulloch, remarks during FutureChurch pilgrimage tour, March 15, 2007.

39. Denzey, *Bone Gatherers*, 83.

40. Ibid. Denzey cites Tertullian, *Ad uxorem* 2.8.35–36: "How beautiful, then the marriage of two Christians, two who are one in hope, one in desire, one in the way of life they follow, one in the religion they practice. . . . They pray together, they worship together, they fast together, instructing one another, encouraging one another, strengthening one another. Side by side they face difficulties and persecution, and share their consolations."

41. Denzey, *Bone Gatherers*, 85.

Février suggests that the scene depicts the education of the woman by a male teacher since it does not include the standard *dextrarum iunctio* formula for both Christian and non-Christian representations of marriage.[42] Early Christian archaeologist Fabrizio Bisconti rejects Février's interpretation of a woman's education. He argues that the scene must represent a liturgical practice since to him it looks ceremonial.[43] For Borg, the images detail the woman's education, motherhood, and *pietas* (religious devotion) with a special focus on the Scriptures.[44]

But parallel representations of the seated woman on the right with the seated bishop/authority figure on the left offer other important clues to the life of this mystery woman. With the exception of Mary, the mother of Jesus, images of a Christian woman seated in high backed chair (*sedis*) are rare in early Christian art. In this fresco, both seated figures are the same size and dressed similarly in white dalmatics with dark stripes (*clavi*), although the "bishop" seems to have a rectangular cloak or *pallium*, probably signifying his office. The artistic similarities between the two figures convey they are roughly similar in status. The center *orans* is almost certainly not a female deacon since there is no literary or epigraphical evidence that there were women deacons in the West until the fifth century.[45] It is more probable that the wealthy woman in this fresco was an enrolled—or possibly an ordained—widow. The liturgical scene on the left may be her ordination or enrollment ceremony. The third-century *Apostolic Tradition* instructs that widows were not to be ordained, thereby attesting that some women must have been or there would have been no need for a rule proscribing it.

Ute Eisen identifies numerous early inscriptions from Rome commemorating ecclesiastically enrolled widows. For example, the engraving to "the widow Flavia Arcas" found at the catacombs of

---

42. Paul A. Février, "Les peintures de la catacombe de Priscille: deux scènes relatives à la vie intellectuelle," *Mélanges d'archéologie et d'histoire* 71 (1959): 301–19, as cited by B. Borg, *Crisis and Ambition*, 254.

43. Fabrizio Bisconti and Donatella Nuzzi, "Scavi e restauri nella regione della 'Velata' in Priscilla." *Rivista di archeologia cristiana* 77 (2001): 74, as cited by B. Borg, *Crisis and Ambition*, 254.

44. B. Borg, *Crisis and Ambition*, 254.

45. Madigan and Osiek, *Ordained Women*, 141.

Priscilla is one of only a few Christian inscriptions dating to the second century. It reads:

[Φλαβι]α Αρκας Χηρα ητις
[εζησε]ν αιτη πε μητρι
[γλυκυ]τατη Φλαβια Θεοφιλα
Φυγατηρ εποιησεν

The widow Flavia Arcas, who lived eighty-five years.
Flavia Theophila, her daughter erected (this epitaph)
to the sweetest of mothers.[46]

Here, the Greek word *widow*—Χηρα—is actually a title, "since the designation of women as widows was not customary in the inscriptions of the period."[47] Eisen cites Louis Duchesne and Carl Kaufmann, who "long ago recognized the inscription for the widow Flavia Arcas as the oldest evidence for an enrolled widow, and thus at the same time as the oldest epigraphical attestation of a member of the Church hierarchy."[48] A late fourth-century Latin inscription found in Rome's cemetery of St. Saturninus might shed even more light on our puzzling fresco. It reads:

Rigine vene merenti filia sua fecit
vene. Rigine matri viduae que sedit vidua annos LX et eclesa
numqua(m) gravavit, unibyra, que
vixit annos LXXX, mesis V,
dies XXVI.

For the well-deserving Regina her daughter has placed this stone.
The Mother Regina, the widow, who "sat" as widow for sixty years
and was not a burden to the Church, univira [never remarried],
who lived eighty years and five months and twenty-six days.[49]

---

46. Eisen, *Women Officeholders*, 143.
47. Ibid., 144; see n. 5: Louis M. O Duchesne, *Christian Worship. Its Origin and Evolution. As Study of the Latin Liturgy up to the Time of Charlemagne*, trans. M. L. McClure (London: SPCK, 1956). Carl Maria Kaufmann, *Handbuch der altchristlichen Epigraphik*, 293.
48. Eisen, *Women Officeholders*, 144.
49. Ibid., 145. Eisen cites Carlo Carletti for the inscription: *Iscrizioni cristiane di Roma. Testimonianze di vita cristina (secoli III-VII)*, BPat 7 (Florence: Centro internazionale del libro, 1986), 146: "Lastra marmorea ora perduta: sulla sinistra `e graffita una colomba posata su un ramo" (A marble slab now lost. On the left an engraving of a dove on a palm branch).

According to Eisen, the connection between the two formulaic phrases, *vidua* and *sedit*, signal that Regina was an enrolled widow. As evidence, she cites other inscriptions that use these formulas to signify a church officeholder. One describes a presbyter in this way:

hic quiescit Romanus p(res)b(yter),
qui sedit p(res)b(yter) ann(os) XXVII, m(enses)X.
dep(ositus) X kal(endas) augus(tas)
Con(sulatu) Severini v(iri)c(larissimi). i[n pace]!

here rests Romanus the presbyter,
who "sat" as a presbyter twenty-seven years and ten months.
buried here on the tenth kalends of August
during Consulate of Severinus a most illustrious man. In peace![50]

Yet another inscription from Ferentino testifies that an enrolled widow exercised her office at a basilica and had her "seat" of honor there.[51] The word *sedis*, then, appears to be associated not only with the office of the bishop, but also with other offices in the church, including presbyters (elders) and enrolled widows.

The beautiful fresco in the *Velata* cubiculum may well commemorate an ecclesiastical widow who, like Grapte in the second century, was a woman of stature who ministered in the third-century church at Rome. Her iconography recalls the vision given to the shepherd of Hermas, who was commanded to write "two little books and send one to Grapte and one to Clement" (Herm. Vis. 2.4.3). Grapte was a second-century female leader whose responsibilities involved all the house-church communities at Rome. She was to "instruct the widows and the orphans," and may herself have been a widow. Hermas sharply criticizes Rome's deacons, who "despoil the living of widows and orphans," in contrast to Grapte who ministers to them. While the memory of Grapte has been largely lost to us, the third-century women who prayed and were interred at the catacombs of Priscilla

---

50. Carlo Carletti, *Iscrizioni cristiane inedite del cimitero di Bassilla ad S. Hermetem* (Vatican City: Tipografia Poliglotta Vaticana, 1976), cited by Eisen, *Women Officeholders*, 146.

51. Linus Bopp, *Das Witwentum als organische Gliedschaft im Gemeinschaftsleben der alten Kirche: Ein geschichtlicher Beitrag zur Grundlegung der Witwenseelsorge in der Gegenwart* (Mannheim: Wohlgemuth, 1959), cited by Eisen, *Women Officeholders*, 146.

probably remembered her well and sought to model their own lives on hers.

We should not necessarily assume that the baby held by the deceased is her own child. One ministry of wealthy Christian widows in ancient Rome was to care for unwanted newborns exposed to die. Like the fourth-century Regina, whose inscription is careful to say she "*was not a burden to the Church,*" the woman in the *Velata* cubiculum was not financially dependent on the church to survive. She or her family commissioned this expensive funerary fresco to commemorate what she valued most: ordained or enrolled ministry in the church, learning, Scripture, prayer, prophecy, and care for orphans.

BITALIA IN PACE: CATACOMBS OF SAN GENNARO

Figure 4.7. *Bitalia in Pace*. Portrait fresco of "Bitalia in Peace" depicted with four gospels and standing at what may be an altar. Dates to the late fourth or early fifth century. Catacomb of San Gennaro, Naples. Photo: akg-images/De Agostini Picture Library/A. Dagli Orti.

Deep within an ancient burial ground at the church of Our Lady of Good Counsel at the catacomb of San Gennaro in Naples is an arresting fresco above the burial spot of a woman named Bitalia (see figure 4.7). The painting, which dates to the fourth or fifth century, bears mute testimony to a woman apparently remembered at the very least for her ministry of the word. Bitalia gazes solemnly at us standing behind a table, or, as some believe, an altar, with arms extended in prayer. Her head is partially covered by a short veil and she wears a black garment with close fitting sleeves overlaid with a red tunic, perhaps a cloak, some would say a chasuble. The most arresting element of this carefully wrought portrait are two open books hovering above her with crimson bookmarks cascading down. Three of the four open pages are carefully inscribed in Latin: *Joannis, Markus, Matteus*. The words "*in pace*" inscribed on the back wall tell us that Bitalia now rests in peace.

What we can know of Bitalia's ministry is limited to archaeological and contemporaneous historical and epigraphical records. Still, there is quite a lot of information that can be gleaned, especially from the latter two sources, when one places the various types of evidence in conversation with one another. Bitalia's standing posture in a clearly religious setting indicates she is a woman of authority in the fourth- or fifth-century church. Worship has now moved from house churches with their reclining banquet style of worship into the more formal public space of the basilica, where worshippers stood for at least part of the time. Bitalia's short veil and narrow sleeves are more consistent with women's attire of later antiquity than the unveiled head, *dalmatic*, and *stola* found in earlier centuries. The gospels above her head are in the form of codices (books), which by this time have replaced the scrolls prevalent in Christianity's early centuries. New Testament codices did not appear in Latin until Jerome and his contemporaries translated the New Testament from the Greek in the late fourth century.[52]

Bitalia was a woman of some means because only the wealthy were both literate and had sufficient money to decorate their tombs. Since

---

52. Raymond E. Brown, D. W. Johnson, and Kevin G. O'Connell, "Texts and Versions," in *The New Jerome Biblical Commentary*, ed. Raymond E. Brown, Joseph A. Fitzmyer, and Roland E. Murphy (Englewood Cliffs, NJ: Prentice Hall, 1990), 1095.

catacomb art invariably conveys the most important things about a person's life, the presence of the books of the Gospel listed by name is highly significant. Bitalia seems to have been intimately involved in teaching and proclaiming the good news for the Christian community within which she ministered. It is curious that only John, Mark, and Matthew's names are visible. Even presuming that part of the fourth open page was destroyed, it seems odd that fragments of the Luke inscription would not be visible, since the right side of the page and overlapping red bookmark streamers are undamaged. Given the tendency of Luke's Gospel to heighten Peter's leadership at the expense of the leadership of Mary of Magdala, it is tempting to speculate that Bitalia chose not to include Luke's text, though this is a larger hypothesis than the evidence can support.[53] Dorothy Irvin argues that Bitalia is a female presbyter celebrating Eucharist at the altar.[54] She says this because she sees evidence for two cups on the table and a flat loaf of bread under Bitalia's right elbow in the fresco. While Irvin's interpretation might at first appear somewhat imaginative, there are literary and epigraphical data to support her claim.

FLAVIA VITALIA, *PRESBYTERA SANCTA*

Our corroborating epigraphical data begins with another woman who is a contemporary of our Neapolitan Bitalia. Her name is Flavia Vitalia and her inscription, found in modern day Croatia, is an official document dating to 425. It describes her as a *matrona* (matron) and *presbytera sancta* (holy presbyter). Here is a translation of the full inscription:

> Under our Lord Theodosius, consul for the eleventh time, and Valentinian, most noble man of Caesar, I, Theodosius bought [a burial tomb] from the matron [*matrona*] Flavia Vitalia the holy presbyter[a] for three golden solids.[55]

---

53. Brock, *Mary Magdalene*, 32–35.
54. Dorothy Irvin, *Calendar 2003*.
55. Madigan and Osiek, *Ordained Women*, 196.

The title *matrona* tells us that Flavia Vitalia was a freeborn married woman who was also a presbyter, that is, a religious leader in her community. After Constantine permitted freedom of religious practice, presbyters assumed primary responsibility for overseeing Christian burial sites. Hence, Flavia Vitalia has been designated as a keeper of the tombstones. That she is also called "holy" tells us something of the high esteem in which she was held by her fellow Christians.

ABOUT THE TITLE "PRESBYTER"

The title "presbyter" has a long history in the church. First-century Christians avoided using the Greek term "priest" (*hieros*) for their religious leaders, preferring to use titles taken from everyday life. Some of these included *diakonos* (minister), *apostolos* (missionary), *presbyteros* (elder), *didaskalos* (teacher), *episcopos* (overseer), and *prophetēs* (prophet).[56] By the fifth century, however, "presbyter" had become more formalized and meant the person had been commissioned and, in some cases, ordained with a laying on of hands for leadership in the church. Some commentators dismiss all inscriptions for women *presbyterae* as signifying honorary titles for the wives of clerics, not actual church office. While there is data to support this with some women in some historical periods, it is not true for others. In fact, we only know that women held formal presbyteral office in their own right because of writings by male church leaders who sought to ban the practice.

OPPOSITION TO FEMALE PRESBYTERS

Fortuitously, at least for present day advocates of expanded roles for women in Christianity, condemnations by churchmen provide historic evidence not only that women presbyters existed but that they were banned because of the belief that females were created subordinate to males, something no longer held as church doctrine today. As

---

56. Karen Jo Torjesen, *When Women Were Priests: Women's Leadership in the Early Church and the Scandal of Their Subordination in the Rise of Christianity* (San Francisco: HarperSanFrancisco, 1993), 5–6.

we saw in chapter 2, the late fourth-century churchman, Epiphanius, vehemently opposed female presbyters. He selectively cited Hebrew and early Christian texts that suggested the inferior status of women's (Gen 3:16, 1 Cor 11:8, and 1 Tim 2:12–15) while ignoring texts suggesting the opposite (Gal 3:28 and Gen 1:27). According to Ute Eisen:

> Epiphanius's central purpose is to establish that women had never held the rank of presbyter, i.e., priest, which would have authorized them to celebrate the Eucharist. . . .
>
> In his argument Epiphanius attempts to show that women who held different titles (deaconesses, widows, *presbytides*) really exercised the same office, namely that of deaconess. . . . This picture of a subordinate Church office for women was the result of Epiphanius's concept of creation theology, which determined women's inferiority to men.[57]

Canon 11 of the Council of Laodicea (ca. 341–81) attests that ordained women leaders, called *presbytides*, acted as presidents of their congregations. Women's leadership in Laodicea could easily have been well established, dating to Nympha's first-century house church. Colossians 4:15 has Paul sending "greetings to the brothers and sisters who are in Laodicea and to Nympha and the church that meets in her house." By the fourth century, rather than recognize women church leaders whose ministry dated to the time of Paul, churchmen forbade them to be installed in the church (Canon 11). Canon 44 forbade women entry to the sanctuary. According to Ute Eisen and Ida Raming, these prohibitions provide compelling evidence that there were fourth-century women within the mainstream church in the East who led the assembly and presided at the eucharistic celebrations. They were not only to be found in schismatic groups but also in the Great (mainstream) Church.[58]

---

57. Eisen, *Women Officeholders*, 122.

58. Eisen, *Women Officeholders*, 121–22, and Ida Raming, *The Exclusion of Women from the Priesthood: Divine Law or Sex Discrimination? A Historical Investigation of the Juridical and Doctrinal Foundations of the Code of Canon Law, Canon 968,1*, trans. Norman R. Adams (Metuchen, NJ: Scarecrow, 1976), 22.

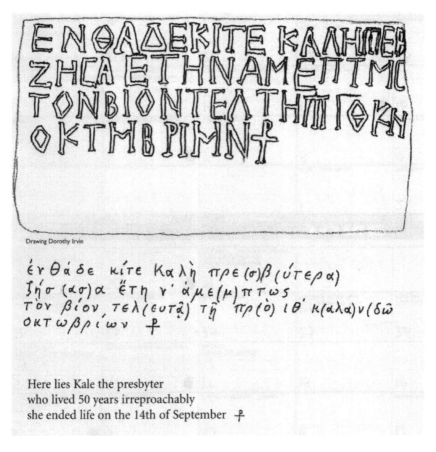

ἐνθάδε κίτε Καλὴ πρε(σ)β(ύτερα)
ζήσ(ασ)α ἔτη ν' ἀμε(μ)πτως
τὸν βίον, τελ(εύτα) τῇ πρ(ὸ) ιθ' κ(αλα)ν(δῶ
ὀκτωβρίων ⳨

Here lies Kale the presbyter
who lived 50 years irreproachably
she ended life on the 14th of September ⳨

Figure 4.8. A reproduction by Dr. Dorothy Irvin of a fourth- or fifth-century inscription found on a tombstone in Centuripae, Sicily. Used with permission.

WOMEN PRESBYTERS IN THE EAST

In Asia Minor, Greece, and Egypt respectively, Eisen has studied inscriptions dating from the second to fourth centuries for three women leaders: Ammion the Presbyter, Epikto the *Presbytis*, and Artemidora the Presbyter. Ammion the Presbyter's early third-century inscription was found in Phrygia in Asia Minor as part of a group of commemorations named by the local bishop, Diogas. In English, *Epikto the Presbytis*'s inscription reads: *Angel of Epikto, presbytis*. She led the community of Christians on the Greek island of Thera in the second or third century. Artemidora the Presbyter's second- or third-century inscription is from a label for her mummy found in Egypt: "(Mummy of) the presbyter Artemidora, the daughter of Mikkalos (and the) mother Paniskiaina. She has fallen asleep in the Lord." The *Testamentum Domini*, which possibly originated in Egypt, twice mentions women presbyters explicitly, providing further validation for Artemidora's title.[59]

TWO OTHER CONTEMPORARIES OF BITALIA IN THE WESTERN CHURCH

In the fourth and fifth centuries in Southern Italy and Sicily we find two more women presbyters who were contemporaries of Bitalia, in addition to Flavia Vitalia mentioned earlier. Kale, *presbytera*, is a woman from Centuripae, Sicily, who led her community in the fourth or fifth century (see figure 4.8). She is remembered in this translated inscription: "Here lies Kale presbyter, who lived fifty years blamelessly. She died on the nineteenth kallends of October [September 14]." Kale's inscription contains the abbreviation "PREB," which also appears in other Greek and Latin inscriptions. While it could mean "older woman," this was not a designation used on inscriptions in Sicily.[60] Since no husband is named, Kale held the *presbytera* title in her own right, designating her Christian leadership. Leta the *Presbytera* is a woman from the small town of Tropea in Calabria. Her late fifth-century tombstone reflects the love and honor in which her husband held her:

> Sacred to her good memory Leta the Presbyter lived 40 years, 8 months, 9 days, for whom her husband set up this tomb. She preceded him in peace on the day before the Ides of May.[61]

Leta's title was originally interpreted to mean she was the wife of a priest. Yet her husband does not bear an ecclesiastical title.

---

59. Eisen, *Women Officeholders*, 116–28.
60. Ibid., 128–31.
61. Madigan and Osiek, *Ordained Women*, 193–95.

POPE GELASIUS IS UPSET

Giorgio Otranto's groundbreaking research into an early letter from Pope Gelasius I constitutes significant evidence for women priests in the fifth and early sixth centuries. In 494, Pope Gelasius I sent a lengthy letter "to all episcopates established in Lucania [modern Basilicata], Bruttium [modern Calabria—in the ankle and toe of Italy]—and Sicilia [modern Sicily]."[62] His letter included twenty-seven decrees addressing pastoral concerns in the various communities, including internal church organization; relationships between priests, deacons, and bishops; the discipline of priests; and qualifications for ordination. Four of the decrees addressed women's concerns, including the consecration of virgins, the veiling of widows, and, significantly, his great unhappiness about the priesthood of women:

> Nevertheless we have heard to our annoyance that divine affairs have come to such a low state that women are encouraged to officiate at the sacred altars, and to take part in all matters imputed to the offices of the male sex, to which they do not belong.[63]

Otranto is careful to explain that the word *cuncta* in the Latin

> comprises all the attributes of the male services: liturgical, juridical, and magisterial. The functions exercised by women at the altars, therefore, can refer only to the administration of the sacraments, to the liturgical service, and to the public and official announcement of the evangelical message, all of which comprise the duties of ministerial priesthood.[64]

Otranto also points to the writings of a tenth-century bishop, Atto of Vercelli, who, in response to a question, wrote that women did receive sacred orders in the early church but that the practice was prohibited by the Council of Laodicea in the latter half of the fourth century. According to Otranto, "Atto's statement is a striking and significant testimony of female priesthood in antiquity." He further

62. Mary Ann Rossi and Giorgio Otranto, "Priesthood, Precedent and Prejudice: On Recovering the Women Priests of Early Christianity," *Journal of Feminist Studies* 7, no. 1 (1991): 80.
63. Ibid., 80–81: "Nihilominus impatienter audivimus, tantum divinarum rerum subisse despectum, ut feminae sacris altaribus ministrare firmentur, cunctaque non nisi virorum famulatui deputata sexum, cui non competunt, exhibere."
64. Ibid., 82.

questions why the scholarly specialists of the period have ignored the evidence for so long: "Perhaps when scholars have become more dispassionate, this picture will provide fuller documentary support for the question of the admission of women to the priesthood."[65]

Even though male church leaders in both the East and West regularly opposed the practice of female presbyters, there is substantial inscriptional and literary evidence that women leaders with priestly titles regularly served local churches. When male church leaders argued against female presbyters, they did so on the grounds that women were created subordinate to men, a belief widely held by men in the church at the time. It is therefore all the more remarkable to find literary and inscriptional evidence that women did exercise such roles despite the constraints imposed by an increasingly misogynist clerical culture.

A minimalist interpretation of Bitalia's fresco would point to her desire to be remembered as a woman of prayer, teacher of Scripture, and proclaimer of the word. When we combine the literary evidence from Pope Gelasius I with the epigraphical evidence from Kale, the *presbytera* in Sicily; Leta, the *presbytera* in Calabria; and Flavia Vitalia, the *presbytera sancta* from Dalmatia, it becomes plausible that Bitalia's expressive fresco in Naples may indeed be that of a fifth-century woman priest "officiating at the sacred altars." The weight of the argument, however, rests with the epigraphical and literary evidence since it is problematic to try to determine any specific church office based solely on the fresco art.

VENERANDA AND PETRONELLA: WOMEN OF THE WORD

In a beautiful setting on the Via delle Sette Chiese near the Via Ardeatina, the gentle green landscape of the catacombs of Domitilla rises to greet us. Hidden underground is a spacious fourth-century basilica renovated by Pope Damasus (366–84) to honor Nereus and Achilleus, two Roman soldiers, as the story goes, who were martyred by Diocletian for refusing to torture Christian believers.

65. Ibid., 92–93.

Figure 4.9. Late fourth-century fresco with a portrait of the deceased Veneranda accompanied by "Petronella, martyr." In Roman art, scrolls in a *capsa* (basket) and codices typically signify learnedness and authority. Here, they probably also represent the Hebrew and Christian Scriptures. Photo akg-images/De Agostini Picture Library/ V. Pirozzi.

But before Damasus built the basilica honoring the male martyrs, these burial grounds were part of the estate of a woman named Flavia Domitilla, whose memory dates to the first century. Although there were many women named Domitilla in the Flavius family, an early historian, Dio Cassius, tells us that the first-century wife of one Flavius Clemens was exiled after her husband was executed for "Judaizing." Some scholars believe this accusation reflects early Christian proselytism in Rome, since first-century Roman understanding of Christianity was intimately linked to its Jewish origins.[66] Domitilla (whom later Christian tradition also claimed as a martyr) was one of many female patrons who donated ancestral lands for the burial of Christians who could not otherwise afford it. Other Christian catacombs tracing their origins to the generosity of prominent female patrons include the catacombs of Priscilla, Commodilla, and the crypts of Lucina and Balbina in the catacombs of Callixtus.[67] According to Carolyn Osiek, there were "significant numbers of women who owned land and were in the position of head of household with responsibility to provide burials for the *familia*, which then extended to others, especially the needy members of the Christian community."[68] With this as background, let us examine what is perhaps the loveliest painting of early women leaders in all of catacomb art (see figure 4.9).

Most scholars date Veneranda's burial to 356 CE, although it may have occurred as late as 460. The 356 dating derives from an inscription on a neighboring tomb.[69] The painting is located in a small cubiculum immediately behind the apse of the basilica. We know the deceased Veneranda must have been wealthy because of the elaborately frescoed detail of her memorial and its prime location near the martyrs Nereus, Achilleus, and, as Veneranda believed, Petronella. The painting shows two women dressed in clothing from two different historical periods. Above the head of the deceased, is the word Veneranda, meaning "she who is to be venerated." Her companion is named simply "Petronella, martyr." The date of Veneranda's death—January 7—is also inscribed, but not the year. To the viewer's right are signs of the women's learnedness and, as I argue, early Christian ministry. A codex with red ribbons streaming down is likely associated with Veneranda, whereas Petronella's ministry is

66. Osiek, "Roman and Christian Burial," 252.
67. Ibid., 255–57.
68. Ibid., 270.
69. Denzey, *Bone Gatherers*, 126n8: "The 356 date comes not from Veneranda's grave, but from an epitaph for another grave in her cubiculum."

probably associated with the scrolls contained in a special basket called a *capsa*, with a lid and a shoulder strap. Carrying Scripture scrolls within a *capsa* was common in the early centuries of Christianity whereas codices appeared later. Petronella's hairstyle and clothing are more typical of earlier centuries in the common era while Veneranda's are more consistent with later periods.[70]

In the following discussion, I argue that the visual and inscriptional evidence suggests Veneranda was a Christian woman of the late fourth century who both remembered and revered the earlier ministry of the martyr Petronella. Most catacomb experts believe Petronella's tomb was located near Veneranda's, though it has yet to be discovered.[71] Catacomb paintings invariably point to what the deceased or their families would like us to remember about them. In a nearby cubiculum, we find a painting of the *fossore* (gravedigger) Diogenes, easily identified by the buckets and digging implements that were the tools of his trade.[72] Much like Diogenes, Dorothy Irvin posits that the presence of the codex and *capsa* in the Veneranda fresco signify the ministries exercised by two women in early Christianity, one of whom, Veneranda, modeled her ministry on that of her forebear, Petronella.[73] Conventional commentators, however, give the painting a different emphasis. Philip Pergola suggests the painting represents the martyr Petronella leading Veneranda to paradise. Consider this excerpt from his commentary:

On [Veneranda's] right a bunch of red flowers alludes to the Garden of Eden where the deceased is led in by a young woman with tunic and palla. This is Petronella mart(yr) as is written near her head. Petronella points with her left hand to a round casket that is open and full of scrolls, on top, an open book symbolizes the Divine Law contained in the Scriptures, faithfully observed by the deceased in order to earn her eternal reward, to which contributes also the intercession of the devout Veneranda.[74]

70. Dorothy Irvin, "The Archaeology of Women's Traditional Ministries in the Church 300–1500 AD," in *Calendar 2004* (St. Paul, MN: Self-published, 2004).

71. Mancinelli, *The Catacombs of Rome and the Origins of Christianity*, 25.

72. Philippe Pergola, *Christian Rome: Early Christian Rome; Catacombs and Basilicas, Past and Present* (Rome: Vision, 2000), 25.

73. Irvin, *Calendar 2004*.

74. Philippe Pergola, *Roman and Italian Catacombs: Domitilla* (Vatican City: Pontificia Commisione di Archeologia Sacra, 2002), 41–43.

This interpretation seems incomplete, however, when the viewer considers the interpersonal dynamics of the artistic rendering. Both women are focusing on the scrolls to which Petronella points on her left, not on the roses that Pergola believes represent paradise on her right. In the context of a burial site honoring a Christian martyr, it is likely that the scrolls signify the Hebrew and Christian Scriptures. As Petronella points to the *capsa* filled with scrolls, she looks at Veneranda, whose gaze is also fixed on the scrolls, not on the roses. Petronella may well be leading Veneranda into paradise, but there seems to be something else going on. Why is the attention of both women (and by extension, our attention) focused on the Scriptures? Veneranda's connection to the Scriptures is interpreted passively as faithful observance rather than active proclamation. Yet, we know from literary, epigraphical, and funerary reliefs that women were active teachers and exercised authority in the fourth-century church. It is not surprising then, that funerary remembrances would portray them accordingly. What is surprising is that these remembrances were created in the midst of efforts to suppress women's initiative and leadership in that same church (see chapter 2).[75] Significantly for our immediate study, there is no parallel commentary about male leaders passively following Scripture to earn their heavenly reward. A short distance from Veneranda's memorial, we find a painting of the apostle Paul holding a scroll with a *capsa* at his feet (see figure 4.10). Yet Paul's painting is described this way:

> The apostle is depicted, as was usual at that time, bald and with a pointed beard; at his feet there is a casket (*capsa*) full of hand-written scrolls (*volumina*): he holds one of them—symbol of the doctrine—with both hands.[76]

75. Denzey, *Bone Gatherers*, 176; and Torjesen, *When Women Were Priests*, 5–6.
76. Pergola, *Roman and Italian Catacombs*, 53.

Figure 4.10. This fourth-century fresco depicts Paul holding a scroll with a *capsa* (basket for scrolls) at his feet. Catacombs of Domitilla. Photo: Pontifical Commission of Sacred Archaeology.

The presence of the *capsa* in the Pauline painting makes a strong case for our interpretation of the Veneranda and Petronella fresco-with-*capsa* as representing a first- or second-century minister of the word (Petronella) akin to Paul. If the interpretation of the *capsa* and scroll in the painting can be linked to the exercise of author-ity—showing early Christian scrolls as a "symbol of the doc-trine"—then a similar interpretation can be attested for Petronella based on the same iconography.[77] To what can we ascribe the differ-ence in interpretations? One possibility is the contemporary difficulty in believing (and therefore seeing) that women served in authori-tative roles in the early church. Another is the historical tendency of catacomb scholars to reinforce church-approved interpretations of catacomb art and artifacts even when scientific analysis proves church sanctioned explanations to be false.[78]

While we have some notion of who Veneranda might have been, who was Petronella? Although Christian tradition long believed her to be the daughter of the apostle Peter, this is a case of mistaken identity. The only early literary evidence attesting that Peter had a daughter is a second-century apocryphal work, the Acts of Peter. This text does not give Peter's daughter a name nor does it describe her as a martyr. Rather, it describes her as beautiful, a virgin, and sick with palsy. Peter's followers appeal to him to heal her, which he finally does, only to command her to "return to your infirmity" since it will help preserve her virginity.[79] How then, did we come to believe Petronellae Mart was Peter's daughter? A famous nineteenth-century archaeologist, Giovanni Battista de Rossi, knew from earlier church records that in the eighth century a sarcophagus containing Petronella's remains and bearing the inscription Aur. Petronellae Filiae Dulcissime had been moved from the Domitilla catacomb to a spe-cial chapel in Saint Peter's basilica. During a sixteenth-century ren-ovation of Petronella's chapel in Saint Peter's, two witnesses saw the inscription on her ancient, strigillated sarcophagus for the last time

77. While Petronella is not depicted holding a scroll as Paul does, many Christian sarcophagi reliefs portray women with scrolls (see chapters 6 and 7).

78. In brief, the official church held that graves of the martyrs were identified by glass or ceramic containers of blood affixed outside the graves. Even though a chemical analysis was published proving the red coloration was rust, in 1863, the church reaffirmed a 1668 decree say-ing the containers held blood. See Amy K. Hirschfield's discussion of the 1860 "Phial of Blood Controversy" in her chapter "History of Catacomb Archaeology," in Brink and Green, Com-memorating the Dead, 25–26.

79. Acts of Peter 1.128 (M. R. James, The Apocryphal New Testament [Oxford: Clarendon, 1924], reprinted on Early Christian Writings, http://tinyurl.com/y7rxauto). See also Denzey, Bone Gatherers, 129–30.

before it was crushed for use in the chapel floor. They interpreted the "Aur." on the inscription not as part of her name, Aurelia, as it would have been read in antiquity, but as *aureae* or golden, as it would have been understood by educated people in the early Middle Ages. So it was that a common funerary inscription in late antiquity, "For a most sweet daughter: Aur. (Aurelia) Petronellae," came to be translated as the "golden Petronella," Peter's daughter.

Some have argued that since Petrus (Peter) was not a Latin or Greek name, Petronella could only be interpreted one way—as the daughter of Saint Peter. But religion historian Nicola Denzey and catacomb expert Phillip Pergola point to another ancient Roman family name: Petronius, from which the cognomen Petronella was more likely derived. It is possible that Petronella was a relative of Titus Flavius Petronius, the great-grandfather of the Christian consul, Flavius Clemens, who, as mentioned earlier, was executed by the first-century emperor, Domitian. The Flavii were descended from the senatorial Aurelii family, which could explain how Aurelia Petronella, came to be honored and remembered in the family burial grounds of Flavia Domitilla. Neither Denzey nor Pergola, however, believes the Petronella now enshrined in Saint Peter's was a martyr, let alone Peter's daughter. Denzey suggests she may have been a wealthy *matrona* who financed an early fourth-century burial chapel honoring Nereus and Achilleus, as well as her own memorial, on the cemetery grounds of her kinswoman Domitilla. For Denzey, Petronella did this to "broadcast her benevolence and her piety."[80] Just a few generations later, the historical *matrona* Petronella was forgotten while believers like Veneranda began—apparently without precedent—to revere her as a martyr. Pergola believes that sometime after 313, Petronella received a "privileged inhumation . . . of a holy woman of great merit, who died at the moment of, or a little bit after, the construction of the basilica."[81] He apparently bases this opinion on earlier beliefs about the location of the original sarcophagus

---

80. Denzey, *Bone Gatherers*, 140.

81. Philippe Pergola, "'Petronella martyr': une évergète de la fin du IVe siècle?," in *Memoriam Sanctorum Venerantes: Miscellanea in onore di Monsignor Victor Saxer*, ed. Eugenio Alliata (Vatican City: Pontificio Istituto di Archeologia Cristiana, 1992), 628, as cited in Denzey, *Bone Gatherers*, 133.

of Petronella. However, neither Denzey's nor Pergola's explanation resolves the question of why Veneranda identified Petronella as a martyr on her funerary fresco if she had not remembered her as such. I suggest two other possibilities. Given the original location of Petronella's tomb near the martyred soldiers Nereus and Achilleus, is it possible that Petronella was also martyred under Diocletian (284–305) and buried near them? We know that a special basilica honoring Petronella, Nereus, and Achilleus already existed at the Domitilla site in the early fourth century.[82] This is not to be confused with the later fourth-century renovation by Pope Damasus. When Damasus renovated the Domitilla basilica, he dedicated it to Nereus and Achilleus alone, thereby demoting Petronella, although he could not stop those who continued to venerate her cult.[83]

A second possibility is that Petronella was martyred sometime between the late first to early third centuries. I favor this explanation because in Veneranda's visual memorial, Petronella's clothing and hairstyle are more consistent with earlier Roman dress, as is the presence of the *capsa*. Of course, this analysis may only tell us that Veneranda, who commissioned the burial fresco, believed Petronella to be an early woman minister and martyr, not that she necessarily was one. There is other evidence, however. Our sixteenth-century eyewitnesses said Petronella's sarcophagus was strigillated and had four dolphins carved onto it. This sarcophagus style is consistent with earlier centuries CE in Rome. Denzey correctly argues that sarcophagi were frequently reused, so that alone cannot be used for dating the year of Petronella's death. But if Petronella was indeed a wealthy, fourth-century Christian *matrona* and "holy woman of great merit," as Denzey and Pergola argue, it seems unlikely that she would reuse an earlier pagan sarcophagus at a time when elaborate carvings of Christian sarcophagi were flourishing (see chapters 6 and 7).

Petronella's name does not appear in the fourth-century Roman calendar of martyrs' feasts, the *Depositio Martyrum* (354). The *Catholic*

82. Pergola, "Petronella Martyr," 628, as cited in Denzey, *Bone Gatherers*, 126.

83. Pergola, *Roman and Italian Catacombs*, 18–20. Denzey (*Bone Gatherers*, 134) also notes that Pope Siriacus (384–99 CE) recognized Petronella's cult and renovated her grave, enclosing it together with those of Nereus and Achilleus. Petronella would be demoted in later years when this memorial again became the Church of Nereus and Achilleus.

Encyclopedia states that this supports a late first- or early second-century dating of Petronella's martyrdom because no martyrs prior to the third century were included in the *Depositio*, except for Peter and Paul.[84] However, Nereus and Achilleus do not appear in the *Depositio* either, and their martyrdoms date to the early fourth century. All three appear in the sixth-century *Hieronymian Martyrology*. Nicola Denzey suggests another explanation:

> Petronella's absence from the church's official sanctioned list of martyrs reveals a fundamental disconnection between whom people actually venerated and [those] whom Rome's bishops advocated venerating. Part of this may have been gendered. The official list is dominated by male saints, with only four of forty-six recognized martyrs being women. Veneranda's painting suggests that even in 354, memory traditions of "unrecognized" martyrs such as Petronella still lay in the hands of women.[85]

I find Denzey's contention that the Veneranda/Petronella painting may be "emblematic of what historian Lucy Grig has called 'private rather than ecclesiastical piety'" compelling.[86] It is plausible that individual Christians, particularly women, begin "constructing the meaning of the saints for themselves through devotional acts that included commissioning inscriptions and paintings."[87] This may have been the case for Veneranda's memorialization of Petronella, as well as for other women in this time period. By the time Veneranda commissioned her memorial, Petronella may have been remembered both as martyr and a revered woman of the word for at least two centuries in the "private space" of her extended family's burial lands.

I am inclined, therefore, to support the thesis advanced by Dorothy Irvin that Veneranda was an early Christian woman who viewed her own ministry as following in the footsteps of Petronella, her foremother in the faith. There is precedent for this type of memorialization on a fourth-century inscription discovered in 1903 on the

---

84. Johann Peter Kirsch, "St. Petronilla," in *The Catholic Encyclopedia*, vol. 11 (New York: Robert Appleton, 1911), reprinted by Alphonsus Maria Arata Nunobe on New Advent, http://tinyurl.com/yd3ykj7x.

85. Denzey, *Bone Gatherers*, 146.

86. Ibid., 142.

87. Ibid.

Mount of Olives in Israel (see figure 2.3). The Greek tombstone has been translated as: "Here lies the slave and bride of Christ, Sofia the Deacon, a second Phoebe. She fell asleep in peace on the 21st of the month of March . . ."[88] This suggests that the fourth-century Christian community in Jerusalem understood Sofia's ministry to be part of a three-hundred-year-old tradition dating back to the Phoebe named in Paul's letter to the Romans (Romans 16). Phoebe probably carried Paul's letter to Rome, and Paul validates her ecclesial authority: "I commend to you our sister Phoebe, a deacon of the Church at Cenchreae. I ask you to receive her in the Lord in a way worthy of his people and to give her any help she may need from you, for she has been the benefactor of many people, including me" (Rom 16:1–2).[89]

In the end, we will probably never know with certainty who the "real Petronella" was. But that may not be nearly as important as recognizing that from earliest history, Christians reverenced the spiritual and ecclesial authority of women. At least some women, such as Sofia the Deacon and possibly Veneranda, modeled their ministry on their early Christian foremothers, proudly leaving their legacy in the archaeological record.

CATACOMB COMMEMORATIONS AND FEMALE AUTHORITY

In the *Velata* fresco at the catacombs of Priscilla, a woman is artistically portrayed as equal to the male authority figure judging from the chairs (*cathedrae*) on which each sits. The deceased is probably an enrolled widow, but her authoritative status is iconically portrayed as equal to that of the male who sits opposite her. In the same catacomb, the *Fractio Panis* fresco depicts a woman hosting or presiding at a largely female funerary meal. The fresco's iconography includes plausible eucharistic elements in its commemoration of the deceased. In the *Bitalia in Pace* fresco located at Naples, a woman is portrayed exercising biblical authority to teach and perhaps preside at the altar,

88. Madigan and Osiek, *Ordained Women*, 90.

89. It is notable that for both Phoebe and Sofia, the Greek word *diakonos* is used, a masculine ending. *Diakonos*, the same word Paul used to describe his own ministry, had various meanings in the first century, but it seemed to designate one as an official representative of the church.

if corresponding literary sources are also considered. At the catacombs of Domitilla, a late fourth-century woman, Veneranda, commissioned a funerary fresco to portray her ministry as a "woman of the Word," in line with that of Petronella, her early Christian foremother. Although the study of Christian catacomb female figures has just begun, the preceding analyses suggest that early Christian women were memorialized as learned—probably in the Hebrew and Christian Scriptures—and exercising ecclesial authority. We have only been able to arrive at this conclusion by analyzing contemporary archaeological, inscriptional, and literary evidence together.

5.

Commemorating the Dead:
Roman Funerary Customs and Practices

To embark on a study of late ancient Roman funerary practices is to undertake a fascinating journey into the history and culture of the late Roman Empire. The following overview of Roman and Christian burial practices provides the context for the next chapter's analysis of portraits on Christian sarcophagi. These artifacts show both women and men in authoritative portrayals featuring scrolls, codices, and biblical stories. Such portrayals did not emerge in a vacuum. When Christian sarcophagi first arrived on the scene (ca. 290–300 CE), Romans had been burying their dead in elaborately sculpted caskets for over 150 years. Most early Christians were either converted gentiles or, in the first or second century, Godfearers from the Jewish diaspora. Both groups were shaped by and immersed in Greco-Roman society where art played an important role in spreading and consolidating cultural identity. This is especially true in the second sophistic period, which extended from the late first century and reached its zenith in the second and early third century.[1] While some

1. The first sophistic period dates to the mid-fifth century BCE in Greece, where itinerant professional teachers and intellectuals known as sophists educated wealthy, nonelite Greek men in virtue/excellence so as to advance their prospects in Greek society. They attracted opposition from the aristocracy, who thought education belonged only to them. George Duke, "The Sophists (Ancient Greece)," *Internet Encyclopedia of Philosophy*, http://tinyurl.com/y8yameeq.

administrative and military-minded Romans had previously looked upon Greek culture with a certain amount of disdain, during the second sophistic era, the empire enthusiastically adopted Greek philosophical and artistic ideals, educational values, and a shared Greco-Roman mythology. Jaś Eisner comments:

> One of the conspicuous achievements of the Second Sophistic was the empire's reformulation as a culturally integrated whole. The peoples of the entire empire, from Britain and Spain to Egypt and Syria, shared not only a single currency, an economy, an army and a government, but also an ideology of common Greco-Roman myths, of public rituals (such as the games), and of religious practices (including the cult of the emperor).[2]

Greco-Roman culture was highly visual. Elegantly sculpted and painted statues, colorful mosaics, and graceful paintings embellished public baths, fountains, libraries, the walls and floors of shops, gymnasia, public arenas, temples, and public buildings, as well as private homes and villas. Public art honored gods and goddesses, the emperor, military heroes, and the wealthy male and female aristocrats who financed civic amenities such as libraries, fountains, and public baths. This is the world in which Christians were born, grew up, lived, worked, and died. Christians were part of their culture and their culture was part of them. It is therefore unsurprising that Christian burial customs and tomb art reflect their Greco-Roman heritage. Eventually, their funerary art would also reflect the transformative impact of their Christian beliefs.

From the reign of Augustus Caesar (63 BCE–14 CE) to Constantine (306–337 CE), scholars estimate the population of the Roman Empire was probably relatively constant at roughly 60 million people.[3] Citing numerous sources, sociologist Rodney Stark estimates that "the actual number of Christians in the year 300 CE lay within the range of 5–7.5 million" people.[4] Although population numbers for this period are notoriously difficult to establish, scholarly con-

---

2. Elsner, *Imperial Rome*, 6.
3. Stark, *Rise of Christianity*, 6. Citing numerous sources Stark says that 60 million is "the most widely accepted estimate."
4. Ibid., 6.

sensus is that during the first three centuries CE, between 750,000 and 1 million people of all religious affiliations lived in the city of Rome. When surrounding suburbs are included, the total population of Rome is believed to have been between 10.5 and 14 million.[5] Yet, archaeologists can account for only 150,000 burials in the vicinity. Scholars are therefore cautious about theorizing from such a tiny fraction (1.5 percent) of funerary remains. The sample becomes even more skewed because historians and researchers prefer to study commemorative monuments and epitaphs rather than unmarked, anonymous graves.[6] Material remains such as sarcophagi, grave goods, catacomb art, and other artifacts tell us mainly about the more privileged segments of the population. These include the imperial family, senatorial and equestrian classes, freedmen and freedwomen, and their *familia*, including in some cases slaves who, in this social system, were valued property. The abundance of material evidence from tombs and funerary artifacts—more than any other aspect of the Roman world—supplies irreplaceable sociological and historical information, especially when literary evidence from the same period is unavailable.[7] For example, very little would be known about nonelite groups in Rome such as freedmen, freedwomen, and children, without evidence from their tombs. Freedmen and freedwomen were former slaves who had been manumitted. Ancient Roman administrators did not keep statistics about morbidity and mortality rates, but we know they were far higher than is the case today. Efforts to estimate death rates based on tomb inscriptions are unreliable. Most burials were anonymous and many excavated tombs with one epitaph were found to contain several sets of remains. Nevertheless, after studying crude death rates from selected cities in England and Mumbai before antimalarial and antibiotic drugs became available, Walter Scheidel writes: "We may safely assume that the Crude Death Rates at [imperial] Rome regularly reached or even exceeded 60 per 1000 and that mean life expectancy at birth fell below 20 years."[8] As many

5. Bodel, "From Columbaria to Catacombs," 179.
6. Ibid.
7. Richard Saller, introduction to Brink and Green, *Commemorating the Dead*, 1.
8. Walter Scheidel, "Germs for Rome," in *Rome the Cosmopolis*, ed. Catharine Edwards and Greg Woolf (Cambridge: Cambridge University Press, 2003), 174–75.

as fifty thousand corpses per year had to be disposed of, many in *puticuli*, or anonymous public burial pits.[9] While death rates cannot be calculated from tomb inscriptions, it is possible to study the seasonal distribution of deaths based on dates found on tomb epitaphs. In late ancient Rome, 38 percent of four thousand attested inscriptional deaths occurred during August, September, and October, for a mean death rate 1.8 times higher than the remainder of the year.[10] After an exhaustive study of plausible disease trajectories, Scheidel concludes:

> [At] least from the late Republic onwards the disease community of Rome was dominated by hyper endemic malaria, and other diseases developed accordingly.
> . . . [A]bove all gastro-intestinal disorders and probably also pulmonary diseases were regularly exacerbated by malaria and rendered more lethal than would otherwise have been. As a result, foetuses, small children, pregnant women and adult immigrants faced particularly grave risks.[11]

Because Rome's estimated annual birth rate of forty per thousand could not keep up with the death rate, the city needed a huge influx of immigrants each year simply to maintain the population.[12] Immigrants came from all parts of the empire, some voluntarily, but many, if not most, had little or no choice in the matter. These included slaves who were paraded through the city as spoils of war and subsequently sold, and impoverished freeborn peasants forced to immigrate to the city simply to survive.[13] Voluntary immigrants included traders, government officials, wandering philosophers, preachers, retired soldiers, freedmen and freedwomen, and perhaps some freeborn peasants with modest means.[14] Female slaves were rarely given freedom until after their childbearing years, owing to the householder's need to continually replenish slaves for their household.[15]

---

9. Willem Jongman, "Slavery and the Growth of Rome: The Transformation of Italy in the Second and First Centuries BCE," in Edwards and Woolf, *Rome the Cosmopolis*, 106–7.
10. Scheidel, "Germs for Rome," 162.
11. Ibid., 173.
12. Ibid., 176.
13. Jongman, "Slavery," 122.
14. Scheidel, "Germs for Rome," 176.
15. See Jongman "Slavery,"117–18.

Upon arrival, all immigrants found a crowded, disease-ridden city that nevertheless had several advantages, such as free grain distribution and access to the public games. But life was short and precarious, leading Keith Hopkins to describe Rome as "a huge death trap which consumed both goods and people."[16]

Figure 5.1. Funerary altar of Luccia Telesina. Photo © Vatican Museums, inv. 1877. All rights reserved.

16. Keith Hopkins, "Rome, Taxes, Rents and Trade," in *The Ancient Economy*, ed. Walter Scheidel and Sitta von Reden (Edinburgh: Edinburgh University Press, 2002), 190–230.

A BRIEF HISTORY OF ROMAN FUNERARY CUSTOMS

Care of the dead was important in Greco-Roman culture. In Roman religious belief, a corpse had to be hidden from the light of day or the living would suffer dire consequences. A funerary monument was sacred space and protected by law because nearness to the dead was associated with nearness or contact with divinity.[17] Both inhumation and cremation were practiced before the founding of the republic, although cremation was the usual practice until the early second century when inhumation became increasingly popular.[18]

For those who were cremated, ash chests and grave altars honored their memory (figure 5.1). These were normally housed in aboveground, often richly decorated, mausoleums, cemeteries, and columbaria. Columbaria are buildings with special niches to hold ash chests and urns containing cremains. Society's elite, such as the imperial, senatorial, and equestrian classes, invested in lavishly decorated tomb memorials to emphasize their wealth and status. The elite classes were not unique in building elaborate memorials. In the second century, cemeteries, used primarily by freedmen and their descendants, contained mausoleums with two-storied facades, marble fountains, mosaic floors, and courtyards. These provided a luxurious space for funerary banquets that could accommodate large numbers of people.[19]

The reasons for the rising popularity of inhumation are obscure, but Glenys Davies points to a "considerable number" of children's sarcophagi decorated with iconography suitable for children. These date to the early second century. She suggests "there might be a positive correlation between the death of a loved child and the choice of inhumation as a burial rite, that some parents did consider inhumation a gentler and less traumatic option in such circumstances."[20] Contemporary scholars no longer support the mid-twentieth-century assumption that burial practices changed because of changing

17. Osiek, "Roman and Christian Burial," 246–47.
18. Glenys Davis, "Before Sarcophagi," in *Life, Death and Representation: Some New Work on Roman Sarcophagi*, ed. Jaś Elsner and Janet Huskinson (New York: de Gruyter, 2011), 23.
19. B. Borg, *Crisis and Ambition*, 272.
20. Davis, "Before Sarcophagi," 47.

religious beliefs and attitudes about the fate of the body and soul after death.[21] It is not clear why the practice changed.

Roman law forbade burials within city walls. High mortality rates and a chronic shortage of burial space led to steady expansion of above ground cemeteries where possible, and multiple burials of cremains and bodies in single columbaria and sarcophagi respectively. The second century saw a transition to building extensive, open-ended systems of underground tombs, called catacombs, throughout the suburbs.[22] Catacomb networks have been estimated to extend for one thousand kilometers (621 miles) beneath the suburban regions of Rome and to have provided burial space for six million people.[23] For the most part, the catacombs were extensions of underground, privately owned family burial spaces called hypogea that had been dug below surface mausoleums and cemeteries when space ran out. Gravediggers, known as *fossores*, burrowed networks, often in a fishbone pattern, from the soft volcanic soil that hardened on contact with air. Catacomb networks were also carved in former cisterns, quarries, and underground water channels that had dried up because of a lowered water table.[24]

By the early third century, ash chests and grave altars had largely disappeared, and the usual funerary monument for those who could afford it was a sarcophagus.[25] The vast majority, who could not afford sarcophagi, were buried, usually without identification, in graves called loculi that layered the walls of catacomb corridors (figure 5.2). As in aboveground burial sites, larger spaces, called hypogea, included smaller rooms called cubicula. Half-moon wall excavations called *arcosolia* were common (figure 5.3). These accommodated elite and other privileged groups whose carefully decorated sarcophagi now served as monuments to deceased *familia* members, much as mausoleums and ash altars did above ground. These larger, more expensive spaces dot catacomb corridors with no apparent pattern except that surface access is sometimes more direct.

21. Ibid., 23–24. See also Bodel, "From Columbaria to Catacombs," 181.
22. Bodel, "From Columbaria to Catacombs," 181.
23. Shaw, "Seasons of Death," 101.
24. B. Borg, *Crisis and Ambition*, 274.
25. Davis, "Before Sarcophagi," 22.

Figure 5.2. *Loculi* and *arcosolium* (on right) lining corridors at the catacombs of Priscilla. Photo Eric Vandeville/akg-images.

Figure 5.3. Decorated *arcosolium* (excavated sarcophagus space) with trench grave found in the catacombs of SS Marcellino e Pietro. Photo: Pontifical Commission of Sacred Archaeology.

Burial spaces were protected by Roman law and could be inherited or sold. Two kinds of tombs were recognized: those belonging to the *familia* (*sepulchra familiara*)—including the male or female head of household, members of their blood family, and the family's freedmen, freedwomen, slaves, and others attached to the household—and those belonging only to the family's heirs (*sepulchra hereditaria*). This second type included blood heirs and potential heirs but excluded unrelated household members. The last successors of both types were permitted to designate other heirs, and the founder of a tomb could specify exceptions to the normal rules. Osiek points to an inscription in a third century hypogeum in the catacomb of Domitilla where the owner says he is reserving space only for burials of Christian family members.[26] Most surviving tombs in Italy are familial, and it was expected that the heads of household would provide for the burials of all in the *familia*. Besides burying members of the extended household over several generations, the head of household could extend burial rights to others outside the household. A tomb could also be owned by more than one person, with several owners holding the property and burial rights together.[27]

CHRISTIAN BURIAL CUSTOMS AND FEMALE PATRONS

Designated burial sites for Christians are suggested in texts written by several early third-century church leaders—Tertullian, Dionysius of Alexandria, Origin, and Hippolytus of Rome.[28] Hippolytus's (*Refutatio omnium haeresium* 9.12.14) account is the most famous, and for our purposes perhaps the most interesting. He denounced his rival Callixtus, a deacon who had been placed over the private burial grounds of Zephyrinus (198–217), the reigning bishop of Rome.[29] In 1850, archaeologists explored this complex and found the tombs of nine bishops of Rome dating from 230 to 274. The cemetery is now called the catacombs of Callixtus even though Callixtus himself was not subsequently buried there. The complex is among the oldest Christian burial sites in Rome, and tombs of the early popes can still be seen today. In the third century, however, it was not yet an official burial

26. Osiek, "Roman and Christian Burial," 247.
27. Ibid.
28. Ibid., 243–44.
29. Ibid., 244.

place controlled by the church. Osiek notes, "There is today common agreement that all of the burial areas that were to become Christian catacombs began as private property and private burial areas, in most cases at a time before any Christian identity can be documented."[30] Thus, while there is literary evidence of common burial sites for Christians in the third century, archaeological evidence remains elusive. Analysis of tomb art and grave goods from Roman catacombs has on occasion found non-Christian, Christian, and Jewish tombs interspersed in the same area. In many, if not most, pre-Constantinian burial complexes, it can be difficult to distinguish a Christian grave from a non-Christian one. There are reasons for this. First, the number of Christians in Rome in the early third century was very small, probably under seven thousand people, or 1 percent of the population.[31] Surviving grave artifacts from this period would be very scarce indeed. Second, since Christian funerary art was just beginning to evolve from Greco-Roman art, identifying a "Christian" grave based solely on the artwork is problematic. Unmistakably Christian images did not become prevalent until after Constantine's Edict of Milan decreed tolerance for Christians who would not offer sacrifice on behalf of the emperor. Constantinian policies subsequently made Christianity not only legal but prestigious.

At the dawn of the fourth century, an estimated 10.5 percent of the Roman Empire was Christian.[32] By mid-century, probably due at least in part to imperial patronage, an estimated 56 percent of the empire was Christian.[33] Communal Christian burial sites in the catacombs surpassed all other groups, and we find a flowering of identifiable Christian art in both catacomb frescos and sarcophagi friezes. As more and more Christians sought to be buried close to the martyrs, bishops and deacons began to assume responsibility for administering catacomb sites rather than leaving this duty to private heads of household. Now every catacomb had its own memorial to specific martyrs, and special cemetery basilicas were constructed over or near the mar-

30. Ibid., 245.

31. Robert M. Grant, *Early Christianity and Society: Seven Studies* (San Francisco: Harper and Row, 1977), as cited in Stark, *Rise of Christianity*, 9.

32. Stark, *Rise of Christianity*, 7.

33. Ibid., 7.

tyrs' graves. These accommodated an ever-increasing number of pilgrims, as well as family and community funerary banquets honoring the dead that, in good Roman fashion, frequently lasted through the night.[34]

But before the rise of the cult of the martyrs, what would eventually become Christian burial areas had first been privately owned. These private burial sites were sometimes the property of *collegia*, or burial societies, a collective of Romans who joined together to guarantee proper burials, including funerary banquets, for their members. More often, well-to-do heads of household—including many prominent women—owned private burial lands. Osiek found that "some of the actual persons involved in the creation of the Christian burial sites may have been elites, such as a Flavia Domitilla or a Priscilla married into the Acilii Glabriones."[35] Christian women in Rome owned land, developed burial complexes, and were heads of the household, "with responsibility to provide burials for the *familia*, which then extended to others, especially the needy members of the church."[36] It is significant that the catacombs continued to be named for the female patrons who donated the land—Domitilla and Priscilla in this instance—since popular male martyr cults eventually developed at each of these sites (see chapter 8).[37] Other catacombs associated with women patrons include Commodilla, Lucina, Balbina, Thecla, Bassilla, Agnes, Felicitas, and others. Male patrons are also associated with Roman catacombs. These include Calepodius, Callixtus, Sebastian, Novatian, Hippolytus, and others.[38]

Like others in their Greco-Roman milieu, Christians honored and mourned deceased loved ones with special funerary banquets held near their graves. These celebratory meals had a long history in the Mediterranean world dating from the fifth century BCE to the early fifth century CE. As we saw in chapter 4, family and friends banqueted at funerary meals at various times during the first year after

---

34. Osiek, "Roman and Christian Burial," 245. Early church fathers vainly tried to stop these funerary revelries.

35. Ibid., 257.

36. Ibid., 270.

37. For example, the cults of Achilleus and Nereus at the Domitilla catacombs and Felix and Philip at the catacombs of Priscilla.

38. Ibid., 255.

the death of the deceased and in subsequent years on his or her birthday. Romans also honored deceased ancestors during the February *Parentalia* when business was suspended, the temples were closed, and marriages were not held. In May or June, family members brought roses to the graves of relatives in a festival known as the *Rosalia*, which may be one reason why roses so often appear on tomb walls or coverings.[39] Families could also commemorate their ancestors privately inside the home. These important commemorations

> ensured well-being and honor for the dead, purification for the living, and order, continuity and prosperity for the empire. Such a private cult of the dead involved the entire household, including slaves, freedmen, and freedwomen; it was the responsibility of household members and their descendants to ensure that their forbears would not be forgotten or dishonored through the regular practice of commemorative banquets and rites.[40]

Numerous depictions of funerary banquets have been found on catacomb frescos and sarcophagi reliefs, both Christian and non-Christian. The celebrations involved imbibing wine, toasting the dead, and eating more or less sumptuously, depending on the social status of the family. To accommodate mourners, cemeteries offered permanent stone tables, hearths for cooking, and systems of water fountains for purification and clean up.[41] Ash urns, sarcophagi, and tablets covering graves have been found with small holes through which wine was poured in the belief that the deceased was present.[42]

As heads of households, Christian women hosted funerary meals. Tulloch painstakingly analyzed portrayals of female Christian hosts found on early fourth-century frescos in the catacomb of Marcellino and Pietro (figure 4.4). Her findings suggest that their status was no longer tied to "a legal relationship to the *paterfamilias*," in contrast to similar portrayals of non-Christian Roman women. Instead, Tulloch says, "It is visually indexed by the women's role in relation to her

---

39. Jensen, "Dining with the Dead," 118.
40. Janet H. Tulloch, "Family Funerary Banquets," in *A Woman's Place: House Churches in Earliest Christianity*, ed. Carolyn Osiek and Margaret Y. MacDonald, with Janet H. Tulloch (Minneapolis: Fortress Press, 2006), 168.
41. Jensen, "Dining with the Dead," 120.
42. Tulloch, "Family Funerary Banquets," 172.

household, as someone who has reared children and provided hospitality for family, close relatives, and friends."[43]

Figure. 5.4. Detail of women leading a funerary meal. The deceased father and son are shown in the center. The inscription reads "a toast to (*mix me*) peace." Catacombs of Pietro and Marcellino. Fourth century CE. Photo: Pontifical Commission of Sacred Archaeology.

Until the fourth century, management of private burial lands was mostly in the hands of the head of the *familia* or the *collegia*. But bishops eventually wrested ownership and administration of Christian burial sites from heads of household. They then assumed the role of patron and benefactor, funneling financial resources from lay patrons toward care of the poor. In addition, bishops and deacons administered moral and spiritual beneficence through the rising cult of the martyrs and ongoing control of sacraments.[44] These factors, combined with the power vacuum that formed when Constantine moved the capital of the empire to Constantinople, account for the rapidly accelerating power of Roman bishops throughout the fourth century and beyond. Even with increasingly centralized authority, fourth-century bishops exercised little or no control over the funerary practices of ordinary Christians. After reviewing the meager literary

43. Ibid., 192.
44. Ibid., 269.

evidence for official church involvement with the dying, Éric Rebillard concludes, "In late antiquity there was no Christian rite for the dying and the presence of the clergy at the deathbed of Christians was at best optional."[45] There are no liturgical documents for funeral rituals before the eighth century. Both Augustine and John Chrysostom frequently criticize rich Christians for expensive funerals and burials, but neither offers an alternative. Augustine does not provide rules for a Christian ritual nor does he picture the clergy at the home of the deceased. In fact, a canon from the Council of Hippo (393) forbids Christians to bring the corpse of the deceased to the church, arguing that the Eucharist cannot be celebrated in the presence of a corpse.[46] After reviewing all available information on mourning practices and associated rites, Rebillard concludes: "I believe that a useful distinction can be made between 'Christian funerals' and the 'funerals of Christians.' The former did not exist in Late Antiquity: there was neither a Church-sanctioned ritual for death, nor an attempt by the Church to impose uniformity. Family wishes and local traditions prevailed."[47]

Christian patronage in donating and developing private burial places for the needy did not release local towns and cities from this responsibility. In exchange for tax exemptions, Constantine delegated the church at Rome and Constantinople to bury the poor, presumably regardless of their religious beliefs.[48] Still, "There is no late antique ecclesiastical regulation concerning who can be buried where, except when the burial is to be in a space controlled by the Church."[49] The church only controlled burial spaces very close to the martyrs (*ad sanctos*). These privileged burials were reserved for clergy and lay nobility.[50] In late antiquity, bishops had little or no control over the burials of most Christians.[51] We can therefore assume that the selection of funerary art on catacomb frescos and sarcophagi

---

45. Éric Rebillard, "The Church, the Living, and the Dead," in *A Companion to Late Antiquity*, ed. Philip Rousseau (West Sussex: Wiley-Blackwell, 2012), 222.
46. Ibid., 223.
47. Ibid., 224.
48. Ibid.
49. Ibid.
50. Ibid., 225.
51. Ibid., 224.

carvings was left to the discretion of individual Christians and their patrons or families.

NON-CHRISTIAN SARCOPHAGI

In early second-century Italy, the increased demand for burial in a sarcophagus came about rather suddenly as privileged elites and upwardly mobile freeborn sought inhumation rather than cremation. The custom would last until the early fifth-century when we see a sudden end of large-scale, high quality sarcophagus production in Rome, though some local centers in Europe continued using local stone for a while longer. Why people started to use sarcophagi and why they stopped ordering new ones is unclear, though both phenomena are no doubt "tied to wider changes in aesthetics, material production and burial practices in late antiquity."[52] While production of new sarcophagi ceased, many old sarcophagi were reused both in late antiquity and throughout history. A pre-owned sarcophagus might come to serve as a casket for saints' relics, a tomb for a wealthy Italian merchant, a classical façade, and/or an artistic display adorning the estate of a wealthy family.[53] This loss of archaeological context creates immense challenges for art and social historians. Even so, Elsner sees sarcophagi as rich fonts of information about spiritual beliefs, life, and culture of both elite and aspiring middle classes in late antiquity:

> Sarcophagi are our richest single source of Roman iconography—translating the realms of Greek and Roman myth, the subjects of Roman public art, some themes of spiritual or directly religious content into images that were designed to resonate in the most personal and intense of private contexts, when a family mourned for its deceased. . . . Their visual negotiation of the ideals, realities and fantasies of Roman people, both the deceased and their mourners . . . makes them of quite exceptional importance for understanding Roman culture.[54]

---

52. Elsner, introduction to *Life, Death and Representation*, 3.
53. Ibid., 4. See also Janet Huskinson, "*Habent sua fata*: Writing Life Histories of Roman Sarcophagi," in Elsner and Huskinson, *Life, Death and Representation*, 56–81.
54. Elsner, introduction to *Life, Death and Representation*, 14.

Stine Birk points to two characteristics of Roman sarcophagus production that make these caskets "unique as a source of information for exploring social change."[55] First, since the coffins were created by workshops continuously from the second to the fourth century, changes in the iconography can "illustrate changes in mentality and the complex interplay between pagan and Christian cultures."[56] Second, a large number of pieces are individualized with a portrait attesting to the direct involvement of the owner in selection of design motifs.[57] Both factors "make sarcophagi a valuable source of historical and cultural inquiry, and indeed complementary to the testimony of the literary sources of the period."[58]

It is difficult to quantify how many Roman sarcophagi were created in late antiquity. Jaś Elsner estimates there are over ten thousand surviving examples of Roman sarcophagi, although the number could increase to roughly twenty thousand if fragments (many unpublished) are included.[59] Ben Russell identifies "between twelve thousand and fifteen thousand of all types datable to the second and third centuries."[60] It is certain that sarcophagus production continued into the sixth century. A contemporary three-volume work compiled by German archaeologists includes plates and descriptions of 2119 Christian Roman sarcophagi and fragments preserved from Italy, France, Dalmatia, Algeria, and Tunisia.[61] These date from the late third to the early sixth centuries. Another two volumes containing plates of Christian sarcophagi from Spain, Constantinople, and the eastern Mediterranean are yet to be published.[62] Recent scholarship suggests an average survival rate of all sarcophagi at 20 percent.[63]

55. Birk, *Depicting the Dead*, 10.
56. Ibid.
57. Birk (*Depicting the Dead*, 10n16) catalogues 677 portrait entries, which "is not a complete collection but a representative corpus of what I would estimate to be around 90 percent of the preserved material."
58. Ibid., 11.
59. Elsner, introduction to *Life, Death and Representation*, 1.
60. Ben Russell, "The Roman Sarcophagus 'Industry': A Reconsideration," in Elsner and Huskinson, *Life, Death and Representation*, 127.
61. Deichmann, Bovini, and Brandenburg, *Rom und Ostia* (RS 1); Dresken-Weiland, *Italien* (RS 2); and Christern-Briesenick, *Frankreich, Algerien, Tunesien* (RS 3).
62. See "Wissenschaftsprojekt Türkei," Spätantike Archäologie und Byzantinische Kunstgeschichte E.V., http://tinyurl.com/ydgddhe9.
63. Russell, "Roman Sarcophagus 'Industry,'" 127.

Extrapolating from Russell's estimate of twelve thousand to fifteen thousand surviving third-century tombs, one could estimate a rough production total of between sixty thousand and seventy-five thousand sarcophagi during the nearly two centuries of peak production (defined as 120–310 CE). This would yield an average production of 317 to 395 Roman caskets per year.[64] The use of an average can be misleading, however, since it suggests that an equal number of sarcophagi were produced every year, which is unlikely. Sarcophagus production probably started with smaller numbers in the early second century, becoming more popular with more tombs being sculpted in the third and early fourth centuries (see table 6.6 for dating of Christian portrait tombs).

Figure 5.5. Marble sarcophagus lid with reclining couple, ca. 220 CE. Courtesy Metropolitan Museum of Art, Purchase, Lila Acheson Wallace Gift, 1993.

Production of sarcophagi was extremely labor intensive and required significant skill. Marble was cut from quarries near Rome (Metropolitan), as well as quarries in Athens (Attic) and Asia Minor (Dokimeion). Quarrying and shaping of a medium size, unsculpted sarcophagus chest could take a skilled quarryman and two assistants as long as a month. Scholars estimate the sculpting of the most elaborate Attic sarcophagi, including chest and the *kline* lid (reclining deceased

---

64. This is my calculation based on Russell's estimate that the survival rate was about 20 percent rather than the earlier 2–3 percent postulated by Guntram Koch in *Sarkophage der römischen Kaiserzeit* (Darmstadt: Wissenschaftliche Buchgesellschaft, 1993).

couple) could take four sculptors an entire year (see figure 5.5).[65] The only known price of a sarcophagus comes from a late third-century undecorated limestone piece listed at 15 *solidi*. This is equivalent to 150 late first-century denarii, which is roughly five times the minimum annual subsistence figure of 29 denarii.[66] An elaborately carved marble sarcophagus would cost much more, with the price being determined by the amount and quality of decoration and the quality of the marble. Sculpted caskets with marble imported from Athens or Asia Minor would have been out of reach for all but the wealthiest individuals. Russell notes that in Rome,

> The most commonly attested purchasers of sarcophagi were individuals of middling to high rank in the military or civil administration; elsewhere, priests, town counsellors and tradesmen are recorded—only rarely are persons of lower status identifiable. For most of these individuals, a sarcophagus would have been a massive, once in a lifetime, investment in the monument by which posterity would judge them.[67]

Figure 5.6. Rough-cut garland sarcophagus from quarry near Ephesus in Asia Minor. Photo by author.

65. Russell, "Roman Sarcophagus 'Industry,'" 122, 128.
66. Ibid., 122.
67. Ibid., 122–23.

All sarcophagi were produced in special workshops. The three main parties involved were the customer, who specified what he or she wanted on the sarcophagus; the quarry workshop located in Greece, Asia Minor, or Rome that extricated the marble from the ground; and the sculpting workshop that finished the frieze decoration from the marble chests supplied by the quarry workshop. The sculpting workshop was usually located in cities closer to the clientele. If the marble was quarried at a distance, such as in Athens or Asia Minor, the quarry workshop would likely carve a blank chest with roughed out decorative elements to make it lighter, and then ship it to the sculpting workshop for completion (see figure 5.6). While there were many standardized, popular iconic figures used in both non-Christian and Christian sarcophagi, Russell attests that personalization of each memorial could and did occur at any time during the process:

> At every stage of the production process changes could be made, speci-fications altered, or complications arise. Equally, from quarry to finished article any single sarcophagus could follow a number of different tra-jectories. There is no single, one-size-fits-all, model that can adequately account for this heterogeneity. The decisions of innumerable individual customers determined the pattern of sarcophagus production.[68]

For Romans, whether Christian or not, a sarcophagus was a monu-ment filled with meaning, not just a container for a corpse. Planning for how one wished to be remembered was an important process. Most sarcophagi were purchased beforehand by an owner who chose iconographical motifs to best represent the departed—often a spouse or a child—and, in many cases, the owner as well. A number of coffins were commissioned to include two portraits—one of the owner or patron and the other of the departed, loved family member. Women could and did commission sarcophagi as well. Portraits could be carved directly onto the sarcophagus lid, onto mythological figures, into a round frame called a *clipeus*, onto figures bearing scrolls or depicting magistrates, muses, or philosophers, or combinations of the aforementioned. Most portrait sarcophagi commemorate just one or two people, though some have multiple portraits. Portrait figures could be sculpted immediately or left in a roughed-out, unfinished

68. Ibid., 142.

condition, presumably for carving after death but sometimes purposefully left blank.[69] Sometimes roughed-out portraits were never completed, or a sarcophagus could be exchanged or sold to another whose portrait would then be carved on it. Sarcophagi may also contain multiple remains from the same family even though just one or two individuals are identified via inscription or portrait.[70] If death occurred suddenly, the monument could be purchased with the desired iconic motifs selected by the owner and later personalized, with further carving carried out after the sarcophagus was placed in a necropolis or catacomb hypogea.[71]

Sarcophagi could be and were placed in a wide variety of settings, ranging from open-air monuments and mausoleums, to catacomb hypogea, wall niches, and *arcosolia*, as well as burial in the ground. If placed in a catacomb, they were generally surrounded by richly decorated walls and ceilings replete with mythical figures, roses, vines, peacocks, shepherds, and other motifs evoking peaceful, pleasant environs. Since some buried caskets could not be seen, several scholars doubt that "the sophisticated messages that art historians and archaeologists have extracted from the reliefs' iconographies could ever have been appreciated by their ancient patrons."[72] But Barbara Borg, after an exhaustive review, argues that the purpose of completely burying a sarcophagus was to avoid robbery since many contained expensive grave goods. She found that numerous unburied sarcophagi were elevated by small platforms to render the tomb more visible to viewers and concluded that caskets with reliefs were frequently the most significant part of a catacomb tomb and its decoration.[73]

---

69. Birk, *Depicting the Dead*, 56–58.
70. B. Borg, *Crisis and Ambition*, 202–6.
71. Ibid., 139–41.
72. B. Borg, *Crisis and Ambition*, 213: "[Jutta] Dresken-Weiland, *Sarkophagbestattungen* 193–4, for instance suggests that the imagery of most Roman sarcophagi was not terribly important to their patrons."
73. Ibid., 213, 236.

FUNERARY FUNCTIONS
OF MYTHOLOGICAL ALLEGORIES

To study Greco-Roman sarcophagus art is to uncover a rich world of meaning, frequently hidden from modern eyes. It is rare today to find even well-educated people who are conversant with classical mythology, which is an important key to Roman funerary art. Romans grew up steeped in mythological stories much as Jews and Christians today learn biblical stories from childhood. An exhaustive discussion of mythological sarcophagus art and what it meant in the context of three hundred years of late antique Greco-Roman culture is beyond the scope of this book. The interested reader is referred to works by art historians, who have devoted their lives to studying this fascinating topic.[74] What follows is a broad-brush overview of some key thematic motifs and their interpretation. This exploration will contextualize our study of how and why Christians, especially Christian women, may have chosen and interpreted their own sarcophagus art.

Zanker and Ewald identify three major "thematic fields" of the mythological allegories on Roman sarcophagi: themes with a direct connection to dying that bring together motifs of lamentation, grief, and comfort; themes that evoke "visions of felicity and bliss"; and themes that "focus on the prestige of the deceased, and praise for their successes and virtues."[75] Greco-Roman art may evoke all three themes on the same sarcophagus, though usually one or the other predominates. For example, the sarcophagus art of the second to early third century reflects the drama of death and mourning and is filled with tragedy and pathos. Mythic portrayals abound as mourners lament, identifying their own tragedy with those of mythical gods and heroes. Borg identifies a change in the interpretive use of myths by sarcophagi patrons in the third century. In the second century, mythic images were used to "enhance the event of the funeral [lament, mourning, and comfort] and elevate the deceased and their

---

74. See Paul Zanker and Björn C. Ewald, *Living with Myths: The Imagery of Roman Sarcophagi*, trans. Julia Slater (Oxford: Oxford University Press, 2012); Elsner, *Imperial Rome*; B. Borg, *Crisis and Ambition*; Elsner and Huskinson, *Life, Death and Representation*.
75. Zanker and Ewald, *Living with Myths*, 55.

families but in a very general manner."[76] By the third century, Borg observes that sarcophagus myths and iconographies are intentionally manipulated to reflect the messages the patron wished to convey. Portraits of the deceased plainly liken them to legendary heroes. Themes of lament over loss and death are "marginalized" and "praise for the deceased became the primary message."[77]

Figure 5.7. Marble garland "seasons" sarcophagus with Theseus and Ariadne (in each loop of the garland). 130–50 CE. New York Metropolitan Museum of Art.

While scholars have conducted in-depth studies of the meaning of hundreds of mythological figures found on non-Christian sarcophagi, we will explore just a few.[78] A second-century marble sarcophagus now at New York's Metropolitan Museum of Art (figure 5.7) emphasizes comforting themes of felicity and bliss because of the cosmic order signified by nature's perennially changing seasons. Garlands are among the most popular images used on Greco-Roman sarcophagi. It was customary for mourners to festoon the tomb with garlands of fruit and flowers. The front of this sarcophagus features four cupids carrying a huge garland with plants and fruits from spring (flowers), summer (ears of corn), autumn (grapes and other fruit), and winter (olives). The cupids themselves are crowned with seasonal wreathes, and the lid of the casket has a seasonal motif, with carts

76. B. Borg, *Crisis and Ambition*, 177.
77. Ibid., 177.
78. See n. 75 of this chapter. Barbara Borg (*Crisis and Ambition*, 161–77) traces changes between second- and third-century interpretations of the following mythical figures on multiple pagan sarcophagi: Hades and Persephone, Endymion and Selene, Theseus and Ariadne, Adonis and Aphrodite, Amazonomachy, Pelops and Oinomaos, Meleagor, and Hippolytos.

being drawn by beasts associated with a specific season: bears with spring, lions with summer, bulls with fall, and boars with winter. To the Roman mind, nature evoked tranquility, abundance, and happiness.[79] Those who commissioned this sarcophagus wanted themes of peace and happiness to predominate.

A subtheme of this casket is the myth of Theseus and Ariadne, whose story is carved in each of the three loops of the garland. Theseus was the son of Aethra and Aegeus, who were the queen and king of Athens. According to the myth, each year Athenians were required to send seven boys and seven girls to the Isle of Crete where they would be sacrificed to a half-man, half-bull creature called a Minotaur. The Minotaur was kept inside a labyrinth owned by Minos, the king of Crete. Our hero, Theseus, is determined to slay the creature and save the youths. When he arrives on Crete, Minos's daughter, Princess Ariadne, falls passionately in love with him. She shows Theseus a clever way to escape the labyrinth after he slays the Minotaur. After exiting the labyrinth, Theseus, Ariadne, and the freed children flee to the island of Naxos where Theseus, for reasons unknown, abandons Ariadne while she sleeps. She will eventually be awakened by the god Dionysus and become his immortal bride. Depicted from left to right, the garland vignettes show Ariadne giving a thread to Theseus at the entrance to the labyrinth, Theseus slaying the Minotaur, and Theseus abandoning the sleeping and soon to be immortalized Ariadne.[80]

There are no sculpted portrait features on this second-century sarcophagus to aid us in interpretation. A reasonable guess could be that this memorial was commissioned to memorialize a couple. Both the heroism and abandonment of Theseus are recalled—perhaps signifying the surviving wife's sense of abandonment by her beloved, courageous husband. Now she must await her own death/awakening to rejoin him. An alternative interpretation is that the grieving husband commemorates the love and ingenuity of his deceased wife and is comforted by reflecting that, like Ariadne, she is now immortalized with the gods. Both interpretations are plausible, especially if the tomb was commissioned while the spouses were still alive. In any

---

79. Zanker and Ewald, *Living with Myths*, 163.
80. Ibid., 404.

case, the multiple images of changing seasons on this work point to a predominant theme of cosmic order, peacefulness, and bliss.

SCENES FROM DAILY LIFE
(*VITA HUMANA*) SARCOPHAGI

Scenes from daily life, or the so-called *vita humana* sarcophagi, were also a popular way of memorializing the deceased. The first-century memorial of a miller, Publius Nonius Zethus, is a good example (see figure 5.8). Found in Ostia and now at the Vatican Museums, the cinerary urn holder that Publius chose housed his remains and those of his relatives. The reliefs depict scenes from a miller's work: on the left, a donkey turns a grindstone, while on the right are pots, sieves, and other tools of the trade. Another example of a *vita humana* memorial is a portrait relief of a physician carved onto an early fourth-century sarcophagus now at the Metropolitan Museum of Art in New York (see figure 5.9). The tomb owner is shown seated with an open scroll demonstrating that he is a person of learning and stature. The case on the cabinet top contains surgical tools indicating his profession. Other scrolls and a basin for bleeding patients within the cabinet offer further proof. The deceased's style of dress and a Greek inscription (warning of a stiff fine and "eternal punishment" if anyone buries another in the grave) indicate the deceased was one of many Greeks who lived in Italy. Warnings against grave robbers are frequently found on ancient funerary artifacts.

Figure 5.8. Cinerary urn holder for a miller's family with *vita humana* scenes. First century CE. Photo © Vatican Museums, inv. 1343. All rights reserved.

Figure 5.9. Sarcophagus relief of a physician. Fourth century CE. Courtesy of New York Metropolitan Museum of Art.

Figure 5.10. Mythological sarcophagus of married couple with portraits carved onto lid and onto figures of Achilles and Penthesilea, opposing leaders in the battle between Greeks and Amazons. Mid-third century CE. Photo © Vatican Museums, inv. 933. All rights reserved.

Figure 5.11. Detail, portraits of deceased carved onto mythological figures of Achilles and Penthesilea. Mid-third century CE. Photo © Vatican Museums, inv. 933. All rights reserved.

PORTRAITS ON MYTHOLOGICAL SARCOPHAGI

Romans carved portraits on funerary monuments as early as the first century BCE, and extending well into the fourth century.[81] Portrait figures on sarcophagi become increasingly prevalent from the late second century onward as inhumation became more popular. Zahra Newby comments: "The trend toward portraiture seems to occur on both mythological and non-mythological frieze sarcophagi roughly concurrently . . . and reaches its height in the third century, continuing even later on some sarcophagus types."[82] While second-century mythological sarcophagi focus on the drama of death and mourning, in the third century a new desire for more explicit praise led to the addition of portrait features likening the departed to mythical heroes.[83] A mid-third-century sarcophagus in the Vatican Museums contains a total of four likenesses of a married couple, two carved on the lid and two sculpted directly onto the mythological figures of Achilles and Penthesilea in the battle between the Greeks and the Amazons (figure 5.10). This is an excellent example of the owners' manipulation of a myth to convey a different message than one would suppose. Unlike the straightforward allegory of Theseus and Ariadne, described above, the story on this relief has been artfully crafted to convey the passionate love of the deceased couple now writ large with mythic power. According to the story, the queen of the Amazons, Penthesilea, pledges to fight Achilles to the death in defense of Troy. After a great battle, Achilles slays Penthesilea but falls in love with her just as he deals her the mortal blow. In the second century, this mythic battle between Greeks and Amazons was a popular funerary portrayal because it is "a parable of bravery and steadfastness," exemplifying manly virtue.[84] While second-century depictions have "a large number of equal groups in varied and dramatic positions," third-century portrayals of this myth, such as our example here, "show a group singled out in the midst

---

81. Peter Stewart, *Statues in Roman Society: Representation and Response* (Oxford: Oxford University Press, 2003), 92, as cited in Birk, *Depicting the Dead*, 14.

82. Zahra Newby, "In the Guise of Gods and Heroes: Portrait Heads on Roman Mythological Sarcophagi," in Elsner and Huskinson, *Life, Death and Representation*, 193.

83. B. Borg, *Crisis and Ambition*, 177.

84. Zanker and Ewald, *Living with Myths*, 47.

of the fighters, larger than the other figures, who can be recognized as the tragic lovers Achilles and Penthesilea" (figure 5.11).[85] A new interpretation now comes to light:

> Hero and heroine are no longer fighting. . . . On six of these sarcophagi, both protagonists have portrait heads, and they all show Penthesilea being held in a particularly unnatural theatrical position. She is presented to the viewer rather than embraced by Achilles, who is also turned as far towards the viewer as the subject allows. . . . The beauty, courage, love and care of the mythic heroes are not just meant as mythical paradigms for the beauty, virtus, love and care of the deceased couple, strikingly ignoring the fact that it was Achilles who killed the woman, but they are also proudly presented as such.[86]

Given the wide divergence between the traditional interpretation of this myth and what it now conveys, it is clear that sarcophagus workshops and their patrons counted on a

> highly sophisticated ability to see the essential point behind the way the tale is related . . . particularly when it is not primarily the story itself which is being used to evoke a comparison, but a specific virtue or the specific feelings of the mythological figures, in which case the unfolding of the tale is actually a distraction.[87]

As is apparent from the preceding, one function of portraits on mythological sarcophagi is to elevate the deceased into an idealized, heroic realm. Indeed, all sarcophagi portrayals, whether they include portraits or not, reflect an idealization of the deceased and cannot be counted upon to describe real-life situations. Nevertheless, they do tell us what people wanted to idealize and are thus a source of information about the cultural values of any given period. Another important consideration in interpreting mythological sarcophagi is that any one myth may have multiple meanings depending on the viewer. Zanker and Ewald point out:

> The different ways in which the observer can approach the images and the range of possible associations open to him mean that there is a special quality to the way in which the images speak. Their "openness" enabled

85. Ibid.
86. B. Borg, *Crisis and Ambition*, 170.
87. Zanker and Ewald, *Living with Myths*, 47.

the observer to be drawn in. In contrast to the "propaganda" images of imperial art, he was not bound by a single narrowly defined message.[88]

Likewise, Newby suggests that "while the precise messages of many of these [mythological] sarcophagi must remain obscure to us, they attest to the continued flexibility and multivalency of mythological imagery in the funerary sphere and its possibilities for the expression of human values, hopes and beliefs."[89]

Eventually, mythological images were essentially abandoned, making way for the widespread use of portraits on *vita humana* (scenes from daily life) and other types such as *paideia* sarcophagi. Concern for social status is now the primary message.[90] Portraits in popular hunting-scene motifs evoke comparisons with the emperor or other high-ranking elites, rather than admired gods and heroes. Office-holders, such as magistrates, are memorialized with images directly related to their offices, supplementing the *vita humana* style with new elements meant to elevate their stature. For example, from the mid-third century, magistrates are portrayed leading parades, presiding over law courts, and heading public games. Clothing and other accoutrements indicate status, with figures wearing classical togas, senatorial shoes, and signet rings.[91]

PAIDEIA SARCOPHAGI

As previously noted, during the second sophistic era, Romans came to have a very high regard for Greek education, including liberal arts, rhetoric, philosophy, and the sciences. By the second century, this appreciation of wide-ranging learnedness, or *paideia*, "had long informed the curriculum of Roman school boys, occupied the elite in their leisure, and stimulated ambitious freedmen."[92] One important route to upward mobility was demonstrating one's *paideia*, or learnedness, at symposia and banquets. These lavish and lengthy meals were held in rooms replete with frescos, mosaics, and even

88. Ibid., 49.
89. Newby, "In the Guise," 225.
90. B. Borg, *Crisis and Ambition*, 180.
91. Ibid., 186–87.
92. Ibid., 193.

tableware alluding to Greek myths, all of which provided concrete evidence of the host's *paideia*. The banquet or symposium was a perfect place for clients to impress potential patrons "in a kind of ritualized intimacy" that involved extensive philosophical discussion and debate (see figure 1.3).[93] The value of *paideia* was such that even the emperors presided over speeches and debates of the learned.[94] By the third century, "advertising one's *paideia* not only became ever more popular . . . but also an appropriate status symbol for all social classes."[95]

Figure 5.12. Eight muses are shown standing, with the ninth, representing the deceased, seated with a musical instrument facing her husband, who holds an open scroll. This couple wished to be remembered for their wide-ranging learning or *paideia*. The standing muses (always female) would become a prototype for Christian *orans* figures. Mid-third century CE. Photo © Vatican Museums, inv. 976. All rights reserved.

To signify the deceased's *paideia*, sarcophagi portraits depict figures holding scrolls or codices and surrounded by philosophers, muses, or both. Elsner believes, "Of all the private objects which signaled their owner's wealth and *paideia*, perhaps the supreme examples . . . were books."[96] Originally, texts were written on papyrus rolls that were either rolled around a small rod called a *rotulus* or simply rolled up.

93. Elsner, *Imperial Rome*, 102.
94. Ibid., 104.
95. B. Borg, *Crisis and Ambition*, 193.
96. Elsner, *Imperial Rome*, 110.

At end of the first century, a new type of book was invented called a codex. While some codices were made from papyrus, most were made of folded leaves of animal skins, called vellum, which was much more durable. Two advantages of a codex were that it could accommodate considerably more text than a scroll and that it was easier to handle. A big disadvantage was expense. Two fifth-century codices of Virgil's works, now in the Vatican Library, required the skins of 74 and 205 sheep respectively. Both scrolls and codices were used jointly until the fourth century when the codex became more prevalent.[97] Christians who wished to advertise their own learning and *paideia* imitated pagan sarcophagi figures holding scrolls, albeit in the context of the Christian stories sculpted onto their own sarcophagi (see figure 5.14).

Figure 5.13. Deceased woman is shown center and also shown with seated philosophers on each side. She holds a scroll, "possibly an allusion that she was part of an intellectual circle" (per Vatican Museums descriptor). 230–40 CE. Photo © Vatican Museums, inv. 871. All rights reserved.

97. Ibid., 110–12.

Figure 5.14. Deceased woman pictured with a scroll signifying her learning. Shepherd and sheep evoke bucolic setting. Possibly Christian. Third century CE. Photo by author.

MARITAL STATUS, GENDER, AND "LEARNED WOMEN"

While second-century sarcophagi were sometimes used for more than one person, it is difficult to evaluate the prevalence of this practice owing to a scarcity of inscriptions, portraits, and information about archaeological contexts. On third-century sarcophagi, portraits and inscriptions are much more frequent, and therefore scholars are able to make inferences with greater confidence. Borg notes an "extraordinary number" of sarcophagi sculpted explicitly for couples. Examples include two portraits that are carved onto mythical figures (figure 5.11), so-called *kline* sarcophagi that have a reclining couple on the lid (figure 5.5), and many caskets with a round *clipeus* on the front with a portrait of the couple (figures 7.1 and 7.2). People of the same sex, parents with children, and brothers and sisters were also memorialized with portraits.[98] Stine Birk recently completed an extensive study of non-Christian portrait sarcophagi made in Rome. Learned women (usually but not always depicted with a scroll) were the "most popular form of self–representation for women" (figures

98. B. Borg, *Crisis and Ambition*, 203–4.

5.13 and 5.14).[99] Further, according to Birk's analysis, representations of learned female figures were found almost as frequently as male learned figures.[100] We will consider Birk's work in greater detail in the next chapter as it has significant bearing on our own study.

Figure 5.15. Christian sarcophagus with figure of Jonah reclining under the leafy plant (see Jonah 4:6). This image derives from iconic pagan portrayals of Endymion. 280–300 CE. RS 1, no. 35. Photo © Vatican Museums, inv. 31448. All rights reserved.

99. Birk, *Depicting the Dead*, 120.
100. Ibid., 86.

BUCOLIC SARCOPHAGI

Toward the end of the third century, the notion of an idyllic, peaceful country life became increasingly popular. So-called "bucolic" sarcophagi were carved with images of shepherds, sheep, and trees, evoking a peaceful country scene. Occasionally, figures from *paideia* sarcophagi, such as muses and philosophers holding scrolls, are integrated into these bucolic scenes, "linking them with ideas of contemplation, wisdom and spiritual guidance."[101] Such integrations were attractive to Christians, who eventually adopted them into their own iconography. Most bucolic sarcophagi, however, have no direct indication of the Christian faith. A happy, peaceful life was an ideal shared by many Romans, regardless of their religious beliefs.[102]

In the past Christian and pagan sarcophagi were studied as two completely separate art forms. But today's scholars study them together because they were "produced in the same places by the same workshops for very similar patrons and clients."[103] After Constantine's Edict of Toleration, so many caskets with biblical themes were ordered so quickly, it is reasonable to suppose that Christians had already been patronizing sarcophagus workshops for some time, albeit choosing the traditional images described above.[104] As discussed in chapter 3, once Christianity became not only recognized but prestigious, biblical images began to appear in abundance on funerary art. Multiple figures from the Hebrew and Christian Scriptures adorn sarcophagi chests and lids sometimes carved so closely together, it can be difficult to identify the transition from one scene to the next. Significantly, even though Christians ordered their caskets to be carved with biblical figures, there was "no desire to distance themselves from the usual iconography."[105] The image of Jonah, for example, is usually modeled after that of the mythical Endymion, a popular Greco-Roman funerary figure (figure 5.15).[106] Felicity Harley points to the

101. B. Borg, *Crisis and Ambition*, 202.
102. Ibid.
103. Elsner, introduction to *Life, Death, and Representation*, 9.
104. Zanker and Ewald, *Living with Myths*, 260.
105. Ibid., 263.
106. Ibid. Endymion was a shepherd loved by the moon goddess Selene. According to one tradition, Zeus offered him anything that he might desire, and Endymion chose an everlasting

much-studied Christian sarcophagus of the Roman prefect Junius Bassus on which the central figure is Christ enthroned in glory (figure 6.12): "This Christ-figure embodied those facial characteristics familiar to viewers as belonging to the divine Apollos."[107]

Elsner sees early Christian funerary art as "marking a Christian identity of resistance" particularly during the years of persecution in the third and early fourth centuries. Popular images such as Daniel in the lions' den, the three men in the fiery furnace, and Susannah evoke divine deliverance from persecution and false accusation for those who persevere in faith.[108] Many images give evidence of typological exegesis in which figures from the Hebrew Scriptures become "types" that prefigure salvation through Christ. For example, Jonah's deliverance from the belly of the whale is seen as a foreshadowing of the resurrection. Likewise, Abraham's willingness to sacrifice Isaac is viewed as a prototype of God's self-giving love in surrendering his beloved child, Jesus, to the powers of death. Other popular frieze images are miracle stories such as the healing of the man born blind, the wedding feast at Cana, the raising of the son of the widow of Nain, the cure of the paralytic, and the raising of Lazarus. Gradually, typological figures from the Hebrew Scriptures give way to more triumphal and dogmatic themes focusing on Christ portrayed on a throne as ruler of the world, teacher, and giver of the new law. Images of apostles such as Paul, and especially Peter, as the preeminent recipient of the law are increasingly prevalent (figure 5.16).

In the fourth century, then, we see a marked change in the iconography of sarcophagus commemorations. The use of mythological allegories to evoke love, devotion, and praise for the achievements of the departed has all but disappeared. Gone too are references to lamentation and mourning, images of male courage, strength, and virility, and images of pleasure and enjoyment.[109] In their place are praying and proclaiming figures surrounded by biblical images that

sleep in which he might remain youthful forever. He was placed in a cave where Selene would visit him each night. Endymion and Selene were popular subjects for sarcophagi in late antiquity, when greater interest in an afterlife came to the fore.

107. Felicity Harley, "Christianity and the Transformation of Classical Art," in Rousseau, *Companion to Late Antiquity*, 308–9.

108. Elsner, *Imperial Rome*, 139.

109. Zanker and Ewald, *Living with Myths*, 265.

convey transcendence and a divine power that brings miraculous healing, deliverance from persecutors, and victory over death. Perhaps Zanker and Ewald summarize it best:

> The ruler now derives his legitimacy from Christ, and myth no longer has a role to play. But the home remains the place [where] . . . mythological images continue to be valued, but they represent primarily a claim to culture and the preservation of tradition; they have lost the function of paradigms, which they fulfilled for so long.[110]

Figure 5.16. Detail of Christ enthroned above a personification of heaven giving open scroll of the law (*traditio legis*) to Peter. 350–75 CE. Courtesy Fabbrica di San Pietro in Vaticano.

110. Ibid., 266.

6.

Crispina and Her Sisters:
Portraits on Christian Sarcophagi

An underlying assumption of this book is that late third- through fifth-century Christian portrait funerary art is an important source of information about women. It can help us discover whether some early Christian women viewed themselves—or their contemporaries viewed them—as persons who exercised religious authority and influence. The funerary commemoration of one fourth-century woman, Crispina, is a good example. She is one of the rare Christian women whose name is inscribed on the sarcophagus lid fragment bearing her portrait (see figure 6.1).[1] Crispina is the primary, idealized figure, since her portrait is placed centrally on the lid with her head extending outside the frame of the relief. She is shown between two palm trees, cradling a codex monogrammed with the Chi Rho symbol for Christ.[2] The iconography tells us that she was a learned woman, and judging by the tender way she cradles the monogrammed codex, she loved Christ and the Scriptures that proclaim him. Palm trees evoke eternal, heavenly life and also function as iconic remembrances of the

1. The name Crispina was common in late antiquity, so it should not be assumed that this artifact, found in Rome, is from the sarcophagus of Saint Crispina, who was martyred in Africa during the Diocletian persecution.

2. The monogram contains the first two letters of "Christ" in Greek (ΧΡΙΣΤΟΣ, Christos), chi (Χ) and rho (Ρ), used as a Christian symbol. See Ken Mafli, "Christian Symbols—The Chi Rho Symbol," Glass House Theology, March 2, 2013, http://tinyurl.com/yat8rocy.

biblical Susanna, who is often portrayed between two trees on Christian sarcophagi (see figure 6.2).[3] Crispina and her family had significant wealth to be able to afford this elaborately carved memorial. To the viewer's right are two unidentified young male figures, the first of whom seems to lean away from Crispina, perhaps looking askance at a female religious role model (see figure 6.3). He is a person of status because he is shown with a scroll and a two-fingered speech gesture across his chest. Both figures are unconnected to the religious scenes to the viewer's right. As often occurs with other extraneous male figures, sarcophagus experts Deichmann, Bovini, and Brandenburg do not identify either man as an "apostle" or "disciple," so it is difficult to know much beyond what the art evokes.[4] Both men are frowning, but since all of the other figures in the relief are also frowning, this is probably the artist's style.

Figure 6.1. Portrait of deceased Crispina cradling a codex embellished with Christogram. Lid of mid-fourth-century Christian sarcophagus. RS 1, no. 32. Photo © Vatican Museums, inv. 31552. All rights reserved.

3. RS 3, nos. 40, 41, 108.
4. RS 1, no. 135.

Figure 6.2. Typical image of Susanna between two olive trees. Lecherous elders peer at her from behind the trees. This image appears on what is probably a mother-son sarcophagus, which has another image of Susanna and Daniel at the stoning of the elders as well as Miriam prominently leading a young boy and the Israelites across the Reed Sea. Mid-fourth century. RS 3, no. 41. Courtesy of Musée d l'Arles Antique: Sarcophage de la chaste Suzanne.

Figure 6.3. Right side of Crispina's sarcophagus lid (left side is lost). L to R: two unidentified male figures, unconnected to biblical scene on viewer's right, one of whom seems to lean away from central Crispina portrait; multiplication of the loaves (note in-facing "apostle" figures); arrest of Peter; Peter baptizes jailers with miraculous water. RS 1, no. 32. Photo © Vatican Museums, inv. 31552. All rights reserved.

To the right of the male figures is a relief of the multiplication miracle. Jesus, in a center frontal depiction, holds a loaf in his right hand and a fish in his left while in-facing male "apostles" gaze at him from either side. This in-facing "apostle" pose enhances the status of the center figure. To the right of the multiplication scene is a relief of Peter being arrested by two soldiers. The final relief on the right depicts Peter's legendary miracle wherein he is said to have struck the wall of his jail cell, miraculously supplying water to baptize his jailers. This apocryphal story may have come from the Acts of Peter, and it is popular on fourth-century Christian funerary art.[5] The vignettes of Jesus and Peter suggest that the learned and devout Crispina was remembered for teaching about Christ and Peter, who was beloved by the church in Rome. The male figure who seems to be leaning away from her suggests that the witness of this female religious role model was not universally well received, although this is probably more than visual data alone can support.[6]

In this chapter, we will discuss an analysis of 2119 images and descriptors of third- to fifth-century sarcophagi and fragments. This research was conducted over three years and includes all images currently available for Christian sarcophagi and loculus plates.[7] Hugo Brandenburg estimates that around 1500 Christian sarcophagi were produced in Rome, mostly in the fourth century, compared to 6000 non-Christian sarcophagi dating from the second through the fourth centuries.[8] While there is much to be learned from studying these intriguing caskets, this investigation focuses on Christian portraits and what can be discovered from the iconography chosen by the deceased person and/or patron who commissioned them. Special

5. Robin Jenson, Living Water: Symbols and Settings of Early Christian Baptism (Leiden: Brill, 2010), 77.

6. The left half of Crispina's sarcophagus lid has been lost. This description covers only the right side of the lid. Two other lid fragments that do not belong with this lid are nevertheless displayed with it on the left in RS 1, no. 135 and in the Pio Cristiano Museum.

7. A loculus plate is a covering for niche tombs found in the catacombs. It could be made of marble slabs or bricks.

8. Hugo Brandenburg, "Osservazioni sulla fine della produzione e dell'uso dei sarcofagi a rilievo nella tarda antichità nonché sulla loro decorazione," in Sarcofagi tardoantichi, paleocristiani e altomedievali: Atti della giornata tematica dei seminari di archeologia Cristiana, École Francaise de Rome, 8 maggio 2002, ed. Fabrizio Bisconti and Hugo Brandenburg (Vatican City: Pontificio Istituto di Archeologia Cristiana), 1–34, cited in Janet Huskinson, Roman Strigillated Sarcophagi: Art and Social History (Oxford: Oxford University Press: 2015), 207.

attention is paid to commemorations of Christian women. I am greatly indebted to Stine Birk for her extensive study of 677 non-Christian portraits on Roman sarcophagi.[9] Aside from being helpful in shaping the methodology for this study, Birk's findings are a valuable point of reference in comparing Christian portraits to non-Christian portraits on Roman sarcophagi.

Both Birk and art historian Janet Huskinson, have written extensively about the significance of sarcophagus art and what it might have meant to Romans in general and Roman women in particular. Birk observes that in late antiquity: "An increased focus on the self and an awareness of the value of remembrance means that sarcophagi were generally made as personal monuments, an aspect of Roman funerary culture that is revelatory of the importance of individuals, as they negotiated their roles and identities in life and death."[10] Huskinson describes the function of sarcophagus art:

> Although it is ultimately impossible to be certain of the beliefs held by those who used or viewed them, sarcophagi provide good evidence about role models because funerary commemoration as a genre was an important vehicle for self-representation: it offered special opportunities for people to represent ideals that were valued by themselves as individuals and also by the society in which they lived. This was also true for Christian patrons at this time.[11]

For Huskinson, a role model is "a figure chosen not merely to commemorate the individual dead but to offer a collective example to the Christian community in terms of beliefs and the conduct of their lives."[12] Her research into late third-century secular images such as the philosopher, *orans*, and ram bearer indicated that as Christian influence increased, these conventional Roman images acquired a "specifically Christian value." The conventional philosopher dressed in a *pallium* (cloak) and, holding a scroll, became a role model for learning, while the *orans* figure modeled both learning and religious

---

9. Birk, *Depicting the Dead*.
10. Ibid., 12.
11. Janet Huskinson, "Degrees of Differentiation: Role Models on Early Christian Sarcophagi," in *Role Models in Ancient Rome: Identity and Assimilation*, ed. Sinclair Bell and Inge Lyse Hansen (Ann Arbor: University of Michigan Press, 2008), 287.
12. Ibid., 288.

devotion. The ram bearer/good shepherd came to symbolize love of Christ and of neighbor. These secular images now offer "models for ideal Christian activities of learning, teaching and contemplative reading."[13] The new role models are a "fusion of symbolism" that allowed Christians to integrate Roman cultural values with their faith because, "by linking figures of learning and culture to religious symbols, they brought these aspects of their lives into a Christian spiritual dimension."[14] If Birk and Huskinson are correct, an exploration of portraits on Christian sarcophagi will advance our understanding about how early Christian women (and some men) identified themselves and their roles within fourth-century Christian communities.

Among art historians, it is axiomatic that each sarcophagus is a work of art with its own unique meaning and message. Globally quantifying discrete characteristics of Christian portrait sarcophagi as is done in this study, risks diluting important information to be gleaned from studying each sarcophagus in all its glorious particularity. The dilemma is not unlike those undertaking biblical studies. One can examine a gospel text for the number of times a certain Greek word is used to better understand the author's meaning each time that word appears in any given chapter or parable. Such an approach has the potential to enhance the overall interpretation of the gospel. An unavoidable downside is that the unique message of any specific passage may lose some of its power and vitality in the process. Still, quantitative analysis has the advantage of providing information at the macro level that is often otherwise inaccessible. Birk's study of non-Christian portrait sarcophagi is a case in point. She catalogued 677 portrait sarcophagi, which she estimates to be 90 percent of the preserved materials in this category. Of these, 208 were found to commemorate single men, 199 commemorated single women, 186 commemorated couples, 80 commemorated children, and the remaining 4 were of unknown sex.[15] Birk's quantification uncovers several important facts, not least of which is that solo male and female portrait commemorations were roughly equal—and this at a time when written historical references to women are rare.

13. Ibid., 295.
14. Ibid., 297.
15. Birk, *Depicting the Dead*, 120.

Without quantifying the data, this important information could have been lost. Particularly pertinent to this book is Birk's discovery that learned women (usually, but not always, portrayed with a scroll or codex) were the most popular form of self-representation for non-Christian women: "Out of around 382 sarcophagi with women individualized through a portrait . . . about 160 sarcophagi commemorate women through a learned figure" (see figure 5.13).[16] Further, Birk found that representations of learned female figures occurred almost as frequently as male learned figures.[17]

As does Birk's, this investigation analyzes iconographical elements of Christian portraits quantitatively and individually or qualitatively (see Crispina discussion above). The purpose is to discover if archaeological evidence suggests that the deceased was commemorated as a person of influence and authority within his or her Christian social network. A brief synopsis of several salient outcomes may be helpful before turning to a more detailed treatment. An analysis of 2119 images and descriptors identified 247 Christian sarcophagi, sarcophagus lids and fragments, and loculus plates containing 312 portraits.[18] Of these, 156 commemorated individual/solo women, 47 commemorated individual/solo men, 64 commemorated couples, 20 commemorated children, and 9 were too damaged to classify according to sex. An additional sixteen self-representations on seven sarcophagi were classified as "embedded," but these were not included in the statistical analysis for reasons that will be explained. The 312 Christian portraits were examined for the presence of learned elements (such as scrolls), posture (*orans*—outstretched praying arms); and hand gestures (oratorical, recommending, or acclaiming). Ubiquitous and somewhat mysterious in-facing "apostle" figures were also analyzed. Various cohorts were compared and contrasted, including individual

16. Ibid., 77. This number includes portraits of couples in which, invariably, only the male holds a scroll. See ibid., 75: "the learned woman symbolizes status and qualities that relate to the intellectual sphere, in the spirit of the time of the Second Sophistic. Therefore the category *learned woman* encompasses Muses, women with lyres, women as philosophers, and, not least, women with scrolls."

17. Ibid., 86.

18. The designation "Christian" was applied narrowly only to artifacts with biblical figures. See appendix N for listing by dates.

male and female portraits, couple and solo portraits, and non-portrait Christ configurations.

In striking contrast to Birk's findings, there were three times as many individual/solo female Christian portraits compared to individual male Christian portraits. Twice as many solo female portraits were accompanied by in-facing "apostle" figures compared to solo male portraits. In what follows, I suggest that the in- facing "apostle" motif serves to bolster the authority of the central figure, whether it is Christ or a portrait of the deceased. These findings supply impressive evidence that many Christian women chose to commemorate themselves—or their family and friends chose to commemorate them—as role models with influence and authority within their Christian social networks. With this introduction, let us now turn to a discussion of the methodology and procedures used in this study before discussing specific motifs.

METHODOLOGICAL APPROACH

Photographs and descriptors of 2119 sarcophagus artifacts contained in the three volumes of Repertorium der Christlich-Antiken Sarkophage comprise the initial study cohort.[19] The term "sarcophagus artifact" in this study signifies a complete sarcophagus with lid, the lid only, fragments of sarcophagi and/or lids, and loculus plates or fragments. The term does not include grave goods found inside the coffin. Occasionally, the term coffin is used interchangeably with sarcophagus. Wealthy families throughout the empire purchased Roman-made sarcophagi, and as the Repertorium volumes attest, they were in demand in provinces far afield from Rome. While most artifacts are sarcophagi or fragments of sarcophagi, there are also a number of loculus plates used to cover catacomb burial niches. Friedrich W. Deichmann's volume 1 of the Repertorium (RS 1) includes images and descriptors of sarcophagi artifacts housed in Rome and Ostia. Repertorium volume 2 (RS 2), edited by Jutta Dresken-Weiland, describes sarcophagus artifacts from Rome and Ostia not found in volume 1 and includes those in Dalmatia and

19. See RS 1, RS 2, and RS 3.

museums around the world. Repertorium volume 3 (RS 3), edited by Brigitte Christern-Briesenick, describes sarcophagi found in France, Algeria, and Tunisia. Images are listed in this work according to the Repertorium volume (1, 2, or 3) and the image number found there. For example, the caption in figure 6.2, is listed as "RS 1, no. 32." This means the photograph is listed as image 32 in the first Repertorium volume.

PROCEDURES

Each image was first reviewed for the presence of a portrait or possible portrait figure, and then for various other characteristics, such as gender, age, presence of Christian elements, *orans*, and other learned elements, including scrolls, codices, and *capses*. These impressions were entered into a *FileMaker Pro 13* database and then verified with descriptors by the authors of the RS volumes. Any needed adjustments were made accordingly. In addition to the gender identifications provided by RS authors,[20] Birk's criteria for age and gender were included in portrait analysis. Birk assigned gender based on hair length (long hair or veils for women and short hair for men) and length of clothing (long dress for women, short dress for men). Age was determined by iconographical characteristics, inscriptional evidence, and sometimes the size of the sarcophagus. If the RS described the casket as a *Kinder* (children) sarcophagus or if the inscription indicated the departed was less than nine years of age, the portrait was categorized as belonging to a child.[21] Likewise, per Birk's suggestion, if the portrait had chubby cheeks and a child's body, it was categorized as belonging to a child.[22] In a few instances, I differed with some aspects of the RS analyses of Christian portrait sarcophagi. These will be noted as they occur.

Every sarcophagus artifact that had portrait characteristics was given an individual record. Not every sarcophagus or fragment described in the RS volumes had a photographic image. Some only

---

20. "*Weibl*" indicating female, "*Männl*" indicating male, "*Knaben*" indicating a young boy, "*Madchen*" indicating a young girl, and "*Kinder*" indicating children.

21. Birk, *Depicting the Dead*, 158.

22. Ibid., 160.

had written descriptors, others were drawings. If a descriptor or drawing indicated that a portrait figure was present, a separate record was created for each with the description added to the database. All *orans* figures were studied. Occasional unique figures that appeared to be representations of the deceased embedded in biblical scenes were also studied. If no portrait was in evidence, most complete or nearly complete Christian sarcophagi and some large Christian fragments were also given individual records. This was done to create a cohort for later comparison of Christian sarcophagus artifacts containing portraits with those that did not. In all, 762 sarcophagus artifact images were entered for classification in the database. Excluded images were mostly small fragments without portrait figures, fragments of inscription tabula, sarcophagi without figures, or coffins and fragments with decorative vegetal elements without portrait features. According to Repertorium authors, over 75 percent of all sarcophagus artifacts entered into the database were made in Roman workshops. Of the 247 demonstrably Christian portrait sarcophagus artifacts identified, 86 percent were created in Roman workshops, according to those same authors.

CLASSIFYING SARCOPHAGUS ARTIFACTS

Table 6.1: Is This a Christian Sarcophagus Artifact?[23]
Criteria for Classification

(NOTE: For purposes of this study, only artifacts from categories A, B, E, F, and G were classified as "Christian." Categories are mutually exclusive.)

A. Explicitly Christian	Features explicit scenes from either the Hebrew or Christian Scriptures or both.
B. Probably Christian	Features a portrait with two in-facing male figures, variously described as "Peter and Paul," "apostle," or "male figure," but without explicit scriptural/biblical scenes.
C. Possibly Christian	Includes one or more ram bearer figures[24] but without evidence of biblical scenes, in-facing "apostle" figures, Christian inscription,

---

23. The term "sarcophagus artifact" in this study includes a complete sarcophagus with lid, the lid only, fragments of sarcophagi and/or lids, and loculus plates or loculus fragments. The term does not include grave goods found inside the coffin.

Christogram, or cross.

D. No Biblical Figures	No evidence of Christian identity (no biblical scenes, ram bearers, or in-facing "apostle" figures).
E. Christian Inscription	No biblical scenes but does have Latin and Greek inscriptions with Chi Rho symbol or explicitly Christian phrases such as "servant of Christ," "handmaid of God," "in the peace of Christ," or "Holy Spirit." Scholars are divided as to whether the phrase *in pace* (in peace) is exclusively Christian, and so portraits with these inscriptions were not included.[25]
F. Christogram or G. Christian Cross	No biblical scenes but sarcophagus artifacts with these symbols were categorized as Christian since both were used exclusively by Christians. However, if (as often happened) a Christogram was later applied over a clearly Roman tomb, the artifact was not included.

Specific criteria were developed to classify an artifact as Christian (see table 6.1). For purposes of this study, the sarcophagus artifact was categorized as "Christian" only if it displayed figures from the Hebrew Bible and/or early Christian writings, in-facing "apostle" figures, a Christian inscription, a Christogram, or a cross. Scholars disagree on whether the phrase *in pace* (in peace) can be considered to be exclusively Christian. Dennis E. Trout believes the phrase "signals Christian identification."[26] Stine Birk agrees that *in pace* "showed [Christian] religious affiliation."[27] Barbara Borg examined a well-known catacomb fresco of five *orans* figures in the catacombs of Callixtus inscribed with *Arcadia in Pace* (Arcadia in peace) but finds it "impossible to identify the religious background" of the catacomb patrons "in the absence of any Christian signs or symbols."[28] Carolyn Osiek agrees with Borg that the phrase is not exclusively Christian.[29]

---

24. Ram bearer must be Orpheus type with sheep on shoulder or two at feet. Christians quickly adopted the ram-bearer figure from Roman iconography to represent Christ the Good Shepherd. If a tomb has a ram bearer with an *orans* figure, for example, it is difficult to know if it is a Christian tomb, since both figures were common in Roman sarcophagi iconography and later adopted by Christians.

25. See "Classifying Sarcophagus Artifacts" in chapter 6.

26. See Dennis E. Trout, "Inscribing Identity: Latin Epigraphic Habit in Late Antiquity," in Rousseau, *Companion to Late Antiquity*, 175.

27. Stine Birk, "Sarcophagi, Self-Representation, and Patronage in Rome and Tyre," in *Patrons and Viewers in Late Antiquity*, ed. Stine Birk and Birte Poulsen (Aarhus, DNK: Aarhus University Press: 2012), 111.

28. B. Borg, *Crisis and Ambition*, 269.

29. Carolyn Osiek, personal correspondence with author, July 26, 2015.

Therefore, sarcophagus artifacts that had only an *in pace* inscription without other Christian identifiers were not included in this analysis (see appendix A).[30]

As we saw in chapter 3, late third-century Christian art adapted standard Roman iconography such as the philosopher, *orans,* and ram-bearer figures to symbolize, respectively, Christian learnedness, both learnedness and piety, and Christ as the Good Shepherd. Because it can be difficult to say with certainty that sarcophagi with this iconography are Christian, portraits were identified as Christian only if the sarcophagus artifact also included biblical figures and/or clearly Christian symbols such as a cross or a Chi Rho symbol. Excluded from the Christian portrait cohort were sarcophagus artifacts without biblical figures, those classified as "uncertain," and those classified as "possibly Christian" (see table 6.1). While it is very likely that many of the "possibly Christian" sarcophagus artifacts were from coffins of Christians, there is no way to know with certainty. Similarly, it is quite probable that a number of the "no biblical figures" fragments came from Christian sarcophagi, but again, there could be no certainty. Since my purpose is to study portrait figures on Christian sarcophagi, I classified the artifacts strictly.

When initial analysis was completed, a total of 558 sarcophagus artifacts, dating from the late third through the late fifth centuries, were classified as Christian (see table 6.2). Of these, 247 were classified as Christian portrait artifacts because they included one or more portraits (see table 6.3). An additional 33 Christian "possible portrait" artifacts were eliminated because it was impossible to say with certainty that they were portraits (see table 6.4). As previously noted, the final study cohort consists of 312 portraits found on 247 Christian portrait sarcophagus artifacts (see table 6.5). This figure includes 156 portraits of solo/individual women, 47 portraits of solo/individual

---

30. A total of thirty-six *in pace* inscriptions were identified (see appendix A). Of these, twenty-two had additional identifiers confirming Christian identity. Ten had conventional non-Christian iconography without biblical figures or Christian symbols. Four artifacts had either uncertain or possibly Christian identities. One of these is a drawing of a strigillated (wavy lines) sarcophagus with a *dextrarum iunctio* (marriage) scene in which the usual non-Christian iconography of the god Concordia or Juno has been replaced with scrolls (RS 1, no. 688 [drawing]). This could point to Christian identity, but it is difficult to speculate without other identifiers.

men, 20 children portrayals, 16 "embedded" portraits, and 64 couple portrayals that were counted as one portrait even though two figures are displayed. In 9 reliefs, the portrait intent was clear, but the artifact was too damaged to classify. Couple portraits are discussed in depth in chapter 7.

Table 6.2. Outcomes of Classification of Funerary Artifacts (n=762)[31]

Category	Number
A. Explicitly Christian (Biblical Figures)	483
B. Probably Christian (In-Facing "Apostle")	49
C. Possibly Christian (Ram Bearer vs. "Good Shepherd")	78
D. No Biblical Figures	122
E. Christian Inscription	10
F. Christogram	14
G. Christian Cross	2
H. Uncertain[32]	4
Total All Categories (Includes Portraits)	762
Total "Christian" (Categories A, B, E, F, and G; Includes Portraits)	**558**

31. Actually, a total of 826 records were created. Of these: (1) 762 are separate records of a single artifact to be analyzed in depth. Many of these were on RS pages with 2–10 images of other artifacts. Thus, a separate record was not created for all 2119 artifact images. (This explains the smaller number of database records compared to total artifact images reviewed.) (2) 49 records are of pages containing multiple artifact images without any portrait figures. (3) 14 records are duplicates. (Either the artifact appeared in more than one place or several images of the same artifact were displayed on two separate plates.) (4) 1 record was "modern"—pictorial decoration created in modern times and therefore not included.

32. Four artifacts were classified as uncertain: (1) drawing with too many errors / artwork unclear (RS 3, no. 472); (2) fragmented lid with slight similarities to other lids with biblical figures but too unclear to classify (RS 3, no. 288); (3) reconstruction of fragmented front is speculative (RS 1, no. 749); and (4) Chi Rho Christian symbol may have been added later (RS 1, no. 790).

Table 6.3: Identification of Likely Portrait Artifacts (n=392)

Category	Christian Artifact Has One or More Portraits	Unclear that Christian Artifact Has a Portrait (Eventually Eliminated)
A. Explicitly Christian (Biblical Figures) (Includes 6 "Embedded")	202	25
B. Probably Christian (In-Facing "Apostle")	33	3
C. Possibly Christian (Ram Bearer but No Explicit Biblical Figures)	51	4
D. No Biblical Figures	92	15
E. Christian Inscription	5	1 (? Reuse)
F. Christogram	6	3
G. Christian Cross	2	1 (? Reuse)
H. Uncertain[33]	1	1 (RS 3, no. 288)
Total Artifacts with Portraits— All Categories	392	53
Total Christian Artifacts with One or More Portraits (Categories A, B, E, F, and G Only)	247[34]	33

33. Of the four artifacts classified as "uncertain" in this table, I considered just one of these to be a possible portrait: RS 3, no. 288. It is unclear if the figure is Susanna or *orans* female between two "apostles" because artifact is too fragmented to classify.

34. One eliminated (RS 3, no. 453) from analysis because only a small portion of the rim of a portrait *clipeus* on a tomb with Christian scenes was visible. It was therefore impossible to determine anything about absent portrait figures though the *clipeus* indicated the presence of a portrait.

Table 6.4: Why "Unclear" Potential Portraits on Christian Sarcophagi Were Eliminated (n=33)

1. *Orans* figures could not be identified as portraits with reasonable certainty   16

(damage/no head visible, drawing, accompanied by ram-bearer figure, female portrait *orans* vs. biblical figure, experts undecided, etc.)
Gender/type: 12 solo female (1 child), 1 solo male, 2 unknown
Images: RS 1: nos. 464, 651, 691, 746, 748, 980, 987
RS 2: nos. 15, 164, 241
RS 3: nos. 198, 223, 365, 464, 487, 491

2. Uncertain if artifact is an embedded portrait or a biblical figure   6

Gender/type: child and mother (?); husband with wife (?); solo male, solo female, and embedded child (?); parents (male and female)
Images: RS 1: nos. 21, 24, 527
RS 2: nos. 122, 202, 243

3. Uncertain if figure is portrait or "apostle"/biblical figure   3

Gender/type: Couple (female and male) not in *clipeus*; 2 male "apostles" in *clipei* vs. *dextrarum iunctio*; solo male vs. "apostle."
Images: RS 1: no. 232
RS 3: nos. 262, 474

4. Christogram or cross incised on reused tomb   3

Gender/Type: Family? Female, male child; female and male not in clipeus (drawing); 2 males
Images: RS 2: nos. 92, 289, 292

5. Skirt only visible on standing female figures   3

Gender/Type: All female (4 female figures total—RS 1, no. 871 has two standing female figures and one male *togatus*)
Images: RS 1: no. 871 (2 standing female)
RS 2: no. 12
RS 3: no. 253

6. Female portrait reported missing by RS descriptor   1

Gender/Type: Female
Image: RS 3: no. 199

7. Severe fragmentation, only *clipeus* edge is visible, no figures visible   1

Gender/Type: Unknown
Image: RS 3: no. 453

Total eliminated   33

Table 6.5. Christian Sarcophagus Portraits by Type
(312 portraits on 247 artifacts; see appendix C for RS listings.)

Portrait Type	Number
Individual/solo adult female	**156**
Female portrait—non-orans	60
Female portrait—orans	55
Female "probable portrait"—orans	41
Individual/solo adult male	**47**
Male portrait—non-orans	35
Male portrait—orans	9
Male "probable portrait"—orans	3
Couple (male-female duo counted as one portrait)	**64**
Couple portrayal with female orans	4
Couple portrayal with male orans	2
Children	**20**
Child portrait—orans	8
Child "probable portrait"—orans	2
Embedded (on 7 sarcophagi—not included in statistics)	**16**
Adult female	9
Adult male	3
Couple (philosopher-muse type-drawing)	1
Children (all male)	3
Unknown[35]	**9**
Unknown "probable portrait"	1
Total Christian Sarcophagus portraits	**312**
(includes 64 couple portrayals counted as one portrait)	
Total excluding embedded, unknown, and "probable portraits"	241

35. While portrait intent is clear, the relief is too damaged to classify: RS 1: nos. 536 ("probable"), 636; RS 2: nos. 71, 95, 180, 182, 300; RS 3: nos. 493, 644.

As we saw in chapter 5, Romans did not hesitate to embed their own portraits onto mythological figures to commemorate the meaning of their lives and of their deaths (see figures 5.10 and 5.11). Several examples of embedded Christian portraits were identified, even though earlier investigators believed Christian sarcophagus art had no embedded self-representations.[36] Embedded portraits were not included in the statistical analysis but will be discussed separately in chapter 7. Neither were children's portraits included in the statistical analysis for reasons that will be discussed in chapter 7.

A WORD ABOUT DATING

Table 6.6 Christian Portrait Sarcophagi Distribution by Dates (n=247)

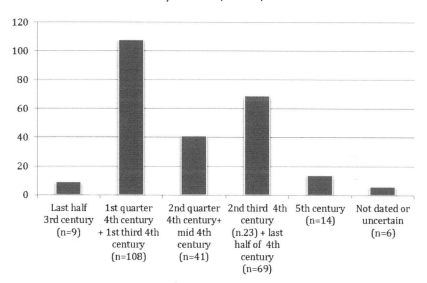

Date ranges per RS descriptors. Portraits in each group are mutually exclusive, although date ranges overlap. The majority of tombs (n=181 or 73 percent) date to before 366 CE. See appendix N for portrait listing by date.

36. Huskinson, "Degrees of Differentiation," 293; Huskinson, *Roman Strigillated Sarcophagi*, 231; Stine Birk, "The Christian Muse: Continuity and Change in the Representations of Women on Late Roman Sarcophagi," in *Akten des Symposiums Römische Sarkophage. Marburg, 2.-8. Juli 2006*, ed. Karin Kirchhainer, Heidemarie Koch, and Guntram Koch, Marburger Beiträge zur Archäologie 3 (Marburg: Eigenverlag des Archäologischen Seminars der Philipps-Universität, 2016), 63–72.

The 312 portraits found on 247 Christian portrait sarcophagus arti-facts in this study date from the mid-third century to the late fifth century, with a significant majority (88 percent) dating to the fourth century (see table 6.6). Stine Birk's review of Christian portraits in Rome and Ostia led her to conclude that after about 330 CE Christian portrait figures essentially "disappeared" because now "religion and not the individual and the family was the central factor in the construction of identity."[37] But Birk had researched Deichmann et al.'s 1967 RS 1 only. This present study includes Deichmann's pioneering work as well as the two subsequent RS volumes by Dresken-Weiland and Christern-Briesenick. These experts analyzed sarcophagi and loculus plates from Rome and Ostia that were not described by Deichmann, as well as sarcophagi found in Dalmatia, Tunisia, France, and museums around the world. A review of this expanded cohort reveals that over half (125 of 247) of Christian portrait sarcophagus artifacts were dated after 325 by RS experts (see appendix N for listing by dates).[38]

Even though most portrait sarcophagi were carved in Rome, many were made for clients outside of Italy, especially Gaul. Of the 125 Christian sarcophagus portraits made after 325, half (62) are at sites outside of Italy, while just 14 Christian portraits created before 325 are outside of Italy. It is hard to know how to evaluate this data, since after the invasion of Rome, the city became "the marble quarry of Europe," and many portrait sarcophagi may have been lost or moved. Still, the question of whether Rome workshops sculpted

---

37. Stine Birk, "Using Images of Self-representation on Roman Sarcophagi," in *Using Images in Late Antiquity*, ed. Stine Birk, Troels Myrup Kristensen, and Birte Poulsen (Philadelphia: Oxbow, 2014), 43.

38. In *Depicting the Dead*, Birk lists 667 Roman-made non-Christian portrait sarcophagi from a total of 6000 sarcophagi made in Rome in the imperial period. She estimates her portraits represent 90 percent of the preserved material. This study found 247 Christian portrait sarcophagi (strictly defined) dating from the late third century to the late fifth century. There were another 143 sarcophagus artifacts with portraits that did not meet strict criteria as "Christian." So, if we consider the 2119 artifacts listed in the RS volumes as the universe of preserved material, the proportion of Christian portrait sarcophagi (strictly defined) compared to non-portrait sarcophagi matches that of Birk's study (roughly 11 percent). If one counts as Christian the remaining 143 portrait-sarcophagus artifacts listed in the RS volumes (for a total of 390), proportionately more Christian portrait sarcophagi were created (18 percent) compared to non-Christian portrait sarcophagi (11 percent). My numbers include sarcophagus artifacts from all over the empire, however, although most are Roman made. An important caveat is that this is a very inexact science and one is at severe risk of comparing apples and oranges!

proportionately more Christian portrait sarcophagi for the provinces after 325 CE might be worth further investigation.[39] The portrait dating detailed above indicates that Christian women and men used portraits on their sarcophagi into the fifth century. This suggests that portraits continued to be a way for Christians to negotiate their identities as individuals and families who were both Roman and Christian.

Let us now turn to an in-depth analysis and discussion of early Christian sarcophagus portraits. In what follows, we will first discuss contemporary research and interpretative issues about portraits and characteristic iconographical motifs found on early Christian portraits. Some motifs are common to both non–Christian and early Christian reliefs and some are specific to Christian reliefs. The outcomes of this investigation, including significant statistical findings, will then be reviewed before discussing pertinent conclusions. Photographic examples and a holistic reading of selected sarcophagi are integrated throughout the text.

OF PORTRAITS AND PATRONS

Figure 6.4. Strigillated "tub" sarcophagus with unfinished portrait face of a deceased woman. She is depicted as an *orans* flanked by in-facing "apostle" figures with early Christian and Hebrew Bible scenes on each end (left: raising of Lazarus; right: Peter baptizes jailers). RS 1, no. 67. Photo © Vatican Museums, Pio Cristiano, inv. 31517.

39. There is scholarly debate over whether later fourth- and fifth-century Christian strigillated sarcophagi in southern France were locally made or exported from Rome. The question remains unresolved. Huskinson (*Roman Strigillated Sarcophagi*, 42) favors the opinion that they were Roman exports after their publication by Christern-Briesenick in RS 3.

Figure 6.5. Close up of portrait of female patron with right hand in a speech gesture while holding a scroll in her left hand. Face is unfinished. Sarcophagus of Sabinus. 300–325 CE. RS 1, no. 6. Photo © Vatican Museums, Pio Cristiano, inv. 31509. All rights reserved.

Figure 6.6. Sarcophagus of Sabinus. Inscription for male deceased, Sabinus the "well deserving spouse." Note unfinished portraits of female on lid and central *orans*. If an inscription was present, it was sometimes thought unnecessary to have a portrait of the deceased. 300–325 CE. RS 1, no. 6. Photo © Vatican Museums, Pio Cristiano, inv. 31509. All rights reserved.

Huskinson defines a portrait as "an 'image of self representation' rather than only those with personal features."[40] Birk states the common denominator for a portrait "is that one or more figures on each relief has been individualized."[41] Thus, contemporary scholars employ a range of definitions for what exactly qualifies as portrait. Is there a difference between self-representational images without "personal features" and relief figures that are "individualized"? Are these concepts mutually exclusive? After looking at hundreds of portraits, I suggest they are not. Some portrait faces are left unfinished even though the figures have distinctive clothing and hairstyles (figures 6.5 and 6.6). Others have generic clothing such as a tunic and *palla* (a woman's cloak often pulled over her head in public) and roughed-in facial features (figure 6.4). Still others have unique jewelry, shoes, and faces carved in distinctive detail (figures 6.7 and 7.2). Yet, experts who analyzed each of these renditions in situ regard them all as self-representations, and I agree.

For Christian *orans* figures, there is some ambiguity about what constitutes a portrait. This investigation defines a portrait as a self-representation of the deceased (and his or her patron, if present) that has been carved onto a sarcophagus or loculus plate. Birk clarifies it best:

> In the end, none of the portraits on sarcophagi are portraits according to a modern definition. The important thing about the Roman portraits is that they individualize a figure with the purpose of constructing an image of a specific person. A modern portrait is supposed to capture some of the person's inner character—an ancient portrait is used as a means of constructing an idea/identity of a person.[42]

The notion that ancient funerary portraits were created to construct the idea or the identity of a person supports our hypothesis that we can discover something about the social and religious roles of early Christians, especially Christian women, by studying their funerary art. Funerary commemorations provide important data about how

40. Huskinson, *Roman Strigillated Sarcophagi*, 117.
41. Birk, *Depicting the Dead*, 205.
42. Stine Birk, email to author, June 1, 2016.

early Christians self-identified and who their families and friends understood them to be.

The deceased's portrait is often found on the casket itself but may also appear on the lid. Sometimes the deceased has two portraits of him or herself, one on the lid and one on the front of the casket. Occasionally portraits are also found on either narrow side of the rectangular casket. Solo portrait busts may appear in a round frame called a *clipeus*, or in front of a *parapetasma*, a veil-like curtain behind the portrait head. The *parapetasma* is frequently held by two cupids—even on Christian sarcophagi, since Christians did not hesitate to adopt Roman funerary iconography common to their culture. On Christian sarcophagi, portraits also appear on numerous *orans* figures as well as free-standing figures—usually, but not always, located in the center front of the sarcophagus. Male and female figures, often but not always married, also appear in individual *clipei* or before a *parapetasma* (see figures 7.1 and 7.5).

A patron is the person who commissioned and paid for the sarcophagus and chose the decorative motifs that symbolize the virtues and values held by the portrait subject.[43] The patron may be the deceased person herself, who chose funerary motifs while alive, or close family members such as a spouse or parent, or even a close friend. A portrait of the patron may also appear on the sarcophagus, in addition to the deceased if the deceased was not her own patron. The patron's portrait commonly appears on the lid.[44] Except for sarcophagi with a married couple in a central *clipeus*, most portrait sarcophagi hold one and sometimes two individual portraits. When there are two different portraits carved onto the same sarcophagus, one is frequently the surviving spouse or parent (who is the patron) even though he or she may not necessarily be buried in the same coffin.[45] On sarcophagi with two portraits, it can be difficult to distinguish which is the deceased and which is the patron. In this case, the inscription, if intact, is helpful since usually the patron or dedicator

---

43. Birk, "Sarcophagi, Self-Representation," 107.
44. Birk, *Depicting the Dead*, 27.
45. Ibid., 25–26.

is in the nominative case while the one commemorated in the dative case.[46]

The sarcophagus of Sabinus is a good example of a coffin with two portrait images (figures 6.5 and 6.6). One is a female figure with a scroll and speech gesture on the left side of the lid (figure 6.5). The other is a female *orans* whose face is unfinished, shown between two in-facing "apostle" figures on the casket itself. Without the inscription, one would surmise that this sarcophagus is that of a deceased woman whose portrait appears on both the casket and on the lid. Alternatively, the lid figure might have been a learned woman patron who originally commissioned the sarcophagus to honor the deceased female *orans*. Neither interpretation fits with the inscription: "To the well deserving husband Sabinus who lived 44 years ten months and 13 days. [May he rest] in peace."[47] Initially, Repertorium experts wondered if, as often happens, the sarcophagus lid belonged to a different casket. This interpretation was discarded because the calligraphy on the inscription on the upper rim of the casket—"buried on the 6th kalends of May"—matches that on the lid.[48] While it seems surprising to have two female self-representations on a sarcophagus with an inscription commemorating a male spouse, it is possible that Sabinus originally commissioned this coffin and then died unexpectedly. Or Sabinus's wife could have commissioned it intending to have his portrait on the lid and hers on the *orans* figure. Conventional iconography showing a hunt scene to the right of the lid tabula is often found on sarcophagi commemorating Roman men. In this instance, the female spouse who provided the inscription is probably the patron seen on the left side of the lid in a scroll-speech gesture portrayal. If Sabinus's wife (our patron) had died first, the patron portrait on the lid would likely have been his. Another possibility is offered by Barbara Borg, who found that portraits and inscriptions could function as

46. Carolyn Osiek, personal correspondence with author, December 2, 2016: "The patron or dedicator is in nominative case; the one commemorated in dative case—usually. So and so to so and so. But the order of the two can be either way. I can think of more examples I've seen where dedicator in nominative is first, then 'to so and so' in dative." In *Depicting the Dead* (25), Stine Birk writes that the first name listed is the deceased and the second the patron, but this is apparently not always the case.

47. "Sabino / coniugi / qui vixit / ann(os) XLIIII / m(enses) X d(ies) XIII / b(ene) m(erenti) in pace."

48. "d(epositus) VI k(alendas) Mai." See RS 1, no. 6.

equivalents on sarcophagus monuments. If a portrait of the deceased was displayed, an inscription was not always believed to be necessary. A second family member without a portrait—as in the Sabinus sarcophagus—could be commemorated with an inscription.[49]

The scenes on either side of the female *orans* figure (figure 6.6; from L to R) include Peter's miracle obtaining water from a rock to baptize his jailors, Peter's arrest, the miracle at Cana, the healing of the blind, the multiplication of the loaves, and the raising of Lazarus with Mary of Bethany at Jesus's feet. Note that Christ holds a scroll in nearly every scene, and in two scenes he holds a wand (Cana and Lazarus). Roman culture did not have a category for "miracle." Their wonder workers were magicians, so in Roman sarcophagus art, Jesus is often portrayed with a wand. It was important to early Christians to use images from their own culture to signal the stature and power of Christ and other biblical figures. The learned and devout female patron who commissioned this sarcophagus wanted it to reflect core Christian beliefs in the miracles of Jesus, including healing the blind, bringing wine from water, feeding the hungry, and most importantly, bringing life from death. To this influential Roman woman, Peter's faith in the face of suffering seems to be an important sub theme.

BLANK OR UNFINISHED PORTRAITS

Early researchers hypothesized that when portrait faces were left blank or partially carved (figures 6.4 and 6.5), the purchaser planned to carve the deceased's likeness at a later time. But after finding an "astonishing number" of 201 unfinished portraits on 677 non-Christian portrait reliefs, Stine Birk theorizes that blank portraits were preserved in high numbers because they acquired meaning (and corresponding social value) for viewers over time. Since the portrait is a representation of the deceased and not necessarily a true likeness of the person at any one point in life, says Birk, their appearance is "just

49. B. Borg, *Crisis and Ambition*, 206. Borg cites a Roman sarcophagus from mausoleum H in the Vatican necropolis: "According to the inscription on the tabula, it was dedicated by two sons to their father Titus Caesenius Severianus, but a female bust with an unfinished portrait figures in the relief to the right."

as negotiable as all the other metaphorical images used to represent virtues on funerary monuments. . . . This means that the faceless figure maintained the same function as the figure with a portrait since both types of portraits symbolized the deceased individual."[50] Birk suggests that for some third-century Romans, "The blank portrait and the faceless head symbolize a conception of death in which the body and soul have different destinies. The figure with the roughly carved head thereby becomes a physical statement of the individual that once existed."[51]

Since blank portraits function essentially the same as detailed portraits in symbolizing the deceased person, they are included in this analysis. A total of forty-six early Christian portraits were left blank or otherwise unfinished (see appendix B). Of these, twenty-nine were solo/individual female portraits, two were male portraits, and the gender of one portrait could not be certainly identified. The remaining fourteen were unfinished couple commemorations that were counted as one portrait each even though they obviously had two figures—one male and one female—sometimes in a *clipeus* or before a *parapetasma* and sometimes not. The facial characteristics of an additional sixty-seven Christian sarcophagus artifacts with one or more portraits could not be certainly identified as blank or unfinished.[52] Representations of the deceased on these samples, however, could be classified according to sex, age, *orans* postures, in-facing figures, and learned characteristics; hence, they are included in this study.

50. Birk, *Depicting the Dead*, 58.
51. Ibid.
52. These images could not with certainty be identified as blank for the following reasons: damage or visible wear (46), reworked or revised (5), or known only through drawings or written descriptors (16).

IDENTIFYING EARLY CHRISTIAN PORTRAITS:
THE *ORANS* DILEMMA, ANALYSIS, AND OUTCOMES

Figure 6.7. Detail portrait relief of Marcia Romania Celsa, a "most illustrious woman" whose elaborate fourth-century sarcophagus includes many stories from the Hebrew Bible and Christian writings. Note that deceased is portrayed in a frontal, *orans* posture with a scroll bundle at her feet and in-facing "apostle" figures whose hand gestures "introduce" her. RS 3, no. 37. Musée de l'Arles Antique, Sarcophage de Marcia Romania Celsa. © R. Bénali, L. Roux.

Although the *orans* figure was briefly addressed in chapter 3, interpretive challenges related to sarcophagus portraiture require the more comprehensive discussion that follows.[53] For centuries, and even today, numerous interpreters viewed *orans* figures as symbols of the soul rather than necessarily representing an actual deceased person.[54] This perspective meant that Christian women who chose an *orans* for

53. I follow Janet Tulloch's practice of using the term *orans* to designate a figure of either sex. Grammatically, a single male figure is an *orant*, a single female figure is an *orante*. The plural of the feminine singular term is *orantes*. Tulloch, "Art and Archaeology," 288.

54. Ibid., 286–94; Maurice M. Hassett, "Orans," *Catholic Encyclopedia (1913)*, vol. 11, November 5, 2013, http://tinyurl.com/ycaqy7ep; Dresken-Weiland, *Bild, Grab und Wort*, 38–76, cited in Birk, *Depicting the Dead*, 89–90.

their funerary commemorations became essentially invisible. Other investigators have shown unequivocally that there are portrait features on Christian *orans* figures gracing sarcophagi (figure 6.7).[55] Far from being disembodied "souls," contemporary interpreters now understand portrait *orans* as representations of the deceased, and as such, they symbolize the values and virtues with which the departed identified.

Janet Huskinson, an expert in the transitional period from non-Christian to Christian sarcophagus iconography, notes that the early Christian *orans* evolved from the classical figure of *pietas* that a Roman wife brought to a marriage.[56] A proper Roman matron was expected to conduct religious rituals and offer sacrifice to the gods on behalf of the family and the emperor. Early non-Christian sarcophagi depict standing female figures conducting these rituals in conjunction with their male partners. Eventually, as we saw in chapter 5, standing female figures with scrolls became much more prevalent. By the late third century, the female *orans* had "emerged as a significant free-standing figure in her own right. Christians could see her as symbolizing the state of prayerfulness that led to salvation, or the Christian soul. But with her similarity—and interchangeability—with other female images of learning, and occasional portrait features, the identity of the *orans* often remains open."[57]

Stine Birk interprets the *orans* as an "expression of a new form of virtue (i.e. piety in relation to Christian belief) combined with the traditional cultural understanding of how to express ideas through iconographic language."[58] She notes that the *orans* combines learned female and muse iconography on non-Christian sarcophagi. In non-Christian iconography, muses were always female. Given these connotations, she describes the evolving *orans* as "an ideal representation of a certain kind of woman who possesses, *pietas*, intellectual status, and authority."[59] Birk also finds equivalence between learned women

55. Birk, "Using Images," 42; Huskinson, *Roman Strigillated Sarcophagi*, 220; RS 1; RS 2; and RS 3.

56. Huskinson, *Roman Strigillated Sarcophagi*, 198.

57. Ibid.

58. Birk, "Using Images," 44. Birk also cites Tulloch, "Art and Archaeology," 286–87.

59. Birk, "Using Images," 44.

and *orans* portrait figures on early Christian sarcophagi. She points to the many depictions of women with scrolls surrounded by biblical figures. Such a woman looks "as if she is preaching or teaching the men on either side of her" (see figures 6.9 and 8.1).[60] Similar portraits of female *orans* in the midst of biblical figures confirm "the close connection between the symbolic meanings of the two female figures. The *orans* is a personification of piety and faith. At the same time she embodies intellectuality and literary knowledge, now related to Christian religious texts instead of the usual philosophical ideology."[61] Female portraits with *orans* and/or learned iconography suggest roles that were open to women in early Christianity: "She could apparently teach, preach or act as a spiritual leader—even for men."[62] Ever the careful scholar, Birk cautions against assuming that the person who chose this funerary iconography "was necessarily a religious leader herself." She suggests that

> by using the motif she placed herself in an ideal female role. This role contains ideals and norms that all reflect currents in society. . . . [I]n this formative period of Christianity in Rome it seems there were other possibilities for women to negotiate their social role than those represented in the Christian literary tradition. These possibilities are symbolized by the individualized female portrait figures: the traditional Roman way of showing social status and power was transferred to Christian ways of constructing identity.[63]

As will be seen, the most popular female self-representation on Christian sarcophagi were in-facing "apostle" configurations, the *orans* figure, and other "learned woman" motifs, such as portrayals with a scroll or codex and/or a *capsa* (basket for carrying scrolls). While the early Christian literary record gives a largely negative witness about women who exercised authority, this present investigation suggests that numerous fourth-century Christian women were remembered as exercising it—with its corresponding status and power—or these iconic motifs would not have been chosen to signify female role models idealized by early Christians. Further (contra Birk), at least

---

60. Birk, *Depicting the Dead*, 90.
61. Ibid. Also, Birk cites Dresken-Weiland, *Bild, Grab und Wort*, 38.
62. Birk, *Depicting the Dead*, 90.
63. Ibid.

some of the Christian sarcophagi with learned and in-facing "apostle" motifs probably did belong to early Christian women who exercised authority in their lifetimes. For example, one early fourth-century frieze sarcophagus has a portrait of an uncharacteristically rotund deceased woman who is shown holding a scroll in her left hand with biblical stories arrayed on either side of her (see figures 7.13 and 7.14). Her distinctive hairstyle is barely covered by a veil, her clothing is richly draped, and she is wearing shoes. She needs no speech gesture because her mouth is partly opened as if speaking to viewers on her left (figure 7.14). This is a uniquely individualized portrait.

THE *ORANS* DILEMMA

Because of historical scholarly ambiguity about whether or not Christian *orans* figures only symbolize the soul or if they actually represent portraits of the female deceased, specific criteria were developed for identifying Christian *orans* portraits (see table 6.7).[64] If the RS volume identified the *orans* figure as a portrait or as the deceased grave owner, the *orans* was designated as a portrait in the database.[65] Nearly all *orans* figures in RS 3 were classified as "grave owners" and were therefore designated as portraits. If the *orans* face was left unfinished or blank, it was assumed to have been left blank by the sarcophagus workshop either because it was awaiting a portrait upon the person's death or because the patron deliberately chose to leave it blank.[66] These were therefore designated as portraits. Since it is probable that an *orans* figure with both an identifying inscription and in-facing "apostle" iconography was intended to represent the deceased, this combined configuration was classified as a portrait.[67] One female pair of *orans* was classified as individualized portraits because one had younger features while the other was given obviously older features.[68]

---

64. All *orans* figures were verified in the iconographic registers for RS 1 and RS 3. RS 2 has no such register, however these *orans* figures were confirmed by the written descriptors from that volume.

65. Described as "*Verstorbene*" or "*Grabinhaber*" in RS volumes.

66. Birk, *Depicting the Dead*, 58.

67. RS 1, no. 672; RS 2, no. 101.

68. RS 1, no. 972.

A total of seventy-eight Christian *orans* figures were classified as portraits (see table 6.5). These include eight child *orans* and six *orans* figures in couple portrayals.

Table 6.7: Criteria for Categorizing Christian *Orans* Figures as Portraits

Category and Criteria	Number
Yes (*orans* is Christian portrait)	78

- If described as a portrait in RS descriptors
- If specifically described as deceased or grave owner in RS ("*Verstorbene*" in RS 1 or "*Grabinhaber*" in RS 3)
- If blank *orans* face is described as unfinished (*bossiert*) or variation (indicates face was originally meant to be a portrait)
- Presence of obvious distinct physiognomy (for example, two female *orans*, one older, one younger [RS 1, no. 972])
- Identifying inscription together with in-facing "apostle" figures (RS 1, no. 672; RS 2, no. 101)

Yes – probable portrait (*orans* is probably a Christian portrait)	46

- If individualized features of clothing, hairstyle, jewelry, dove, *capsa*, scroll bundles, etc. are present
- If in-facing companion/"apostle" figures are present
- If solo standing figure on front frieze with adjoining biblical figures
- If in *clipeus* or on lid in space normally designating patron or deceased

Unclear (*orans* cannot be said with reasonable certainty to be a Christian portrait)	16

- If featured with generic ram bearer (vs. "Good Shepherd") without any individualizing characteristics listed above
- If too highly fragmented, damaged, or found only in an unclear drawing
- If largely reworked at a later time

Total *orans* figures on (possibly) Christian artifacts analyzed and classified	140
Total clearly Christian *orans* portraits and probable portraits	**124**

ABOUT *ORANS* "PROBABLE PORTRAITS"

The remaining Christian *orans* figures were carefully reviewed for signs of individualization. These were designated as "probable portraits" if they displayed personalized characteristics such as distinctive hairstyles, clothing, jewelry, or signs of learnedness (*capsa* or scroll bundle). They were also designated as "probable portraits" if an inscriptionless *orans* was accompanied by in-facing "apostle" figures, a solo standing figure was surrounded by biblical scenes, or the *orans* appeared in a *clipeus* or lid space normally reserved for the patron or deceased. Upon completion of this analysis, forty-seven Christian *orans* were classified as "probable portraits," including two child figures. Sixteen *orans* on early Christian sarcophagus artifacts were unclear and eliminated from final analysis (see table 6.4, no. 1). While it seemed necessary to separate out the *orans* "probable portraits" for statistical purposes, the distinction is insignificant since recent scholarship suggests *orans* such as these are representations of the deceased. For example, Birk believes that as Christian funerary iconography evolved, the focus on religious belief became more important than emphasis on the individuality of the deceased:

> It becomes more difficult to distinguish portraits from generic heads during the 4th century. . . . It seems as if it were no longer important to make the portraits realistic: symbolic representation of the deceased is sufficient for him or her to be associated with the ideals and virtues embodied in the scene.[69]

After excluding "unknown," "embedded," and *orans* "probable portraits," from the original group of 312 likely Christian portrait sarcophagus artifacts, the remaining 241 portraits make up the primary cohort for the quantitative and qualitative analyses that follow (see table 6.5). This cohort includes a total of 115 individual/solo adult female depictions, 44 individual/solo adult male depictions, 18 child depictions, and 64 couple depictions. Since the 44 adult *orans* "probable portraits" described in detail above meet our study's definition of a portrait as a "self-representation of the deceased," they were added

69. Birk, "Using Images," 43.

to the primary cohort but tested separately for any statistically significant differences compared to the primary cohort. When *orans* "probable portraits," were added, a total of 156 individual/solo adult female portraits were identified compared to 47 individual/solo adult male portraits (see table 6.8).

Table 6.8: Individual/Solo Adult Christian Portraits by Gender[70]

Female	No.	Male	No.
Adult solo/individual female[71]	115	Adult solo/individual male[72]	44[73]
*Adult female non-*orans *portraits*	*60*	*Adult male non-*orans *portraits*	*35*
Adult female (non-couple) portrait orans	*55*	*Adult male (non-couple) portrait* orans	*9*
Adult female *orans* "probable portrait"	41	Adult male *orans* "probable portrait"	3
Total individual/solo female portraits	156	Total individual/solo male portraits	47

DIFFERENTIATING "COUPLE" AND SOLO/INDIVIDUAL PORTRAITS

Couple portraits have one male and one female figure (who are often, but not always, married) in various standardized representations (see table 7.1). In couple reliefs, it was culturally expected that the male

70. For listing of RS images, see appendix C. In eight portrait artifacts, it was not possible to identify gender with certainty due to severe damage or fragmentation.

71. Solo female portrait (including *orans* portraits) or individual female portrait(s) on tombs with multiple portrait portrayals including families. In general, a solo portrait is the only portrait on a tomb while individual portraits are non-couple renditions on tombs with multiple portraits. I did not separate these numerically. Does not include child or obvious male-female couple portrayals.

72. Includes solo male portrait (including *orans* portraits) or individual male portrait(s) on tombs with multiple portrait portrayals including families. Does not include child or obvious male-female couple portrayals. In RS 2, no. 149, in addition to the two married representations found there, I included only one male portrait that is likely to be the male deceased (left side of sarcophagus) since the four other male figures are servant or "office" portrayals.

73. Includes three portraits that have a "male head carved onto a female body" and one male portrait on the lid of a tomb also containing a female *orans* classified as "probable portrait" (RS 1, no. 771).

would be depicted with signs of authority such as a scroll or a speech gesture. Since, with rare exceptions, the male is always portrayed hierarchically in such reliefs, it was necessary in this study to differentiate carefully between couple portraits and individual or solo portraits. An individual portrait is defined as one found with multiple other portraits on sarcophagus artifacts, but not in a standardized couple configuration. A solo portrait is defined as the only portrait on any given sarcophagus. In conducting the statistical analyses, however, no numerical differentiation was made between solo and individual portraits since both are independent reliefs that stand on their own, unrelated to a spousal portrayal. These have been described with a slash—individual/solo—or used interchangeably until this point in the text. However, to simplify things in the analyses that follow, the term "solo" will be used for both categories with the stipulation that this also includes individual portraits.

CRITERIA FOR INCLUDING PORTRAIT FRAGMENTS

In general, Stine Birk omitted sarcophagi from which only the fragment with the portrait was preserved, although she did include those "in which it was possible to identify the original motif of the fragment."[74] In this study, all fragments that had a discernible portrait large enough to identify the gender and learned characteristics of the subject were included. It was hypothesized that every sarcophagus had an equal opportunity to be fragmented, and therefore, theoretically, one should find an equal number of male and female portraits on fragments. Birk apparently identified entire sarcophagi as "male portrait" or "female portrait," whereas in this study each portrait was counted separately because some sarcophagi had multiple portraits of different genders.

---

74. Birk, *Depicting the Dead*, 205.

WHY STATISTICS? SOLO FEMALE PORTRAITS OUTNUMBER MALE PORTRAITS

An important finding of this study is that the number of solo female early Christian portraits outnumbered solo male early Christian portraits by three to one. But was the difference in the observed number of solo female Christian portraits compared to solo male portraits statistically significant? To validly compare differences between these mathematically diverse groups, statistical testing is necessary. For example, if one simply reported that there were forty solo portraits of Christian females with scrolls or *capses* (containers for scrolls) compared to twenty-five solo males with scrolls or *capses*, one might wrongly assume that there were proportionately more solo learned (scroll-bearing) female portraits on Christian sarcophagi compared to learned male portraits. Such an interpretation does not consider that, theoretically, there are also three times as many opportunities for a solo female portrait to have a scroll compared to a solo male portrait.[75]

EARLY CHRISTIAN SOLO PORTRAITS: SUMMARY OF STATISTICAL ANALYSIS

An important working hypothesis in this investigation is that the likelihood of an early Christian solo portrait containing iconography commemorating a woman is equal to the likelihood that it would commemorate a man. If this hypothesis is correct, one would expect an equal number of solo female and solo male portraits. Instead, solo female portraits outnumbered solo male portraits by three to one. Of 203 adult solo portraits on early Christian sarcophagi, 156 were portraits of women and 47 were portraits of men (table 6.8). Therefore, the observed proportion of solo female portraits is 156/203 = 0.768, or 76.8 percent. The observed proportion of solo male portraits is 47/203 = 0.232, or 23.2 percent. Appropriate statistical tests were conducted to determine whether the proportion of female solo portraits

75. I am indebted to Thomas H. Short, PhD, PStat, who provided statistical consultation, calculations, and interpretations so that I could meaningfully compare various iconographical characteristics of male and female portraits.

is significantly different from 0.5, or 50 percent. Since the observed percentage of females is 76.8 percent, the proportion of females in the population of solo portraits that is represented by the sample is significantly larger than 0.5, or 50 percent. The likelihood that this finding is due to chance is less than 1 in 1000. These findings did not change when "probable portraits" were excluded (see appendix C).

EARLY CHRISTIAN SOLO PORTRAITS: DISCUSSION AND CONCLUSIONS

Unlike Stine Birk's study of Roman sarcophagi in which women and men were commemorated in equal numbers, this investigation found three times as many solo female portrait commemorations on early Christian sarcophagi compared to solo male commemorations. This outcome is surprising when compared to Birk's outcomes. Likewise, Brent D. Shaw's investigation of early third- to early seventh-century Christian funerary inscriptions in the city of Rome found that the proportion of male and female dated inscriptions was essentially equal (males, n=1918; females, n=1815).[76] Over half of the Christian inscriptions (n=approximately 1825) date to before the sacking of Rome (410 CE), making them roughly contemporaneous with the portrait sarcophagi studied here.[77] Shaw discovered the inscriptions were representative of "the great mass of common persons" in Rome, although a few belonged to persons in the aristocracy.[78]

Of the 558 early Christian sarcophagus artifacts (classified strictly) in the present study, 247 contained one or more portraits, of which 156, or 76.8 percent, were female. Of the remaining 311 Christian sarcophagus artifacts without verifiable portraits, 20 funerary inscriptions were identified. These were equally distributed between males and females. This sampling of inscriptions is too small to draw any

76. Shaw, "Seasons of Death," 100–138. Shaw's findings do not support Rodney Stark's sociological thesis that there were more women than men in early Christianity. See Stark, *Rise of Christianity*, 128.

77. An overwhelming majority of Christian portrait sarcophagi (228 of 247, or 95 percent) were made in Rome or sculpted in the Roman style, suggesting roughly comparable populations in inscriptions and portrait sarcophagi linked to the city of Rome.

78. Of the aristocratic titles, twenty-eight belonged to men and fifteen belonged to women.

conclusions about the gender of those buried in the remaining 291 sarcophagus artifacts that had neither an inscription nor a verifiable portrait. Therefore, it is risky to infer on the basis of material remains from Christian sarcophagi that there were more higher status Christian women than higher status Christian men in late antiquity. That said, neither should one assume that the portrait sarcophagi analyzed here all belonged to early Christian elites. Freed and freeborn women and men could and did acquire sufficient wealth through various financial and business undertakings to afford elaborate sarcophagi that commemorated their virtues and values.

What is clear, however, is that more early Christian women chose to be commemorated with portraits than did Christian men at statistically significant levels. This finding supports the conclusions of Carolyn Osiek, Margaret Y. MacDonald, Rodney Stark, and Peter Lampe discussed in chapters 1 and 2. Osiek and MacDonald's detailed, multidisciplinary study demonstrated that Christian women were substantially more influential in the Roman patronage system and domestic social networks than previously recognized. Stark's sociological methodologies suggest that Christian women "filled leadership positions" and enjoyed a higher status within the Christian subculture than non-Christian women enjoyed within the non-Christian culture. Lampe found that in wealthy aristocratic families (who could also afford such sarcophagi), the women were more likely to be Christian than the men.[79] That the material remains of early Christian portrait sarcophagi support what these researchers had originally theorized constitutes a significant addition to what can be known about Christian women and men in late antiquity.

ANALYZING PORTRAIT MOTIFS: LEARNEDNESS, SPEECH GESTURES, AND IN-FACING "APOSTLES"

With the main portrait cohorts identified, it became possible to study their iconological motifs. Two goals for studying portrait motifs are

---

79. Lampe, *From Paul to Valentinus*, 149.

1. to discover what they might signify about the Christians who chose them; and

2. to discover any significant differences between male and female portraits depicted with any given motif.

The following motifs were investigated:

1. "Learned" motifs such as the presence of scrolls, codices, and *capses* or scroll bundles, as well as *orans* figures

2. Speech gestures

3. In-facing "apostle" figures with their assorted characteristics

The aforementioned portrait motifs were identified, tabulated, and categorized as belonging to a male or female portrait. Since motifs can occur alone or in combination (such as a scroll with a speech gesture), various combinations were also compared and tested where appropriate. Statistical testing determined whether there were significant differences between male and female cohorts. Since both Christ figures and portrait figures are shown with in-facing "apostle" figures, various cohorts of these groupings were also identified and statistically tested.

In what follows, we will first review what scholars understand to be the meaning of each motif within Greco-Roman and Christian cultures. Computational and statistical findings for each motif will then be summarized in the body of the text. Each motif section will close with a brief discussion of the findings and how they relate to our topic of women and authority in early Christianity. Listings of RS images and statistical computations for various cohorts are found in corresponding appendices.

ABOUT "LEARNED" PORTRAIT MOTIFS

From their research of Roman funerary portraits from the first through the fourth centuries, both Birk and Huskinson found significant changes in female iconography that point to a corresponding change in female social identity. In the first and second centuries, female funerary representations highlight beauty, fidelity, and marital harmony. With the rise of the second sophistic period (first century through mid-third century), female portraits began to include scrolls, lyres, *orans* figures, and other signs of learnedness. Soon, learned figures became the most popular iconographic representations for female deceased, just as they were for male deceased.[80] By the middle of the third century, female busts with a scroll had become a regular occurrence, and, together with an increasing popularity of female full-length figures with scrolls, this pattern "suggest[s] collective acceptance that this scroll carrying image was also possible for the contemporary woman."[81]

But what do scrolls signify? Scholars believe that in third- and fourth-century society, funerary scrolls point to the departed's "status and power," associating him or her with knowledge and the intellectual virtues of upper-class Rome.[82] The fact that males and females holding scrolls on funerary reliefs appeared at the same time suggests an "overall acceptance" of women as learned, and therefore "male and female virtues were presented as one and the same."[83] Lest we assume parity existed between the sexes, however, it is important to note that hierarchical relationships persisted in couple depictions. On non-Christian sarcophagi with two separate portrait figures, a female could hold a scroll as long as it was not in a marital relief with her husband. In marital depictions, only the male holds the scroll (see chapter 7 for a comprehensive discussion of couple portraits).[84] In the early Christian context, the presence of a scroll, codex, or *capsa* also suggests the deceased's learnedness about the Hebrew and Christian Scriptures.[85]

As noted elsewhere, Birk found that learned figures were the most popular representation for non–Christian Roman women. She classified female portraits as "learned" if they included these motifs: muse,

---

80. Birk, *Depicting the Dead*, 59, 76.

81. Janet Huskinson, "Women and Learning: Gender and Identity in Scenes of Intellectual Life on Late Roman Sarcophagi," in *Constricting Identities in Late Antiquity*, ed. Richard Miles (New York: Routledge, 1999), 199.

82. Birk, *Depicting the Dead*, 76.

83. Ibid.

84. Ibid.

85. Ibid., 90.

orans, scroll, or a musical instrument. She also included two reliefs depicting female philosophers indicated by a seated (usually male) figure with a tunic or naked chest or standing figure wearing a *himation*.[86] Male learned portraits were less varied, but they could be shown as poets, philosophers, or holding a scroll.[87] Birk also found that learned non-Christian women were most often represented alone on sarcophagi, whereas learned non-Christian men were found almost as frequently in couple depictions as in solo depictions.[88] In quantifying learned female figures Birk did not include reliefs of marital sarcophagi or *clipeus* busts of a couple in the statistics, because she found "in these motifs the woman is never represented as learned."[89] Unlike their non-Christian counterparts, however, this study discovered a few portraits of Christian couples in which the woman is depicted with a scroll (see figures 7.5 and 7.7).

There are many sarcophagus portraits of early Christian women with scroll/*capsa* iconography (see table 6.9). This suggests that Christian women in the fourth century were commemorated as persons of "status and power," educated, and, at the least, active in teaching and explaining Scripture (see figure 6.9).[90] In analyzing early Christian figures with scrolls and *capses*, this investigation adopted Birk's methodology and separated out couple portrayals from solo portrayals. Because Birk considers portrait *orans* as learned figures on non-Christian sarcophagi, this study included Christian portrait *orans* depictions in its analyses of learned figures (see table 6.10). Early Christians adapted Roman iconography to express their own beliefs. Just because the *orans* figure came to represent Christian piety does not therefore mean that it lost its original connotation of learnedness. Yet, since early (and some contemporary) interpretations of the Christian *orans* figure do not include connotations of learnedness, separate analyses were conducted for solo portrait figures with scrolls (or codices) and *capses* (or scroll bundles) and solo portrait figures

86. This is a square outer garment draped over the left shoulder and worn as a cloak. It originated in Greece.
87. Ibid., 86.
88. Ibid., 88.
89. Ibid.
90. Ibid., 90.

with an *orans* configuration. A final analysis added portraits with *orans* configurations to portraits with scroll and *capsa* motifs in order to create and evaluate a comprehensive "learned" category. (For computational purposes, henceforward the term "scroll" will be understood to include codices and the term "*capsa/capses*" should be understood as including scroll bundles).

Table 6.9: Portrait Figures with Scrolls or *Capses* by Gender[91]

Type of Learned Portrait[92]	Scroll	*Capsa* or Scroll Bundle	Total
Solo Female	27	9[93] (includes 7 *orans*)	36
Solo Male	22	2[94] (includes 1 *orans*)	24
Couple: Female with Scroll	6[95]		6
Couple: Male with Scroll[96]	43[97]		43
Solo Female *Orans* "Probable Portrait"	0	4	4
Solo Male *Orans* "Probable Portrait"	0	1	1
Uncertain[98]	8	1	9

91. As found on individual, couple, family (defined as including at least one adult and one child) and multiple portrait tombs (more than two portraits, usually no children). For listing by RS volume and image number, see appendix D.

92. No embedded portraits had learned iconography.

93. One figure had both a scroll and *capsa* (RS 1: no. 221). Seven *orans* figures also had a scroll bundle or a *capsa* (RS 1: no. 195; RS 3: nos. 37, 70, 75, 355, 366, 497).

94. Three figures had both scroll and *capsa* for two additional learned figures, one of which was an *orans*.

95. In six unconventional couple reliefs, the female is depicted with a scroll: RS 1: nos. 120, 811; RS 2: nos. 12, 123, 148; RS 3: no. 77. A woman was not expected to have a scroll or a speech gesture in marital depictions.

96. Even though the RS volumes describe these as married depictions, it is possible that six could have been mother-son portrayals with son holding scroll. The beardless head of the male figure appears smaller than the female's. I still counted these as couples since I only had access to photographs. Nevertheless, this probably deserves further investigation: RS 1: nos. 112, 385; RS 2: no. 108; RS 3: nos. 40, 41, 555.

97. In one portrayal (RS 3, no. 51) a male is shown holding a scroll, and a scroll bundle is shown in the center of a *dextrarum iunctio* scene, replacing the pagan figure Hymenaeus frequently found in this depiction on Roman tombs. For this statistical analysis, the male with a scroll was included but the scroll bundle was not since it theoretically could have belonged to either the husband or wife.

All Learned Females (Includes 6 Couple Portrayals and 4 *Orans* "Probable Portrait")	46
All Learned Males (Includes 43 Couple Portrayals and 1 *Orans* "Probable Portrait")	68
All Solo Learned Females (Scroll-*Capsa*)	**40**
All Solo Learned Males (Scroll-*Capsa*)	**25**

Table 6.10: All Learned Portrait Portrayals by Gender (*Orans* Figures Added to Scroll and/or *Capsa* Depictions)[99] *(See appendix F)*

Type of Learned Portrait[100]	Scroll	*Orans* Only	With *Capsa* or Scroll Bundle at Feet	Total
Solo learned female—non-*orans*	27		2	29
Solo learned female—*orans*		48	7	55
Total learned solo female (without *orans* "probable portraits")	**27**	**48**	**9**	**84**
Solo female *orans* "probable portrait"		37	4	41
Adjusted total learned solo female (with *orans* "probable portraits")	*27*	*85*	*13*	*125*
Solo learned male—non-*orans*	22		1	23
Solo learned male—*orans*		8	1	9
Total learned solo male (without "probable portraits")	**22**	**8**	**2**	**32**
Solo male *orans* "probable portrait"		2	1	3

98. Unable to identify gender due to damage or expert uncertainty. See RS 1, no. 135—experts question if the figure is an embedded portrait or biblical figure.

99. As found on individual, couple, family (defined as including at least one adult and one child) and multiple portrait tombs (more than two portraits). For listing by RS volume and image number, see appendixes C and D.

100. No embedded portraits had learned iconography.

Adjusted total learned solo male (with "probable portraits")	*22*	*10*	*3*	*35*
Couple: Female with scroll or *orans* posture	6[101]	4		10
Couple: Male with scroll[102] or *orans* posture	43[103]	2		45
Uncertain[104]	8	1		9
All learned female (includes 10 couple portrayals)				135
All learned male (includes 45 couple portrayals)				80

EARLY CHRISTIAN PORTRAITS WITH SCROLLS AND *CAPSES*: SUMMARY OF STATISTICAL OUTCOMES

Hypothetically, each solo male or solo female portrait on Christian sarcophagi has an equal chance of being shown with a scroll, a *capsa*, or both. If this is correct, one would expect portraits of solo females with a scroll and/or *capsa* to be proportionate to portraits of solo males with the same configuration. A total of forty solo female portraits with scrolls/codices or *capses* were identified (see table 6.9). Twenty-seven hold scrolls while an additional thirteen are shown with a scroll bundle or a *capsa* at their feet. Four are *orans* "probable portraits."[105] This compares with twenty-five solo learned male portraits, of which

101. In six unconventional couple reliefs, the female is depicted with a scroll: RS 1: nos. 120, 811; RS 2: no. 12, 123, 148; RS 3: no. 77. A woman was not expected to have a scroll or a speech gesture in marital depictions.

102. Even though the RS volumes describe these as married depictions, I believe seven could have been mother-son portrayals with son holding scroll. The beardless head of the male figure appears smaller than the female's. I still counted these as couples since I only had access to photographs. Nevertheless, this probably deserves further investigation.

103. In one portrayal (RS 3, no. 51) a male is shown holding a scroll, and a scroll bundle is shown in the center of a *dextrarum iunctio* scene, replacing the pagan figure Hymenaeus frequently found in this depiction on Roman tombs. For this statistical analysis, the male with a scroll was included but the scroll bundle was not since it theoretically could have belonged to either the husband or wife.

104. Unable to identify gender due to damage or expert uncertainty. See RS 1, no. 135—experts question if the figure is an embedded portrait or biblical figure.

105. One figure had both a scroll bundle and a *capsa*.

twenty-two are depicted with a scroll and three with a *capsa* at their feet. One of the latter is an *orans* "probable portrait."[106]

Therefore, of 156 solo female portraits, 40 (25.6 percent) contained a scroll, a *capsa*, or both. Of 47 solo male portraits, 25 (53.2 percent) contained a scroll, a *capsa*, or both. Appropriate statistical tests found that proportionately more male portraits had scroll/*capsa* depictions compared to female portraits and the difference is statistically significant. On the other hand, when just the sixty-five scroll-*capsa* portrait portrayals are considered (rather than all solo portraits), there were no statistically significant differences in the proportions of males and females with this motif. This finding did not change when "probable portraits" were excluded (see appendix D). For purposes of this study one must acknowledge that despite the different statistical "lenses" viewing these portrait sarcophagi, there is no denying that a large number of women are shown with learned iconography that is the same as that used on male portraits.

EARLY CHRISTIAN PORTRAITS WITH *ORANS* CONFIGURATIONS: STATISTICAL SUMMARY

Since the Christian *orans* originated with Roman muse figures, it is unsurprising that most *orans* figures on Christian portraits are female. Of 108 Christian portrait *orans* figures the vast majority (96) are female while only 12 are male. It should be noted that 11 female *orans* portraits and two male *orans* portraits also have scrolls, codices, *capses*, or scroll bundles as part of their portraits, as if to emphasize the learnedness of the devout *orans* (see figure 6.7). For this reason, care was taken to avoid counting the same portrait twice. An examination of whether there were significant differences between solo female *orans*-only (no scroll or *capsa*) and solo male *orans*-only portraits was conducted (see table 6.11). Of 156 solo female portraits, 85 were portrayed as *orans*-only figures without a scroll or *capsa*. Of

---

106. As expected, in couple portrayals many more males—forty-three to be exact—are shown holding a scroll, for a total of sixty-eight learned males. Six females in couple portrayals are unconventionally shown with a scroll for a total of forty-six learned females (RS 1, nos. 120, 811; RS 2, nos. 12, 123, 148; RS 3, no. 77).

47 solo male portraits, 10 were portrayed with this configuration. As one would expect, the proportions for female *orans*-only portraits are statistically significantly greater. These portraits were 2.6 times more likely than solo male portraits to be depicted in an *orans*-only posture, and the likelihood that this difference is due to chance is less than 1 in 1000. This finding did not change when "probable portraits" were excluded (see appendix E).

Table 6.11: *Orans*-Only Solo Portrait Figures by Gender
(See appendix E for statistical computations.)

Type of Portrait	Orans (without Scrolls or Capses)
Female *orans*	48
Female *orans* "probable portrait"	37
Total female	**85**
Male *orans*	8
Male *orans* "probable portrait"	2
Total male	**10**

EARLY CHRISTIAN PORTRAITS WITH SCROLL, *CAPSA*, AND *ORANS* CONFIGURATIONS: SUMMARY OF STATISTICAL OUTCOMES

Turning to an analysis of all Christian learned portraits, we hypothesized that all portraits on Christian sarcophagi have an equal chance of being shown with one or more of the following learned iconographical elements—a scroll, a *capsa*, and/or an *orans* depiction (table 6.10). If this hypothesis is correct, one would expect portraits of females depicted with learned iconography, such as a scroll, *capsa*, or *orans* posture, to be proportionate to portraits of males with these configurations. For this analysis, we first considered solo male and solo female portraits and then added couple portraits. Of 156 solo female portraits, 125 (80.1 percent) were portrayed with learned iconographical elements, including a scroll, a *capsa*, and/or an *orans* depiction. Of 47 solo male portraits, 35 (74.5 percent) were portrayed with these iconographical elements. Appropriate statistical tests found no statistically significant differences between proportions of solo learned male figures and solo learned female figures. These findings did not change when "probable portraits" were excluded (see appendix F)

Both solo and couple learned portrayals were combined and analyzed for the presence of scroll and *capsa* depictions as well as *orans* configurations (see table 6.10). Out of 220 possible portraits (156 solo + 64 female half of couple), a total of 135 learned female portraits with these depictions were identified. Out of 111 possible portraits (47 solo + 64 male half of couple), a total of 80 learned male portraits were identified. Appropriate tests revealed no statistically significant differences between proportions of all learned male figures and all learned female figures portrayed with a scroll, *capsa*, or *orans* configurations. When *orans* "probable portraits" were excluded, however, the proportion of male portraits is larger. The likelihood that the latter finding is due to chance is 2 in 1000 (see appendix F).

EARLY CHRISTIAN "LEARNED" PORTRAITS: DISCUSSION AND CONCLUSIONS

On Christian sarcophagi, both solo male and solo female portraits are shown with scrolls and *capses*. Appropriate statistical tests found no statistically significant difference in the proportions of solo male and solo female Christian portraits with scroll and/or *capsa* motifs. At first glance, this would seem to mimic Stine Birk's findings that on non-Christian sarcophagi, both men and women were equally represented with learned motifs.[107] However, Birk included other motifs to signify learnedness besides scrolls. In Birk's analysis, learned women also included *orans*, muse figures, and musical instruments. We therefore separated out the scroll-bearing male and female portraits in Birk's sample in order to make an "apples to apples" comparison.[108] Birk identified 97 solo female portraits with scrolls and 62 solo males with

---

107. Birk, *Depicting the Dead*, 75, 86.
108. I based my numbers on those listed in appendix C of Birk's *Depicting the Dead*, 200–201.

scrolls for a total of 159 solo portraits with scrolls. After appropriate statistical testing, Birk's sample was found to have proportionately more solo female portraits with scrolls than solo male portraits. The difference was statistically significant, and the likelihood that this finding was due to chance is just 7 in 1000.[109] As noted above, on Christian sarcophagi this was not the case. There was no statistically significant difference between the proportions of Christian solo female portraits and Christian solo male portraits depicted with scrolls and *capses*. When Christian *orans* figures were added to the sample, the proportions of Christian solo female and solo male "learned" depictions replicate Birk's original findings, namely that both men and women were equally represented with learned motifs.

When couple portraits with all learned motifs were added to solo portraits, there was no statistically significant difference between proportions of learned male figures and learned female figures. Only when the *orans* "probable portraits" were removed from the combined couple-solo portrait analysis was there a statistically significant difference between male and female learned portraits. The proportion of male figures was larger. This is explained by the fact that in married depictions, the male nearly always holds a scroll while the female does not. This investigation found forty-three males holding scrolls in married depictions, and just six females holding them. When the (largely female) *orans* "probable portraits" were removed from the combined cohort, male learned figures with scrolls proportionately increased while the (largely female) *orans* learned figures decreased. This leads to the observation that in all Christian portrait sarcophagi (both couple and solo portraits), males are more likely to be depicted with scroll iconography whereas females are more likely to be depicted as *orans* figures. Still, since "probable portraits" are also representations of the deceased, there remains no statistically significant difference in the proportion of male and female learned portraits when all couple and solo depictions are combined.

These findings suggest that the fourth-century Christians who commissioned these sarcophagi adopted and adapted the iconography

---

109. A two-sided exact binomial test found a statistically significant P-value of 0.007 for 97 females out of 159 portraits. This means that the likelihood that this finding was due to chance is just 7 in 1000.

of their Roman culture in commemorating both deceased women and men with scrolls, *capses*, and in *orans* postures. Just as in the non-Christian context, this iconography represented values of status, power, learnedness, and religious devotion, but now within a Christian context.[110] Both early Christian women and Christian men were commemorated and idealized as persons of status, power, learnedness, and religious devotion. When their portraits include biblical scenes, a scroll or *capsa* may also signal their learnedness about the Hebrew and Christian Scriptures. Considering the many proscriptions of women exercising religious authority in the fourth century (and previously), one would expect to find proportionately fewer representations of Christian women idealized as persons of power and status, but this is not the case. I agree with Birk's well-founded opinion that "the continuation of the representation of learned woman in Christian sarcophagi reliefs suggests late antique women played a greater role in formation of Christianity than previously supposed."[111]

SARCOPHAGUS OF MARCIA ROMANIA CELSA

Figure 6.8. Full sarcophagus of Marcia Romania Celsa, a "most illustrious woman." See text for biblical scenes. Early fourth century. RS 3, no. 37. France: Musée de l'Arles Antique, Sarcophage de Marcia Romania Celsa. © R. Bénali, L. Roux.

The well-known sarcophagus of Marcia Romania Celsus exemplifies a learned woman of "power and status" who, if we accept the above correlation, was learned in the Hebrew and Christian Scriptures and

110. Birk, *Depicting the Dead*, 75–85, 90.
111. Ibid., 183.

exercised religious authority. Marcia is depicted in an *orans* posture with a scroll bundle at her feet indicating her piety, learning, and scriptural literacy. Found in Arles, France, this early fourth-century sarcophagus was one of many Christian sarcophagi commissioned after Constantine's Edict of Toleration in 314. Arles was established as a Roman colony in 46 BCE. With proximity to the Mediterranean Sea to the South and the Rhone River to the North, the city became a key communications route between Rome and the rest of Gaul, and soon acquired a typical Roman cityscape, including an amphitheater, triumphal arch, Roman circus, and theatre. One of the best-known Roman antiquities in Arles is the sarcophagus of Marcia Romania Celsa, located in the Musée de l'Arles Antique (see figure 6.8). In the round *clipeus* on the lid, we find this inscription:

> XVII Kalendas apriles hic quiescet in pace Marcia Romania Celsa clarissima femina que vixit annos XXXVIII, menses II, dies XI. Flavius Januarinus vir clarissimus ex consule ordinario coniugi bene merenti posuit.

The English translation reads:

> On the 17th kalends of April here rests in peace Marcia Romania Celsa, most illustrious woman who lived 38 years, two months, eleven days. Flavius Januarinus, illustrious man, ordinary consul, set up this monument to his most deserving spouse.

This is the final resting place of Marcia Romania Celsa, the highly esteemed spouse of Flavius Januarinus, who has the title ordinary consul, the highest rank in the Roman Empire after that of the emperor. Consuls were elected or appointed for one year. At the time of Constantine, this title had become largely honorific, though it was granted only to elites who had achieved prominence through significant public service, or military fame.[112] Marcia Romania Celsa was a member of an elite and politically influential family as both the inscription and her elaborate sarcophagus reliefs attest.

Scenes from the Hebrew and Christian Scriptures on both upper and lower registers tell us immediately that Marcia's is a Christian sar-

---

112. "Roman Consul," Wikipedia, 2016, http://tinyurl.com/ya94tqsl; "Consul: Ancient Roman Official," *Encyclopedia Britannica*, July 20, 1998, http://tinyurl.com/ya3vewfm.

cophagus. In the center of the lower register is a portrait of a partially veiled woman, clad in a tunic, dalmatic, and shoes, whose arms are raised in an *orans* posture evoking both her religious devotion and her learnedness (see figures 6.7 and 6.8). At her feet, a scroll bundle probably represents biblical texts and reinforces her learned status. Distinctively wavy hair parted in the center signals that this is a portrait. To her right and left are two in-facing "apostle" figures with hands extended in what the RS describes as an "introduction" gesture.[113] Arrayed on either side of Marcia are vignettes based on early Christian writings. To the viewer's right are three scenes from the life of Jesus: the multiplication of the loaves, the healing of the blind man (note his guide staff), and the raising of Lazarus respectively. On the left are three scenes from the life of Peter: a composite prediction of Peter's denial and his commissioning (notice the small rooster at Peter's feet), Peter's arrest, and his water miracle in jail. Jesus carries a small rod in the multiplication and Lazarus scenes, signifying miraculous events. The small female figure at the base of Lazarus's tomb is Mary, the sister of Lazarus shown here kissing Jesus's feet. Some fourth-century Christians believed that the woman at Simon's house who anointed and kissed Jesus feet (Luke 7:36–50) and Mary of Bethany, who anointed his feet with ointment (John 12:1–8), were the same person, but this opinion has been discounted.[114] Christ carries a scroll in the healing of the blind scene and Peter's denial/commissioning scenes, while Peter carries a scroll in the water miracle portrayal. It was important to early Christians to depict biblical figures as learned persons on par with the great philosophers of their day. Also notable are the "apostle" figures flanking Christ in the multiplication scene and in Peter's denial/commissioning. These are quite similar to those flanking Marcia. The implications of this iconography will be discussed below, as will the two-fingered "speech gestures" shown by Peter in the arrest scene and Christ in Peter's commissioning portrayal.

On the lid of Marcia's sarcophagus are two vignettes often found

---

113. *Einführungsgestus*, see RS 3, no. 37. A similar gesture is sometimes described by RS experts as *Empfehlungsgestus* (recommendation), see RS 3, no. 75, or *Geleit* (escort), see RS 3, no. 57. Yet another related gesture is called *Gestus der Fürsprache* and translates as intercession.

114. Thurston, *Women in the New Testament*, 88–89, 104–5.

on lids of Christian sarcophagi. To the left of the inscription *clipeus* is a relief from the Hebrew Bible depicting Shadrach, Meshach, and Abednego, who were thrown into the fiery furnace by Nebuchadnezzar, king of Babylon, when they refused to worship his golden image (Daniel 3). As the story goes, Nebuchadnezzar was astonished to see "four men unbound and unhurt walking in the fire; and the fourth looks like a son of God." And so it is that we see three male *orans* figures in Phrygian hats, with a fourth in their midst shown with a speech gesture. This figure is described as an "angel" in the RS, but it is plausible to surmise that fourth-century Christians saw him as a precursor of Christ. To the right of the *clipeus* is a relief of the visit of the magi from the east (Matthew 2). Three men (again in Phrygian hats) and their camels approach Mary, who is seated on a throne holding the Christ child in her lap. Mary's iconography is similar to depictions of the much-beloved Egyptian goddess Isis, who is usually portrayed seated on a throne with her son Horus on her lap. Again, we have an additional male figure with a speech gesture in this relief. He is Balaam, a pagan prophet, who predicted that "a star shall come out of Jacob and a scepter shall rise out of Israel" (see Numbers 22–24). Early church fathers Justin Martyr, Irenaeus, and Origen attributed a messianic meaning to Balaam's prophecy, suggesting that the magi were familiar with his prediction that a star and a new ruler would come out of Israel. This interpretation was known to early Christians who incorporated it into their funerary art.[115]

Marcia's sarcophagus suggests she was remembered not only as a wealthy woman of status but for her learnedness, biblical authority, and faith. A theological reflection about the iconography on her sarcophagus suggests that mourners may have been reminded that even the worst of betrayals, such as Peter's, can not only be forgiven but can lead to a deeper walk with the risen Christ. Though imprisoned, Peter baptizes his jailers with miraculous water, and a pagan prophet foretells the Messiah. In life and in death, Marcia proclaims Christ's power over corruption and disease. Just as God raised Lazarus from the dead and brought Shadrach, Meshach, and Abednego out

---

115. Wayne Jackson, "Did Balaam Prophesy Concerning the Messiah?" *Christian Courier*, accessed June 20, 2017. http://tinyurl.com/y8a2f2wa.

of the fiery furnace, so Marcia, and those reflecting on her sarcophagus, will be raised to new life. Marcia is indeed a "most illustrious woman" whose Christian faith, learnedness, and religious authority shine brightly beyond the grave.

ANALYZING PORTRAIT MOTIFS: SPEECH GESTURES

Anyone studying early Christian sarcophagi will soon notice two-fingered "speech gestures" on both portraits and biblical figures that are strange and unfamiliar to modern eyes (see figure 6.9). People living in the twenty-first century have little understanding of the importance of oratory and rhetoric in the predominantly aural societies of antiquity. The speech gesture is one of many used by public speakers, politicians, philosophers, and actors to enhance the impact of the spoken word. A precise understanding of these ancient signals can be elusive. Gregory S. Aldrete's interesting book *Gestures and Acclamations in Ancient Rome* investigates the characteristics of non-verbal communication (mainly hand gestures) in Roman oratory. He writes: "Rome's political and social life revolved around face-to-face public interactions, of which speechmaking before large audiences was the central feature."[116] In an age without microphones, nonverbal forms of communication were important if ruling elites were to win over the common people who played "a significant role" in political decision-making. Aldrete reviews gestures described in ancient handbooks on rhetoric that were written to prepare upper-class young men for public life. He compares three volumes by Cicero (106–42 BCE) and the *Insitito Oratoria* by Quintilian (35–100 CE) with the *Illustrated Terence Manuscripts*. He describes the *Manuscripts* as "a visual analogue to the rhetorical handbooks."[117] Publius Terentius Afer (Terence) was a former slave and a famous Roman playwright whose comedies were first performed around 170–160 BCE. He is perhaps best remembered for his famous quotation "I am human, and nothing of that which is human is alien to me."[118]

116. Gregory S. Aldrete, *Gestures and Acclamations in Ancient Rome* (Baltimore: Johns Hopkins University Press, 1999), 73.
117. Ibid., 67.
118. Terence, *Heauton Timorumenos* (Henry Thomas Riley, *The Comedies of Terence* [New

Later manuscripts of Terence's plays included drawings of actors making a variety of oratorical gestures for individual scenes. While the oldest illustrated copies date from the ninth to the twelfth century, scholars Leslie W. Jones and C. R. Morey believe the ninth-century version faithfully reproduced gestures that dated to the fifth century or earlier.[119] Significantly, Aldrete finds "in the illustrations for these plays, many of the gestures made by these comic actors are exactly those used by orators as described by Quintilian."[120] Further, Aldrete found the speech gesture to be the most common hand gesture in the Terence illustrations. He describes it as "the right arm being outstretched with the index and middle fingers extended and held together, while the thumb and other fingers are curled into the palm."[121] Generally, the gesture is directed to one other character, though sometimes two actors each direct it to the other. Unfortunately for our purposes, Quintilian does not describe the speech gesture found in the *Terence Manuscripts*. Although speech gestures occur frequently in *Manuscript* illustrations, the meaning is not altogether clear. Aldrete believes "they may have been used to add emphasis to narration or argument."[122]

German RS scholars invariably describe these two-fingers-extended motifs as *redegestus* or "speech gestures." Janet Huskinson points to a full-length female figure with a scroll in her left hand and the right "raised in an oratorical gesture" in the center of an early fourth-century strigillated sarcophagus (RS 1, no. 1004).[123] In her opinion, reliefs of women in these "learned" or "oratorical" poses constitute a repeated use of "traditional tokens of masculinity," that helped "create a new stereotype of female virtue for women depicted alone."[124] Huskinson questions if these changes in female portraiture

York: Harper & Brothers, 1874], reprinted on Perseus Digital Library, http://tinyurl.com/y77owpyv).

119. Leslie Webber Jones and C. R. Morey, *The Miniatures of the Manuscripts of Terence Prior to the Thirteenth Century*, 2 vols. (Princeton: Princeton University Press, 1931), 45, cited in Aldrete, *Gestures and Acclamations*, 55–57.

120. Aldrete, *Gestures and Acclamations*, 54–57.

121. Ibid., 63.

122. Ibid.

123. Huskinson, "Women and Learning," 200. I classified this sarcophagus as "possibly Christian" because of two ram bearer figures on either end.

124. Huskinson, *Roman Strigillated Sarcophagi*, 142.

represent qualities of a new female identity independent of male models, observing that the sarcophagi images on strigillated sarcophagi "offer no clear answer." She found many female portraits depicting women who "have authority in their own right," but despite the popularity of muses and the Christian *orans* as powerful female role models, normative male iconography was still a powerful force: "Images of the couple fell back on traditional distinctions: men were usually the only ones to hold a scroll, and women were still sometimes shown in feminine, Venus-style dress."[125]

SOLO PORTRAITS WITH SPEECH GESTURES: SUMMARY OF OUTCOMES

This study hypothesized that all solo male and female portraits on Christian sarcophagi have an equal chance of being shown with a speech gesture. If this hypothesis is correct, one would expect solo female portraits to be proportionate to solo male portraits with this gesture. Of sixty solo female non-*orans* portraits, twenty-two were depicted with a speech gesture. Of thirty-five solo male non-*orans* portraits, eleven were depicted with a speech gesture (see table 6.12). Appropriate mathematical testing revealed no statistically significant difference in the proportions of solo male and female depictions shown with a speech gesture (see appendix G).

Table 6.12: Adult Portraits with Speech Gestures by Gender
All orans *portrait figures are excluded since by definition they do not have a possibility of speech gesture. (See appendix G for listing of images.)*

Type of Speech Depiction	Number
Couple: female with speech gesture	5
Couple: male with speech gesture[126]	22
Solo female with speech gesture[127]	**22**

125. Ibid., 142. It is worth noting, however, that women are depicted with scrolls in a number of Christian couple portrayals. See chapter 7 and figures 7.4 and 7.6.
126. Includes eight "partial" (two fingers holding top of scroll).
127. Includes two "partial" (two fingers holding top of scroll).

Solo male with speech gesture[128]	11
Male child with speech gesture	3
Uncertain identity	5

SOLO PORTRAITS WITH BOTH SCROLL AND SPEECH GESTURES: SUMMARY OF OUTCOMES

Since there were so many portrait reliefs in which the deceased was shown with both a scroll and a speech gesture, it seemed important to take a closer look at these scroll-speech portrayals. We hypothesized that all male and female portraits on Christian sarcophagi have an equal chance of being shown with both a scroll and a speech gesture. If this hypothesis is correct, one would expect solo female portraits shown with both a scroll and a speech gesture to be proportionate to solo male portraits with this configuration. Of sixty solo female non-*orans* portraits, twenty contained both scroll and speech configurations. Of thirty-five non-*orans* solo male portraits, nine contained both scroll and speech configurations (see tables 6.5 and 6.13). While solo female non-*orans* portraits were 1.3 times as likely as solo male non-*orans* portraits to contain both scroll and speech configurations, appropriate mathematical tests revealed no statistically significant difference in the proportions of solo male and solo female portraits with both a scroll and speech gesture (see appendix H).

Table 6.13: Adult Portraits with Both Scroll/*Capsa* and Speech Gestures by Gender[129]
(See appendix H for listing of images.)

Type of Depiction	Number
Couple: female with both scroll/*capsa* and speech gesture	3
Couple: male with both scroll/*capsa* and speech gesture	22

128. Includes one "partial."
129. By definition, *orans* have both hands extended, so there were no combination scroll and speech portrayals on *orans* figures. Learned *orans* are so classified because they have scroll bundles or *capses* at the feet.

Solo non-*orans* female with both scroll/*capsa* and speech gesture   20

Solo non-*orans* male with both scroll/*capsa* and speech gesture   9

Unable to identify   5

BIBLICAL SCENES AND SCROLL-SPEECH ICONOGRAPHY: MORE ANALYSIS

In looking carefully at portraits with scroll-speech iconography, the quantitative analysis discussed above may risk missing the forest for the trees. A qualitative evaluation of the twenty-nine sarcophagi with scroll-speech motifs found just one of nine male portraits situated in the midst of two or more biblical scenes. Yet ten of the twenty female portraits were shown in this configuration, sometimes dramatically so (see figures 6.9, 6.10, 8.1, and 8.3). Six of the nine male portraits are minimally engaged with biblical scenes (see table 6.14). Four of the 6 are typical scroll-speech bust portrayals with only a Jonah scene (in Endymion pose).[130] Two other male portraits are on state sarcophagi in which the scroll-speech motif is found in "office" or business scenes. None of the twenty solo female portraits with scroll-speech iconography are found in office scenes, but ten are in the midst of two or more biblical scenes about which the deceased woman may be teaching or proclaiming.

Table 6.14: Iconographical context of solo portraits with scroll-speech gestures

Gender and Number of Portraits	Bust— Jonah scene	Office Scene (Nonbiblical)	Portrait amidst Two or More Biblical Scenes	Portrait with In-Facing "Apostles"	Portrait with One Biblical Scene (Not Jonah)
Male	(n=4)	(n=2)	(n=1)	(n=1)	(n=1)

130. See figure 4.15. Jonah reclining under the gourd plant was among the earliest Christian reliefs. In the absence of biblical figures (as in these examples), non-Christians may not have easily identified the deceased as a Christian owing to the popularity of the Endymion motif in Roman iconography.

(n=9)	RS 1: nos. 629 (male in mandorla), 708 (fragment), 756 (male head on bust of woman), 795 (partial lid)	RS 2: nos. 149, 428	RS 3: no. 305	Istanbul Tomb of Flavius Eutyches[131]	RS 1: no. 801 (partial lid: three in fiery furnace)
Female	(n=3)	(n=0)	(n=10)	(n=3)	(n=4)
(n=20)	RS 1: nos. 83, 629, (female on lid) 985.		RS 1: nos. 14, 25, 33, 85, 143, 176, 621, 838 RS 2: nos. 1232, 181,	RS 1: no. 982 RS 2: nos. 105, 123[132]	RS 1: nos. 147 (lid only), 221, 443 RS 2: no. 414 (Christ next to standing female with scroll and speech) RS 3: no. 436

One possible conclusion is that it can be difficult to determine whether typical Roman "authority" iconography—such as portraits with scroll and speech gestures—signifies secular authority or religious authority. A thorough examination of these twenty-nine portraits leads to the thesis that only portraits with scroll-speech iconography portrayed in the midst of two or more biblical scenes could plausibly be said to represent religious or spiritual authority. With this working hypothesis, one would expect all portraits with scroll-speech iconography to have an equal opportunity to be shown in the midst of two or more biblical scenes. Appropriate mathematical tests found no statistically significant difference between the proportion of female scroll-speech portrayals in the midst of two biblical scenes compared to the proportion of male portrayals with the same configuration. Still, it is notable that female portraits with scroll-speech iconography are 4.5 times as likely to be shown in the midst of two or more biblical scenes compared to male portraits (see appendix I).

131. Istanbul Musei: fifth-century tomb of Flavius Eutyches (male portrait holding a scroll with partial speech gesture, flanked by Peter, Paul, and two muses).
132. Portrait has both two or more biblical scenes and in-facing "apostle" motif.

Given all of the above, one wonders if solo male portraits with scroll-speech iconography without biblical scenes are more likely to signify the exercise of secular authority whereas solo portraits with scroll-speech iconography in the midst of two or more biblical scenes are more likely to signify the exercise of religious authority. Since the sample size is small, this interpretation is admittedly speculative, but it may be worth further investigation if new Christian portraits with similar motifs are discovered.

SOLO PORTRAITS WITH SPEECH GESTURES: DISCUSSION AND CONCLUSIONS

Solo portraits of Christian women with authoritative iconography such as scroll and speech gestures occur in similar proportions to solo portraits of men with this iconography. This is a surprising finding. In light of the vigorous criticism women who exercised ecclesial authority received from male church leaders, one would expect to see very few Christian women depicted with these iconic "power and status" motifs.

Figure 6.9. Early fourth-century frieze sarcophagus with full-sized standing portrait of female deceased with a codex and speech gesture with biblical scenes on both sides. See text for explanation of biblical scenes. Note in-facing "apostle" figures flank Jesus in the multiplication and entry into Jerusalem scenes, and in-facing heads flank Peter in the water miracle scene. RS 1, no. 14. Photo © Vatican Museums, Pio Cristiano, inv. 31537. All rights reserved.

Figure 6.10. Detail of fourth-century portrait of deceased woman holding a scroll with right hand in speech gesture. Note her mouth is partially open as Christ figure gazes at her. RS 1, no. 14. Photo © Vatican Museums, Pio Cristiano, inv. 31537. All rights reserved.

An investigation of all Christian portrait sarcophagi (not only the strigillated ones Huskinson studied as mentioned above) suggests that Christian women chose both scroll and speech iconography to represent a new female identity of biblical learnedness and preaching or teaching authority. It is striking that they did so in the context of churchmen who persistently evoked 1 Timothy 2:11–12, to discourage female preaching and teaching: "Let a woman learn in silence with full submission. I permit no woman to teach or to have authority over a man; she is to keep silent." Sarcophagus reliefs of women surrounded by biblical scenes, with hands in a speech gesture and holding scrolls, offer a poignant and powerful witness that male admonitions to be silent were not heeded. There is a reason. For five centuries, the wildly popular Acts of Paul and Thecla had been circulating throughout the Christian world. By the fourth century, hundreds of women and men were traveling great distances to visit Thecla's shrine in Asia Minor. Why? Thecla was a heroine, a model to early Christians, and to Christian women in particular. She taught, she baptized, and she witnessed to the Christian gospel in the public arena despite attempts to kill her for it. In Acts of Paul and Thecla, Paul commissions Thecla to "go and teach the word of God."[133] For centuries, women had pointed to Thecla's leadership as validation for their own exercise of authority on behalf of the gospel (see chapter 2). There is good reason to surmise that an unknown number of women commemorated on early Christian sarcophagi believed themselves authorized to teach and evangelize as Thecla had.

One prominent example of another woman exercising biblical authority is an early fourth-century frieze sarcophagus of a deceased woman now located in the Pio Cristiano Museum in the Vatican Museums (see figures 6.9 and 6.10).[134] This sarcophagus dates to 300–335 CE. In the portrait, the deceased woman holds a valuable codex—probably a book of Scripture—rather than a scroll. Her right hand, with the first and second fingers extended, is in a typical speech gesture. Even though the right hand has been repaired, judging from the angle of her arm and the codex in her left hand, it is clear that a speech gesture was part of the original carving, and the RS descriptor identifies it accordingly. This portrait of a deceased woman, standing in the midst of scriptural scenes with a codex, her mouth partly open,

133. Acts of Paul and Thecla 2.41 (M. R. James, *The Apocryphal New Testament* [Oxford: Clarendon, 1924], reprinted in Early Christian Writings, http://tinyurl.com/ydeofur4).

134. The Pio Cristiano Museum contains over three hundred sarcophagi and fragments that date from around 250 CE to the beginning of the fifth century CE. It is the most comprehensive collection of early Christian archaeological discoveries in the world.

and a speech gesture suggests that either she or her family wished her to be associated with the virtues of knowledge of the Scriptures and authority to proclaim or teach. The stories surrounding her are, from left to right, Peter's water miracle in jail, Peter's arrest, the vision of the prophet Ezekiel, with "Christ-Logos" raising the dead, the healing of the man born blind, the multiplication miracle, and Jesus's entry into Jerusalem.

It is notable that both Peter (arrest scene) and the prophet Ezekiel have speech gestures. Two other apparent speech gestures—Jesus's hand in the entry into Jerusalem and the left soldier in Peter's arrest scene—are later supplements and are not named as such by Deichmann though he does confirm it for the deceased woman.[135] It is apparent that a speech motif is assigned to important figures (Peter and Ezekiel) within the overall relief, as well as to our deceased Christian woman. Jesus's healing of the blind man identifies a two-finger gesture, but it is not the typical speech gesture and might be a hybrid signifying both speech and healing touch. Many biblical figures with scrolls are also apparent on this frieze, including Peter, Jesus, and an unidentified male background figure in the entry to Jerusalem scene. In-facing "apostles" are shown here around Jesus in the multiplication and Jerusalem scenes and around Peter (heads only) in the water miracle scene on the viewer's far left. The placement of these in-facing "apostles" (or male heads) around prominent New Testament figures is not insignificant and will be discussed at length below. It is touching that the Christ figure to the deceased's left actively engages her as she teaches or proclaims and as he simultaneously heals the blind man. This Christian woman is commemorated as a person with scriptural learning and authority to preach about God's miraculous power at work in Peter even as he faces arrest, and in Jesus who heals even as he faces suffering in Jerusalem.

135. RS 1, nos. 13, 14.

ANALYZING PORTRAIT MOTIFS:
IN-FACING "APOSTLE" FIGURES

An important iconographical characteristic of Christian portraits is the ubiquitous in-facing "apostle" motif found on so many sarcophagi. Christian portraits flanked with in-facing male figures include male and female *orans*, as well as portraits of both genders shown with scrolls, codices, *capses* and scroll bundles, and occasional speech gestures. An important thesis of our investigation is that this uniquely Christian iconography says something about the authoritative status of the deceased person in the center. With rare exceptions, the in-facing figures are bearded or beardless males found on both strigillated (figure 6.11) and frieze sarcophagi (figure 6.6). They also flank reliefs of Christ, both in triumphal depictions, that were dubbed "magistrate" (figure 6.12), and in biblical narratives on frieze sarcophagi, such as the multiplication of the loaves, identified as "non-magistrate" (figures 6.3 and 6.6). Roman strigillated sarcophagi often have a portrait of the deceased in a central panel while the end panels feature shepherds, male philosophers or *orans* figures. On explicitly Christian strigillated sarcophagi, the central panel is usually a portrait of the deceased or Christ, while the end panels usually contain either a male "apostle" figure or biblical scenes (figures 6.4 and 6.11). These panels are separated with wavy (strigils) or straight (fluted) lines, hence the name.

Figure 6.11. Note both in-facing "apostles" have acclaiming gestures and a scroll bundle at their feet, while the central female *orans* portrait is shown between two palm trees with a *capsa* at her feet. The palm trees evoke the biblical Susanna and paradise. Last third of the fourth century. RS 3, no. 355. France, Mouriès (Bouches-du-Rhône). Courtesy of Chateau de Servanes.

Figure 6.12. Detail of sarcophagus of Junius Bassus. Dates to 359. RS 1, no. 680. Courtesy Fabbrica di San Pietro in Vaticano.

Figure 6.13. Fragment of so-called amateur philosopher's sarcophagus or sarcophagus of Plotinus. Third century. Photo © Vatican Museums, Museo Gregoriano Profano, inv. 31537. All rights reserved.

We have already discussed several frieze sarcophagi with continuously carved biblical figures on the front and sometimes on the sides and back (figures 6.6 and 6.8). On frieze sarcophagi, in-facing figures immediately flank portraits of the deceased and are sometimes also found flanking one or several biblical figures depicted in the relief (figure 6.6). The biblical figure most frequently shown with in-facing figures is Christ, portrayed in both "magistrate" and "non-magistrate" depictions. In "magistrate" depictions, Christ is seated on a throne or standing on a mountain. He is often shown handing a scroll to Peter (but occasionally to Paul), in what is called a *traditio legis* scene, wherein Christ entrusts the tradition of the Christian Law to these apostle leaders (figure 6.12). In "non-magistrate" scenes on frieze sarcophagi, Jesus performs miracles with full size in-facing "apostle" figures, who look on from either side (figures. 6.3, and 6.9). Another biblical leader often shown with in-facing "apostles" is Peter (figure 6.9—viewer's left end), although Moses, Daniel, Abraham, and Noah also occasionally have in-facing male figures.[136] Sometimes the in-facing "apostle" iconography is simply evoked with in-facing heads rather than a full body relief. In figure 6.6, Peter's water miracle scene on the left has two small in-facing heads in the background, and in the multiplication scene, Jesus has four in-facing male figures—two heads in shallow relief as well as two full size "apostle" figures. The in-facing "apostle" figures themselves display a number of characteristics such as holding a scroll or various hand gestures including speech, acclaiming, and recommending or accompanying gestures. These were analyzed in some depth and will be discussed later.

Art historians and sarcophagus experts have varied interpretations of what the in-facing figures in Christian iconography signify. How they are named seems to be determined by what any given scholar views as their function. Jutta Dresken-Weiland sees them as "apostles," "angels," or "saints" and believes their function is to accompany the soul of the deceased (usually signified by the central *orans* figure) on its journey to the afterlife. She notes that while the bearded man with a scroll and speech gesture is easily recognized from the philosophical iconography, "no such reference can be found for the protecting and accompanying figures surrounding the *orans*."[137] She points to the prevalence of demons and angels as companions of the deceased in both the Greco-Roman and early Christian world, as well as Christian graffiti "in the *triclia* under San Sebastiano, in which Peter and Paul are invoked," as providing important context. Likewise, she observes that numerous early Christian texts allude to both the intercession of saints and the prevalence of Christian burials *ad sanctos* (near the martyrs or saints).[138] The "lack of 'paradisiacal' elements such as birds and palm trees," however, leads her to opine that

136. Partial listing: Abraham: RS 3, nos. 35, 403; Daniel: RS 1, nos. 16, 39 (note heroic naked Daniel figure is taller—embedded portrait?), 40, 44, 144; Moses: RS 1, nos. 44, 771 (vs. embedded portrait?); and Noah: RS 3, no. 427.
137. Dresken-Weiland, *Bild, Grab und Wort*, 53. Translated by Roseanne Lundberg, Verbatim Translations.
138. Ibid., 56.

the deceased is in good hands in a safe, positively defined place, but has not yet reached 'heaven' or is not in complete communion with Christ. . . . The *orans* between companions is the image of theological reflection on what is to be expected after death, how it may continue.[139]

To my knowledge, Dresken-Weiland has not addressed what the many in-facing male figures flanking Christ depictions might signify.

Janet Huskinson cautions against "ideology that may color the assessment [of the images], especially in terms of modern attributions or interpretative assumptions. . . . [Examples] of this are the snap identifications of female praying figures as 'souls,' of philosophical-looking men as 'apostles,' or of a male and female couple as necessarily 'man and wife.'"[140] Huskinson sees portraits with in-facing figures as "an effective space filler and as such gets repeated time and time again."[141] She believes this Christian iconography derives from two examples of muses on earlier Roman portrait sarcophagi. On a mid-third-century sarcophagus in the Vatican Museums, on the viewer's left, a seated female with a lyre is depicted as the ninth muse (see figure 5.12). Surrounding her are three standing muses (two in-facing) while the other five muses are also in typical standing poses across the front of the sarcophagus. On the other end, facing the seated woman, is a seated man with a scroll and an oratorical gesture.[142] In yet another late third-century example cited by Huskinson, a male figure with scroll, *capsa*, and speech gesture is portrayed as the ninth muse.[143] He stands in the center of the casket before a *parapetasma* and is flanked by standing female muses with in-facing heads.

In Huskinson's analysis, Christians changed the Roman composition of an individual flanked by two muses to a "praying woman [*orans*] between two saints."[144] She variously characterizes in-facing figures on Christian sarcophagi as "holy men," "saints," and "reverential supporters."[145] She also classifies the previously ambiguous *orans* and "Good Shepherd" reliefs as "unequivocally Christian" when

139. Ibid., 58.
140. Huskinson, "Women and Learning," 191.
141. Ibid., 200.
142. Ibid., 194, fig. 9.1.
143. Ibid., 196, fig. 9.2.
144. Huskinson, *Roman Strigillated Sarcophagi*, 228.
145. Ibid., 220–21.

depicted centrally and surrounded by biblical scenes or in-facing figures.[146] Huskinson's recent work focuses on Roman strigillated sarcophagi. She believes Christian in-facing reliefs originated on frieze sarcophagi and cites many examples of Christian strigillated sarcophagi in which the end "saint" figures acclaim central portrayals that include portrait, *orans*, or a Christ relief (figures 6.11 and 6.12). For her, flanking figures "were heavily dependent on the central image for their action and even for their *raison d'être*. Their main role was as reverential supporters."[147] In Huskinson's study of strigillated Christian sarcophagi, the male in-facing figures were "almost always depicted as bearded and middle aged without portrait features," and she finds it "quite possible" that some ancient viewers read in-facing figures in *traditio legis* portrayals as Peter and Paul.[148] Unlike Dresken-Weiland, Huskinson does not interpret these "saint" figures as accompanying the soul into the afterlife. Rather, she sees them as "omni-purpose 'holy men,' who provide a bridge between human experience and the divine by acclaiming the rule of God and by surrounding Christians, the living and the dead, with their intercessions and prayerful support."[149] To my knowledge, Huskinson has not addressed differences between what in-facing figures signify on portrait reliefs compared to Christ/Jesus portrayals.

IN-FACING "APOSTLE" MOTIFS AND AUTHORITY

Other experts in Roman and early Christian archaeology interpret Roman reliefs with in-facing male figures in ways that further nuance our understanding of Christian reliefs, particularly with regard to the authority of the central subject. Foremost among them is Felicity Harley, who suggests that a portrait portrayal on a mid-third-century Roman sarcophagus would later become iconic for Christian authority representations. For Harley, "The early Christians were neither dismissive of the 'noble inventions' of the ancients, nor hesitant in

146. Ibid., 200.
147. Ibid., 221.
148. Ibid.
149. Ibid., 222.

utilizing them for their own pictorial and educational needs."[150] She compares two images, one from a fragment of a Roman sarcophagus (the so-called sarcophagus of Plotinus or "philosopher's sarcophagus") that dates to 280 CE (figure 6.13), and the "similarly enthroned Christ" central image of the sarcophagus of Junius Bassus (figure 6.12). Her comparison leads us "to understand how a primary set of visual attributes could be used to indicate the leadership role of an individual and his learned status in the ancient world."[151] Harley points to a number of elaborate late third-century Roman sarcophagi that, like figure 6.13 above, illustrate how prominent deceased individuals were publicly recognized for valuing intellectual pursuits and philosophy. Both the iconic frontality (figure faces viewer) used in imperial monuments and "the visual symbolism associated with the philosopher," demonstrate the extent to which

> the inference of rigorous philosophical training had become essential in conveying the superior status and authority of the deceased. The prestige accorded to learning, especially philosophical learning, helped to convey the authority of the individual concerned. Christians needed to draw and did draw, on this symbolism to present their own leader in a recognizable guise: that of a figure who promised salvation through learning, but who also worked miracles.[152]

The muses flanking the central figure in the Roman sarcophagus (figure 6.13) imply a connection beyond the temporal order, although both are portraits of female members of the deceased's family, one portrayed as Polyhymnia on the viewer's right and the other portrayed as Calliope on the left.[153] The central male figure is seated on a chair with an open scroll on his lap and a scroll bundle at his feet. His body faces frontally, with legs slightly apart as he gazes thoughtfully to his right. Turning to the image of Christ (figure 6.12), we see a very similar seated frontal configuration, with an open scroll in his left hand, a rightward gaze, and what Harley calls a "gesture of instruction," in his (now broken away) right hand. Flanking the seated Christ, says Harley, are two "apostles [who] stand looking at

150. Harley, "Christianity and the Transformation," 311.
151. Ibid.
152. Ibid., 312.
153. B. Borg, *Crisis and Ambition*, 195.

him with the same intent as the philosopher's muses." She suggests Peter and Paul could be "an amalgam of muse and co-philosopher, Paul [on viewer's left] shown clasping his own scroll." Harley concludes, "Christians were, in other words, remarkably astute in their appropriation of a visual language for their own ends."[154]

Barbara Borg does not agree that the iconography of the central male in figure 6.13 is strictly that of a philosopher, because he wears elite clothing that differs markedly from the bare-chested figure on the viewer's far left whose iconography typifies the Cynic philosophical school. Instead, Borg convincingly argues that the iconography of the central figure points to his authoritative and even magisterial status: "The type of figure used for his characterization was taken not from philosophical iconography but from monarchical and magisterial representations, as a result his claim is that of an authoritative figure, possibly a magistrate."[155] Paul Zanker and Björn Ewald also analyzed the "philosopher's sarcophagus" (figure 6.14). They agree with Borg that the central figure "is wearing not the garb of the philosopher but a toga," and that "the frontal view, derived from official state art, was designed to stress his authority as the subject of this portrayal."[156] One other clue about the authority or prominence of any given figure is its frontality, that is, the extent to which it directly faces the viewer.

In this investigation, the descriptor "apostle" is used for in-facing figures because it is the term most frequently used by RS experts and because it fits well with our interpretive conclusions about what the figures signify. The aforementioned scholarly opinions about the authoritative character of in-facing figures suggest that they represent something more than "holy men" accompanying the deceased into new life. If Dresken-Weiland is correct that accompanying "saints," "apostles," and "holy men" signify protection and accompaniment in the deceased's journey to the afterlife, what can then be said about this iconography when applied to Christ? Her interpretation does not consider similar in-facing "apostles" on Christ portrayals where they appear to have a different connotation.

154. Harley, "Christianity and the Transformation," 312–13.
155. B. Borg, Crisis and Ambition, 196.
156. Zanker and Ewald, Living with Myths, 252.

As Harley and Borg suggest, iconography with "apostles" flanking Christ in magisterial representations [on a throne or mountain] point to the risen Christ's status as one with authority. But what can be said about the many in-facing "apostles" shown on non-magisterial Jesus portrayals on both frieze and strigillated sarcophagi? In these portrayals—usually scenes from the earthly life of Jesus—I suggest that flanking "apostle" figures draw the viewer's attention to Jesus, the central figure, thereby enhancing his significance and, by extension, his authority. In the same way, I contend, in-facing "apostles" draw the viewer's attention to central portraits of deceased Christians—both female and male—in order to enhance their status and authority as well.

Figure 6.14. Detail of so-called sarcophagus of "Crescens" with Peter and Paul iconography. Note center female *orans* with Peter on left (with speech gesture) and Paul on right (with a receding hairline and left hand in recommendation gesture). The small kneeling woman to the viewer's right is the healing of the woman with the flow of blood, and on the left is the miracle of Cana. First quarter of the fourth century. RS 1, no. 11. Photo © Vatican Museums, Pio Cristiano Museum, inv. 31484. All rights reserved.

Figure 6.15. Detail from mid-fourth-century columnar sarcophagus with Jesus and in-facing "apostle" figures described as Peter (on viewer's left) and Paul with a receding hairline (on viewer's right). Jesus shown with a scroll in his left hand while the right hand is in a speech gesture. Mid-fourth century. RS 1, no. 51. Photo © Vatican Museums, Pio Cristiano Museum, inv. 31499. All rights reserved.

Figure 6.16. Front of mid-fourth-century columnar sarcophagus with middle niche showing Jesus and in-facing "apostle" figures described as Peter and Paul. Biblical scenes left to right: multiplication of loaves, Peter's denial (note Peter with hand to chin in a "gesture of sorrow or apology" and Jesus with "teaching gesture" and a rooster at his feet), center scene, Cana miracle (note double in-facing figures), and healing of paralytic. RS 1, no. 51. Photo © Vatican Museums, Pio Cristiano Museum, inv. 31499. All rights reserved.

Figure 6.17. Detail of so-called sarcophagus of Stilicho: Christ shown in authoritative iconography, seated as a magistrate with codex and speech gesture and in-facing Peter and Paul. Paul is on right with high forehead and long, thin beard. Stilicho was a Roman general who twice saved the Roman Empire from certain defeat by the Goths. This frieze sarcophagus has a lid and decorations on four sides, though only the front section is shown here. This is described by the Pio Cristiano Museum as: "Christ enthroned with the Apostles; at his feet the deceased [Stilicho and his wife] adoring Christ by a lamb." About 380–400 CE. RS 2, no. 150. Photo courtesy of Basilica di S. Ambrogio di Milano.

"PETER" AND "PAUL" DESCRIPTORS FOR
IN-FACING "APOSTLE" FIGURES

A number of in-facing male figures bear what RS experts describe as "apostle" iconography. In descriptors describing the reliefs as "Peter and Paul," Paul is shown with a high forehead or receding hairline and a pointed beard, while Peter has a full head of hair and a fluffier beard (figures 6.14, 6.15, and 6.17). In other reliefs, one "apostle" may be bearded while another is beardless (figures 6.6 and 6.7), or both may be beardless (figure 6.4). Both beardless and bearded male "apostle" figures regularly appear in biblical scenes, though not always in in-facing poses. Since sarcophagus figures, especially prominent ones, were frequently revised in later centuries, it can sometimes be difficult to determine if today's artistic representations are original. Care was taken to select two examples with "Peter and Paul" iconography that, at least to my knowledge, have not been revised. One is from the early fourth century (figure 6.14) and one from the mid-fourth century (figures 6.15 and 6.16). Both were made in Rome. Together with the late fourth-century so-called sarcophagus of Stilicho (figure 6.17) these sarcophagi constitute evidence that Peter and Paul iconography appeared on Christian sarcophagi throughout the fourth century. Portrait sarcophagi with Peter-Paul iconography continued even into the fifth century. The sarcophagus of Flavius Eutyches in the Istanbul Archaeology Museums features a male portrait with scroll and speech gesture, flanked by Peter and Paul—who also hold scrolls—and two female muse figures on each end. (Even in the fifth century, non-Christian motifs appear alongside biblical figures on Christian sarcophagi.)[157] The point in examining sarcophagus iconography of Peter and Paul is to suggest that the Christian women (and some men) who chose in-facing "apostle" iconography for their memorial portraits may have done so to validate their own authority to proclaim the gospel. Who better to affirm religious authority

---

157. Gitte Lønstrup Dal Santo, "Bishop and Believers—Patrons and Viewers: Appropriating the Roman Patron Saints Peter and Paul in Constantinople," in Birk and Poulsen, *Patrons and Viewers*, 237–57. On page 249 is a photograph of the fifth century sarcophagus of Flavius Eutyches.

within Christian social networks than these two preeminent martyrs of the church in Rome?

The preceding discussion does not eliminate the possibility that in-facing "apostles" also signify to some viewers saintly intercession or accompaniment. It does suggest that these are not the only possible meanings. One of the many blessings of great art, especially great religious art, is its capacity to evoke diverse responses from intended viewers. Contemporary research has demonstrated that women were significantly more influential in the growth of early Christianity than previously appreciated. It is therefore reasonable to suggest that Christians in the fourth century chose to commemorate themselves or their loved ones as spiritually influential women (and a few men) with an authoritative iconography that befitted their ministries. This includes portraits with speech gestures, scrolls, *capses*, and other signs of learnedness such as *orans* portrayals. I submit that portraits with in-facing "apostle" figures also point to the deceased's influence and authority. This may especially be the case when in-facing "apostles" appear simultaneously with learned iconography on Christian portraits.

A LEARNED WOMAN BETWEEN TWO "APOSTLES"

Figure 6.18 is a mid-fourth-century portrait of an unidentified woman shown in a frontal position dressed in a tunic with her *palla* drawn over her head. In the RS descriptor, Deichmann tells us that while the woman's head was revised, only the outer garments of the "apostle" figures were supplemented.[158] The woman holds a scroll, and although her head turns to the right, her gaze is directed more centrally toward the viewer. Deichmann describes the male figures on each side of her as "apostles."[159] The "apostle" on the viewer's left places his arm affectionately on the woman's right arm in a gesture very similar to the wife's in a spousal portrayal (see figures 7.1 and 7.2). His longer face and pointed beard suggest iconography linked to the apostle Paul. The "apostle" on the viewer's right holds a scroll

158. RS 1, no. 80.
159. RS 1, no. 80.

in his left hand and his mantle with his right. He has a squarish head with a shorter beard, and taken together with the scroll, the relief suggests the apostle Peter. He follows the woman's gaze toward the viewer, while Paul's gaze is directed to the right. Experts in images from late antiquity tell us to pay attention to what is being evoked by the art. That these two "apostles" carefully attend to the woman with the scroll hints that she or her family wished to be remembered, at the least, as a well-respected woman who was learned in the Scriptures. Her frontal posture between two in-facing figures with head turned slightly to the right is reminiscent of the magistrate portrayal in the "philosopher sarcophagus" and of Jesus on the Junius Bassus sarcophagus. Taken together with the tenderly respectful "apostle" figures, the art suggests that she was remembered as a woman who exercised authority within her Christian community.

Figure 6.18. This deceased woman holds a scroll and is flanked by "apostles" who attend to her respectfully. This frieze was cut off the front of a strigillated sarcophagus and dates to about 350 CE. From the cemetery of San Sebastian, then in the Christian Museum of Benedict XIV (restored by B. Cavaceppi in 1757). RS 1, no. 80. Photo © Vatican Museums, Pio Cristiano Museum, inv. 31512. All rights reserved.

PORTRAITS WITH IN-FACING "APOSTLE" MOTIFS: SUMMARY OF STATISTICAL FINDINGS

All female and male portraits accompanied by in-facing "apostle" figures were examined in some depth. Hypothetically, both male and female adult portraits have an equal opportunity to be depicted with in-facing "apostle" figures. If this hypothesis is correct, one would expect male portraits with in-facing "apostle" figures to be proportionate to female portraits with the same configuration. In all cases, however, the proportion of female portraits with in-facing "apostle" portrayals dramatically exceeded male portraits at statistically significant levels. Outcomes of statistical analyses are summarized immediately below (see also appendix J).

FINDINGS FOR ALL PORTRAITS WITH IN-FACING "APOSTLE" MOTIFS

Of 156 solo female adult portraits, 73 had in-facing "apostle" figures. Of 47 solo male portraits, 10 had in-facing "apostle" figures (see table 6.15). Solo female portraits were 2.2 times as likely as solo male portraits to contain in-facing "apostle" figures. This is highly significant since the likelihood that this finding is due to chance is just 2 in 1000. Even with "probable portraits" excluded, solo female portraits were 2.13 times more likely than solo male portraits to contain in-facing "apostle" figures. The likelihood that this finding is due to chance is 1 in 100.

Table 6.15: Solo Adult Portraits with In-Facing "Apostle" Figures by Gender
(See appendix J for listing of images and statistics.)

Gender of Center Figure		Married[160]
Female	73	3 of 73
Female central—non-orans	7	
Female central—orans[161]	43	
Female central—orans "probable portrait"[162]	23	
Male	10	1 of 10
Male central—non-orans[163]	3	
Male central—orans	6	
Male central—orans "probable portrait"	1	
Couple / *dextrarum iunctio* central	3	
Female child *orans* (excludes one with in-facing parents)	1	
Male child *orans* (includes one "partial" [one side shown due to damage] and one *orans* "probable portrait")	4	
Uncertain[164]	2	

FINDINGS FOR *ORANS* PORTRAITS WITH IN-FACING "APOSTLE" MOTIFS

Of 156 solo female portraits, 66 were *orans* figures with in-facing "apostle" figures. Of 47 solo male portraits, 7 were *orans* figures with in-facing "apostle" figures (see table 6.15). For all *orans* portraits with in-facing configurations, female *orans* were 2.84 times more likely to have in-facing companion figures compared to male *orans*. Again,

160. Identified by tomb inscription.
161. Includes six artifacts in which just one in-facing "apostle" figure is visible due to damage.
162. Includes six reliefs in which just one in-facing "apostle" figure is visible due to damage.
163. Includes two male head on female torso and one "partial" (one side only due to damage). Excludes one male with in-facing muse figures.
164. RS 1, no. 748—able to identify in-facing figure but not gender or age of central figure; RS 1, no. 675—drawing and unable to determine in-facing configuration with certainty.

this is a highly significant difference since the likelihood that this finding is due to chance is less than 1 in 1000. Even when "probable portraits" are excluded, the rate of in-facing "apostle" figures on all solo female *orans* portraits significantly exceeds the rate of similar depictions on solo male *orans* portraits. In this cohort, female *orans* portraits were 2.74 times as likely to have in-facing companion figures compared to male portraits. The likelihood that this finding is due to chance is 4 in 1000.

PORTRAITS WITH IN-FACING "APOSTLE" MOTIFS: DISCUSSION AND CONCLUSIONS

Fourth-century Christians who commissioned sarcophagi with in-facing "apostle" figures were far more likely to put this iconography on solo female portraits than on solo male portraits. What could this mean? If one interprets the in-facing figures as saints who accompany the deceased into the afterlife or intercessors with the divine, it seems odd that significantly fewer male portraits display this iconography compared to female portraits. One would expect to find no significant difference between male and female commemorations depicting the deceased with holy ones accompanying them into the next life. If, however, one interprets the in-facing figures as enhancing the status and spiritual authority of the central figure, there is a plausible explanation for why this motif would be more popular with Christian women. Persistent tension about female ministerial initiative in the early church surfaces repeatedly in Christian literary sources into the fifth century (see chapters 1 and 2). To validate their own religious authority, women serving the fourth-century church may have chosen sarcophagus iconography to evoke the universally agreed upon authority of "apostle" figures. For these women, it could only help to have preeminent martyrs and apostles like Peter and Paul affirm their authority to preach and teach about the biblical scenes so gloriously displayed on their sarcophagi.

IN-FACING "APOSTLE" MOTIFS:
MORE ABOUT HAND GESTURES

Aside from speech gestures, let us briefly discuss three other hand gestures here, since they are featured in an examination of characteristics of in-facing "apostle" figures on portrait and Christ portrayals below. The first gesture is a hand outstretched to the hip level frequently made by in-facing "apostles" on portraits of the deceased, such as that of Marcia Romania Celsa discussed above (figure 6.7). Jutta Dresken-Weiland sees this as signifying "protection," "intercession," or "accompaniment."[165] I have named it as a recommendation or introduction gesture since these are the most common descriptors used by RS experts who describe the pose as *Empfehlungsgestus* (introduction)[166] or *Einführungsgestus* (recommendation).[167] Still another term is *Geleit* (escort),[168] and a related gesture is called *Gestus der Fürsprache* (intercession—literally: "speak for" gesture). All of these gestures involve hands pointing downward, sometimes directly downward, as in RS 1, no. 776, in which an "apostle" places his hand on the shoulder of a blind man in *Gestus der Fürsprache* as he presents him to Christ. Another word, *Weisegestus*, is sometimes used interchangeably with *Empfehlungsgestus*. All of which is to say that experts have differing intuitions about the gesture's significance. It is not described in early oratorical manuals, and while it appears in the Terence illustrations, it is not described therein. The exact meaning seems somewhat fluid and will be explored in what follows.

Two other hand gestures are less puzzling. What I have dubbed an "apology" gesture, the RS volumes describe as *Gestus der Betrübnis* (gesture of sorrow). On Christian sarcophagi, it is most frequently found in reliefs of Peter's betrayal and commissioning, signified by a rooster at Peter's feet (see figure 6.17).[169] This gesture is found in the *Terence* illustrations, and Aldrete explains that the open palm to face

165. Dresken-Weiland, *Bild, Grab und Wort*, 53. Translated by Roseanne Lundberg, Verbatim Translations.
166. As in descriptor for RS 3, no. 37.
167. RS 3, no. 75.
168. RS 3, no. 57.
169. See also RS 1, nos. 40, 42, 376, and others.

gesture derives from Roman oratory and theatre actors. He describes it variously as a gesture of humility (orators) or of apology, modesty, or regret (actors).[170] The last gesture to be considered is the simplest, the gesture of acclamation. It probably derives from a common first-century Roman oratorical gesture denoting adoration or invocation wherein a front-facing figure stretches out "both arms toward the person or object of veneration."[171] On Christian sarcophagi just one arm or hand is extended, usually toward Christ, but occasionally to the Christian deceased (see figures 6.11 and 6.12).

IN-FACING "APOSTLE" CHARACTERISTICS: CHRIST PORTRAYALS COMPARED TO PORTRAITS OF THE DECEASED

Table 6.16: Characteristics of In-Facing "Apostle" Figures on Adult Portraits Compared to Similar Christ Portrayals
(See appendix K for listing of images of Christ with in-facing male figures.)

Central Figure	Total	In-Facing Learned (with Scroll, *Capsa*, Etc.)	"Apostle" or "Peter and Paul"	Recommend or Introduction Gesture	Speech Gesture	Acclaim Gesture
Christ–Magistrate Central Figure[172]	48	31	38	4	10	28
Non–Magistrate Christ Central[173]	118	45	69	6	14	19

170. Aldrete, *Gestures and Acclamations*, 62.
171. Ibid., 9–10, 13.
172. Includes portrayals of central Christ figure seated on chair, standing on mountain, or in otherwise elevated posture portrayed with two in-facing "apostle"/companion figures. Over half of these (26 of 48) are *traditio legis* scenes in which Christ is handing a scroll to either Peter (20 times) or Paul (3 times) or both (once).
173. These tombs have portrayals of non-elevated Christ with in-facing figures. Consequently, this iconography is more similar to that of portraits with in-facing figures.

All Christ Central[174]	166	76	107	10	24	47
Percentage		*46%*	*64%*	*6%*	*14%*	*28%*
Female Non-Orans *Portrait*	7	2	3	1	4	1
Female Orans *Portrait*	43	17	34	18	9	4
Female Orans: *"Probable Portraits"*	23	11	12	7	5	3
All Female Central	73	30	49	26	18	8
Percentage		*41%*	*67%*	*36%*	*25%*	*11%*
Male Non-Orans *Portrait*	3	2	2	0	1	0
Male Orans *Portrait*	6	4	5	2	1	1
Male Orans: *"Probable Portrait"*	1	1		1	1	
All Male Central	10	7	7	3	3	1
Percentage		*70%*	*70%*	*30%*	*30%*	*10%*

Similarities and differences between portraits of deceased Christians with in-facing "apostle" figures and portrayals of Christ with in-facing "apostle" figures (see table 6.16) were then investigated. There were 166 examples of Christ with in-facing "apostle" figures compared to 73 female portraits and 10 male portraits with this configuration. This suggests that the in-facing "apostle" motif was similarly

174. Four artifacts were severely damaged and were not included here. The 166 artifacts examined had companion figures with one or more identifiable characteristics as listed. The in-facing "apostle" portrayal was found in 60 multiplication scenes with 25 noted in other biblical stories. In addition, Christ was not infrequently shown with unidentified in-facing figures in the background (25 portrayals), or sometimes with heads only (16 portrayals). For an example of the latter, see figure 6.6 (RS 1, no. 6: note two pairs of in-facing figures—one just heads—in multiplication scene) and figure 6.8 (RS 3, no. 37). For an example of the former, see figure 7.13 (RS 1, no. 13).

applied to both Christ and to deceased Christians and presumably functioned similarly with regard to the central figure. To determine if the in-facing "apostle" motif did function similarly in the two cohorts, specific characteristics of in-facing figures were then examined. Each in-facing "apostle" on all female and male portraits was examined for the presence or absence of the following:

a. Learnedness: in-facing figure depicted with a scroll or *capsa* (figure 6.18)
b. RS describes in-facing companion figure as "apostle" or "Peter and Paul" (figure 6.15)
c. In-facing figure shown with a recommendation or introduction gesture (figure 6.7)
d. In-facing figure has a speech gesture (figure 6.14)
e. In-facing figure shown with an acclaiming gesture (figure 6.11)

In-facing "apostles" on Christ-central portrayals were also examined for these five characteristics. Christ portrayals were further subdivided into "all Christ portrayals" (n=166) and "non-magistrate" Christ portrayals (n=118). The latter excluded Christ shown on a throne or a mountain with in-facing figures, often described by the RS as Peter and Paul. These are frequently *traditio legis* (transmission of the Law) scenes and typically depict Christ handing a scroll to either Peter or Paul (see figure 6.13). Non-magistrate Christ portrayals on the other hand, exhibit greater similarity to depictions of male and female central figures with in-facing "apostle" figures. These portrayals show Jesus in a miracle or healing context with in-facing "apostles" to either side or in the background (figures 6.3, 6.6, and 6.16).[175] This subdivision was created to check for possible differences between in-facing portrayals if Christ was shown as an elevated, triumphal magistrate figure or in a depiction similar to portraits of female and male deceased with in-facing companion figures. Another goal was to discover if there were differences between male and female portraits with in-facing "apostle" characteristics compared

---

175. There were many non-magistrate Christ portrayals with in-facing "apostle" figures, and I may have missed a few despite my best efforts.

to Christ-central portrayals. Appropriate statistical testing was used to detect associations between variables (see appendix K).

IN-FACING "APOSTLE" CHARACTERISTICS ON CHRIST PORTRAYALS COMPARED TO PORTRAITS OF THE DECEASED: SUMMARY OF STATISTICAL OUTCOMES

For the "all Christ" group (both magistrate and non-magistrate reliefs), there were no statistically significant associations between male, female, and Christ figures and the presence or absence of the following groups of characteristics: (a) learned (in-facing figure holds a scroll), (b) "apostle"/"Peter and Paul" descriptor, and (d) speech gesture.

Statistically significant associations were found in (c) recommendation/introduction gesture and (e) acclaiming gesture. For the recommendation/introduction gesture, there is a statistically significant association between the male, female, and Christ figures and the presence or absence of this gesture. The proportion for "all Christ portrayals" is substantially lower than the proportions for females and males. This finding indicates that in Christ-central portrayals, sarcophagi artists did not show companion figures with introduction or recommendation gestures at the same rate as in male and female central portraits. This further suggests that to the fourth-century Christians who commissioned these sarcophagi, Christ figures literally needed no introduction (by in-facing companion figures or anyone else), while male and female deceased did require introductory gestures.

For the acclaim gesture, there is a statistically significant association between the male, female, and Christ figures and the presence or absence of this gesture. The proportion for all Christ figures with in-facing acclaim gestures is substantially higher than the proportions for females and males. This finding indicates that sarcophagus artists portrayed in-facing figures with acclaiming gestures in Christ-central depictions at a higher rate than in male and female central depictions. This further suggests that to the fourth-century Christians who commissioned these sarcophagi, in-facing acclaiming gestures for Christ-central figures were more popular than for deceased male and female central depictions.

For the Christ non-magistrate group, there were no statistically significant associations between male, female, and non-magistrate Christ figures and the presence or absence of the following groups of characteristics: (a) learned (in-facing figure holds a scroll), (b) "apostle"/ "Peter and Paul" descriptor, and (e) acclaim gesture.

For the recommendation/introduction gesture (c), there is a statistically significant association between male, female, and non-magistrate Christ central figures and the presence or absence of this gesture. The proportion for non-magistrate Christ figures is substantially lower than the proportions for females and males. This finding indicates that in non-magistrate, Christ-central portrayals, sarcophagus artists did not show companion figures with recommendation gesture at the same rate as in male and female central portrayals. This further suggests that to the fourth-century Christians who commissioned these sarcophagi, non-magistrate Christ figures literally needed no introduction (by in-facing companion figures or anyone else), while male and female deceased did require them.

For the speech gesture (d), there is a statistically significant association between the male, female, and non-magistrate Christ figures and the presence or absence of the speech gesture. All three of the proportions seem somewhat different from one another. The statistical test used for this analysis is not able to indicate specific significant differences between the proportions, only that there is some association between the type and the presence or absence of the speech gesture. That all three proportions seem different from one another is at the limit of the specific information that can be determined statistically. Still, it is worth noting that the rate of female-central portrayals whose in-facing "apostles" had a speech gesture is twice that of non-magistrate Christ-central figures. Likewise, the rate of male-central figures with in-facing speech gestures was 2.5 times the rate of non-magistrate Christ figures with this gesture. This finding suggests that the fourth-century Christians who commissioned these sarcophagi were more reluctant to sculpt speaking in-facing "apostle" figures for Christ than for deceased men and women. This reluctance probably points to the respect and reverence believers had for Christ.

IN-FACING "APOSTLE" CHARACTERISTICS ON LEARNED AND NON-LEARNED PORTRAITS COMPARED WITH CHRIST PORTRAYALS

It seemed worthwhile to explore whether there were any statistically significant differences in characteristics of in-facing "apostle" figures when the central figure had learned iconography. For example, if the deceased was holding a scroll, or had a speech gesture, would the flanking "apostle" figure be more likely or less likely to have a scroll or speech gesture? To find out, in-facing "apostle" figures on all central portraits with learned female and learned male depictions were examined for the presence or absence of the five previously named characteristics. In this instance, "learned figures" were defined as central male and female depictions containing a scroll, scroll bundle, or a *capsa*. In-facing "apostle" figures on non-magistrate Christ portrayals were also examined for the presence of the same characteristics. Non-magistrate Christ portrayals were chosen for comparison because of their greater similarity to portraits of male and female central figures with in-facing "apostles" (see table 6.17). Appropriate statistical testing was applied to detect associations between variables (see appendix L).

Table 6.17: Characteristics of In-Facing Companion/"Apostle" Figures on Learned (Scroll-*Capsa*) Portraits Compared to Non-Learned Portraits and Non-Magistrate Christ Portrayals

Central Figure	Total	In-Facing Learned (with Scroll, *Capsa*, Etc.)	"Apostle" or "Peter and Paul"	Recommend or Introduction Gesture	Speech Gesture	Acclaim Gesture
Non-magistrate Christ central[176]	118	45	69	6	14	19
Percentage		*38%*	*58%*	*5%*	*12%*	*16%*
Non-learned female portrait central	39	12	30	17	10	2
Percentage		*31%*	*77%*	*44%*	*26%*	*5%*
Learned female center[177]	11	7	7	2	3	3
Percentage		*64%*	*64%*	*18%*	*27%*	*27%*
Non-learned male portrait central[178]	6	3	5	2	1	0
Percentage		*50%*	*83%*	*33%*	*17%*	*0%*
Learned male center	3	3	2	0	1	1
Percentage		*100%*	*67%*	*0%*	*33%*	*33%*

176. Non-magistrate portrayals were chosen for comparison because of their greater similarity to central male and female figures with in-facing "apostle" figures. Magistrate portrayals nearly always include Peter and Paul with a scroll and acclaiming gestures.

177. Calculations based on findings from analysis of fifty female portraits. There were no learned portrayals in the female *orans* "probable portraits" cohort.

178. Calculations based on findings from nine male portraits. There were no learned portrayals in the male *orans* "probable portraits" cohort.

For female-central depictions, there were no statistically significant associations between female learned, female non-learned, and non-magistrate Christ depictions and the presence or absence of characteristics in four of five groupings including: (a) learned (in-facing "apostle" figure holds a scroll), (b) "apostle"/"Peter and Paul" descriptor, (d) speech gesture, and (e) acclaim gesture. Statistically significant associations were found only in the recommendation/introduction gesture (c), where proportions in female learned, female non-learned, and non-magistrate Christ depictions seem to be quite different from one another. The odds that this finding was due to chance are less than 1 in 1000. The statistical test employed does not indicate specific significant differences between the proportions, just that there is an association between the type of figure and the presence or absence of the recommendation/introduction gesture. That all three proportions seem quite different from one another is all the specific information that can be determined.

Nevertheless, in this analysis, female non-learned figures were 2.4 times as likely to have "apostles" with recommendation gestures compared to female learned figures, and 8.5 times as likely to have "apostles" with recommendation gestures compared to Christ figures, whereas learned female figures were just 3.6 times as likely to have recommendation gestures compared to Christ figures. This finding leads one to ask whether the fourth-century Christians who commissioned these sarcophagi judged that female deceased with scrolls or learned iconography as being less in need of recommendation or introduction.

Owing to the very small numbers for in-facing characteristics found in male-central depictions, statistical conditions for inference were not satisfied in any of the five cases. Therefore, I report briefly on these results with the caveat that they are questionable at best. For the central-male portrait depictions, there were no statistically significant associations between male learned, male non-learned, and non-magistrate Christ depictions and the presence or absence of characteristics from the following groupings: (a) learned (in-facing companion figure holds a scroll), (b) "apostle" or "Peter and Paul" descriptor, (d) speech gesture, and (e) acclaim gesture. A statistically significant association was found only in the recommendation ges-ture cohort (c). Here, the proportion for male non-learned central figures whose in-facing "apostles" have a recommendation gesture is substantially higher than the other two proportions. Since the condi-tions for inference in this case are not satisfied, it is unwise to specu-late on what this might mean. It may be worth noting, however, that as with the learned female figures in this configuration (see above), proportionately fewer male learned figures have in-facing "apostles" with a recommendation gesture. This may suggest that any deceased, whether male or female, shown holding a scroll is less likely to be shown with "apostles" recommending or introducing him or her.

IN-FACING "APOSTLE" CHARACTERISTICS ON CHRIST PORTRAYALS AND MALE AND FEMALE PORTRAITS: DISCUSSION AND CONCLUSIONS

Figure 6.19. Stained glass window portraying Pope St. Pius X with the book of the Gospels in his left hand and his right hand in a two-fingered teaching/speech gesture. The iconography demonstrates the authoritative status the speech gesture combined with a gospel text would come to represent. Author's photograph from a Catholic church in Cleveland.

In evaluating in-facing "apostles" on deceased portraits compared to similar in-facing depictions on Christ central portrayals, perhaps the most telling observation is that there are few differences in iconographical characteristics except for an understandably higher incidence of the acclaiming gesture and a lower incidence of the recommending gesture on Christ portrayals. There were no statistically significant associations between deceased portrait portrayals and Christ-central portrayals whose in-facing figures displayed learned iconography, speech gestures, and "apostle" or "Peter and Paul" descriptors. Notably, the recommendation gesture was not entirely absent on Christ portrayals, though it did occur less frequently than in portraits of the deceased. These observations support our thesis that in-facing "apostle" figures on Christ portrayals function similarly to in-facing figures on portraits of the deceased—namely, to enhance the status and authority of the central figure, whether it be Christ or a deceased Christian.

SUMMARY

A comprehensive examination of 2119 images and descriptions in three volumes of sarcophagus artifacts related to early Christianity yielded 247 sarcophagus artifacts containing 312 Christian portraits of deceased women and men. One hundred fifty-six solo female portraits were identified compared to forty-seven solo male portraits. The likelihood that this statistically significant difference is due to chance is less than 1 in 1000. Therefore, the material remains from Christian sarcophagi strongly support contemporary sociological and literary scholars who theorize that in the early church, Christian women were of higher social status than men and substantially more influential in the Roman patronage system and domestic social networks than previously recognized.

The portrait artifacts in this study date from the mid-third century to the late fifth century, with most (88 percent) dating to the fourth century. Earlier studies of sarcophagi found in Rome had suggested that after 330 CE, Christian portraits essentially disappeared. This study included all published images of Christian sarcophagi, including those found outside of Rome. It found that over half of all Christian portrait artifacts date to after 325 CE, and that Christians used portraits on their sarcophagi into the fifth century.

Roman sarcophagus art was meant to construct the idea or the identity of the deceased person and commemorate their values and virtues. It provides important information about how early Christian women and men self-identified and about how they were viewed by their families and friends. This research analyzed specific motifs on Christian portrait sarcophagi that signify the status, influence, and authority of the deceased, including scrolls, *capses*, speech gestures, *orans* postures, and in-facing "apostle" figures. It examined couple portraits, solo portraits, and their relationships to biblical iconography. Most Christian couple portraits followed Roman iconographical conventions in showing only the male with a scroll (and often a speech gesture), signifying his place at the top of the spousal hierarchy. Experts in non-Christian Roman sarcophagi found no couple portrayals in which a learned woman (with a scroll) is represented with an unlearned man. On Christian funerary remains, however, this study found a number of portrayals of women with scrolls or speech gestures, which suggests a certain role reversal (see chapter 7). When we recall that in the early church, higher status Christian women routinely married men of lower status, it makes sense that their funerary art would sometimes reflect this reality.

Solo male and solo female portraits with scrolls and speech gestures were examined, and no statistically significant differences were found between the proportions of solo male and solo female portraits with these signs of learnedness, influence, and authority. This is surprising in the context of churchmen who repeatedly sought to discourage female preaching and teaching. It is notable that twenty Christian women were commemorated with both scroll and speech iconography, suggesting the emergence of a new female identity of biblical learnedness and teaching authority. Scroll-speech iconography would come to have enduring significance in church history into the present day. A photograph of a stained-glass window in a contemporary Catholic church in Cleveland exemplifies the authoritative status this iconography would come to represent (see figure 6.19).

Previously, some scholars of early Christian art interpreted *orans* figures primarily as souls rather than portrayals of the deceased, but contemporary scholarship cites ample evidence of portrait features on both male and female *orans* figures, with most being female. The Christian *orans* originated from standing female muse figures in Roman iconography, so they carry connotations of learnedness as well as piety. In this study, eighty-five solo portraits of female *orans* were shown without accompanying scroll or *capses*, compared to just ten solo portraits of male *orans* with the same configuration. Three of the male *orans* were originally female torsos with a male head carved over it, suggesting that in some sarcophagi workshops, the template for *orans* may have been a female figure (see chapter 7). Solo female portraits were 2.6 times as likely as solo male portraits to be depicted in an *orans*-only posture (without accompanying *capsa*). The likelihood that this difference is due to chance is less than 1000 to 1. When all Christian portrait sarcophagi were examined (including couple portraits where male scroll holders predominate), male portraits appear more likely to be depicted with scroll iconography while female portraits are more likely to be depicted as *orans* figures.

A comparison of solo male and solo female portraits with all learned motifs—specifically *orans* posture, scrolls, and *capses*—revealed no statistically significant differences between proportions of solo male portraits and solo female portraits shown with these signs of status and learnedness. Fourth-century Christians adopted and adapted the iconography of their Roman culture in commemorating both deceased women and men with scrolls, *capses*, and in *orans* postures. Both Christian women and Christian men were commemorated and idealized as persons of status, authority, learnedness, and religious devotion. When portraits were in proximity to biblical scenes, a scroll or *capsa* could also signal learnedness about the Hebrew and Christian Scriptures.

In-facing "apostle" figures on portraits of the deceased have been variously interpreted as saints, apostles, or angels who accompany the soul of the deceased into the afterlife (Dresken-Weiland), or as "effective space fillers" and "reverential supporters" (Huskinson). But since these in-facing "apostle" figures are even more prevalent on Christ reliefs, such interpretations are incomplete at best. Surely, Christ doesn't need accompanying into the afterlife. Felicity Harley believes a portrait portrayal on the "philosopher's sarcophagus," a third-century Roman sarcophagus, became iconic for how Christians represented Christ's authority. Barbara Borg convincingly argues that the iconography on the central figure of this non-Christian sarcophagus points to his authoritative, indeed magisterial, status. For both Harley and Borg, the in-facing "apostles" flanking Christ in magisterial representations point to his status as one with authority.

The many in-facing "apostles" flanking Christ in miracle reliefs on both strigillated and frieze sarcophagi serve to draw the viewer's attention to the central figure of Christ, thereby enhancing his significance and authority. A central thesis of this exploration is that that in-facing "apostles" motifs function similarly on portraits of Christians to enhance their significance and authority. In this study, solo female portraits were 2.2 times as likely as solo male portraits to contain in-facing "apostle" figures. The likelihood that this finding is due to chance is just 2 in 1000. If one subscribes to the notion that the in-facing "apostles" were meant to accompany deceased Christians in the next life, it is odd that significantly fewer male portraits display this iconography. One plausible explanation for the popularity of this motif with early Christian women is that it served to validate female religious authority at a time when churchmen were silencing women in the Christian assembly. A close comparison of five characteristics of in-facing "apostle" motifs suggests they function similarly on both Christ portrayals (n=166) and solo Christian adult portraits (n=83). Over 25 percent of Christian solo male portraits adopted the *orans* posture and in-facing "apostle" motifs so prevalent on female sarcophagi. It is instructive that authoritative (and essentially female) iconography was adapted to commemorate deceased men at a time when male church officials were chastising women for exercising religious authority.

Early Christian literary sources repeatedly cite 1 Timothy 2:11–12 in bitterly criticizing women for teaching, baptizing, and leading eucharistic meals. A study of fourth-century portrait motifs on Christian sarcophagi reveals that women were remembered as exercising significant ecclesial authority—with its corresponding status and power—or these iconic motifs would not have been chosen to signify female role models idealized by early Christians. This investigation of portraits on Christian sarcophagi validates Janet Tulloch's prescient observation, "unlike the early Christian literary tradition, in which women are largely invisible, misrepresented, or omitted entirely, female figures in early Christian art play significant roles in the transmission of the faith."[179]

179. Tulloch, "Art and Archaeology," 302.

7.

More Portraits on Christian Sarcophagi

This chapter examines portraits of both couples and children, as well as selected characteristics of solo male portraits. We will also take a look at several sarcophagi that appear to have portraits embedded within scenes from the Hebrew and Christian Scriptures. Until recently, embedded portraits were thought to be nonexistent on Christian sarcophagi. The implications for understanding female iconography in each of the aforementioned portrait types will also be addressed.

PORTRAITS OF COUPLES

Excellent examples of double register Christian sarcophagi with central portrait *clipei* of married couples can be found in the Vatican's Pio Cristiano Museum. In figure 7.1, the center *clipeus* shows a married couple in a typical pose with the male holding a scroll with both hands and what is probably a speech gesture. He wears an expensive *contabulata* toga (sash across his chest) while the woman has a partial veil over an individualized hairstyle. Both faces are unfinished. In addition to the *clipeus*, we find a front facing female *orans* between "apostles" on lower left of register. The face of the female *orans* is also unfinished. The upper register contains biblical scenes starting from the left with the multiplication of the loaves. This is followed by what is called a "rooster scene" in which Peter's commissioning and betrayal are remembered simultaneously (note that Peter has his hand to his chin in a "gesture of sorrow," which frequently appears in this vignette).[1] The "rooster" scene is a popular motif on early Christian sarcophagi. Some suggest this is because not every Christian was brave enough to accept martyrdom during the Diocletian persecutions. Jesus's forgiveness of Peter despite his denial would be a healing balm to many a struggling believer. Just in front of the *clipeus* is a relief of Moses receiving the law. Biblical scenes to the right of the *clipeus* in the upper register include the sacrifice of Isaac, the healing of the blind man, and the raising of Lazarus with Mary of Bethany kneeling at Jesus's feet.

Figure 7.1. This elaborate double-zoned sarcophagus shows a married couple in the central *clipeus*. The man is in an expensive *contabulata* toga and the woman has a distinctive hairstyle and clothing. Both faces are unfinished. Note the female *orans* (whose face is also unfinished) with in-facing "apostle" figures in lower register on viewer's left. See text for description of scriptural scenes. Early fourth century. RS 1, no. 39. Photo © Vatican Museums, Pio Cristiano Museum, inv. 31546. All rights reserved.

Starting at the lower left register, a female *orans* stands between two "apostle" figures whose hands are in "recommendation" gestures. To

1. The *Repertorium* volumes often describe this gesture as one of sorrow *Gestus der Betrübnis* (see, for example, RS 1, nos. 40, 42, 376, and others. According to Gregory Aldrete (*Gestures and Acclamations*, 62), the open palm to face gesture derives from Roman oratory and play actors. He describes it variously as a gesture of humility (orators) or of apology, modesty, or regret (actors).

her right, we find the arrest of Peter (note Peter's right hand in a speech gesture). This is followed by three personifications of spring, summer, and winter. While somewhat unusual on a Christian sarcophagus, the seasonal personifications supply evidence that Christians continued to use popular scenes from Greco-Roman iconography. To the right, the naked Daniel is shown in a standardized relief as an *orans* flanked by two lions and two in-facing bearded male figures. These are frequently identified as the prophet Habakkuk and an angel. On mythological Roman sarcophagi, nakedness signaled the heroic status of the mythic figure, in this case applied to the biblical Daniel. Then follow the miracle at Cana, the healing of the paralytic, and Peter's water miracle baptizing his jailers. In every scene but one (multiplication of the loaves and fish), Jesus is shown holding a scroll, while Peter holds a scroll in every scene in which he appears. Jesus, Peter, and other biblical figures frequently carry scrolls since it was important to early Christians to signal the status and learnedness of their spiritual leaders. Jesus holds a wand in the multiplication and Cana scenes while Peter holds one in the jail scene (lower register right). As we have seen, for Romans, miraculous events are related to magicians or wonder workers, hence the wand.

This elaborately crafted sarcophagus may originally have been planned to commemorate both spouses, although the female *orans* suggests a special commemoration for a woman. The *orans* next to biblical figures suggests that, besides being a devoted Roman *materfamilias*, the deceased spouse is also learned in Scripture and recommended to us, the viewers, by two in-facing apostle figures sculpted with physiognomies reminiscent of Peter on the left and Paul (with a receding hairline) on the right.

Portrait busts of a couple in a central *clipeus* or shell are often seen on the front of Roman sarcophagi, both non-Christian and Christian (figure 7.2). Typically, the male is shown in the foreground on the viewer's right, holding a scroll with one hand. Often, the forefinger and middle finger of the other hand are extended in a typical oratorical or speech gesture and sometimes touching the end of the scroll. The woman is shown in the background and on the viewer's left. Her left arm is placed affectionately around the man's shoulder with the right arm extending across her body to touch her spouse's elbow. Portraits of this type normally commemorate a deceased spouse, not necessarily the couple. On Roman sarcophagi, the coffin itself was often destined for the woman, so the man is usually the patron.[2]

Figure 7.2. Close-up portrait of a *clipeus* couple. The woman is partially veiled and wears a tunic, a *palla* drawn over her head, and a jeweled necklace. Her left hand extends affectionately over to her spouse's left shoulder and her right stretches over his chest as if to acclaim him. The man wears an expensive toga and holds a scroll in his left hand with his right in a typical oratorical or speech gesture. RS 1, no. 40. Photo © Vatican Museums, Pio Cristiano Museum, inv. 31551. All rights reserved.

Another common married-couple depiction is the *dextrarum iunctio* marriage scene in which the standing pair join right hands (figure

2. Birk, *Depicting the Dead*, 25.

7.6). Non-Christian *dextrarum iunctio* scenes often depict the goddess Juno or, some say, Concordia in the center background and a small figure standing in the center foreground representing Hymenaeus, the Greek god of the wedding. On Christian sarcophagi, the deceased couple is also frequently shown worshipping at the feet of a triumphant Christ who occupies the center front (figure 6.17). As noted in chapter 6, male and female figures that are often (but not always) married couples may appear separately on lids or other parts of the sarcophagus.

ANALYZING MALE-FEMALE COUPLE PORTRAITS

Table 7.1: Male-Female Couple Christian Portraits
(For listing of images, see appendix M.)

Type and Characteristics of Male-Female Portrait	Number
Man and woman in same clipeus	28
Each in separate *clipei, parapetasma* on lid or casket portrayal	8
Dextrarum iunctio (marriage iconography)	8
Married couple worshipping at base of triumphant Christ	11
Other couple portrayals (end figures or standing figures)	8
Embedded couple/family portrayal (RS 3, no. 323)	1
Total male-female couple portraits[3]	**64**
Unusual male-female configurations	
Female-male role reversal?[4]	7
Possible mother-son rather than married portrayal? (male head appears younger and/or smaller than female's)[5]	8

3. Includes artifacts with one male-female couple portrait in either a *clipeus* or a *parapetasma*, *dextrarum iunctio* portrayals, separate male-female *clipei* on one lid, and standing end figures. Also includes male-female couple portraits found in family and "multiple portrait" tombs.
4. RS 1: nos. 120, 811; RS 2: no. 12, 123, 148; RS 3: no. 51, 77.
5. RS 1: nos. 112, 385 650; RS 2: no. 108; RS 3: nos. 40, 41, 81, 555.

A total of sixty-four male-female couple portrait commemorations were found on Christian sarcophagus artifacts and categorized accordingly (see table 7.1). Interestingly one commemoration was an embedded family portrayal (see figure 7.16).[6] Included in "other couple portrayals" are male and female end figures, male-female couple portraits found in "family reliefs" (more than two portrait figures including a child), and "multiple portrait" reliefs that have both a male and female in a standardized couple depiction as well as individualized solo portraits. Although RS experts nearly always describe the male in couple portraits as a husband, there are a number of reliefs in which the beardless head of the male figure holding a scroll appears smaller and younger than the female (figures 7.3 and 7.4). This apparent incongruity suggests some male-female pairs were mother-son portrayals with the young man seen in an idealized pose. Such depictions were still counted as couple portrayals in this study, however, since the topic requires further exploration. It is interesting that the other portrayals on the Arles sarcophagus prominently feature biblical women (RS 3, no. 41—figures 6.2 and 7.4). Susanna appears twice (see figure 6.2), and two women appear in an Exodus scene in the lower register wherein Miriam leads a young boy as well as the Israelites across the Reed Sea. All of which is to say that these may be clues that this was not a married couple at all but a mother who witnesses to biblical justice and salvation for herself and her son. This question deserves further investigation.[7]

Stine Birk's study of learned females with portraits on Roman (non-Christian) sarcophagi found no reliefs that "show a learned woman represented with a non-learned man; this combination does not exist."[8] Yet, I found seven distinctly unconventional marital portrayals on early Christian sarcophagi that suggest a certain role reversal. Six of the seven involve women holding scrolls in couple portrayals. For example, an early fourth-century sarcophagus lid in the Pio Cristiano Museum at the Vatican Museums depicts a male and female in front of a *parapetasma*, with the female holding a scroll with a

---

6. RS 3, no. 32.
7. See note 96 on table 6.9 for listing of six possible mother-son portrayals.
8. Birk, *Depicting the Dead*, 79.

speech gesture while the male is shown as an *orans* figure (figure 7.5).[9] The obscure Greek inscription asks God to remember the woman, Eugenies, who died at fifty-seven years of age after forty-one years of marriage, leaving four surviving children. While the inscription does not say who commissioned the monument, it may have been the surviving children who depict their father as a deceased *orans*.[10] An early fourth-century sarcophagus at the Camposanto in Pisa shows a man and woman in one *clipeus* (RS 2, no. 12). Both are shown with a scroll and a speech gesture, but in a significant reversal, the woman is shown on the viewer's right (unfortunately no image is available). In conventional *clipeus* couple configurations, the woman is always shown on the viewer's left (see figures 7.1 and 7.2). Dresken-Weiland hypothesizes that the Camposanto pair was not married but kinfolk.[11] Another possibility is that they were ministerial leaders, with the woman the more prominent of the duo. In two other marital portrayals, one in the Rome's Musei Capitolini (RS 1, no. 811) and the other in Perugia (RS 2, no. 123), the female is depicted with both a scroll and a speech gesture whereas the male is shown only with a scroll or codex but no speech gesture. Two other sarcophagi in Tolentino (RS 2, no. 148) and Arles, France, (RS 3, no. 77) each have separate portrait busts of a married couple. On each, the female figures hold scrolls, as do the male figures. The male figures also have a speech gesture signifying that the usual spousal hierarchy remains intact in these portrayals, at least in part.

9. RS 1, no. 120.
10. I am indebted to Carolyn Osiek for translation and interpretation help for this puzzling Greek inscription. She notes that a Greek epitaph in fourth-century Rome is unusual. It suggests the deceased were recent immigrants and wealthy enough to purchase a nice sarcophagus. Email to author, October 23, 2016.
11. RS 2, no. 6.

Figure 7.3. In this *clipeus* relief fragment, the male head appears noticeably smaller than the female's, leading one to wonder whether it could be a mother-son portrayal with the son in an idealized role. The sacrifice of Isaac scene is below the *clipeus* and may suggest a mother's grief and belief in salvation for her son (see "Sarah" in table 7.4). Later fourth century. RS 1, no. 112. Photo © Vatican Museums, Pio Cristiano Museum, inv. 31567. All rights reserved.

Figure 7.4. A *clipeus* relief on a double register sarcophagus in which the male head appears noticeably smaller than the female's, leading one to wonder whether it is a mother-son portrayal with the son in an idealized role. Late fourth century. RS 3, no. 41. Courtesy Musée de L'Arles Antique, Sarcophage de la chaste Suzanne.

Figure 7.5. This unusual couple configuration depicts the deceased woman, Eugenies, shown with a scroll and speech gesture to left of an adult male who is shown as an *orant*. Both faces are individualized. Early fourth-century sarcophagus lid. RS 1, no. 120. Photo © Vatican Museums, Pio Cristiano Museum, inv. 31586. All rights reserved.

Figure 7.6. The second frame from the right is a *dextrarum iunctio* (joining of right hands) or marriage scene. Note the woman has a speech gesture in both central scenes while the man does not. Side panels (not shown here) are explicitly Christian scenes (multiplication of the loaves and scene of Peter reading). Late fourth-century sarcophagus. RS 3, no. 51. Musée de l'Arles Antique: Sarcophage des Dioscures, MDAA. © M. Lacanaud.

In yet another Arles sarcophagus (figure 7.6), the two female portraits are taller than either male portrait and the woman alone is shown with speech gestures. This late fourth-century sarcophagus was Roman made for a high-ranking patron in Arles, France, which was a prominent provincial Roman city. Some experts believe this family was "at least of the equestrian order" while another suggests the young soldier's distinctive footwear (*calcei patricii*) even points to senatorial status.[12] The two central scenes portray two separate events in the lives of a married couple. The left center scene is a farewell configuration in which a regal woman with head partially veiled and an individualized hairstyle places her right hand on the shoulder of a beardless young man in soldier's clothing and elite footwear (*calcei patricii*). The woman wears elegant clothing with a high-waisted belt, perhaps evoking the muse iconography frequently seen on Roman sarcophagi. Neither figure holds a scroll, but the woman's left hand has a speech gesture. This vignette may well commemorate a young wife's farewell to her equally young equestrian husband as he rode off to battle. The next vignette (on the viewer's right) commemorates a *dextrarum iunctio* marriage scene, but the usual background figure of Juno or Concordia has been replaced with a scroll held by the man. Likewise, the small Hymenaeus figure often seen between the couple

12. RS 3, nos. 37, 38.

in non-Christian marriage depictions has now become a scroll bundle. In this second scene, the man is bearded, dressed in an elaborate toga and sandals, and carries a scroll in his left hand. An equally elaborate head covering partially conceals the woman's distinctive hairstyle, and she is again shown with a speech gesture. It is significant that in each of these two central scenes, the female figure is taller than the male figure and is shown with a speech gesture while the man is not.

On each of the end scenes, the heroic nakedness of Dioscuri demigods Castor and Pollux—the Greek gods of horsemanship—serve to elevate the status of the departed soldier spouse. Matching the central male figures, the left horseman is beardless, and the right bearded. It could also be that this sarcophagus commemorates both a husband and a soldier son, but this cannot be known with certainty. On both narrow sides (ends) of this casket, in shallow relief, are two Christian scenes—the multiplication of the loaves and a scene described as Peter reading before his arrest (not pictured). The unusual combination of both Christian and non-Christian themes on the same sarcophagus is relatively rare but not unknown.[13] In some cases, the scriptural end scenes were sculpted later when a Christian reused a pagan sarcophagus.[14] One hint that a Christian may have originally commissioned this Arles sarcophagus is that the scroll bundle at the couple's feet (perhaps symbolizing the Christian Scriptures) has replaced the pagan deity Hymenaeus often found in *dextrarum iunctio* iconography.

This sarcophagus suggests a "mixed marriage" between a Christian woman and a pagan man as described by Peter Lampe at the conclusion of chapter 2. Lampe found that in the fourth century most Christian aristocrats were women, while the men in the family remained pagan until their deathbeds. Therefore, a Christian aristocratic wife is probably the patron of this sarcophagus. She chose pagan funerary themes that reflected the virtues and values of her equestrian husband, taking care to retain understated Christian elements, including scriptural scenes on the side of the sarcophagus, and replacing a pagan

13. RS 1, no. 777 and RS 2, no. 90.
14. For example, RS 1, no. 777. See Huskinson, *Roman Strigillated Sarcophagi*, table 9.1. Huskinson notes that the shallow Christian carvings on the sides were added later.

marriage god with a scroll bundle. The iconic characteristics of this interesting sarcophagus, as well as the other unconventional marital configurations previously identified, provide evidence that it was not unknown for a Christian married woman to exercise influence and authority beyond expected gender roles.[15]

THE PROJECTA CASKET

Figure 7.7. Lid of silver toiletry case used by an elite woman for her bath. It has a Christian inscription: "Secundus and Projecta, may you live in Christ." The central *tondo* of this unconventional relief shows a woman with a scroll while the man has none. Mid- to late fourth century. © The Trustees of the British Museum. All rights reserved.

One last example of a married couple portrait in which a woman is depicted in an unconventional way is not found on a funerary relief but on a richly decorated carrying case used by an elite woman to

15. Janet Tulloch (email to author, May 18, 2017) offers another plausible interpretation of figure 7.6: "As a Roman materfamilias with a husband and possible son off to war, this behavior would have been expected of her and her authority was legitimized in the contract [scroll held by the male] signed at the time of marriage."

transport toiletry items for her bath. Elaborate artwork adorns five sides of the beveled, hinged lid and four sides of the matching rectangular pyramid container below. On top of the lid, a medallion held by two cupids encircles a married couple (figure 7.7). On the viewer's left, a bejeweled woman with an elaborately braided hairstyle holds a scroll with both hands. To her right, her richly dressed husband is shown with neither a scroll nor a speech gesture but with his right hand extended across his chest. Even though Venus, the Roman goddess of love, is embossed immediately below Projecta's name, the case bears a Christian inscription: "Secundus and Projecta, may you live in Christ."[16] This silver casket with golden detail dates to the mid- to late fourth century and is one of more than sixty pieces found in 1793 in the remains of a private Roman house on Rome's Esquiline Hill. According to British art historian Jaś Elsner, it is uncertain whether the Christian inscription is original or whether it was added by a later owner, so it is "impossible to say with certainty" that the woman and man actually represent Secundus and Projecta.[17] Still, Elsner notes that allusions to Venus were not unknown in Christian contexts in the fourth century. In 398, a public speech calls upon the beautifying Venus to bless and bring fruitfulness to the union of the young Christian emperor Honorius and Maria, the daughter of general Stilicho.[18]

In 2003, Elsner published an article detailing his own efforts "to examine the casket's extraordinarily rich iconographic programme in relation to its presentation of a woman's role and place in elite society at the end of the fourth century."[19] He finds the motifs on the casket to be "resolutely female centered" because the art clearly indicates a parallel between the central female figure and the figure of Venus, both of whom are shown holding mirrors. For Elsner, the iconography's purpose is in part "to help achieve what its complex iconography advertises—namely the beautification of a woman for her husband's delight. . . . Like the casket itself, the adorned woman is

---

16. SECVNDE ET PROIECTA VIVATIS IN CHRISTO.

17. Jaś Elsner, "Visualising Women in Late Antique Rome: The Projecta Casket," in *Through a Glass Brightly: Studies in Byzantine and Medieval Art and Archaeology*, ed. Chris Entwistle (Oxford: Oxbow, 2003), 23.

18. Ibid., 32.

19. Ibid., 24.

a carefully crafted object of display—a luxury ornament for her husband's possession and pleasure."[20]

It is puzzling that while Elsner notices that the woman is carrying a scroll, it plays no part in his otherwise brilliant interpretation of what the iconography might have symbolized to late antique women and men. He draws interesting parallels between the modest Roman *matrona* ideal with the equally ideal sexual partner symbolized by Venus. Unfortunately his interpretation is incomplete, and this leads inevitably to some overdrawn (not to say woefully androcentric) reflections: "The iconography of the casket is fundamentally woman and marriage-centered, though the referent is the man for whom all this is being prepared. This ties the imagery in the principal social context available to women in late antiquity . . . namely, the process of marriage."[21] Although Elsner assumes the casket was "probably commissioned and paid for by men," he finds he cannot discount some female influence. But for him that influence arises from the desires of the "ruling male," which are reinterpreted, transformed, and come to represent the desires of the household's women.[22] Describing the couple portrayal on the casket's lid, he views the man as "ruling" alongside his wife while the "arrangements for that dominion . . . lie properly with the servants and their mistress on the casket's base."[23]

One is led to wonder to what extent a fourth-century married Christian woman might have valued being a beautiful, sexually desirable partner for its own sake and why the primary referent would only be the man. The unusual marital portrayal of a woman holding a scroll while the man carries none at least opens up the possibility that a woman may have commissioned this toiletry case for herself or for a female loved one. Leaving that question aside, it seems clear that whoever commissioned the toiletry case was careful to portray the female partner as a learned woman whose status may even have exceeded that of her husband. This interpretation undercuts the notion that, on the Projecta casket at least, the husband was "ruling"

20. Ibid., 30.
21. Ibid.
22. Ibid., 31.
23. Ibid.

over his wife. It also fits with the well-documented fact that higher status Christian women frequently married men of lower status in the early church.[24] Finally, the unusual "role reversal" iconography may supply additional evidence that the Projecta casket was commissioned by a Christian since in similar portrayals on non-Christian sarcophagi, the man always holds a scroll while the woman never does.[25] Sadly lost in Elsner's interpretation is any notion that Projecta herself may have valued education and learning equally to beauty and sexual desirability. Is it such a stretch to imagine that even in the fourth century a wealthy Christian wife such as Projecta may have seen herself as beautiful, sexy, educated, and powerful rather than only a sexual object for her husband? The self-identity of elite Christian married women—like that of their non-Christian sisters—had been evolving for many generations and the complex iconography on the Projecta casket may be an important witness to this evolution.

PORTRAITS OF CHILDREN

In her review of non-Christian, Roman-made sarcophagi, Stine Birk identified eighty portraits of children, so identified if "either an inscription or a portrait informs us that it is a commemoration of a child." If the inscription said the child was less than nine years of age, the portrait was classified as belonging to a child. If there was no inscription, Birk applied characteristics such as a round face, "voluminous cheeks," a protruding mouth, and short hairstyle to identify the portrait as a child's. Since virtually all children are portrayed with short hairstyles, it can be difficult to distinguish the sex.[26] In twenty-eight (of eighty) non-Christian child portraits, the child was depicted as a learned figure with a scroll.[27] This may at first seem surprising except that child funerary motifs were "chosen in order to fulfill the expectations of the adults."[28] Children's sarcophagi, like all sarcophagi, were also meant to enhance the status of the family, and "an

---

24. Lampe, *From Paul to Valentinus*, 121.
25. Birk, *Depicting the Dead*, 79.
26. Ibid., 160, 198.
27. Ibid., 198.
28. Ibid., 157.

obvious function of children's sarcophagi was that they were put up to construct the identity of the family as much as to commemorate the child."[29] When a child is commemorated as a learned figure, the purpose was to show parental aspirations for that child's future:

> The learned boy or child-philosopher can, therefore, be read as an allegory of the parent's hopes for their son's future. These hopes should be interpreted more in terms of status than a future profession. Through this visual construction of memory, the parents present an ideal child, and take the opportunity to promote themselves.[30]

Birk reports finding four girls portrayed with scrolls, although boy portraits with scrolls are far more frequent.[31]

This investigation found a total of twenty Christian portraits of children. Birk's criteria for identifying child portraits as described above were used, along with the German designation *Kind* (child) sarcophagus as classified by RS authors. Sex identifications found in the RS volumes were also added to the criteria. A total of thirteen Christian portraits of boys and seven Christian portraits of girls were identified. Two figures were "probable *orans*" portraits, one male and one female (see table 7.2).

Table 7.2: Individual Child Portraits by Gender[32]
(See appendix C for listing of images.)

Female	No.	Male	No.
Female child portraits (*includes four portrait* orans *figures*)	6	Male child portraits (*includes four portrait* orans *figures*)	12[33]
Female child *orans* "probable portrait"	1	Male child *orans* "probable portrait"	1
Grand total female child portraits	7	Grand total male child portraits	13

29. Ibid., 158.
30. Ibid., 168.
31. Ibid.
32. Artifact designated as "*kinder*" (children) sarcophagus in RS or listed as under nine years old on inscription, unless portrait has adult features, in which case it is classified as such (RS 1, no. 664).
33. Includes one male child portrait *orans* with male head over a female body.

Table 7.3: Child Learned Figures[34]
(See appendix D for listing of images.)

Type of Learned Portrait	Scroll	*Capsa* or Scroll Bundle	Total
Male child	6	1[35]	7
Female child	0	0	0

Seven portraits had learned elements in which the deceased child was portrayed with a scroll or *capsa* (see table 7.3). It is notable that none of the female child portraits were depicted with a scroll. One wonders if this is a variation of the expectation that only males uphold the status of the family and therefore only boy children would be portrayed in a learned posture. Figure 7.8 shows the *clipeus* detail of a mid-fourth-century sarcophagus of a male child now housed at the Pio Cristiano Museum. The child has short hair and is holding a scroll in his left hand while his right hand has a speech gesture. The scroll and speech gesture mimic the typical male status iconography found in married couple *clipei* and suggests the elevated status of his family and the stature his parents hoped he would attain as an adult. Immediately beneath the *clipeus* is the scene of the three wise ones from the east visiting Mary and the Christ child. The visit of the magi seems to be a popular scene for children's coffins. Since the iconography on child portraits is essentially a reflection of parental aspirations, they cannot be said to necessarily reflect actual role model or self-identification values of the child itself. For this reason, I did not include child portraits in my overall analyses.

---

34. Under nine years old on inscription or designated as *kinder* sarcophagus.
35. This is a male child *orans* "probable portrait" figure.

Figure 7.8. Detail of central clipeus from the tomb of a male child. Notice that the child holds a scroll and has a speech gesture, reflecting the aspirations of his parents. Mid-fourth century. RS 1, no. 41. Photo © Vatican Museums, Pio Cristiano Museum, inv. 31569. All rights reserved.

SOLO/INDIVIDUAL ADULT MALE PORTRAITS

According to Stine Birk, as Christian sarcophagi began to predominate in the fourth century, "the most popular portraits on Christian sarcophagi were learned women. Only a few male portraits appear and they are mostly in the context of a couple."[36] Likewise, Huskinson's study of Christian strigillated sarcophagi found a trend toward "a predominance of female portraits," while male portraits became "relatively uncommon on these sarcophagi, either as single standing figures, or as busts."[37] Moreover, both experts noticed a wider range of roles for female portrait figures compared to their male counterparts. For instance, on strigillated sarcophagi, Huskinson says, "central standing figures showed women in various situations—prayerful, intellectual or accompanied by other significant figures. . . . In contrast, the most common central portrait type for men was standing alongside their wives in the *dextrarum iunctio*."[38] Birk also points to fewer men with portrait heads on Christian sarcophagi, noting that they are "only seldom represented as protagonists," while "women with portrait heads were more often represented as interacting with other figures, and the *orans* and the learned woman are by far the most frequent examples."[39]

This study confirms the findings of both Birk and Huskinson. Solo female portraits were found to proportionately outnumber solo male portraits by a statistically significant 3 to 1. Proportions of female deceased shown as *orans* and/or with in-facing "apostle" figures exceeded proportions of male deceased with these motifs at statistically significant levels. Solo female portrait figures are also depicted as protagonists who engage viewers and surrounding figures more frequently than do male portrait figures (see table 6.17 and figures 6.9 and 7.13).

36. Birk, *Depicting the Dead*, 120. This is presumably based on Birk's review of RS 1.
37. Huskinson, *Roman Strigillated Sarcophagi*, 227.
38. Ibid., 227. Huskinson cites strigillated sarcophagi from all three *Repertorium* volumes.
39. Birk, "Using Images," 42.

Figure 7.9. So-called "brothers" double-zoned sarcophagus. Unconventional central shell shows two males in what was originally a married couple relief. The man on the right holds a scroll. The torso of the figure on the left was originally female (note right breast) but a male head was created instead. The right hand was revised to make a speech gesture rather than gesture of affection usual to the wife. RS 1, no. 45. Photo © Vatican Museums, Pio Cristiano Museum, inv. 31543. All rights reserved.

Figure 7.10. Early fourth-century lid with biblical scenes. Unfinished portrait in center shows a male holding a scroll. Biblical scenes (left to right) are Jonah, Daniel (with Habakkuk), sacrifice of Isaac, and Jonah reclining under gourd plant. Inscription tabulae are blank, suggesting that this lid may not have been used. RS 1, no. 144. Photo © Vatican Museums, Pio Cristiano Museum, inv. 31483. All rights reserved.

Nevertheless, there are several examples of male *orans* portraits and male learned portraits in which the male figures appear actively engaged, if not always as dramatically as female figures. The mid-fourth-century so-called "brothers" double-zoned sarcophagus is perhaps the most elaborate of all male solo/individual portrait sarcophagi (see figure 7.9). The central shell *clipeus* shows two bearded men in what was originally a married couple configuration.[40] The man on

40. RS 1, no. 45.

the right holds a scroll in his right hand. The male head on the left is carved over a female torso draped in a *palla* with the right breast noticeable beneath the tunic. His hand has apparently been revised into a speech gesture rather than the usual wifely gesture of affection commonly seen in married-couple portrayals. The tomb is replete with scriptural scenes. On the upper zone from left to right we find the resurrection of Lazarus (with Mary of Bethany in a nearly full-size portrayal), the "rooster" scene (signifying the betrayal, forgiveness, and commissioning of Peter), Moses receiving the law (note the hand of God coming from the top of the *clipeus*), the sacrifice of Isaac, and an elaborate Pilate handwashing scene. Pilate is shown sitting on a rock at the end, looking away into the distance with his left hand to his face. In front of him is a balding, unidentified male figure dressed, like Pilate, in a distinctive clip-fastened cloak (called a *paludamentum*) signifying a high-ranking official. In front of him is a partially dressed man, probably a slave, holding a basin and pitcher. A soldier stands with a shield in the background and to his left stands a young man, also of high rank, signified by the cloak clip on his shoulder. Notably absent is a figure of Jesus, but he is evoked by the kneeling Isaac figure. In the lower zone, from left to right, we find Peter's water miracle with his jailers, what Deichmann et al. describe as the "arrest of Moses,"[41] Daniel and the lions (note prophet Habakkuk holding bread), Peter in a "reading scene" with two soldiers looking on, an unidentified standing bearded man holding what may be a *rotulus*,[42] followed by two miracle scenes: the healing of the blind man and the miracle of the multiplication of the loaves.

There are a number of unidentified figures on this sarcophagus who were presumably important to the deceased, although in what way remains obscure. While it is difficult to interpret with any certainty the exact meaning these complex biblical reliefs might have held for viewers, several themes emerge. First, martyrdom at the hands of an unjust state is evoked by Jesus's trial before Pilate, the

41. RS 1, no. 45. While this is clearly an arrest scene, (soldiers' hats are iconic), it is less clear who is being arrested. This is one of only two scenes described as the arrest of Moses that I could find in all three *Repertorium* volumes. The other scene is found in RS 1, no. 35, also described as Moses by Deichmann et al.

42. A type of wooden staff around which was wrapped a scroll.

arrest and jailing of Peter, and the arrest of a young man described as Moses. Second, the Christian view of God's desire to save and liberate from death are suggested by the Lazarus, Isaac, and Daniel scenes. Third, Jesus's miraculous power to bring sight to the blind, forgive ("rooster" scene), and feed a multitude of hungers is prominently featured. Elsner's extensive study of trial scenes on Christian sarcophagi offers an important key for interpreting this sarcophagus. He sees trial scenes as having a "simultaneously apologetic and polemical" edge:

> The scene both affirms Christian triumph and undermines traditional Roman power. The repeated iconography presents a confrontation of two kinds of authority in which the temporal one that does the judging, and will after all put the Savior to death, is nonetheless depicted at the apogee of its weakness with Pilate in the concessive act of washing his hands to show that even he does not concur with the judgment he is himself perforce in the act of passing. . . . The image of the trial—and indeed the total iconographic scheme of these sarcophagi—speaks simultaneously for an assertion of Christian supremacy in the form of the Saviour and an implicit denigration of pre-Christian Roman imperialism in the figure of Pilate.[43]

This elaborate sarcophagus depicts two men commemorated with personal motifs that signal their status and power (scroll) and gifts of preaching or oratory (speech gesture). Taken together with an abundance of biblical themes, it seems clear that these were highly influential Christian men who wished to be remembered for proclaiming a healing, forgiving Christ whose resurrecting power is greater than the power of the state.

A number of individual male portraits with biblical figures are found on sarcophagus lids. The image shown in figure 7.10 is an unfinished portrait of a man depicted in a center shell *clipeus* and holding a scroll. At the viewer's far left is a Jonah relief followed by Daniel and the lions. To the right of the *clipeus* is the sacrifice of Isaac followed by Jonah (in Endymion pose) reclining under the gourd plant. All reliefs suggest the divine power to save from death and destruction. Inscription *tabulae* on either side of the lid are blank, suggesting either that the sarcophagus was never used or that an

---

43. Jaś Elsner, "Image and Rhetoric in Early Christian Sarcophagi: Reflections on Jesus' Trial," in Elsner and Huskinson, *Life, Death and Representation*, 380.

inscription was thought unnecessary. If the sarcophagus was commissioned, the patron/deceased wished to be remembered as an influential, learned man who trusted in God's power to save. If it was a "stock" sarcophagus (one made with a standardized design and awaiting a buyer) we may surmise that there were enough learned, influential Christian men to create a demand for a lid like this one.

The Pio Cristiano Museum houses another early fourth-century lid with a relief of a deceased man holding a scroll (photo not available). This may be a portrait of the learned man Plotius Tertius, since the inscription informs us: "Plotius Tertius and Faustina, servants of God, made (this) for themselves in peace." To the left of the tabula is a scene of the three Hebrews in the fiery furnace with the Jonah cycle on the right. The missing lower casket may have had a portrait of Faustina. This couple wished to be remembered as "servants of God" who proclaim their trust in their God's power over death.

A puzzling characteristic of some solo male portraits is the phenomenon of male heads carved onto an originally female body. A sarcophagus from Arles has a portrait of a beardless male *orans* between two stylized palm trees (unfortunately no photograph is available). He is flanked by two bearded "apostle" figures, the right with his hand in a "recommending" gesture. The male *orans* clothing has been reworked from a dalmatic, suggesting this was originally a female figure.[44] Arrayed on either side, from left to right, are biblical scenes of Jesus raising Lazarus (Lazarus's grave is broken away), the multiplication of the loaves, the healing of the blind man, the "rooster" scene (Peter is shown with a sorrow/apology gesture and Jesus's right hand has speech/proclaiming gesture), the cure of the paralytic, and Peter baptizing his jailers. Christern-Briesenick describes the portrait as having strong facial features with a prominent nose, high cheekbones, a small round mouth, and close-cut hair. She also observes that the "apostles" flanking the *orans* have been placed in the background compared to similar reliefs. They are essentially absorbed by neighboring scenes. This moves the depiction of Jesus's healing of the blind man closer to the *orans* portrait, thereby creating a relationship that Christern-Briesenick describes as "certainly not accidental."

44. RS 3, nos. 20, 21.

Even though this male portrait may have been carved onto an original female torso, the deceased man apparently wanted his sarcophagus commemoration to say something very specific. He seems to have identified in some way with the blind man and may have wished to be commemorated as one who once was also blind but now, because of his belief in Christ, he sees. The healing of the blind is one of the most popular biblical scenes on early Christian sarcophagi (see table 3.2). The use of this motif in relationship to other portrait sarcophagi deserves further exploration. Indeed, discovering if there is a portrait relationship to other popular biblical stories, such as the healing of the woman with the flow of blood, is an interesting question to explore, although beyond the scope of the present work.

Five adult male portrait sarcophagi were identified that sarcophagus experts believe were carved over female figures (see appendix C).[45] Three of these are *orans* portraits and two of the *orans* also have in-facing "apostle" figures (see appendix J).[46] Since proportions of portrait female *orans* and females with flanking "apostle" figures exceed the proportions of similar male portraits at highly significant levels, it is possible that the "template" some sarcophagus workshops used for Christian *orans* and flanking "apostle" portraits was a female figure. Yet nine other male *orans* portraits (two with in-facing "apostles") and three non-*orans* male portraits with in-facing "apostles" were created independently, not from a female template. That some men (or their patrons/families) chose predominantly female iconography (*orans* and/or in-facing "apostles") to commemorate the deceased male suggests that women were not the only ones who valued learning, piety, and religious authority. Men also chose to be commemorated with these motifs. Sarcophagus workshops either adapted their female templates or created new portrait reliefs representing men with popular iconography used mostly by women.

It is unsurprising to find so many female Christian portraits in *orans* depictions since the *orans* derived in part from standing muse figures from Roman iconography (and muses were always female). What are we to make of twelve solo adult male portraits that are also shown

---

45. RS 1, nos. 45, 664, 756; RS 2, no. 68; RS 3, no. 36.
46. RS 2, no. 68 and RS 3, no. 36.

as Christian *orans* figures, three of which were carved over a female body? In her study of strigillated sarcophagi, Janet Huskinson confirms that in the fourth century the traditionally female *orans* figure came to symbolize "prayerfulness, adoration or joy" as well as learnedness. When portrait features were added, the *orans* could also on occasion represent men and boys.[47] Given the fact that Christian literary sources routinely document men chastising women for exercising religious authority, it is instructive that some Christian men adapted authoritative female iconography to signify their own learning, piety, and religious influence. One such man is Licinius Honorius, whose tomb inscription reads:

> To Licinius Honorius most illustrious man who lived about 60 years. [He was] good, pious, a respecter of law. He died in peace 18th kalends of December in the consulship of Fl. Gratianus and Fl. Dagalaifus.[48]

This well-preserved sarcophagus (not pictured), now located in Rome at St. Lawrence Outside-the-Walls, was originally meant to be strigillated, but the inscription occupies the space where the wavy carvings would have been. It dates to 366 CE, which is the year of the consulships of the two high-ranking men named in the inscription. Licinius's portrait is in the center. He is shown as a beardless young man standing in front of a *parapetasma*. Both arms are extended in a typical *orans* posture. He is richly dressed in a special *contabulata* toga and shoes. On the right end stands a bearded, acclaiming male figure who faces inward toward Licinius. He is described as an "apostle or saint" by Dresken-Weiland.[49] On the left end stands another young male figure, also shown in a *contabulata* toga and shoes. He faces inward but has no acclaiming gesture, and there is a scroll bundle at his feet. The interpretation of this figure is unclear. One expert suggests he is a relative or friend of Licinius. What is clear is that Licinius is depicted as a high-ranking Christian man who chose *orans*

---

47. Huskinson, *Roman Strigillated Sarcophagi*, 220.
48. "Licinio Honoro vir clarissimus qui vixit annis plus/minus LX, bonus pius benerans legem decessit in pace XVIII kalends december. Fl Gratiano et FL Dagalaifo conss." RS 2, no. 106 (see descriptor of image on p. 34 of RS 2).
49. Ibid.

iconography and in-facing figures to self-identify as a person of piety and influence.

EMBEDDED PORTRAITS

As we saw in chapter 4, Roman portraits were often embedded in popular mythological figures. Such renditions reflected upon the virtues and values of the deceased and served to elevate his or her status (see figures 5.10 and 5.11). Huskinson and Birk write that early Christian sarcophagi do not have embedded portraits.[50] Others, including this author, find evidence that embedded early Christian portraits do exist and the question remains unsettled. In RS 3, Brigitte Christern-Briesenick identifies a number of embedded figures that appear to be representations of the deceased. Still, she acknowledges that the question of when the deceased are represented as, or directly related to, biblical figures awaits further investigation.[51]

As we have seen, the interpretation of "portrait features" is at times ambiguous. A number of sarcophagi seem to contain representations of the deceased even though they lack intricately carved portrait feature. Examples of representations of the deceased that appear to be embedded in biblical figures can be found in table 7.4. This list is not exhaustive. There are probably more embedded representations awaiting discovery. Except for Noah's family, Jairus, and one philosopher-muse portrayal, all the biblical figures chosen as obvious portrait ideals are female. These include Mary of Magdala, Thecla, Tabitha, Sarah, and Jairus's daughter. Literary accounts from the New Testament and extracanonical sources tell us that Mary of Magdala, Tabitha, and Thecla were remembered, respectively, for first proclaiming the resurrection, ministry to widows, and evangelizing the far-flung communities of Asia Minor. It is unsurprising, therefore, that some Christian women and/or their families chose these female ecclesial role models to represent their virtues and values. Portraits embedded in the "Sarah" and "Jairus's daughter" vignettes seem to be grieving parent commemorations. Space considerations pro-

---

50. Huskinson, "Degrees of Differentiation," 293; and Birk, "Using Images," 42.
51. RS 3, no. 497, with quotation from Christern-Briesenick.

hibit detailed analysis of all embedded portrayals, but I will discuss two typical images in some depth: Tabitha and Jairus's daughter.

Table 7.4: Examples of Deceased Representations Embedded in Biblical Scenes

RS Volume and Number	Biblical Scene(s) and Characteristics	Identity of Portrait Figure(s)	Other Biblical Scenes on Tomb	Date	Ancient Workshop and Today's Venue
RS 1, no. 807	"Mary of Magdala" Frieze sarcophagus with Christ standing in the center shown with a scroll and speech gesture. On his right is a female figure in tunic and hood that RS 1 editors suggest is Mary of Magdala.[52] To my knowledge, this is the only undisputed Mary of Magdala figure identified anywhere by RS experts. Peter is on Christ's left with his right hand over his face in an "apology" gesture and a scroll in his left hand. A rooster is at Christ's feet. Unusually, a small naked child is inserted before the raising of Lazarus scene. These observations suggest that representations of a deceased woman and her child were inserted into biblical scenes. It is notable that a woman— Mary of Magdala— is inserted into the scene commemorating Peter's betrayal and commissioning.	A woman and her child?	Raising of Lazarus; Peter betrays Christ; "Hen Scene"; Cana; Peter arrested; Moses: bush; Moses: law; Ezekiel raising dry bones; Mary of Magdala?	First third of the fourth century	Rome workshop Musei Nationale

52. RS 1, p. 337.

RS 2, no. 420	"Noah's family." Eight figures: Noah, his wife, his three sons, and his three daughters-in-law, as well as assorted creatures. At least two of Noah's sons are shown as children, but all three daughters-in-law are full-grown. Dresken-Weiland writes that there is no known parallel for Noah's family in early Christian sarcophagi.[53] Given the age difference for the sons and daughters-in-law, and the unique braided hairstyles of the daughters-in-law (while Noah's wife is veiled), this tomb may commemorate a family.	Family: a married couple, two young boys, one older boy, and three grown women.		Around 300	Local workshop (Rhine-Moselle) Rheinisches Landes-museum Trier
RS 3, no. 32	"Family" in raising of Jairus's daughter scene (see figure 7.16) A partial front of a frieze sarcophagus comprises three quarters of the original relief. To the right of the central Christ-enthronement scene is the biblical relief of the raising of Jairus's daughter. Unusually, this scene has nine figures with three background heads even though the biblical account names only seven people: Jairus and his wife, their sick daughter, Christ, Peter, James, and John. In this relief, the child is partially reclining on the bed with her left hand placed in Christ's right hand. In front of the bed at Christ's feet is a kneeling woman with curled hair visible	Young daughter, commemorated/ mourned by her mother and father	Peter baptizes jailers; Christ enthroned, flanked by three "apostles" on each side; raising of Jairus's daughter.	First quarter of the fourth century	Rome workshop Musée de l'Arles Antique, France

53. RS 2, p. 130.

beneath her veil, whose hands are outstretched in supplication. Behind the "apostle" next to the headboard is a bearded man with head slightly thrown back, mouth opened and hands raised in surprise. Christern-Briesenick identifies the sick child as the grave inhabitant, the kneeling woman as the child's mother, and the male behind the headboard with elevated hands as the child's father.[54] See text for in-depth interpretation

RS 1, nos. 7, 13, 527 RS 2, no. 10	Four other sarcophagi have "Jairus's daughter" biblical scenes in which various configurations of parents appear. See figures 7.15, 7.17 and chapter 7 for interpretations.				
RS 3, no. 68	"Tabitha" Christern-Briesenick writes that the deceased "grave owner" is probably represented in this biblical scene of the raising of Tabitha (see figure 7.11).[55] The deceased is shown half-raised from her bed and dressed in a tunic, *palla*, and hood that partially covers her wavy hair. Peter stands at the foot of the bed taking her outstretched right arm into both of his hands. Two women, also in hoods, with wavy hair visible, are standing behind her bed. Beneath the bed in front, two diminutive women kneel and plead for Peter's	Deceased woman	Fragment shows Tabitha scene.	Last quarter of the fourth century	Rome workshop Musée de l'Arles Antique, France

54. RS 3, p. 16.

aid. This is thought to be one panel in what was originally a four or five-panel tomb.

RS 3, no. 497	A similar Tabitha tableau is found on the left narrow side of RS 3, no. 497. In this relief, however, there are three small children, one a naked toddler, beneath the bed in front. Tabitha is shown with her hand on the head of the tallest child. On the right narrow side of the same tomb, we find a portrait of a female *orans* between two trees depicted with a *capsa* at her feet. It is probable that this biblically learned woman is represented in the Tabitha scene as well, along with her children, although Christern-Briesenick notes that the whole question of when the deceased are represented as biblical figures or directly related to biblical scenes still needs in-depth investigation.[56]		Healing of the blind man; plea of Canaanite woman; centurion from Capernaum; Tabitha	Last third of the fourth century	Rome workshop St. Marie Madeleine, Saint-Maximin-la- Sainte-Baume, France
RS 3, no. 271	"Sarah" In the sacrifice of Isaac scene on the far right, we find a standing veiled female figure with a hand covering her face in sorrow. Sarah is not named in the biblical account of Abraham's journey to Moriah to sacrifice Isaac. Neither does she appear in scores of other "sacrifice of Isaac" funerary reliefs. Therefore, a grieving	Deceased mother and her child?	Raising of Lazarus; healing of paralytic; healing of blind; multiplication of loaves; sacrifice of Isaac (with Sarah); angels at Mamre; left narrow side: Adam and Eve	First third of the fifth century	Local workshop, southwest France (Tolosane) Saint-Vincent-de-Lucq, France

55. RS 3, p. 234.
56. RS 3, p. 234.

mother may well have inserted herself into the Isaac scene to mourn for her child, who may also be interred here.

RS 3, no. 514	A similar "Sarah" is inserted into the sacrifice of Isaac scene on RS 3, no. 514, a sarcophagus of a female child, represented by a portrait standing *orans* in the center. Notably the center female *orans* has in-facing heads indicating that the in-facing "apostle" motif was copied by local workshops as late as the fifth century.	Child (*kinder*) sarcophagus with embedded portrait of grieving mother as Sarah	Raising of Lazarus; multiplication of loaves; sacrifice of Isaac (with Sarah) combined with Abraham (and Sarah!) and angels at Mamre; L. narrow side: Adam and Eve; R. narrow side: Daniel and lions	First third of the fifth century	Local workshop, southwest France (Tolosane) Musée Saint-Raymond, Toulouse, France
RS 3, no. 297	"Thecla" Tree sarcophagus with seven panels, four of which are vignettes about the arrest and sufferings of Peter and Paul. In the third panel from the left, a young female figure peeks out from behind a tree with her hand in an obvious speech gesture. She wears a tunic and dalmatic and her wavy hair is visible beneath a hood. According to Wilpert, the sarcophagus is the only remaining example of the capture of Paul in Iconium at the behest of Thecla's jealous suitor, Thamyris, as found in the Acts of Paul and Thecla.[57] Experts differ about the identity of the female figure, but the most recent opinion (and one with which I agree) is that	Deceased woman	Thecla; martyrdom of Paul; Peter betrayal and commissioning (aka "Hen scene"); Paul arrested; Peter arrested	End of the fourth century	Rome workshop Saint Victor, Marseille, France

the deceased grave owner
chose to represent herself
as Thecla. Christern-
Briesenick points to the
figure's frontality, outward
gaze, and portrait features
in support of this opin-
ion.[58]

| RS 3, no. 304 | Artist's drawing: seated philosopher (male) and standing muse (female) on lid with biblical scenes. | Couple | Simon Magus and hound; sacrifice of Isaac; healing of blind; woman with flow of blood | Lid only: end of the fourth century (casket dates to the fifth century) | Rome workshop Saint Victor, Marseille, France |
| | Christern-Briesenick suggests that the deceased couple wished to represent themselves in a standardized Roman-couple iconography of a seated philosopher and standing muse.[59] It is unusual to see this Roman iconography surrounded by biblical scenes. | | | | |

"TABITHA"

A late fourth-century sarcophagus fragment found in France at the Musée de l'Arles Antique has a lovely relief of the biblical story of Tabitha (Acts 9:36–43). Unfortunately, no photo is available for what is originally thought to be a four- or five-panel sarcophagus that was made in a workshop in Rome. According to Christern-Briesenick, Tabitha's sculpted scene probably represents the female grave owner. She is shown half raised from her bed and dressed in a tunic, *palla*, and hood that partially covers her wavy hair. Peter stands at the foot of the bed and takes her outstretched right arm into both of his hands. Two women, also in hoods with wavy hair visible, are standing behind "Tabitha's" bed. Beneath and to the front, two diminutive women are

---

57. Monsignor Joseph Wilpert (1899–1944) was a priest-archaeologist and among the first to study Christian funerary art.
58. RS 3, p. 147–48.
59. RS 3, p. 154–55.

shown kneeling and pleading for Peter's aid. Tabitha (Greek: Dorcas) was greatly loved by the "widows and holy ones" at Joppa because of her charitable works, especially making clothing for needy women. When Tabitha died, the disciples quickly sent for Peter who hastened to Joppa immediately. Some scholars believe Peter knew Tabitha well because she was among the "many women" in Jesus's Galilean discipleship (Luke 8:1–3). The deceased fourth-century woman commemorated here was probably recognized for her faith and her care for other women, especially women in need.

A similar late fourth-century Tabitha tableau can be found on the left narrow side of a sarcophagus now housed at St. Mary Magdalene Basilica in Saint-Maximin-la-Sainte-Baume in France (see figure 7.11). But this beautiful Roman-made sarcophagus contains a significantly different Tabitha scene. Rather than two small women kneeling at the bed, we find three small children, one a naked toddler, and "Tabitha," shown with her hand on the head of the tallest child. She wears a long-sleeved tunic, *palla*, and hood with wavy hair visible. Two veiled standing women face her while "Peter" stands at the foot of the bed with hand outstretched to raise her up. On the right narrow side of the same tomb is a portrait of a female *orans* between two trees with a *capsa* at her feet. She is described as the "grave owner." According to Christern-Briesenick, this learned woman and mother is probably also represented in the Tabitha scene, along with her children, and again as the Canaanite woman found on the far right of the sarcophagus front (see figure 7.12). After courageously persuading Jesus to heal her daughter (Matt 15:21–28), this foreigner's "great faith" called Jesus to a new understanding of his mission. Christern-Briesenick suggests the centurion scene on the far left end of the sarcophagus front may represent the husband of the deceased.[60] As with the Canaanite woman, Jesus also praises the centurion's great faith: "Not even in Israel have I found such faith" (Luke 7:9). There is artistic similitude in representing a married man and woman, each with "great faith," on either end of this fascinating tomb. In the center is a damaged *crux invicta* (victorious cross) relief signifying Christ's victory over death and sin. Other biblical scenes

60. Ibid., 234.

include the healing of the man born blind and the "rooster" scene commemorating Peter's betrayal and commissioning. Our learned female *orans* is revealed as a wife, mother, and woman of authority who skillfully chose to commemorate herself and her loved ones as persons with great faith in Christ's healing power and victorious love.

Figure 7.11. Late fourth-century depiction of reclining Tabitha (on right) that probably represents the deceased grave owner, also shown as *orans* figure on the left with a round *capsa* (Acts 9:36–43). RS 3, no 497. American Academy in Rome, Photographic Archive.

Figure 7.12. Front of late fourth-century "Tabitha" sarcophagus depicting the plea of the Canaanite woman on the viewer's far right and the healing of the centurion's servant on the far left, thought to represent, respectively, the female grave owner and her husband. RS 3, no 497. Photo from American Academy in Rome.

PARENTS MOURNING DAUGHTERS: JAIRUS SCENES

In figures 7.13–7.15, we see an early fourth-century frieze sarcophagus with an individualized frontal portrait of an uncharacteristically rotund "woman of substance" holding a scroll. Her mouth is open as if teaching, perhaps, about the Gospel scenes on either side of her (figures 7.13 and 7.14). Another standing female figure appears in the far-right depiction of the raising of Jairus's daughter (Mark 5:21–43).[61] Here, the mother of the moribund girl vigorously engages surrounding male figures, one of whom (Jairus?) points to the child, as Jesus extends a wand to miraculously raise her up (figure 7.15). The girl is shown wrapped in a shroud and placed in a small sarcophagus with lions' feet, not on a bed as shown in three other Jairus scenes on portrait tombs.[62] This suggests that the influential ecclesial woman commemorated here also lost a daughter who may have been buried with her. Mark's Gospel tells us the girl's parents, along with Peter, James, and John, entered the sick room, but counting Jesus, there are just four male figures in this scene compared with five in the text. It is therefore likely that the pointing male figure is meant to be Jairus (and possibly the deceased girl's father). Two other sarcophagi have full-length female figures in the Jairus scene while three others have tiny female figures kneeling beneath the bed with hands outstretched. Some have full-length standing male figures (Jairus?) as well. All of which is to suggest that deceased girls may also be commemorated or buried in each of these sarcophagi.[63] Unlike most reliefs of biblical scenes, the Jairus renditions are rarely shown in the same way. This diversity suggests that whoever commissioned these sarcophagi adapted the story of Jairus's daughter to meet the needs of the patrons, perhaps parents mourning daughters.

---

61. RS 1, no. 13.

62. RS 1, no. 7; RS 2, no.10; RS 3, no 23.

63. See RS 1, no. 7: There are two females in this Jairus scene: one tiny figure kneeling under the bed and the other standing behind the bed with a male figure standing next to her. The deceased female *orans* is in the center front surrounded by biblical scenes. RS 1, no. 527 is a fragment, so there is no obvious portrait, but the woman in this scene is also standing and the child is shown in a shroud and a sarcophagus. RS 2, no. 10 and RS 3, no. 32 have Jairus scenes in which a small, kneeling female figure with hands outstretched is under the bed.

The prominent learned female on this sarcophagus is commemorated as a woman of active faith, engaged with her husband and with Jesus, whom she trusts to raise up her daughter. Other biblical scenes, from left to right, include the arrest of Jesus and his appearance before Caiaphas, two unidentified bearded male figures (the left with a speech gesture and the right with in-facing figures),[64] the nativity, and Jesus's baptism by John the Baptist. This central portrait of a learned and uniquely sculpted "woman of substance," suggests that the deceased and/or her admirers saw her as one with authority to teach and to proclaim a Christ whose baptism by water and by suffering ushered in salvation and resurrection for all those who believe.

Figure 7.13. Early fourth-century frieze sarcophagus with frontal portrait of a standing deceased "woman of substance" with Gospel scenes on either side. These are (left to right) Caiaphas on chair with Jesus between two soldiers before him, two unknown bearded male figures, (left with speech gesture; right with in-facing background figures is probably Peter), deceased woman with scroll, nativity scene, John the Baptist baptizing Jesus, raising of Jairus's daughter. RS 1, no 13. Photo © Vatican Museums, Pio Cristiano Museum, inv. 31542. All rights reserved.

64. Deichmann et al. suggest this scene is Peter's denial of Christ, presumably in the courtyard at the high priest's house. If so, Peter is probably the bearded male with in-facing figures and folded hands, since in early fourth-century tombs Christ is always shown beardless.

Figure 7.14. Close up portrait of deceased woman with a scroll in her left hand and mouth slightly open as if preaching or teaching biblical stories on either side. RS 1, no. 13. Photo © Vatican Museums, Pio Cristiano Museum, inv. 31542. All rights reserved.

Figure 7.15. Detail of healing of Jairus's daughter scene from figure 7.13. Note the full-size woman (the child's mother?) actively engaged with Christ (with a wand) and a male figure who points to the child (father as Jairus?). This tomb may have also held a deceased daughter, shown here in a shroud and small sarcophagus with lion's feet rather than a bed as in other Jairus scenes. Early fourth century. RS 1, no. 13. Photo © Vatican Museums, Pio Cristiano Museum, inv. 31542. All rights reserved.

Figure 7.16. Embedded family portrait found on partial front of early fourth-century frieze sarcophagus with raising of Jairus's daughter scene on the right. The child on the bed is believed to represent the deceased daughter. The male figure with hands up behind headboard is probably the grieving father. The tiny pleading woman with a distinctively wavy hairstyle showing beneath her veil is probably the child's mother. To the left is a Christ enthronement with six flanking figures identified as "apostles" and Peter's water miracle. RS 3, no. 32. Sarcophage des adieux du Christ, Musée départemental Arles antique. © M. Lacanaud.

Figure 7.17. Early fourth-century frieze sarcophagus front with central portrait *orans* with unfinished face. The tomb may also commemorate her spouse and a deceased daughter on the far left, in the raising of Jairus's daughter scene. To the right of the *orans*, a deceased son could be represented by the unidentified young man with a speech gesture who appears engaged with the two left end scenes: the raising of the son of the widow of Nain and the sacrifice of Isaac. Both stories are about sons threatened with death. RS 1, no. 7. Photo © Vatican Museums, Pio Cristiano Museum, inv. 31440. All rights reserved.

A partial front of an early fourth-century frieze sarcophagus contains another biblical relief of the raising of Jairus's daughter, shown to the right of the central Christ-enthronement scene (see figure 7.16). This scene has nine figures plus three background heads for a total of twelve figures, although the New Testament account names only seven people: Jairus and his wife, their dying daughter, Christ, Peter, James, and John (Mark 5:21–43). This Roman-sculpted relief was apparently created for Christians in Gaul and is now in the Musée de l'Arles Antique. In the Jairus scene, the young girl is partially reclining on a bed with her left hand placed in Jesus's right hand. In front of the bed at Jesus's feet is a kneeling woman whose hands are outstretched in supplication. Her wavy hair is visible beneath her veil. Behind the "apostle" next to the headboard is a bearded man with head slightly thrown back, mouth opened, and hands raised in surprise. Brigitte Christern-Briesenick identifies the sick child as the grave inhabitant, the kneeling woman as the child's mother, and the male behind the headboard with elevated hands as the child's father.[65] At the center of this sarcophagus is Christ enthroned with six flanking "apostle" figures, and on the left end is Peter's water miracle in jail. Other scenes on "fragment A" of this sarcophagus include Shadrach, Meshach, and Abednego refusing to worship Nebuchadnezzar's idol (Daniel 3). On the right end, the frontal standing male figure with a scroll and acclaiming gesture is described as an "apostle" figure by Christern-Briesenick.[66] This sarcophagus has no obvious portrait figures except for the embedded couple and their daughter, represented in the Jairus scene.

Another early fourth-century Jairus frieze was apparently created by the same Roman workshop as the tomb in Arles, but this time for Christians in Italy since it was found in Florence (RS 2, no. 10—not shown here). This complete sarcophagus front has a portrait couple who kneel at Christ's feet in the center enthronement scene with two sets of "apostles" flanking Christ. The sarcophagus also contains a relief of the three refusing to worship Nebuchadnezzar's idol, but there are noticeable differences in the Jairus scene, which is probably another embedded portrait of the family. This relief displays a biblically accurate seven figures, with the "father" shown standing behind the bed with both arms raised as in the Arles relief. The mother is again shown as a kneeling veiled figure pleading at Christ's feet. The

---

65. RS 3, no. 16.
66. One wonders if this could also be an embedded portrait given the frontality of the male figure.

three remaining male figures are apparently "apostles," one with a scroll and one shown with hand to face in either an amazement or apology gesture.

One last Jairus's daughter scene that is well worth a glance is an early fourth-century Roman-made sarcophagus front now in the Pio Cristiano Museum but originally found in the catacombs of Domitilla (see figure 7.17). A portrait of a standing female *orans* graces the center of this tomb. She wears a double veil, tunic, and shoes. To the viewer's right are two scenes: the raising of the son of the widow of Nain and the sacrifice of Isaac (right end). Left of the *orans* is the denial and commissioning of Peter (who holds a scroll in his left hand in the "rooster" scene). In-facing "apostle" figures flank Jesus, whose right hand is in a teaching gesture while his left holds an open scroll. To the left of Peter's commissioning is the scene depicting the raising of Jairus's daughter.

However, in this Jairus tableau, there are just five figures, unlike the five men and two women described in the Scriptures. Notably, three of the five figures are female, including the semi-reclining girl whom Jesus raises up with his right hand in her left. An adult woman without a veil stands behind the headboard with both hands raised, the left in shallow background relief. The right hand and head of this female figure were later supplemented, but her floor-length clothing did not change so we can be fairly confident that this was originally meant to be a female figure. This is not a revision of the male figure at the headboard seen in other Jairus reliefs (figure 7.16). A tiny veiled woman kneels beneath the bed, hands outstretched in supplication. One of these women probably represents the child's mother, but the other is unknown. Perhaps a sister or a respected woman healer stands at her post behind the headboard. On the left side of the bed—between the standing female figure and Jesus—a frontal bearded male with a speech gesture gazes outward. His head and upper body have been supplemented, so his speech gesture and beard are not assured, but the frontality would not have changed, signifying an important figure. This is presumably the girl's father, represented as Jairus. Immediately to the (viewer's) right of the central *orans* figure is a beardless, unidentified young man with a speech gesture who is engaged with the raising of the son of the widow of Nain and sacrifice of Isaac scenes that follow. He may be a deceased son who taught or preached about the Scriptures. This is plausible because the two biblical scenes on the right—the raising of the son of the widow of Nain and the sacrifice of Isaac—both point to the threatened death and resurrection of beloved sons. The raising of Jairus's daughter on the left points to the loss and resurrection of a beloved daughter. As in the Tabitha relief described above (figure 7.12), we again see artistic similitude in biblical scenes representing the virtues and values of the deceased. One interpretation of this sarcophagus is that the central female *orans* was a learned, devout Christian mother and wife who lost both a son and a daughter. She carefully commissioned a memorial that emphasized her and her husband's belief in Christ's power over death and that their family would one day be raised up and reunited. Alternatively, her husband may have commissioned this monument to honor his deceased wife, who was remembered as a role model for the Christian belief in God's power to bring life from death—even the untimely deaths of the couple's daughter and son.

8.

Women and Authority in the Fourth Century: Integrating the Literary Evidence

Since most Christian sarcophagi and catacomb art dates to the fourth century, this concluding chapter explores what can be known from the literary sources about contemporaneous Christian women who lived during this dramatically transformative time in church and empire. Such an exploration offers helpful context for the lives and values of Christian women commemorated in the funerary depictions discussed in chapters 4, 6, and 7. It may also shed light on tantalizing questions: Does the literary record corroborate or oppose what the iconic portrayals in catacomb frescos and sarcophagi suggest? Were contemporaneous women from literary sources role models for the women buried in the sarcophagi and catacombs? Or were the catacomb/tomb women role models for their literary contemporaries? And perhaps most important: did fourth-century Christian women exercise religious and spiritual authority?

Chapters 6 and 7 detailed outcomes of a painstaking analysis of third- to fifth-century Christian sarcophagi in which solo female portraits were found to outnumber solo male portraits by three to one. There were no statistically significant differences between solo Christian women and men depicted with scrolls and speech gestures. These findings indicate that both women and men were idealized as persons of status, authority, learnedness, and religious devotion. Female portraits were statistically twice as likely to be flanked by "apostle" figures, quite possibly to validate their religious authority at a time when churchmen sought to silence them. In short, early Christian sarcophagus iconography suggests that many fourth-century Christian women were idealized as learned figures with authority to, at the least, proclaim and teach Scripture even as male church leaders struggled to curtail this practice.

Who were these "tomb women"? For most, any reconstruction is speculative and necessarily based on the occasional inscription and what can be deduced from their funerary iconography. Generally, the iconography tells us that these early female Christians were learned, pious, and wealthy. Since many women are shown with scrolls and speech gestures in the midst of biblical scenes, we can posit that they were well versed in Scripture and wished to be represented as women with faith in God's power to save and as teachers of Jesus's life and healing miracles. The preponderance of women depicted with in-facing "apostle" figures suggests they also chose to be represented as persons whose spiritual authority was recognized, respected, and validated by early male church leaders, especially Peter and Paul. Their sarcophagus iconography tells us they were, in fact, role models or, in Huskinson's felicitous definition, figures "chosen not merely to commemorate the individual dead but to offer a collective example to the Christian community in terms of beliefs and the conduct of their lives."[1]

THE LITERARY RECORD

What do the literary sources have to say about fourth-century Christian women? As it happens, we have a good deal of historical information since prominent churchmen such as Jerome, Palladius, Gregory of Nyssa, Paulinus of Nola, Augustine, John Chrysostom, Sozomen, and Eusebius wrote about them. We learn about Marcella, Paula,

---

1. Huskinson, "Degrees of Differentiation," 288.

Eustochium, Macrina, Helena, Melania the Elder, Melania the Younger, Olympias, and others from learned churchmen writing biographies (such as Gregory of Nyssa's *Life of Macrina*, Palladius's *Lausiac History*, Sozomen's *Church History*, and the anonymous author of the *Life of Olympias*) and from letters for which the women's side of the correspondence is sadly lost. Therefore, for these texts, our information is filtered through a male lens, that is, what men thought about these historical women and not necessarily what the women themselves thought.

We do have two texts that were written by women. Around 360 CE, Faltonia Betitia Proba used a special literary form called a *cento* in which she adapted Rome's much-loved Virgilian prose to tell the Christian story. In the late fourth century, a Spanish virgin, Egeria, wrote a travel diary for her religious circle in Spain describing her journey to sacred sites in the East. Of the women listed above, only Helena, Proba, and Egeria were not ascetics. While Egeria was a dedicated virgin from Spain, she did not adopt ascetic extremes such as rigorous fasting or enclosure as did other ascetics. Melania the Elder was also born in Spain, although she moved to Rome in her early twenties. Marcella, Paula, Eustochium, Proba, and Melania the Younger were born in Rome. Helena was born in Asia Minor but moved to Rome at about age fifty-six to assume her role as the imperial mother of Constantine. Both Macrina and Olympias lived in the East, Macrina in Cappadocia and Pontus (central and northern Turkey) and Olympias in Constantinople. Since most of our sarcophagi and frescos are from Rome, historical women who lived in Rome or who had close contact with the Roman Christian community would seem most germane to our quest to better understand our "tomb women." However, I chose to explore also what the literary record can tell us about prominent historical women, such as Macrina, Olympias, and Egeria, who lived in other parts of the empire. I did so for two reasons. First, Roman cultural values pervaded the empire and impacted women regardless of where they lived. Second, some fourth-century Roman women, such as Melania the Elder and Paula, not only travelled throughout the empire, they also created monasteries in the East. There seemed little reason, therefore, to restrict our literary review only to those women from the city of Rome.

AN EMPIRE AND A CHURCH TRANSFORMED

Before discussing women found in the literary sources and how they may or may not compare to women commemorated on funerary art, it would be wise to briefly summarize some of the momentous changes that transformed the Roman world—and the church—during the fourth century. This century began with the Great Persecution. Diocletian and Galerius, emperors in the eastern empire, posted a series of edicts demanding an end to all Christian gatherings and ordering the confiscation of all Christian churches, bibles, liturgical books, and sacred vessels. All citizens were ordered to offer sacrifice on behalf of the emperor or be put to death. Many Christians refused and suffered horrible deaths, although such executions occurred mainly in the East. Others found a way around the edict, either by forging documents testifying that they had offered sacrifice when they had not or by relinquishing medical treatises masquerading as sacred scrolls. These actions would eventually lead to the Donatist schism, which held that early Christian leaders who had "apostatized" could not administer valid sacraments. While Emperor Constantius in the West destroyed churches, he did not mandate executions for those who refused to offer sacrifice. In 306 CE, Constantine rose in influence and, after invoking the aid of the Christian God, gained sole power in the West at the Battle of the Milvian Bridge in 312 CE. In the following year, co-emperors Constantine and Licinius (then the emperor in the East) issued the Edict of Milan, which rescinded the prohibition of Christianity throughout the empire. A protracted power struggle ensued that ended with Licinius's defeat in 324 CE. Constantine then became and remained the sole Roman emperor until his death in 337 CE.

In a span of sixty-eight years, the formerly persecuted Christian church rose to unprecedented heights of worldly power and influence owing in no small part to the imperial favor of Constantine, his mother Helena, and the sons who succeeded them. To undo the ravages of persecution, Constantine built basilicas in Rome at the traditional shrines of St. Peter and St. Paul as well as in Bethlehem and the Church of the Anastasis (Resurrection) in Jerusalem.[2] He gave the Lateran Palace to the bishops of Rome as an episcopal residence and commissioned new copies of the sacred Scriptures.[3] Peter Brown supplies an impressive description of these early churches:

> They were gigantic assembly halls, with room for up to 4000 worshippers. . . . What we call a "church" was not an isolated building. It usually stood in a complex of buildings that include a secretarium—an audience-hall—an extensive bishop's palace, warehouses for supplies for the poor, and, above all, an impressive courtyard, of the sort that stood in front of a nobleman's townhouse for charitable banquets, distribution of alms, or simply, for the faithful to meet and catch up with the news of the town.[4]

Christian communities that formerly met in large homes or buildings owned by wealthy benefactors, now found themselves in sumptuous public surroundings. These changes would exacerbate tensions about the public ministry of Christian women. Bishops and clergy, formerly first in line for martyrdom, now received immunity from taxes and compulsory public service. Constantine viewed Christian bishops as the judges or arbiters in their communities: "The bishop, already regarded as the God-like judge of sin among believers, rapidly became the *Ombudsman* of an entire local community."[5] Long recognized for their staunch care of poorer believers, Christians now became the distributors of imperial food and clothing for the populace, effectively turning them "into something like a public welfare system, designed to alleviate and to control, the urban poor." For Brown, "the emergence of the Christian clergy as a privileged and ambitious local group was a decisive change: for it took place in an area that affected the entire structure of the Roman Empire."[6]

Since the bishop was expected to act as an exclusive judge and arbiter, theological disagreements between bishops, clergy, and laity

---

2. Later named the Church of the Holy Sepulcher by the crusaders.
3. Chadwick, *Early Church*, 121–22.
4. Peter Brown, *The Rise of Western Christendom: Triumph and Diversity AD 200–1000* (Oxford: Blackwell, 1996), 38–39.
5. Ibid., 39.
6. Ibid.

were perceived as a threat to the unity of the empire, especially an empire previously unified by sacrifice offered on behalf of the emperor. The ecumenical councils of the fourth century—Nicaea and Constantinople—were convened not by bishops but by emperors Constantine and Theodosius respectively, who hoped to unify a doctrinally fractured church. All the while, the influence and wealth of bishops grew dramatically, and not only from imperial favor. Churchmen also received extravagant benefices from the fabulous wealth of aristocratic Christian families such as those of Olympias, Melania the Elder and Younger, and Paula. Paula should be credited not only for the many scholarly contributions she made to Jerome's translation of the bible from Greek to Latin but also for financially underwriting his decades-long work.

ABOUT SYMBOLIC "HERETICAL WOMEN" IN THE FOURTH CENTURY

Throughout the fourth century, church fathers hotly debated theological issues in an attempt to unify Christian doctrine as the church struggled to integrate new members, many of whom converted out of political expedience. Rhetoric, the mainstay of a proper classical education for Greco-Roman men, soared to new heights (and depths) as Christian factions tried to convince or defeat the opposition. Even though church fathers conceded the orthodoxy of sects such as the Montanists, they vehemently opposed women in leadership roles:

> These people [Montanists] confess, as does the Church, that God is the Father of the universe and the Creator of everything, and they confess everything that the Gospel testifies about Christ, but they bring in new observances by way of fasts and holidays, diets of dry food and radishes, alleging that they have been taught to do so by these women.[7]

Orthodoxy is not at issue here. Women leaders were the issue, and male leaders in the mainstream church found them deeply unsettling. Virginia Burrus's fascinating study of the polemical use of gender

---

7. Hippolytus, *Refutation of All Heresies* 8.19, as quoted in Elizabeth A. Clark, *Women in the Early Church*, Message of the Fathers of the Church 13 (Wilmington, DE: Michael Glazier, 1983), 161.

by fourth-century church fathers revealed a "myriad of symbolic associations generated by the figure of the female heretic."[8] For example, Jerome interpreted 2 Timothy 3:6–7 to mean that women played a "crucial role in the founding of every Christian heresy."[9]

> For among them are those who make their way into households and captivate silly women, overwhelmed by their sins and swayed by all kinds of desires, who are always being instructed and can never arrive at a knowledge of the truth. (2 Tim 3:6–7)

Burrus explains: "By suggesting that women, simply by virtue of their female nature, hover on the brink of heresy as well as unchastity, Jerome lays claim to a powerful means of social control."[10] In short, the fourth century saw a distressing tendency on the part of churchmen to symbolically associate the female sex per se with heresy, even though both Christian men and Christian women were involved in the disparate interpretations of Christianity that would eventually be labeled heretical. Church fathers also used femaleness to denigrate male opponents as "effeminate" while their female counterparts were falsely demeaned as promiscuous and sexually uncontrolled.[11]

Women were especially at risk of being labeled heretics and suspected of unchastity if they assumed the role of teacher.[12] In polemical argumentation, the term "heretical women" would come to symbolize a church that is "chaotic and anarchic," while the obedient (and silent) virgin symbolized "a church that is properly ordered according to the traditional model of the separation and subordination of the private sphere to the public sphere and of women to men."[13] Burrus finds the term "heretical woman" to be ultimately androcentric because "it was produced by and functions within the male arena of rhetorical combat." Such symbolism also functioned to control outspoken women within orthodox communities. It attests to the "strong and likewise threatening role of women within the com-

8. Virginia Burrus, "The Heretical Woman as Symbol in Alexander, Athanasius, Epiphanius, and Jerome," *Harvard Theological Review* 84, no. 3 (1991): 229–48.
9. Ibid., 246, citing Jerome's *Epistula* 133 to Ctesiphon.
10. Burrus, "Heretical Woman," 246.
11. Ibid., 245–46.
12. Ibid., 246. Burrus cites the example of Agape, an influential woman who was labeled a "heretic and suspected of unchastity" after taking on the role of teacher.
13. Ibid., 247.

munities led by these orthodox men."[14] Burrus concludes with this cogent observation:

> I suspect that the boundaries separating heretical women from their orthodox sisters were not, after all, so clear cut: the orthodox women were surely not as docile or the heretical women as monstrous as the church fathers would have liked us to believe.[15]

Underlying the polemics over doctrine is the reality that both male and female patrons were opening their homes—effectively becoming new house churches—for dissident clerics and their communities. This was especially an issue after Theodosius expelled Arians from Catholic basilicas in 360 CE. Likewise, when the Arian bishop Demophilus controlled the basilicas in Constantinople in 375 CE, the orthodox pro-Nicene community gathered with their leader, Gregory Nazianzen, in a private residence converted to an assembly space.[16] Thus, both dissident and orthodox Christians had access to male and female patrons and their "house churches" during doctrinal struggles. Some female patrons, such as Melania the Elder, supported Pelagius and pro-Origen churchmen such as Rufinus. Other female patrons, such as Marcella, supported Jerome and Epiphanius, who opposed Pelagius and reviled Origen's legacy. Marcella and Melania are good examples of outspoken, learned women who had differing perspectives that we will sadly never hear about from their own writings. It is likely that both were negatively impacted by the "female-as-heretic" meme. Such criticism may have been ameliorated somewhat because they were also wealthy patrons helping famous male leaders. It is ironic that women underwrote the very men who created a gendered polemic to keep them in their subordinate place.

POPE DAMASUS AND THE CULT OF THE MARTYRS

Any review of the life and times of fourth-century Christian women would be incomplete without including the infamous Pope Damasus

14. Ibid., 248.
15. Ibid.
16. Harry O. Maier, "Religious Dissent, Heresy and Households in Late Antiquity," *Vigiliae Christianae* 49, no. 1 (March 1995): 51.

(305–384 CE) and his campaign to remake the catacombs into pilgrimage sites for venerating Rome's male martyrs. In 366 CE, Damasus won the papacy after a bloody three-day massacre at the basilica at St. Cecilia that resulted in the deaths of 137 people.[17] Despite being discredited publicly, Damasus was consecrated pope but only after the civil authorities intervened. When a new city prefect came to office a year later, Damasus was formally accused of homicide. The charge was lifted only after wealthy friends intervened with the emperor.[18] Throughout his papacy, Damasus tried to compensate for his lack of moral authority by stressing the dignity of his office as the successor of Peter. He was the first to invoke Matthew 16:18, "You are Peter and upon this rock I will build my Church," to buttress the primacy of the Roman see.[19] Many saw Damasus as an ambitious, worldly man who ingratiated himself into Rome's high society with opulent dinner parties surpassing even those given by the emperor's family.[20] But church historian Henry Chadwick finds a silver lining: "[Damasus] did as much as any fourth century Pope to make it natural for the great upper-class families of Rome to turn to Christianity without feeling that they were doing something disreputable and un-Roman."[21] This is not the place for in-depth analysis of Damasus's papacy other than to say he had a profound impact on the funerary landscape of Rome and on the power and primacy of the papal office. His papacy would also render invisible the memory of early women martyrs and powerful female patrons.

Nicola Denzey gives a meticulous account of Damasus's eighteen-year project to remodel catacomb sites and elevate them to shrines honoring Roman martyrs.[22] In the process, he systematically raised up male martyrs for veneration while demoting female martyrs previously honored at the very same catacomb. Damasus wrote sixty lengthy poems (called *elogiae*) heroizing the male martyrs and seeing to it that they were elegantly inscribed at each newly reconfigured catacomb. As the cult of the martyrs exploded in popularity, Dama-

---

17. Chadwick, *Early Church*, 167. See also Denzey, *Bone Gatherers*, 177–78.
18. Chadwick, *Early Church*, 161.
19. Ibid., 238.
20. Ibid., 161.
21. Ibid.
22. Denzey, *Bone Gatherers*, 195–97.

sus's poetry-in-stone would shape pilgrims' interpretations of what they saw. In effect, Denzey says, "Damasus manipulated and created an official Christian collective memory and self-identity that obliterated powerful women from Roman Christian imaginative horizons."[23] Here are a few examples:

In the Via Salaria, the catacombs of Bassilla were named for a female patron who over time came to be remembered as a virgin martyr rather than a wealthy female patron. Bassilla was one of two female martyrs (Agnes is the other) named in the Codex Calendar of 354. Her cult was very popular well before Damasus came to power in 366. But Damasus's poetic inscription at Bassilla's catacomb does not name her. Instead, he commemorated three male martyrs—Protus, Hyacinth, and Hermes—none of whom are mentioned in the Codex Calendar. Bassilla would soon be lost to history. At the catacombs of Domitilla, Damasus renovated an area that had initially venerated three martyrs—Petronella (a woman) and two soldiers, Nereus and Achilleus (see chapter 4). But his *elogia* inexplicably omitted Petronella and honored only Nereus and Achilleus. Denzey summarizes: "In the end, of Damasus' sixty flowery inscriptions in honor of the martyrs, only one commemorates a woman martyr. Not a single one acknowledges the foundations of a holy site by a woman patron."[24] Damasus's ambitious campaign would eventually transform Rome's founding myth from Romulus and Remus to Peter and Paul.[25] In the process, the church's female martyr-heroines, and wealthy woman patrons, would become all but invisible. Even as many influential female Christian martyrs were lost to history, other Christian women would be remembered, primarily because of the men who wrote about them.

---

23. Ibid., 194.

24. Ibid., 197.

25. See Dennis E. Trout, "Damasus and the Invention of Early Christian Rome," in *The Cultural Turn in Late Ancient Studies: Gender, Asceticism, and Historiography*, ed. Dale B. Martin and Patricia Cox Miller (Durham, NC: Duke University Press, 2005), 299–315.

LEARNED WOMEN AND THE RISE
OF MONASTIC ASCETICISM

MACRINA

While Jerome in the West and Basil of Caesarea in the East are frequently credited for the rise of monasticism, it is actually two women—Marcella and Macrina the Younger—who began living this new Christian lifestyle before they did. Macrina (327–379 CE) was the oldest of ten children born to an aristocratic family in Asia Minor whose forebears had suffered in the Great Persecution of Diocletian. While in labor with her firstborn, Macrina's mother, Emmelia, had a vision in which her child was three times addressed as Thecla. This would become Macrina's secret name. According to Macrina's brother and biographer, Gregory, bishop of Nyssa, the vision was meant "to point out, by the identity of name, a similarity in their choice of life."[26] Her parents saw to it that Macrina was educated in Scripture, particularly the book of Wisdom, the Psalms, and "whatever led to the moral life."[27] When she came of age, Macrina's father, Basil, promised her to a young Christian man who used his rhetorical gifts in law "on behalf of the victims of injustice."[28] At this time, betrothals were considered nearly the equivalent of marriage. When her intended met an untimely end, Macrina refused any other suitors, arguing that marriage could take place only once and that it would be wrong not to keep faith with her deceased fiancé. *Univira* (one spouse) marriages were highly regarded in the Roman world, and her parents acceded to her wish to embrace an ascetic lifestyle rather than find another husband. In his *Life of St. Macrina*, Gregory tells us that when his older brother Basil came home from studying rhetoric, he was "excessively puffed up with the thought of his own eloquence." But Macrina "took him in hand" and led him speedily "towards the goal of philosophy."[29] Basil would later become bishop of Caesarea and embrace an ascetic life himself but not before hammering out

26. Clark, *Women in the Early Church*, 238.
27. Ibid.
28. Ibid., 239.
29. Ibid., 241.

what would become the doctrine of the Trinity with brother Gregory of Nyssa and Gregory of Nazianzus. Macrina's was a remarkably intelligent, learned, and devout family.

Domestic asceticism was popular in both the East and the West, particularly among women. When Macrina's father died, she convinced her mother to allow their entire household to live in an egalitarian manner, with slaves, servants, and nobility treated as equals. Later, she founded a monastery at Annisa in Pontus, which became the prototype for a monastic rule written by her brother Basil. Gregory describes Macrina's monastic sisterhood this way:

> Self-control was their pleasure, not to be known was their fame, their wealth was in possessing nothing and in shaking off all material surplus, like dust from the body; their work was none of the concerns of this life, except in so far as it was a subordinate task. Their only care was for divine realities, and there was constant prayer and the unceasing singing of hymns, extended equally throughout the entire day and night so that this was both work and respite from work for them.[30]

Macrina was at the heart of her large and faithful family. Gregory calls her his teacher and saw his sister as a second Thecla as well as a second Socrates. Such a pairing

> was probably made possible for Gregory by the fact that the Macrina he knew and loved was the Macrina he had always gone to for advice and spiritual guidance and really was the Macrina with whom he had always debated his most pressing philosophical and theological problems.[31]

Gregory was present at Annisa when Macrina lay dying in 379. His profound grief was amplified by the lamentations of her monastic sisters:

> From the girls who called her by the name of mother and nurse, their grief flared out more passionately than from the rest. They were those who had been left prostrate along the roadways at the time of the

---

30. Gregory, Bishop of Nyssa, *The Life of Saint Macrina* (Kevin Corrigan, "Saint Macrina: The Hidden Face Behind the Tradition," *Vox Benedictina* 5, no. 1 [1988]: 13–43; reprinted on Monastic Matrix by permission of Peregrina Publishers, http://tinyurl.com/yaubm57a).
31. Corrigan, "Saint Macrina."

famine; and she had picked them up, nursed them, brought them back to health and guided them personally to the pure, uncorrupted life.[32]

If Basil is the father of monasticism, surely Macrina is its mother.[33]

MARCELLA AND PAULA

The Roman noblewoman Marcella had been gathering women to study Scripture and pray in her aristocratic home on the Aventine for fully forty years before Jerome arrived in 382 CE.[34] Yet, Marcella's creation of a Western monastic lifestyle is rooted in the East. In 340 CE, Athanasius, the bishop of Alexandria, found refuge in Rome after being exiled by pro-Arian forces. His keen advocacy of Egyptian asceticism became popular in Rome. It apparently inspired Marcella who, although a young girl at the time, never forgot her attraction to it. Finding herself widowed after only seven months of marriage, Marcella chose an ascetic spiritual path. Instead of fleeing to the desert, her asceticism would be lived as an urban monastic and scholar in the midst of the busy, cosmopolitan city of Rome. Sophronia, Asella, Principia, and Lea eventually joined her, women whom Mary T. Malone and Rosemary Ruether have described as "mothers of the church."[35] Soon, another group of women from the home of a nearby relative, Paula, arrived at Marcella's house each day to pray, study Scripture, and learn about the monastic lifestyle. And what was that lifestyle? Jerome's letter 127 tells us that Marcella lived at home, rarely going out in public except to visit "the basilicas of apostles and martyrs for private prayer." She fasted in moderation, wore "clothing meant to keep out the cold and not to show her figure," and abstained from meat and wine. It is plausible to imagine that our

32. Ibid.

33. I am grateful to Robin Senior for this lovely phrase found in her essay "Macrina: More than a Deacon," *Women Deacons: Why Not Now?*, FutureChurch, 2016, http://tinyurl.com/y9blqbc5.

34. Mary T. Malone, *Women and Christianity*, vol. 1, *The First Thousand Years* (Maryknoll, NY: Orbis, 2001), 136.

35. Ibid. See also Rosemary Radford Ruether, "Mothers of the Church: Ascetic Women in the Late Patristic Age," in *Women of Spirit: Female Leadership in the Jewish and Christian Traditions*, ed. Rosemary Radford Ruether and Eleanor McLaughlin (New York: Simon & Schuster, 1979), 72–94.

Roman ascetics visited and prayed in the Greek chapel at the cata-combs of Priscilla and before the fresco of Veneranda and Petronilla at the catacombs of Domitilla. Another woman in the Roman monas-tic circle, Fabiola, focused on charitable works as well as biblical study. She financed a homeless shelter and a hospital where she her-self nursed the sick and dying. Fabiola's biblical questions led Jerome to explore Numbers, and like other ascetics of her day, she undertook pilgrimages to Jerusalem and Bethlehem.[36]

In 383 CE, Pope Damasus summoned Jerome to serve as his papal secretary and Scripture scholar in Rome. Marcella quickly invited him to the Aventine, where he taught the women to interpret Scrip-ture and to sing psalms in Hebrew. Thus began a long intellectual and spiritual relationship, which has been described as a "study group," that benefited Jerome at least as much as Marcella and her Aventine sisters.[37] After his patron Pope Damasus died, Jerome moved to Jerusalem in 385 CE. He was apparently fleeing public controversy over the death of Paula's daughter, Blessilla, who prob-ably starved to death from the excessive fasting that Jerome had encouraged. Paula and another daughter, Eustochium, followed him, making numerous stops along the way, one of which was Seleucia, probably to visit the shrine of Saint Thecla.[38] Paula eventually financed and oversaw the building of two monasteries in Bethlehem, one for women, and one for men. She turned the male monastery over to the monks, and this is where, thanks to Paula's patronage, Jerome completed his translation of the Greek Bible into Latin. Jerome tells us that Paula's expertise in Hebrew exceeded his own:

> While I myself beginning as a young man have with much toil and effort partially acquired the Hebrew tongue and study it now unceas-ingly lest if I leave it, it also may leave me; Paula, on making up her mind that she too would learn it, succeeded so well that she could chant the psalms in Hebrew and could speak the language without a trace of the pronunciation peculiar to Latin.[39]

36. Anne Ewing Hickey, *Women of the Roman Aristocracy as Christian Monastics* (Ann Arbor, MI: UMI Research Press, 1987), 41.
37. Ibid., 40.
38. Ibid., 27.
39. Jerome, *To Eustochium*, Letter 108, 27.

Paula would guide the women's monastery where Jerome tells us, "No sister was allowed to be ignorant of the psalms, and all had every day to learn a certain portion of the holy scriptures." When she died in 404 at the age of fifty-six, Paula's funeral was attended by the bishop of Jerusalem, bishops from nearby cities, and apparently every cleric, monk, and female monastic in Palestine, as well as "the whole population of the cities of Palestine." The ceremonies lasted a week with frequent chanting of psalms, "now in Greek, now in Latin, now in Syriac."[40] Because of her great philanthropy to the poor, Paula "left not a single penny to her daughter but, . . . a large mass of debt; and, worse even than this, a crowd of brothers and sisters whom it is hard for her to support but whom it would be undutiful to cast off."[41] Paula's daughter Eustochium assumed these debts as she began to lead the monastery.

After Jerome moved to Bethlehem, Marcella became the resident biblical expert in Rome. She frequently found herself fielding scriptural questions from "priests who were inquiring about obscure and doubtful points."[42] Because churchmen forbade women to teach men, she carefully credited Jerome or another man for her knowledge:

> If an argument arose about some evidence from Scripture, the question was pursued with her as the judge. . . . [But] when she was thus questioned, she used to reply as if what she said was not her own, even if the views were her own, but came either from me or from another man. . . . For she knew the saying of the Apostle, "I do not, however, permit a woman to teach" (1 Tim 2:12).[43]

Nevertheless, Marcella, and probably many of her sisters, did in fact teach men. The Roman women of Marcella's circle were biblically literate and engaged in public debate despite the prohibitions against women speaking in public. During the Origenist controversy,[44] Jerome writes:

40. Ibid., 29, 30.
41. Ibid., 31.
42. Jerome, *To Principia*, Letter 127, 7.
43. Ibid.
44. Historian Henry Chadwick calls Origen (184–254) "a giant among early Christian thinkers" for whom "the only source of revelation is the Bible." See Chadwick, *Early Church*, 181, 184–89.

The holy Marcella, who had long held back lest she should be thought to act from party motives, threw herself into the breach. Conscious that the faith of Rome—once praised by an apostle [in] Romans 1:8—was now in danger, and that this new heresy was drawing to itself not only priests and monks but also many of the laity besides imposing on the bishop who fancied others as guileless as he was himself, she publicly withstood its teachers choosing to please God rather than men.[45]

Marcella's home on the Aventine became a scholarly ecclesial center for influential clergy and laity alike. Along with her educated and devout female community, she was intimately involved in the important church issues of the day. She died in 410, four days after being savagely beaten by Goths who found no riches in her household during the sack of Rome. Jerome's eulogy, written for Marcella's dear friend Principia, praised her love of Scripture:

> Her delight in the divine scriptures was incredible. She was forever singing, "Your words have I hid in mine heart." . . . She remembered also the prophet's words, "through your precepts I get understanding," [Ps 119:104] and felt sure that only when she had fulfilled these would she be permitted to understand the scriptures.[46]

MELANIA THE ELDER

Melania the Elder was born into an aristocratic family in 341 or 342 CE in the Roman province in Spain.[47] At about age fourteen, she married into the influential Valerii clan and gave birth to three children. In 364, her husband, who was probably many years her senior, died. Soon thereafter, she suffered the loss of two of her children. With her young son Publicola, Melania moved to Rome where she was drawn to the ascetic community there. Since Marcella's group of learned ascetic women had already been gathering for several decades, we may assume that Melania found companionship and support as she pursued a new life of simplicity, self-denial, and charitable works. In 372, she decided to go on pilgrimage to visit the desert monastics in the East. Leaving Publicola in the care of a guardian, she

45. Jerome, *To Principia*, Letter 127, 9.
46. Ibid., 4.
47. Hickey, *Women of the Roman Aristocracy*, 44.

set sail for Alexandria in the company of "various highborn women and children," taking "all her movable property" with her.[48] Publicola subsequently married into a distinguished aristocratic family.[49] Along with Melania's own family, he would generously support his mother's huge charitable ventures for more than forty years: "Her scale of charitable works must have been staggering, and she is reported to have fed at one time no less than five thousand monks."[50] Publicola would become the father of Melania the Younger, who, after her brother died, was sole heir to her family's empire-wide estates. She spent much of her life trying to rid herself of the vast wealth she had inherited from both parents.[51]

Once in Egypt, the senior Melania used her wealth and influence to help monks, priests, and bishops in the Nitrian Desert. After Athanasius's death in 373, his Arian successor exiled the pro-Nicene desert monks to Palestine. Melania "followed them and ministered to them from her own money."[52] Eventually the ban on Nicene Christians was lifted, and Melania, with her friend the monk Rufinus, founded a double monastery on the Mount of Olives, again using her own funds. Rufinus later translated the Rule of St. Basil (probably modeled on Macrina's community at Annisa), so it is likely that these monasteries followed Basil's daily schedule. For twenty-five to thirty years, Melania, Rufinus, and the other female and male ascetics in Jerusalem engaged in Scripture study, prayer, charitable works, and hospitality for pilgrims.[53] The monastery also had a scriptorium in which, to support themselves, the ascetics copied both sacred and Greco-Roman classical authors.[54] After leaving Rome in 385, Paula and Jerome stayed with Melania and Rufinus before founding their own monastic houses in Bethlehem.

---

48. Palladius, *Lausiac History* 46.1, transcribed by Roger Pearse, Christian Classics Ethereal Library, 2003, http://tinyurl.com/yb8hhxgq; all quotations taken from here unless otherwise specified.

49. Hickey, *Women of the Roman Aristocracy*, 44.

50. Hagith Sivan, "On Hymens and Holiness in Late Antiquity: Opposition to Aristocratic Female Asceticism in Rome," *Jahrbuch für Antike und Christentum* 36 (1993): 90. Author cites Paulinus, letter 29, 11, for the feeding of five thousand monks at one time.

51. Sivan, "On Hymens and Holiness," 90.

52. Palladius, *Lausiac History* 46.3.

53. Ruether, "Mothers of the Church," 84.

54. Ibid.

During her lifetime, Melania exercised a discerning, loving spiritual authority that included reconciling schismatic monks, leading a prominent churchman back to his vow of celibacy, and teaching and converting men. She was instrumental in resolving a schism at Antioch that involved "some 400 monks . . . and winning over every heretic that denied the Holy Spirit." At the same time, in what must have been a masterful peacemaking move, "they honored the clergy of the district with gifts and food, and so continued to the end, without offending anyone."[55] Evagrius Ponticus, a young deacon from Constantinople who was "held in high honor by the whole city," came to Jerusalem in profound spiritual distress. While in Constantinople, he had a sexual affair with a married noblewoman. Although he wished to repent, after arriving in Jerusalem, "the devil hardened his heart," so he hesitated.[56] Evagrius contracted a fever that lasted six long months before Melania finally intervened:

"Son, your long illness does not please me. Tell me therefore what are your thoughts. For this illness of yours is not without God." Then he confessed to her the whole matter. But she said to him: "Give me your word before the Lord that you will keep to the mark of the monastic life; and, sinner though I am, I will pray that you may be granted a furlough of life." And he consented. So within a few days he got well, and he arose and received a change of clothes at the hands of the lady herself and went away and exiled himself in the mount of Nitria, which is in Egypt.[57]

In Egypt, Evagrius would become "one of the most influential writers on the spiritual life" and a principle proponent of the Origenist way of prayer (see below).[58] Melania also taught about God and the Christian way of life to other men, such as her grandson and the non-Christian husband of her niece Avita. Palladius describes the latter man as "that most blessed and worthy man, Apronianus." After convincing Apronianus to become a Christian, Melania persuaded him "to be continent as regards his wife."[59] Melania the Younger would

55. Palladius, *Lausiac History* 46.6.
56. Ibid., 38.3, 8.
57. Ibid., 38.9.
58. Chadwick, *Early Church*, 181, 185.
59. Palladius, *Lausiac History* 54.4.

soon follow in her grandmother's footsteps. She publicly refuted heresy by effectively countering Nestorianism at the court in Constantinople and taught her pagan uncle about the Christian way, leading to his baptism.[60]

Melania the Elder was also a formidable scholar, well versed in Christian theological, and probably some classical, works:

> Being very learned and loving literature, she turned night into day by perusing every writing of the ancient commentators, including 3,000,000 (lines) of Origen and 2,500,000 (lines) of Gregory, Stephen, Pierius, Basil, and other standard writers. Nor did she read them once only and casually, but she laboriously went through each book seven or eight times.[61]

Paulinus of Nola links Melania's love of study to her asceticism: "Her hard couch . . . becomes soft as she studies, for her pleasure in reading reduces the hardship of that stiff bed."[62] Since Melania read so many works by Origen, some speculate that she was fluent in Greek, although she may have had access to Rufinus's Latin translations.[63] Melania the Elder is thought to have died in Jerusalem in the year 410: "having got rid of her possessions, within forty days she fell asleep in a good old age and profound meekness, leaving behind both a monastery in Jerusalem and an endowment for it."[64]

A WORD ABOUT THE ORIGENIST CONTROVERSY

Influential fourth-century Christian women such as Marcella and Melania the Elder were deeply involved in the ecclesial issues of their day. One of these was the Origenist controversy that arose over the writings of the early third-century theologian Origen (184–254). Historian Henry Chadwick calls him "a giant among early Christian

---

60. Gillian Cloke, *This Female Man of God: Women and Spiritual Power in the Patristic Age, AD 350–450* (New York: Routledge, 1995), 183–84. Cloke cites Gerontius's *Life of Melania the Younger*, 53.

61. Palladius, *Lausiac History* 55.3.

62. Paulinus of Nola, Letter 29 (*Ancient Christian Writers* 36:116), as found in Hickey, *Women of the Roman Aristocracy*, 47.

63. Hickey, *Women of the Roman Aristocracy*, 47.

64. Palladius, *Lausiac History* 54.6.

thinkers" for whom "the only source of revelation is the Bible."[65] In 325, Bishop Epiphanius attacked Origen's orthodoxy. Epiphanius was a rather rigid heresy hunter who published a book, *A Panarion* [medicine chest] *against Eighty Heresies*. Dissension quickly spread to Palestine, where it bitterly divided Jerome and Rufinus as well as their respective patrons, Marcella and Melania.[66] For Origen, Scripture could be interpreted allegorically as well as literally. Biblical contemplation may therefore yield several ever-deepening understandings of the soul's relationship to God wherein a person may be brought into wordless union with Christ. In the fourth century, well after his death, controversy arose between "the Origenists"—who taught that while praying one should not form any definite image or picture of God in human form—and the "anthropomorphists," who believed that God could legitimately be imaged in human form as a powerful paternal figure.[67]

This would have been a vital issue for ascetics such as Marcella and Melania the Elder, whose way of life involved meditating upon Scripture at all times. The two women were on opposite sides of the issue. Marcella strongly supported Jerome, who bitterly opposed Origenism, even though in his earlier life he had praised the brilliant theologian. Melania the Elder supported both her pro-Origenist spiritual son, Evagrius, as well as Rufinus, who had translated Origen's works into Latin but omitted certain sections that were thought to be in error. Marcella sent Jerome a stolen copy of Rufinus's unrevised translation and asked him to quickly send her a refutation so she could speak against Origenism in Rome. Unfortunately, Marcella and the fiery Jerome succeeded in "blackening the reputations of Melania and Rufinus until modern times."[68]

Meanwhile the sixty-year-old Melania the Elder, after hearing that her granddaughter, Melania the Younger, and her husband, Pin-

65. Chadwick, *Early Church*, 100–101.
66. Ibid., 184.
67. Ibid., 185.
68. Ruether, "Mothers of the Church," 85. Ruether writes: "in retrospect, the differences between Jerome and Rufinus appear minor. Both agreed that Origen was a great scholar and theologian whose valuable work needed to be used, but who had strayed into errors that must be corrected. . . . Much of the heat surrounding this controversy was the result of [an] enlarged personality conflict rather than substance."

ion, were intent on pursuing an ascetic way of life, hastened to Rome "afraid lest they should be injured by bad teaching or heresy."[69] Scholars believe Melania the Elder "hoped to save her granddaughter from falling into the hands of the pro-Jerome, anti-Origen faction in Rome.[70] She was apparently successful:

> The younger Melania remained friendly with men whom Jerome considered Origenists. She sheltered Palladius in her home when he came on a delegation to Rome in 404 CE and remained on excellent terms with Paulinus of Nola, whom Jerome never won for his camp."[71]

Clearly, influential Roman women such as Marcella, Paula, and the Melanias were deeply involved in helping to shape the spirituality, theology, and social mission of the fourth-century church. That they did not always agree may simply be a sign of the vitality of their individual visions. In succeeding centuries, monastics would recognize that both types of prayer are legitimate ways of approaching a God who, in the end, is ultimate mystery. One, the so-called *via positiva*," or *kataphatic* prayer, employs thoughts and images as a way into the divine. The other the *via negativa*," or *apophatic* prayer, rests in a sort of "cloud of unknowing" that is beyond thoughts and images. A study by Frederick G. McLeod suggests that most believers find grace in both types of prayer at different times during their spiritual journeys.[72]

OLYMPIAS

We have more historical documentation about Olympias than for most women in the early church.[73] She was born in Constantinople

69. Palladius, *Lausiac History* 54.3.

70. Elizabeth A. Clark, *Ascetic Piety and Women's Faith: Essays on Late Ancient Christianity* (Lewiston, NY: Edwin Mellen, 1986), 74. Clark cites the work of E. D. Hunt, "Palladius of Helenopolis: A Party and Its Supporters in the Church of the Late Fourth Century," *Journal of Theological Studies* 24, no. 2 (1973): 456–80.

71. Clark, *Ascetic Piety*, 74. Clark cites Palladius, *Lausiac History* 61 and Paulinus of Nola, Letter 29.12.

72. Frederick G. McLeod, "Apophatic or Kataphatic Prayer?" Dominican Central Province, January 13, 2015, http://tinyurl.com/y9c8vh2g.

73. Elizabeth A. Clark, *Jerome, Chrysostom, and Friends: Essays and Translations* (New York: Edwin Mellen, 1979), 107–8. The *Life of Olympias* was written by a fifth-century anonymous

in 360–70 CE and orphaned at an early age. Her education was over-seen by Theodosia, the sister of the bishop of Iconium who is believed to have gathered a circle of pious women around her. In 384 or 386 CE, Olympias married an influential man named Nebridius, who was considerably older than she. He died after only twenty months, leav-ing Olympias an extremely wealthy young widow. After Nebridius's death, believing that such great wealth could not be entrusted to the care of a young woman, the emperor Theodosius tried to convince Olympias to marry one of his own relatives, Elpidius. But Olympias refused. She was then falsely accused of reckless expenditure of her money and property, giving the emperor a reason to place it under guardianship until she turned thirty. At the behest of Elpidius, the prefect brought even more pressure on Olympias to remarry, but she again refused.

What was the creative source for Olympias's refusal to abide by imperial conventions for women in her day? The anonymous author of the *Life of Olympias* offers us a clue. Olympias did not agree with "the apostolic rule" then widely cited to make sure young widows remarried: "I wish young widows to marry, run a household" (1 Tim 5:14). Instead, her biographer cites another passage from the same source: "For the law was not laid down for the righteous man, but for the unruly, the impure and the insatiable" (1 Tim 1:9). Olympias's knowledge and love of Scripture permeates her sense of self. With simplicity, she claims her own "righteousness" and quotes Scripture pointing to the importance of conscience over law.[74] This woman is knowledgeable, wise, and courageous in opposing any powers beyond her own that seek to control her or her wealth.

In 391, Theodosius finally restored Olympias's fortune. Why the change of heart? According to historian Peter Brown, poverty was a dangerous reality in Constantinople owing to rapid immigration

---

author. Another ancient source, *Narration Concerning St. Olympias*, was written about 630 by the Sergia, the superior of Olympias's monastery. It recounts miraculous events that occurred when her remains were moved back to her convent. Three other early documents, Palladius's *Dialogue* and *Lausiac History* and Sozomen's *Church History*, also give testimony about Olympias. Last, but far from least, are seventeen letters St. John Chrysostom wrote to her from exile. Sadly, we have no documents written by Olympias herself since none of her letters to Chrysostom survived.

74. *The Life of Olympias* as reproduced in Clark, *Jerome, Chrysostom, and Friends*, 129.

from Asia Minor. It fell to the women of the noble class to serve as "intermediaries of the governing class of the city by ministering to the urban poor."[75] The emperor's wife, Flacilla, tended to the poor, visited them in their hospitals, and fed them through special meals akin to today's soup kitchens. When Flacilla died, a decline in services to the poor led to an ugly riot that ended with the burning down of Archbishop Nectarius's palace. Something had to be done. Nectarius decided to make Olympias a deacon, even though she did not meet the age criteria of sixty years. This solved a number of problems. By allowing Olympias's wealth to replace the social safety net that had disappeared with Flacilla's death, Nectarius would regain control of the impoverished populous.[76]

While political motivations may have led to her diaconal ordination, her new official status also allowed Olympias to fulfill a deep desire to use her fortune for the good of the church and for the poor. No sooner did she regain her wealth than she began to distribute it with prodigality nearly unrivaled in her time. Churches in Greece, Asia Minor, and Syria received generous donations of land and money.[77] Palladius testifies that her support actually maintained Archbishop Nectarius's financial needs so much that he took her advice in ecclesiastical affairs. She also made gifts to "every priest who visited the city and a host of ascetics and virgins."[78] The *Life of Olympias* reports that Olympias donated "10 thousand pounds of gold, 20 thousand of silver and all of her real estate situated in the provinces of Thrace, Galatia, Cappadocia Prima, and Bithynia," as well as the houses belonging to her in Constantinople.[79] Shortly after her ordination, Olympias built a large monastery close to the cathedral of Hagia Sophia. Here, "she enclosed her own chambermaids, numbering 50, all of whom lived in purity and virginity."[80] In addition, three relatives, Elisanthia, Martyria, and Palladia, joined her and were ordained deacons. The *Life of Olympias* recounts that

75. Brown, *Body and Society*, 283.
76. Ibid.
77. Mary Lawrence McKenna, *Women of the Church: Role and Renewal* (New York: P. J. Kenedy, 1967), 85.
78. Clark, *Ascetic Piety*, 113.
79. Ibid.
80. Ibid., 131.

many other Roman women of senatorial families came to live at the monastery so that the number of women living a monastic life numbered 250 in all.

Olympias was also a confidante and benefactor of John Chrysostom, who became archbishop of Constantinople in 398 CE. Chrysostom made enemies among the rich and powerful of the city after he persuaded Olympias to stop giving money to the wealthy and give it to the poor instead. This severely restricted the free flow of funds for entertaining visiting ecclesiastical dignitaries. Founding a leper colony on the edge of a fashionable suburb further estranged Chrysostom from the nouveau riche. Chrysostom's fiery sermons denouncing the abuses of the powerful culminated in banishment in 404 CE to central Asia Minor.[81] Shortly after Chrysostom left Constantinople, arsonists destroyed the cathedral. Pro- and anti-Chrysostom factions blamed each other. Followers of Chrysostom "were accused of arson, summoned by the authorities for investigation, tortured, and even put to death."[82] Even though she protested her innocence, Olympias herself was fined and sent into exile, probably to the city of Nicomedia. From exile, she and Chrysostom exchanged numerous letters of which only Chrysostom's survive. In them, he encourages and praises her:

> [I am] cheered, and brightened, and not a little proud on account of your greatness of soul, and the repeated victories which you have won, and this, not only for your own sake, but also for the sake of that large and populous city (Nicomedia?) where you are like a tower, a haven and a wall of defense, speaking in the eloquent voice of example.[83]

John Chrysostom died in the city of Comana in Asia Minor in September of 407, probably overcome by physical exhaustion from the rigors of exile. The exact year of Olympias's death is unknown, although the date is thought to be July 25 sometime between 410 and 420. Olympias's unparalleled generosity in supporting both powerful bishops and the powerless poor places her among the most well-known and beloved women of her time. While her wealth was a

81. Brown, *Body and Society*, 318.
82. Clark, *Ascetic Piety*, 116.
83. John Chrysostom, *To Olympias*, Letter 3.

factor in her ability to influence powerful men, certainly her holiness gave credibility to the spiritual authority she exercised among the sisters at the monastery adjoining Hagia Sophia. It is a great shame that her letters were not preserved since we may well suspect that she influenced Chrysostom even as he did her. Certainly, her solidarity and support with this beloved bishop is of a piece with other male-female teams working throughout history for the betterment of the church.[84]

WOMEN WHO WERE NOT ASCETICS

PROBA

The life of Faltonia Betitia Proba attests to the diversity of lifestyles and perspectives that existed among influential Christian women in the fourth century. Unlike the female ascetics, Proba was a married noblewoman who saw no need to relinquish husband, children, or wealth to be a faithful follower of Christ. Born no later than 322 CE, Proba died around 370 CE, just before the "golden age of asceticism" (370–380 CE) that characterized the lives of women such as Paula and Marcella.[85] Proba's father, a member of Rome's aristocratic Petronii family, is believed to have been Petronius Probianus, a Roman consul who governed as prefect of the city from 329 to 331 CE. Her husband, Clodius Celsinus Adelphius, would himself become consul and prefect in Rome. Along with the couple's two sons, Adelphius eventually became Christian. His conversion was undoubtedly due to Proba's influence after her own conversion, which may have occurred after the civil rebellion of Magnentius in 353 CE. Both of Proba's sons would eventually attain high offices, including prefect of Rome.

Proba is best known for her poetic *cento*. She has been described as "the only female writer of early orthodox Christianity who has an

---

84. For example, Phoebe and Paul, Paula and Jerome, Melania and Rufinus, Clare and Francis, Mary Ward and her Jesuit supporters, and the male and female martyrs of El Salvador.

85. Clark, *Ascetic Piety*, 146.

entire work still extant."[86] A *cento* is a literary genre well known in the ancient world. It is a type of poetry in which "one pieced together lines or parts of lines from earlier works to create a new meaning: the word 'cento' itself is thought originally to have meant a 'patchwork cloak.'"[87] The Greeks used Homer as the source of their *centos* while Latin speakers used Virgil. It can be difficult for modern people to understand how popular Virgil's poetry was among educated people in late antiquity. Not only did every school child learn and memorize Virgil, but his works were so popular that

> they were discussed at dinner parties, made their way into the theatre, and provided inspiration for tapestries and art of various sorts. . . . It was thought that one could turn to Virgil not just for beauty of style but for "wisdom," rather vaguely defined.[88]

Proba's *cento* skillfully wove together lines from Virgil's *Eclogae*, *Georgica*, and *Aeneid* to depict biblical stories and episodes from the life of Jesus. She had written one earlier *cento* about war, probably the Magnentius rebellion against Constantius II in 353 CE. After becoming Christian, she deemed writing about war had been a mistake.[89] Scholars date the *cento* anywhere from after the Magnentius war to the date of Proba's death in 370 CE. One attractive theory is that she wrote it in 362 CE after the emperor, Julian the Apostate (r. 331–63), issued an edict forbidding Christian teachers to include Christian beliefs in their teaching of classical texts. Julian died soon afterward and subsequent Christian emperors rescinded the edict.

Proba's *cento* became an extremely popular educational tool in late antiquity. It circulated throughout the eastern empire and was used in schools in medieval times even up to the seventeenth century. An education in the classics was the *sine qua non* for up and coming Roman scions. *Centos* such as Proba's provided a way to integrate the

86. Elizabeth A. Clark and Diane F. Hatch, ed., *The Golden Bough, the Oaken Cross: The Virgilian Cento of Faltonia Betitia Proba* (Chico, CA: Scholars Press, 1981), 98.

87. Clark, *Ascetic Piety*, 125.

88. Clark and Hatch, *Golden Bough*, 103. The authors cite Juvenal, *Satires II* 180–81; Petronius, *Satyricon* 68; Domenico Comparetti, *Vergil in the Middle Ages*, trans. E. F. M. Benecke (London: S. Sonnenschein, 1908), 29; Macrobius, *Saturnalia* 5.17.5; and David S. Weisen, "Virgil, Minucius Felix and the Bible," *Hermes* 99, no. 1 (1971): 72.

89. Clark and Hatch, *Golden Bough*, 15.

tenets and values of Christianity within a Greco-Roman classical heritage. She is among the first to use Virgilian verse for Christian purposes, and her *cento* has been judged the best of all Christian *centos* because of its artistry and the acclaim it received.[90] Because Proba's "excessively masculine" figure of Christ is depicted as the prototypical Roman hero, Aeneas, Elizabeth A. Clark believes "we can safely assert, at a minimum, that Rome's aristocratic young men would have made a natural audience for the *Cento*."[91] Since many episodes in Proba's *cento* almost exclusively involve males, and because other scenes use well-known Virgilian lines pertaining to men and boys, Clark suggests that Proba has recast Jesus's teaching to have "special relevance to upper class males," perhaps her own sons.[92]

An exhaustive exploration of all the biblical stories and theological issues contained in Proba's *cento* is not possible here, but we will review a few major themes, especially as they relate to our topic of the spiritual/religious authority of fourth-century Christian women. Perhaps the best place to start is the touching account Proba gives of her own conversion:

Alas for filial devotion,
Alas for the old time faith! What gratitude
Shall I express, if I may set
Small themes beside the great? No hope remained
For me of ever seeing my long ago,
My native land, no hope for me remained
Of liberty, nor concern for salvation. Herein
He gave me first the answer to my seeking,
Took away the toughened stain, left pure
Ethereal intelligence, and sent me
Back into my realm. Him would I pursue
Through fire, though exiled among the Africans,
Through varying misfortunes, through a thousand
Flying darts, wherever and whenever
Fate might fall; and him the One and Only
Would I follow.[93]

90. Ibid., 98–106.
91. Clark, *Ascetic Piety*, 146.
92. Ibid., 145.
93. Faltonia Betitia Proba, *Cento*, 419–30, as translated from the Latin by Clark and Hatch, *Golden Bough*, 8.

Strategically placed just after the biblical account of Jesus's baptism, Proba's account reveals the depth of her sense of being lost and then found, of being cleansed and then graced with "ethereal intelligence" before being sent back to her own earthly realm. Her experience leaves her with a boundless gratitude and a fervent desire to follow Christ no matter the cost.

At the very beginning of the *cento*, Proba claims the prophetic power of the Holy Spirit at work in her. She prays that God will "unloose the utterance of your eternal, sevenfold Spirit and so unlock the inmost sanctum of my heart that I may find all mysteries within My power to relate—I, Proba, prophetess."[94] She then begs God to "Be present" and "make straight my power of mind, / That Virgil put to verse Christ's sacred duties / Let me tell."[95] Proba's fervor burns as brightly as that of her ascetic sisters, although her path is a very different one. In what follows, we will briefly review Proba's selection and presentation of various biblical stories in light of the following questions: Were Proba's biblical stories the same or different from the biblical stories found on catacomb frescos and sarcophagi of fourth-century Christians? Did Proba have a specifically "feminine" take in her biblical interpretations? How does Proba understand and interpret Scripture?

Proba includes thirteen biblical scenes that are also found in catacomb frescos and sarcophagi friezes of fourth-century Christians: Adam and Eve, Cain and Abel, Noah and the flood, the exodus, the nativity with the Magi, the baptism of Jesus, the Sermon on Mount, Jesus's entry into Jerusalem, Judas's betrayal, Jesus's condemnation before Pilate, the resurrection, doubting Thomas, and the ascension. Eight biblical stories are found in the *cento* that do not appear on early Christian funerary memorials: Herod and slaughter of the innocents, Jesus's temptation in the desert, warnings of judgment day, the rich young man, the storm at sea/Jesus walks on water, the cleansing of the temple, the Last Supper, and the crucifixion. Proba's *cento* affirms the popularity of the aforementioned thirteen biblical stories that appear in both funerary art and in her written words.

94. Ibid., 9–11.
95. Ibid., 20.

Does Proba have a specifically female perspective on the Hebrew and Christian Scriptures compared to that of male interpreters? The evidence is mixed. She elevates the figures of both Eve and Mary. Eve is described as a "wondrous gift," who shines "in brilliant light."[96] She is given dominion over the earth along with Adam and is not subject to him. For Clark, "This one feature sets Proba's poem apart from the sentiments of the Church Fathers, who dwell endlessly on Eve's condemnation as the justification for women's secondary status."[97] Mary's role is primary in Jesus's birth and infancy. Joseph is never mentioned, and in any case, Proba's Mary does not need a man to protect her from Herod's wrath. In Proba's narrative, Mary knew beforehand that the king would try to destroy her child and "commissioned that the babe be reared in secret."[98] Proba exalts Mary's maternal role in contrast to many church fathers who discouraged motherhood and childbearing in favor of ascetic virginity.

Only Adam, however, is made in the image of God,[99] and when God chastises the couple for eating the forbidden fruit, Eve is named as "the origin and cause of all these ills."[100] Proba names only one woman—Mary of Nazareth—in her account of Jesus's life. We hear nothing of Jesus's interactions with faithful women followers such as Mary and Martha, Mary of Magdala, the Samaritan woman, the Syro-Phoenician woman, the woman with the flow of blood, and others. Even though Mary of Magdala led the women who first witnessed the empty tomb, no women are named in Proba's account of the resurrection. If Proba's intent was to provide a pedagogical tool to attract aristocratic men to the Christian message, it may not be surprising that she omits stories of women in the Gospels.

Proba sometimes puts words into the mouths of biblical figures that they do not actually say in the Scriptures. This is significant. Such "poetic license" (indeed, the entire *cento* is "poetic license") often signals her effort to integrate certain Greco-Roman aristocratic "family

96. Ibid., 129–30.
97. Clark, *Ascetic Piety*, 133.
98. Proba, *Cento*, 361–62.
99. Ibid., 120.
100. Ibid., 264.

values" and practices within an early Christian context. For example, within the Sermon on the Mount narrative, Proba has Jesus say:

> For they who
> Brooded over acquired wealth, alone, and did
> Not share a portion with their relatives, long
> As life remained; or if they struck a parent,
> and cozened a client in entangling snare, then,
> When cold death has sundered soul from limb,
> Imprisoned, they await their penalty.[101]

Injunctions to honor parents, share wealth with relatives (no mention of the poor), and treat clients fairly reflect Proba's aristocratic class, whose duty it was to care for family first and be just patrons to their clients.[102] Unlike all three Synoptic accounts, Proba's Jesus never commands the rich young man to sell everything he owns and give it to the poor. Instead she has Jesus say: "Learn, O lad, contempt for wealth and also mold yourself as worthy, even of God."[103] Perhaps the most startling of Proba's textual deviations are the vindictive words she has Jesus say from the Cross:

> Yet he, undaunted, said, "What makes you tie
> These bonds? Has overweening racial pride possessed you?
> Some day, for wrongs committed, you will pay
> With punishment unlike this one to me."[104]

In this passage we see most clearly Proba's attempt to portray Jesus as a Greco-Roman classical hero, who would never allow his honor to be violated without reprisal. As such, says Clark, "he would provide an attractive model for young men who were learning what 'honor' meant to Romans."[105]

Proba inserted her interpretation of biblical texts into a popular genre—the Virgilian *cento*—with a view to harmonizing, insofar as possible, the Christian ethos with that of her own Greco-Roman culture. In doing so, she created a remarkably effective evangelizing tool

101. Ibid., 475–81.
102. Clark, *Ascetic Piety*, 141.
103. Proba, *Cento*, 522.
104. Ibid., 621–23.
105. Clark, *Ascetic Piety*, 146.

that would influence many thousands of Christians for centuries to come. Aside from her other praiseworthy attributes, Proba was a missionary who saw the need for enculturation of the Christian message and did something about it. This creative exercise of religious authority would bear rich fruit. In contrast to her sisters who embraced an ascetic lifestyle, there is nothing in Proba's *cento* to indicate that she believed asceticism to be a superior way of being Christian.[106]

To conclude, Clark offers this astute observation:

> Yet because Proba opted for home and family, when those about her were on the verge of casting them off, means that later generations were left with something exceedingly rare: a piece of early Christian literature written not by a theologian, a priest, or a monk, but by a female layperson.[107]

HELENA, EGERIA, AND THE DEACONESS MARTHANA

Pilgrimages to desert monasteries and sacred sites in the Holy Land became very popular after Emperor Constantine's mother, Helena, journeyed to Jerusalem in 326 CE.[108] Helena would be revered by succeeding generations of elite Christian women who, for over one hundred years, commissioned images and monuments to her. Born in 250 CE, Helena was probably not an aristocrat and may or may not have been married to Constantine's father, Constantius, who, in any case, married someone else after Constantine was born. She did not come to Rome until after Constantius's death in 306 CE, and church historian Eusebius tells us she had "authority over the imperial treasury."[109] Helena acquired land in Rome where she, and probably Constantine, built the basilica of Saints Marcellinus and Petrus as well as the adjoining mausoleum where she would eventually be buried. Helena also owned a nearby palace and repaired the local

---

106. Ibid., 141.
107. Ibid., 147.
108. For this segment on Helena, I am indebted to Leslie Brubaker's insightful article, "Memories of Helena: Patterns in Imperial Female Matronage in the Fourth and Fifth Centuries" in *Women, Men, and Eunuchs: Gender in Byzantium*, ed. Liz James (New York: Routledge, 1997), 52–75.
109. Brubaker cites *Vita Constantini* 3.47: PG 20.1107–8 and Sozomen, *Ecclesiastical History* 2.2.

baths—*thermae Helenae*—commemorated for posterity with a public inscription. When she died around 330 CE, monuments in Rome, Bethlehem, and Jerusalem were associated with her. The tradition that she found relics of the true cross is "almost certainly a later invention." Although the cross in question may have been discovered in Constantine's reign, Helena is not associated with it until some sixty years after her death.[110] Church historians remember Helena as a humble woman who personally "waited on" the female ascetics in Jerusalem. She is also praised as a generous benefactor to those in need:

> When she visited the cities of the East, she bestowed befitting gifts on the churches in every town, enriched those individuals who had been deprived of their possessions, supplied ungrudgingly the necessities of the poor, and restored to liberty those who had been long imprisoned, or condemned to exile or the mines.[111]

Despite a dubious aristocratic lineage, Helena became a model for elite Christian women who were required to act within acceptable social roles to maintain the power of their families:

> From the time of her death until the middle of the fifth century, memories of Helena were evoked to buttress family continuity and dynastic stability, on the one hand, and the appropriation of sanctity by elite women on the other.[112]

Over fifty years after Helena's excursion to Jerusalem, a Spanish woman, Egeria, would undertake a three-year pilgrimage to Syria, Mesopotamia, and the Holy Land between 381–384 CE. Aside from what can be deduced from her travel diaries, very little is known about Egeria herself. Scholars assume that she was a dedicated virgin since she had freedom to travel.[113] Her diaries were written for a

---

110. Brubaker, "Memories of Helena," 58.

111. Sozomen, *Church History* 2.2 (Chester D. Hartranft, *Nicene and Post-Nicene Fathers, Second Series*, vol. 2, ed. Philip Schaff and Henry Wace [Buffalo, NY: Christian Literature, 1890], rev. and ed. Kevin Knight for New Advent, http://tinyurl.com/y7rn4sv7).

112. Brubaker, "Memories of Helena," 63.

113. Joyce E. Salisbury, *Church Fathers, Independent Virgins* (New York: Verso, 1991), 84–89. Carolyn Osiek (email to author, March 19, 2017) demurs, noting that elite women, whether married or single, also had freedom to travel. Egeria clearly had significant financial means and social status.

loosely knit community of women that she affectionately addresses as "sisters," "reverend ladies, my sisters," or "light of my heart."[114] While it is unclear whether she was of aristocratic stock, Egeria was influential, since bishops and dignitaries greeted her and escorted her to sacred sites everywhere she went. She must have had significant financial resources to be able to afford a three-year pilgrimage requiring a retinue of male guides and pack animals. Another clue to her elevated status is that Egeria and her entourage are often provided with an escort of Roman soldiers. Although she was probably a dedicated virgin, Egeria seems to have had little to no familiarity with the concept of asceticism until she visited the East. She carefully explains the term "ascetics" to her sisters as a reference to those who are particularly holy as distinguished from regular monks.[115] In fact, for Joyce Salisbury, "the concept of self-punishment itself seems to have been foreign to her since her pilgrimages lacked the self-imposed hardships that marked the spiritual practices of many others."[116]

Egeria vividly describes her visits to biblical sites at Mount Sinai, Mount Horeb, Jerusalem, and Bethlehem, as well as biblical and monastic sites and martyrs' shrines in Syria and Mesopotamia. When they arrive at each destination, "It was always our custom first to say a prayer, then to read a passage from the Bible, sing a Psalm fitting the occasion and finally say a second prayer."[117] Every place she goes, bishops (whom she invariably describes as "very holy men") greet her. Monks welcome her to visit their cells and bestow upon her small gifts. Aside from descriptions of her pilgrimage visits, Egeria meticulously chronicles the liturgical practices in Jerusalem during Lent, Holy Week, Eastertide, and Pentecost. Her diary is valuable to scholars since it provides documentation of liturgical practices in Jerusalem in the fourth century.

In Mesopotamia, Egeria eagerly visits sites in Haran associated with the biblical Rebecca and Rachel. She visits the famous *martyrium* of Saint Thecla in Seleucia (today Silifke on the Turkish coast),

114. Egeria, *Diary of a Pilgrimage*, trans. George E. Gingras, Ancient Christian Writers 38 (New York: Newman, 1970).
115. Ibid., 67.
116. Salisbury, *Church Fathers*, 86.
117. Egeria, *Diary of a Pilgrimage*, 66.

where she finds "nothing but countless monastic cells for men and women."[118] Here she ecstatically greets her "very dear friend," the holy deaconess Marthana, whose way of life is known to "everyone in the East." Egeria writes that Marthana actually "governs (*regebat*) these monastic cells of *aputactitae*, or virgins" who live out their ascetic lives near Thecla's shrine.[119] Here we see a rare fourth-century example of a female deacon exercising governing authority over Christian men as well as women.[120] Egeria prayed at the shrine, listened to the reading of the complete Acts of Thecla, and then "gave unceasing thanks to Christ our God, who granted to me, an unworthy woman, and in no way deserving, the fulfillment of my desires in all things."[121]

WHAT CAN WE KNOW ABOUT FOURTH-CENTURY CHRISTIAN WOMEN?

Let us now return to questions posed at the beginning of this chapter as to what the literary sources about contemporaneous Christian women might tell us about the lives and values of our fourth-century "tomb women."

DOES THE LITERARY RECORD CORROBORATE OR OPPOSE WHAT FEMALE ICONIC PORTRAYALS IN CATACOMB FRESCOS AND SARCOPHAGI SUGGEST?

There is remarkable corroboration in literary sources for what this study posits about the women whose portraits are found on early Christian sarcophagi. Our "tomb women" were well-educated, wealthy, wives, mothers, and, judging from the number of solo female sarcophagi, single women, or widows. They are depicted with scrolls, codices, speech gestures, and surrounded by biblical scenes.

118. Ibid., 87.
119. Ibid.
120. Kevin Madigan and Carolyn Osiek (*Ordained Women*, 40) suggest that *aputactitae* may be a transliteration of the Greek *apotaktitai*. The word may be a native term for a particular kind of monk and nun known for observing "a particularly strict regimen of fasting and self discipline."
121. Egeria, *Diary of a Pilgrimage*, 87.

Their funerary iconography indicates that (at the least) they proclaimed or taught Scripture. Just so, our literary sources attest that Marcella, Macrina, Egeria, Melania the Elder, Olympias, Proba, and others were wealthy, well-educated women. They were lovers of Scripture and scholars who taught both women and men.

There are a few caveats. With the exception of Proba, it is very unlikely that female ascetics commissioned expensive catacomb frescos or elaborately carved sarcophagi for themselves. They were, after all, ascetics and as such would have viewed such funerary display as a counter-witness to their abstemious habits.[122] Their non-ascetic Christian contemporaries and peers such as Proba, however, may well have commissioned elaborate funerary art to memorialize their piety and Christian influence. But we should not assume that all of our carefully crafted sarcophagi and catacomb frescos belonged to elite women. Many freedwomen, especially those who ran their own businesses after being emancipated, would also have amassed enough wealth to afford an expensive funerary commemoration. Descendants of freed persons, moreover, would have had sufficient inherited wealth to afford a costly funerary remembrance. By the fourth century, it was not only the elite senatorial class who had money.

WERE CONTEMPORANEOUS WOMEN FROM THE LITERARY RECORD ROLE MODELS FOR THE WOMEN BURIED IN THE SARCOPHAGI AND CATACOMBS? OR, WERE THE CATACOMB/TOMB WOMEN ROLE MODELS FOR THEIR LITERARY CONTEMPORARIES?

This is a fascinating question. With the exception of Helena, who died in 330 CE, all of our "literary" women died well after 366 CE. Yet, almost three-fourths (73 percent) of portrait sarcophagi with biblical scenes date to before 366 CE, with over half (64 percent) dating to before 350 CE. It is more likely, therefore, that our "tomb

---

122. Constantine's mother, Helena, could have commissioned an elaborate Christian tomb, but what is believed to be her priceless red porphyry sarcophagus was found over two centuries ago. It is now on display in the Vatican Museums. It has no Christian scenes, and scholars suspect it was originally created for a male member of the imperial family. See "Sarcophagus St Helena," Vatican Museums, http://tinyurl.com/y8aefvc5.

women" were role models for our "literary women" (see table 6.6). It is plausible to suppose that Marcella, Paula, Melania the Elder, Fabiola, Proba, and other women closely associated with Rome admired these non-ascetic female role models who may have inspired them in their love and knowledge of the Christian Scriptures.

DID FOURTH-CENTURY CHRISTIAN WOMEN EXERCISE RELIGIOUS AND SPIRITUAL AUTHORITY?

The answer to this question must be yes. Let us briefly revisit the working definitions of authority described in the introduction to this book. The first relates to governance or jurisdiction: "The power or right to give orders, make decisions, and enforce obedience."[123] The second relates more to influence and knowledge: "The power to influence others, especially because of one's commanding manner or one's recognized knowledge about something,"[124] and "the confident quality of someone who knows a lot about something or who is respected or obeyed by other people."[125] It can be difficult to say if any given deceased is portrayed as exercising governing authority from portrait iconography alone unless they are seated on a magistrate's chair, such as we find on the philosopher's sarcophagus (see figure 6.13). On Christian sarcophagi, only Christ or authorities such as Daniel, Pilate, or Caiaphas are portrayed in iconic magistrate configurations. One possible exception is the *Velata* cubiculum at the catacombs of Priscilla where a late third century fresco depicts both a woman and a "bishop" figure seated in chairs, or *cathedras* (see figure 4.6). In the main, we know—not from frescos or sarcophagi but from literary or epigraphical sources—that women exercised governance, serving as enrolled widows, deacons, heads of monasteries, and presbyters. In most instances, such women governed other women, although there are significant exceptions such as the deaconess Marthana in Seleucia (Turkey), who governed (*regebat*) a double monastery at the *martyrium* of Saint Thecla. Macrina also seems to

---

123. *Oxford English Dictionary* (online), s.v. "authority."
124. Ibid.
125. *Merriam Webster Learner's Dictionary* (online), s.v. "authority."

have governed both men and women at her monastery in Cappadocia. In her role as a member of the imperial family, Empress Helena undoubtedly exercised a type of governance authority with both men and women. Paula, Eustochium, Olympias, and the Melanias governed monasteries of women. The "holy presbyter" Flavia Vitalia had primary responsibility for overseeing Christian burial sites in Croatia in the fifth century (see chapter 4). The woman commemorated in the *Velata* cubiculum at the catacombs of Priscilla was probably being enrolled into a church office. The artist depicts her seated in a chair and dressed similarly to the "bishop" figure, also in a chair. She may well have exercised governing authority as an enrolled widow, just as, in earlier centuries, Grapte had authority over the communities of widows and orphans in Rome while her counterpart Clement had authority to speak for Rome's house church communities.[126]

The iconographical evidence of women with scrolls, speech gestures, and in-facing "apostle" figures on sarcophagus reliefs, suggests that many fourth-century women were influential and knowledgeable about biblical texts. At the very least, they exercised significant spiritual and teaching authority. The preponderance of women depicted with in-facing "apostle" figures suggests our "tomb women" wished to be represented as persons whose authority was recognized and validated by male church leaders. Female portraits in catacomb frescos show women whose learnedness and authority are attested via scrolls that probably represent both the Christian and Hebrew Scriptures (see figures 4.9 and 4.10). Deceased women are also shown with authority to preside at funerary meals.

Turning to the literary sources, we see Marcella exercising biblical authority when she clarifies texts for the priests in Rome. She also exercises ecclesial authority by engaging in public debate over the Origenist controversy. Melania the Elder's ecclesial authority publicly reconciled four hundred schismatic monks. Melania the Younger's ecclesial authority publicly countered Nestorianism at the court in Constantinople. Macrina's authority as a spiritual director had a profound influence on her theologian brothers, who went on to craft the doctrine of the Trinity. Melania the Elder's spiritual wisdom and

126. Herm. Vis. 8 (2.4.3).

authority led to the healing of the renowned monastic writer Eva-grius. Proba's literary and biblical authority created a remarkably effective cross-cultural evangelizing tool that would influence Christian men and women for generations. These are just a few examples of the women we know about. Their spirited exercise of authority greatly influenced the early Christian communities of their time as well as those to come in the future. These "mothers of the church" exercised authority at a time when "fathers of the church" forbade women to speak or teach publicly, preferred that women stay at home, and judged women more susceptible to "heresy" than men. Yet Christian women in the fourth century did not keep silent or remain enclosed. They spoke up about important ecclesial issues, taught both men and women, and witnessed freely about the Christ with whom they had thrown in their lot. Judging from the continued proscriptions from church "fathers" (see chapters 1 and 2), some women also regularly baptized and celebrated the Eucharist.

One could reasonably ask from whence came the strength and inner authority that impelled these women of the early church to disregard attempts by male churchmen to suppress their voices? Assuredly, status and wealth would have helped, but their social circumstances cannot be the whole story. I suggest that what impelled women to speak rather than to be silent was their faith experience in the risen Christ.

Figure 8.1. Female portrait sarcophagus dating to first third of the fourth century. Deceased woman holds codex with right hand in speech gesture. Biblical scenes shown here include (left to right) God with Cain and Abel, Christ with Adam and Eve, deceased with codex, healing of the paralytic, healing of the blind, miracle at Cana, and healing of Lazarus. RS 1, no. 25. Photo © Vatican Museums, Pio Cristiano Museum, inv. 31556. All rights reserved.

Figure 8.2. Detail of deceased woman with codex and speech gesture while Christ leans in as if to speak to her. It is reasonable to surmise that the deceased and/or her family members honored her as someone who ministered with the authority of Christ. RS 1, no. 25. Photo © Vatican Museums, Pio Cristiano Museum, inv. 31556. All rights reserved.

Let us reflect on one last sarcophagus that I believe images what at least one Christian woman understood to be the source of her inner authority (see figures 8.1–8.2). This sarcophagus dates to the first quarter of the fourth century. Unfortunately, the lid that may have been inscribed with her name is lost. Let us call her Junia. The bottom casket portion of the sarcophagus is carved with biblical reliefs on the front and both short sides. Several years before Junia died, she, or perhaps her family, commissioned this uniquely sculpted sarcophagus to memorialize her and the values that shaped her identity. Her sarcophagus was not just about social status but, like all Roman funerary monuments, it also reflects her deepest beliefs and how she wished to be remembered.[127] When Junia died, her sarcophagus would have been delivered to her home, where she would lie in state for up to seven days so family members, clients, and friends could pay their respects.[128] After seven days, Junia's body and her sarcophagus would be transported to the burial site, perhaps resting in a fresco-adorned catacomb cubiculum. Mourners would partake of funerary meals on the day of burial, nine days later, and each year on Junia's birthday. At any time from lying in state to the funerary meal commemorations, Junia's friends and family would take time to gaze upon her carefully carved memorial. They entered a liminal space to reflect upon her life, her values, her beliefs, and, inevitably, the meaning of life and death.

Junia's tomb iconography was sculpted to exact specifications. In the center, the deceased Junia's portrait is shown with a codex in her left hand while the right hand forms a speech gesture. Arrayed on either side are biblical scenes from both the Hebrew and Christian Scriptures. Junia, or whoever commissioned her sarcophagus, wanted her to be remembered as learned in the biblical texts and gifted to teach and proclaim them. On the viewer's left are scenes from the Hebrew Scriptures (see figure 8.2). According to Deichmann et al., on the far left, seated on a rock, is God the Father portrayed with a speech gesture and speaking with Cain and Abel, shown with offerings of grapes and a lamb. On Abel's right, Christ stands near Adam and Eve. He holds a sheaf of wheat. Deichmann et al. describe this scene as the fall from paradise coupled with the biblical command that

---

127. Birk, "Sarcophagi, Self-Representation," 108.

128. Katharina Meinecke, "Invisible Sarcophagi: Coffin and Viewer in the Late Imperial Age," in Birk and Poulsen, *Patrons and Viewers*, 103. Meinecke writes: "Obviously, the tomb was not the primary place where a sarcophagus should be seen in the third century and presumably already in the century before. Rather the costly stone coffin must have been presented before the actual burial, most likely during the lying-in-state."

henceforth Adam must till the soil (indicated by a shaft of wheat) in order to live (Genesis 3).[129] On the right, Junia or her patron chose four reliefs from the Christian Scriptures: the healing of the paralytic, the healing of the man born blind, the miracle at Cana, and the raising of Lazarus (see figure 8.1). Lazarus's sister Mary is shown upright with her face looking outward rather than prone as it frequently appears in Lazarus reliefs. This may be an embedded portrait of Junia herself, although such an interpretation awaits further research.

Janet Tulloch's observations provide important context as we reimagine mourners who contemplate Junia's biblical reliefs. Tulloch observed that ancient art was viewed as social discourse meant to "draw the viewer in as a participant,"[130] and that art was understood "to perform meaning(s) not simply embed them" (see chapter 3).[131] Using Tulloch's criteria, it is plausible that Junia wished her loved ones to enter into a liminal space and experience Christ's power to reverse the effects of the fall from paradise—namely, healing the blind and lame, providing an abundance of wine in the new reign of God, and raising Lazarus (and Junia) from the dead. Where did Junia find her authority to witness and teach about Christ? One hint is found in figure 8.2, wherein Junia's face is uniquely sculpted close to the face of Christ who leans in, with mouth open, as if to whisper in her ear.[132]

It is reasonable to conclude that Junia and her family wished her to be remembered as someone who taught with the authority of Christ. Her mourners interacted with her tomb art within the liminal ritual space that she or her loved ones envisioned. Here, they commune not only with the departed Junia but also with the Christ who Christians believe heals and raises up through the meaning evoked and "performed" by the art on Junia's sarcophagus. In other words, Junia exhorts the living to embrace the Christ who authorized her ministry

129. The latter scene is found on at least fourteen Christian sarcophagi and indicates that fourth-century Christians were well acquainted with John 1:1–14 in which Christ is the pre-existent Logos or Word of God. As such, he is portrayed as present when Adam and Eve are expelled from paradise. See RS 1, nos. 21, 25, 40, 43, 44, 46, 241, 772, 840; RS 2, nos. 20, 102; and RS 3, nos. 38, 71, 107.

130. Janet Tulloch, "Art and Archaeology," 298.

131. Ibid., 298; see her footnote 47, which refers to Bal, *Reading Rembrandt*, 270–71.

132. I have not found any other depiction of the deceased in such intimate communication with a Christ figure, although RS 1, no. 14 comes close (see figure 6.9).

and to whom she witnesses from beyond the grave. She joins a sister-hood of Christian women, past and present, who obey an authority that supersedes any who would silence them. Junia is one of countless women who witness that they are made in God's image and called to serve *in persona Christi*.

Appendix A: In Pace Inscriptions (n=36)

IN PACE INSCRIPTIONS ON SARCOPHAGI WITH CHRISTIAN IDENTIFIERS (BIBLICAL SCENES, CHRISTOGRAM, ETC.) (22)

RS 1:[1] nos. 6, 130, 131*, 299*, 304*, 555, 589*, 622, 672, 714*, 769, 771, 823, 834*

RS 2: nos. 102, 105, 106, 148, 181, 244*

RS 3: nos. 37, 650*

IN PACE INSCRIPTIONS ON SARCOPHAGI WITH CONVENTIONAL PAGAN ICONOGRAPHY (10)

RS 1: nos. 87, 238, 311, 557, 833, 1022, 1029*, 1031

RS 2: nos. 163*, 197

---

1. * = non-portrait tomb

IN PACE INSCRIPTIONS ON "POSSIBLY CHRISTIAN" SARCOPHAGUS (2)

RS 1: no. 972

RS 3: no. 635*

UNCERTAIN (2)

RS 1: 688, 790*

CONCLUSIONS

This study found a total of thirty-six *in pace* inscriptions. Of these, twenty-two had additional identifiers confirming Christian identity. Ten had conventional pagan iconography without biblical figures or Christian symbols. Four artifacts had either uncertain or possibly Christian identities. One of these is a drawing of a strigillated (wavy lines) sarcophagus with a *dextrarum iunctio* (marriage) scene in which the usual pagan iconography of the god Concordia or Juno has been replaced with scrolls (RS 1, no. 688 [drawing]). This could point to Christian identity, but it is difficult to speculate in the absence of other identifiers.

Appendix B: Christian Portraits with Uncertain/ Unclear Facial Features (n=113)

BLANK OR UNFINISHED PORTRAIT FACES (46)

Individual/Solo Female

RS 1:[1] nos. 6, 7, 11, 67, 73, 77, 107, 143, 221, 222, 376, 621, 682, 694, 722, 770, 787, 803, 836, 838, 842 (x2), 877, 900, 914 (x2), 985

RS 3: nos. 170 ("not fully elaborated"), 479

Individual/Solo Male

RS 1: nos. 144, 364

Couple

RS 1: nos. 43, 86, 188, 220, 241, 747, 778

RS 2: nos. 12, 102, 103

---

1. * = child

Couple (Mixed Portrayals)

RS 1: nos. 39 (*clipeus* couple and female *orant*—all faces unfinished); 629 (female on lid, male on casket center *mandorla*); 772 (Male face unfinished, female *orans* face individualized—each in separate lid *clipei*);

RS 3: no. 41 (female has unfinished face but male is individualized)

Unknown Gender

RS 3: no. 644

DAMAGED (34)

Individual/Solo Female

RS 1: nos. 177, 397 (no head), 443, 608, 672, 693, 695, 731, 763 (no head)

RS 2: nos. 93, 153

RS 3: nos. 70, 146, 436, 460, 511

Individual/Solo Male

RS 1: nos. 226, 389, 820*, 827, 951*(no head)

RS 2: no. 182 (? if male)

RS 3: no. 493

Couple

RS 1: nos. 44 (no heads), 625, 680

RS 2: nos. 180 (male half of married couple? Head broken away), 298 (no heads)

RS 3: nos. 83, 555

Unknown Gender

RS 1: nos. 536, 636 (no head)

RS 2: nos. 71 (severe damage/no figures), 95 (no head)

VISIBLY WORN (12)

Individual/Solo Female

RS 1: nos. 75, 720, 974

RS 2: nos. 101, 119, 414

RS 3: nos. 22, 57

Individual/Solo Male

RS 1: no. 101

RS 2: no. 236

Couple

RS 2: no. 211

RS 3: no. 291

REWORKED (4)

Individual/Solo Female

RS 1: nos. 15.2, 17, 80, 919

REVISED LATER (1)

Mixed

RS 2: no. 151 (casket only; individual female grave owner and *dextrarum iunctio* portrayals)

DRAWING *(CANNOT DETERMINE IF FACE WAS UNFINISHED OR INDIVIDUALIZED)* (13)

Individual/Solo Female

RS 1: nos. 652, 936, 979, 982, 1007

RS 3: no. 601

Individual/Solo Male

RS 1: no. 736*

RS 2: no. 221

Couple

RS 1: nos. 650, 689, 1010

RS 3: no. 304

Mixed

RS 1: no. 675 (individual male and married couple at base depictions).

WRITTEN DESCRIPTION ONLY *(CANNOT DETERMINE IF FACE WAS UNFINISHED OR INDIVIDUALIZED)* (3)

Individual/Solo Female

RS 1: no. 566

RS 3: nos. 201, 206

Appendix C: Tables 6.5 and 6.8: Christian Portraits by Type and Statistical Analysis of Solo Male and Female Portraits

TABLE 6.5: CHRISTIAN SARCOPHAGUS PORTRAITS BY TYPE

FEMALE

Individual/Solo Adult Female Portrait: Non-*Orans* (60)

RS 1: nos. 6, 13, 14, 25, 33, 80, 83, 85, 135, 143, 147, 176, 195, 221, 397, 443, 621, 629, 682, 692, 693, 695, 768, 803, 811, 836, 838, 896, 982, 985

RS 2: nos. 12, 34, 105, 107 (x2), 123, 150 (x2), 151 (x2), 181, 414

RS 3: nos. 18 (x2), 32, 62 (x2), 65 (x3), 108, 160, 201, 296, 436, 497 (x2), 601, 642 (x2)

Individual/Solo Adult Female Portrait: *Orans* (55)

RS 1: nos. 6, 7, 11, 39, 46, 67, 73, 77, 107, 206, 222, 225, 240 (x2), 376, 565, 608, 672, 694, 722, 770, 787, 842 (x2), 877, 900, 972 (x2), 974, 995

RS 2: nos. 101, 105, 245

RS 3: nos. 22, 33, 34, 35, 37, 57, 69, 70, 75, 118, 170, 218, 352, 355, 359, 366, 368, 460, 479, 497, 511, 642

Individual/Solo Adult Female: *Orans* "Probable Portrait" (41)

RS 1: nos. 15, 17, 37, 60, 75, 120, 177, 555, 560, 566, 638, 652, 670, 674, 720, 731, 763, 771, 841, 855, 914 (x2), 919, 936, 979, 990, 991, 1007

RS 2: nos. 11, 58, 60, 62, 93, 96, 118, 119, 146, 153, 242

RS 3: nos. 146, 515

Female Child (7)

RS 1:[1] nos. 9#, 47*

RS 2: nos. 33#, 34#, 300

RS 3: nos. 32, 514#

MALE

Individual Adult Male Portrait: Non-*Orans* (35)

RS 1: nos. 45 (x2, one carved over original female figure), 101, 130, 144, 172, 226, 389, 622, 629, 708, 756 (male over original female figure), 795, 801, 811

---

1. * = "probable portrait"; # = child *orans*

RS 2: nos. 12, 34, 123 (x2), 149, 236, 256

RS 3: nos. 32, 65, 296, 305, 428, 497, 548, 642 (x5)

Istanbul Musei: fifth-century tomb of Flavius Eutyches, (not listed in RS)[2]

Individual Adult Male Portrait: *Orans* (9)

RS 1: nos. 293, 364, 664 (male head applied to female *orans*; inscript says eight years, nine months, but artifact not described as *kinder* in RS 1 and portrait looks adult)

RS 2: nos. 68 (male over woman with in-facing statue—all three figures originally female), 106

RS 3: nos. 36 (male figure over original female body), 221, 493, 500

Individual Adult Male: *Orans* "Probable Portrait" (3)

RS 1: nos. 99, 776, 827

Male Child (13)

RS 1:[3] nos. 1*, 41, 526, 534#, 662, 736, 811, 820, 823, 896, 951 (? if child *orans*)

RS 2: no. 32#

RS 3: no. 296#

COUPLES (64)

See appendix M for complete breakout

---

2. This sarcophagus has a male portrait holding a scroll with partial speech gesture, flanked by Peter, Paul, and two muses. Identified by Dal Santo, "Bishops and Believers," 253–54.

3. * = "probable portrait"; # = child *orans*

EMBEDDED (13)

Female

RS 1: no. 807

RS 2: no. 420 (x3)

RS 3: nos. 68, 271, 297

Male

RS 2: no. 420 (x2)

Male Child

RS 1: no. 807

RS 2: no. 420 (x2)

Couple

RS 3: no. 304 (philosopher/muse type; drawing)

UNKNOWN (9)

RS 1:[4] nos. *536, 636

RS 2: nos. 71, 95, 180, 182, 300

RS 3: nos. 493, 644

4. * = "probable portrait"

TABLE 6.8: SUMMARY OF STATISTICAL OUTCOMES ANALYZING SOLO (NON-COUPLE) ADULT CHRISTIAN SARCOPHAGUS PORTRAITS BY GENDER

Hypothesis: The likelihood of a Christian sarcophagus portrait containing iconography commemorating a woman is equal to the likelihood that it would commemorate a man. Therefore, if this hypothesis is correct, one would expect an equal number of solo/individual female and solo/individual male portraits.

FINDINGS FOR ALL SOLO ADULT PORTRAITS ON CHRISTIAN SARCOPHAGI

1. Of 203 portraits of individual/solo figures on Christian sarcophagi, 156 were portraits of adult women and 47 were portraits of adult men. Therefore, the observed proportion of female portraits is 156/203 = 0.768, or 76.8 percent. The observed proportion of male portraits is 47/203 = 0.232, or 23.2 percent

2. An exact binomial test was run in order to determine whether the proportion of females in solo portraits is significantly different from 0.5, or 50 percent. The two-sided P-value for this test is less than 0.001, and this is less than commonly used thresholds for significance such as $\alpha = 0.05$. Therefore, the proportion of females in solo portraits is significantly different from 0.5. In fact, since the observed percentage of females was 76.8 percent, we can conclude that the proportion of females in the population of solo portraits represented by the sample is larger than 0.5, or 50 percent.

Conclusion: It is highly significant that 76.8 percent of individual adult Christian sarcophagus portraits were portraits of women. The likelihood that that this finding was due to chance is less than 1 in 1000. For every three women choosing individual portraits for their grave commemorations, approximately one man was so commemorated. This finding coincides with opinions from other scholars that women were of higher status and more influential within the early Christian subculture than commonly recognized, and that in early Christian aristocratic families, the women were more likely to be Christian than the men.

FINDINGS FOR INDIVIDUAL/SOLO ADULT PORTRAITS WITH "PROBABLE PORTRAITS" EXCLUDED

1. Of 159 portraits with *orans* "probable portraits" excluded, 115 depicted females and 44 depicted males. The observed proportion of female portraits is therefore 0.723, or 72.3 percent. The observed proportion of male portraits is therefore 0.277, or 27.7 percent.

2. The two-sided exact binomial P-value for this cohort is less than 0.001. The significance level is the same as always, α = 0.05.

Conclusion: It is highly significant that, even with "probable portraits" excluded, 72 percent of all individual/solo adult Christian portraits are female. The likelihood that that this finding was due to chance is less than 1 in 1000. Both the group with all solo adult portraits and the group with solo adult "probable portraits" excluded indicate highly significant differences between the proportions for solo female portraits and solo male portraits. In both cohorts, the proportion of female portraits is substantially higher than 50 percent and the proportion of male portraits substantially lower. Even after controlling for *orans* "probable portraits," this highly significant difference did not change.

IMPLICATIONS

Since there are so many more individual/solo female portraits on Christian sarcophagi compared to solo male portraits, it was necessary to find a way to validly compare differences between these mathematically diverse groups. It is not enough to simply report raw numbers when the universe of solo female artifacts is so much larger. For example, one can't just say there were 40 solo portraits of females with scrolls or *capses* compared to 25 solo males holding scrolls when there are 156 solo female portraits altogether compared to only 47 solo male portraits. I am indebted to Thomas H. Short, PhD, PStat, who provided statistical calculations and interpretations for each cohort. It then became possible to validly analyze various iconographical characteristics of male and female portraits on early Christian sarcophagi.

Appendix D: Table 6.9: Portrait Figures with Scrolls or Capses by Gender with Statistical Computations

INDIVIDUAL/SOLO FEMALE PORTRAIT WITH SCROLLS (27)

RS 1: nos. 13, 14, 25, 33, 80, 85, 135, 143, 147, 176, 221 (both *capsa* and scroll), 443, 621, 629, 682, 695, 803, 811 (x2: 1 solo portrait counted here, 1 counted in couple portrayals),[1] 836, 838, 982, 985

RS 2: nos. 181, 414 (codex), 105

RS 3: nos. 108, 436

INDIVIDUAL/SOLO FEMALE PORTRAIT WITH *CAPSA* OR SCROLL BUNDLE (9)

RS 1: 195*, 397 (both *capsa* and scroll bundle), 680

RS 3: nos. 37*, 70*, 75*, 355*, 366*, 497*

---

1. In sarcophagi that have portraits depicting men or women in both a solo and a couple portrayal, the couple portrayal is included under the appropriate couple heading, with the solo listed in the solo heading.

INDIVIDUAL/SOLO FEMALE *ORANS* "PROBABLE PORTRAIT" WITH *CAPSA* OR SCROLL BUNDLE (4)

RS 1:[2] nos. 60*, 990*, 979*

RS 2: no. 242*

INDIVIDUAL/SOLO ADULT MALE PORTRAIT WITH SCROLL (22)

RS 1: nos. 45, 130, 144, 172, 226 (with both scroll and scroll bundle), 493, 675, 708, 756 ("male over bust of a woman"), 771, 795, 801 (with both scroll and scroll bundle), 811, 629

RS 2: nos. 106, 123 (x2:, 1 couple, 1 solo), 148 (x2:, 1 couple, 1 solo), 149 (x2: 1 solo, 1 *dextrarum iunctio*)

RS 3: nos. 49, 305, 428

Istanbul Musei: fifth-century tomb of Flavius Eutyches (not listed in RS).[3]

INDIVIDUAL/SOLO ADULT MALES WITH ONLY *CAPSA* OR SCROLL BUNDLE (NO SCROLLS) (2)

RS 1: nos. 293*, 389

FEMALES WITH SCROLLS IN COUPLE PORTRAYALS (6)

In the following six unconventional couple reliefs, the female is depicted with a scroll. It is unusual for a woman to be shown with a scroll in couple portrayals since the male invariably has one while the female does not.

RS 1: nos. 120, 811 (also listed under solo female since there were two female portraits)

2. * = *orans* figure
3. Dal Santo, "Bishops and Believers," 253–54.

RS 2: nos. 12, 123, 148

RS 3: no. 77

MALES WITH SCROLLS IN COUPLE PORTRAYALS (46)

RS 1: nos. 39, 40, 42, 43, 44, 86, 112, 188, 241, 385, 435, 625, 650, 678, 689, 747, 772, 778, 811, 952, 1010.

RS 2: nos. 12, 15, 20, 102, 103, 108, 123 (×2: 1 couple, 1 solo), 148 (×2: 1 solo, 1 married), 149 (×2: 1 solo, 1 married), 151, 245, 298 (both scroll and scroll bundle)

RS 3: nos. 38, 40, 41, 51, 77, 83, 203, 211, 555, 607.

MALE CHILD WITH SCROLL (6)

RS 1: no. 41, 143 (? embedded, standing small figure to right with "chubby cheeks"), 526, 662, 823, 896

(I found no female children depicted with scrolls.)

PORTRAITS WITH SCROLLS: UNCERTAIN IDENTITY (9)

RS 1: nos. 135, 397, 636

RS 2: nos. 71, 95, 123, 180, 182

RS 3: no. 644

STATISTICAL APPENDIX FOR TABLE 6.9: PORTRAIT FIGURES WITH SCROLLS OR *CAPSES* BY GENDER

Hypothesis: Each solo male or solo female portrait on Christian sarcophagi has an equal chance of being shown with a scroll or *capsa* or both. If this hypothesis is correct, we would expect portraits of solo females with a scroll or *capsa* to be proportionate to portraits of solo males with the same configuration.

FINDINGS FOR ALL SOLO PORTRAITS

1. Of 156 solo/individual female portraits, 40 contained either a scroll or a *capsa* or both. Of 47 solo male portraits, 25 contained either a scroll or a *capsa* or both.

2. Under the hypothesis of equal proportions, the overall estimated proportion is $(40\,25) / (156\,47) = 65/203 = 0.320$, or 32.0 percent.

	Scroll/*Capsa*	No scroll/*capsa*	Total	Proportion
Female	40	116	156	0.256
Male	25	22	47	0.532

Solo male portraits were approximately twice as likely as solo female portraits to be depicted with scrolls or *capses*.

Fisher's Exact test was used to determine that the two-sided P-value for testing an association between gender and the presence of a scroll or *capsa* is equal to 0.001, which is less than commonly used alpha levels such as 0.05. This indicates that the proportions of solo images for females and males in the population represented by the images in the sample are statistically significantly different. In fact, the observed proportion of scroll/*capsa* images for males indicates that the proportion for males is larger than the proportion for females. The likelihood that this finding is due to chance is 1 in 1000.

Of the 65 total scroll/*capsa* solo portraits (both genders), 40 portrayed females. This proportion is $40/65 = 0.615$, or 61.5 percent. An exact binomial test for the hypothesis of 50 percent females provides a two-sided P-value of 0.082. The P-value is greater than a commonly used 0.05 significance level. Among the scroll/*capsa* solo portraits, the proportion of females portrayed is not significantly different from 0.5.

This implies that the proportions of females and males portrayed are not significantly different.

Discussion: The two statistical modalities used to analyze scroll/*capsa* motifs on male and female portrait sarcophagi test for two different things. The Fisher's Exact test compared the rates of two populations—females and males—each with scroll/*capsa* iconography. It indicates that the rate of males with scroll/*capsa* motifs was significantly greater than the rate of females so depicted. In other words, proportionately more male portraits were depicted with scrolls or *capses* than female portraits.

The exact binomial test analyzed the proportion of females in the total population of scroll *capsa* motifs found on Christian portrait sarcophagi. When one looks at all occurrences of the scroll/*capsa* motif, more than half occurred with female figures, so the exact binomial test found no significant differences in male and females depicted with scroll/*capsa* motifs. In other words, when a scroll/*capsa* motif occurs on a Christian portrait, females were as likely as males to be shown.

FINDINGS WITH "PROBABLE PORTRAITS" OMITTED

1. Of 115 solo/individual female portraits, 36 contained either a scroll or a *capsa* or both. Of 44 solo male portraits, 24 contained either a scroll or a *capsa* or both.

2. Under the hypothesis of equal proportions, the overall estimated proportion is $(36\ 24) / (115\ 44) = 60/159 = 0.377$, or 37.7 percent.

	Scroll/*Capsa*	No scroll/*capsa*	Total	Proportion
Female	36	79	115	0.313
Male	24	20	44	0.546

With probable portraits excluded solo male portraits were 1.74 times as likely as solo female portraits to be depicted with scrolls or *capses*.

The Fisher Exact test two-tailed P-value is 0.010. The proportions of females and males with a scroll or *capsa* in solo portraits are statistically significantly different. In fact, the proportion for males is greater. The likelihood that this finding is due to chance is 1 in 100.

With probable portraits excluded, of the 60 total scroll/*capsa* solo portraits, 36 portrayed females. This proportion is 36/60 = 0.60, or 60 percent. An exact binomial test for the hypothesis of 50 percent females provides a two-sided P-value of 0.155. The P-value is greater than a commonly used 0.05 significance level. Among the scroll/*capsa* solo portraits, the proportion of females portrayed is not significantly different from 0.5. This implies that the proportions of females and males portrayed are not significantly different.

Appendix E: Table 6.11: Statistical Computations for Orans-Only Portrait Figures by Gender

For listing of all orans images, see appendix C. For listing of orans with scrolls and capses see appendix D.

ORANS-ONLY SOLO PORTRAIT FIGURES BY GENDER

Hypothesis: Each solo male or solo female portrait on Christian sarcophagi has an equal chance of being shown in an orans-only posture (depicted without a scroll or a capsa). If this hypothesis is correct, we would expect portraits of solo females in an orans depiction to be proportionate to portraits of solo males with the same configuration.

Type of Portrait	Orans (without Scrolls or Capses)
Female orans	48
Female orans "probable portrait"	37
Total female	**85**
Male orans	8
Male orans "probable portrait"	2
Total male	**10**

ALL SOLO PORTRAIT *ORANS*-ONLY FIGURES

1. Of 156 solo female portraits, 85 were portrayed as *orans* figures without a scroll or *capsa*. Of 47 solo male portraits, 10 were portrayed with this configuration.

2. Under the hypothesis of equal proportions, the overall estimated proportion is $(85 + 10) / (156 + 47) = 95/203 = 0.468$, or 46.8 percent.

	Orans-Only Configuration (without Scroll or *Capsa*)	Not *Orans*-Only (without Scroll or *Capsa*)	Total	Proportion *Orans*-Only Learned
Female	85	71	156	0.545
Male	10	37	47	0.213

The proportions for female and male *orans* portraits depicted without a scroll or *capsa* are significantly different, with Fisher's Exact test two-tailed P-value less than 0.001. In fact, the proportion for females is greater. The likelihood that this finding is due to chance is less than 1 in 1000. Solo female portraits were 2.6 times as likely as solo male portraits to be depicted in an *orans* posture.

SOLO PORTRAIT *ORANS*-ONLY FIGURES: "PROBABLE PORTRAITS" EXCLUDED

1. Of 115 solo female portraits, 48 were portrayed as *orans* figures without a scroll or *capsa*. Of 44 solo male portraits, 8 were portrayed with this configuration.

2. Under the hypothesis of equal proportions, the overall estimated proportion is $(48 + 8) / (115 + 44) = 56/159 = 0.352$, or 35.2 percent.

	Orans-Only Configuration (without Scroll or Capsa)	Not Orans-Only (without Scroll or Capsa)	Total	Proportion Orans-Only Learned
Female	48	67	115	0.417
Male	8	36	44	0.182

With "probable portraits" excluded, the proportions for female and male *orans* portraits depicted without a scroll or *capsa* are statistically significantly different, with Fisher's Exact test two-tailed P-value = 0.009. In fact, the proportion for females is larger. The likelihood that this finding is due to chance is 9 in 1000. Solo female portraits were 2.3 times as likely as solo male portraits to be depicted in an *orans* posture.

Appendix F: Table 6.10: Summary of Statistical Outcomes for All Learned Portraits, Including Orans, Scroll, and Capsa Depictions

(For listing of all orans *images, see appendix C. For listing of all portraits with scrolls and* capses *see appendix D.)*

Hypothesis: All male and female portraits on Christian tombs have an equal chance of being shown with one or more of the following learned iconographical elements: a scroll, a *capsa*, and/or *orans* depictions.

FINDINGS FOR ALL SOLO PORTRAITS

1. All solo learned figures with *orans*, and scroll/*capsa* depictions (considering *orans* as learned figures) were analyzed. Of 156 individual female portraits, 125 were portrayed with learned iconographical elements, including a scroll, a *capsa*, and/or *orans* depictions. Of 47 individual male portraits, 35 were portrayed with these iconographical elements.

2. Under the hypothesis of equal proportions, the overall estimated proportion is (125 + 35) / (156 + 47) = 160/203 = 0.788, or 78.8 percent.

	Learned	Not Learned	Total	Proportion Learned
Female	125	31	156	0.801
Male	35	12	47	0.745

The two-tailed P-value from Fisher's Exact test is 0.419, indicating that there is no statistically significant difference in the proportions of learned female figures and learned male figures when *orans* portraits are included as learned representations.

FINDINGS FOR SOLO PORTRAITS WITH "PROBABLE PORTRAITS" OMITTED

1. Of 115 solo female portraits, 84 were portrayed as *orans*, or with a scroll, a *capsa*, or both. Of 44 solo male portraits, 32 were portrayed as *orans*, or with a scroll, a *capsa*, or both.

2. Under the hypothesis of equal proportions, the overall estimated proportion is $(84 + 32) / (115 + 44)$ = 116/159 = 0.730, or 73.0 percent.

	Learned	Not Learned	Total	Proportion Learned
Female	84	31	115	0.730
Male	32	12	44	0.727

With probable portraits omitted, the two-tailed Fisher exact text P value of 1.000 indicates that there is no statistically significant difference between the proportions of solo male learned portraits and solo female learned portraits when *orans* figures are added to the scroll-*capsa* learned depictions.

FINDINGS FOR COMBINED COUPLE AND SOLO
LEARNED PORTRAYALS (*ORANS*, SCROLL, *CAPSA*)

1. All solo and couple learned portrayals were combined (adding *orans* to learned figures along with scroll and *capsa* depictions). This resulted in 135 learned female portraits with all of these depictions out of 220 possible portraits (156 solo + 64 female half of couple). Likewise, 80 learned male portraits had all of these depictions out of 111 possible portraits (47 solo + 64 male half of couple).

2. Under the hypothesis of equal proportions, the overall estimated proportion is (135 + 80) / (220 + 111) = 215/331 = 0.650, or 65.0 percent.

	Learned	Not Learned	Total	Proportion Learned
Female	135	85	220	0.614
Male	80	31	111	0.721

When couple and solo portraits are combined, the two-tailed P-value for Fisher's Exact test of 0.067, indicates that there is no statistically significant difference between proportions of male and female figures depicted in all learned postures (scroll, *capsa*, *orans*).

FINDINGS FOR COMBINED COUPLE AND INDIVIDUAL/
SOLO LEARNED (*ORANS*, SCROLL, *CAPSA*)
PORTRAYALS: EXCLUDING "PROBABLE PORTRAITS"

1. Excluding *orans* "probable portraits" in the analysis of all solo and couple learned portrayals combined resulted in 94 female portraits with these *orans*-scroll-*capsa* depictions out of 179 possible portraits (115 solo + 64 female half of couple). There were 77 male portraits with these depictions out of 108 possible portraits (44 solo + 64 male half of couple).

2. Under the hypothesis of equal proportions, the overall estimated proportion is (95 + 75) / (179 + 108) = 170/287 = 0.592, or 59.2 percent.

	Learned	Not Learned	Total	Proportion learned
Female	94	85	179	0.525
Male	77	31	108	0.713

The two-tailed P-value for Fisher's Exact test is 0.002, indicating that there is a statistically significant difference between the proportions of male and female learned figures when both couple and solo portraits are analyzed and *orans* "probable portraits" are excluded. The proportion of male figures with all learned depictions is larger. Male portraits in this cohort, including male-female couples, are 1.36 times as likely to have *orans* or scroll learned iconography as female portraits. The likelihood that this phenomenon is due to chance is 2 in 1000. In married depictions, 43 males hold scrolls while only 6 females do. When largely female *orans* "probable portraits" are removed, male learned figures proportionately increase. This suggests that in all Christian portrait tombs (couple and solo portraits), males are more likely to be depicted with scroll iconography while females are more likely to be depicted as *orans* figures.

Appendix G: Table 6.12: Speech Gestures on Christian Portraits and Statistical Outcomes

SOLO ADULT FEMALE PORTRAIT
WITH SPEECH GESTURE (22)

RS 1:[1] nos. 6, 14, 25, 33, 83, 85, 143, 147, 176, 221, 443, 621*,[2] 629, 838, 982, 985

RS 2: nos. 105, 123, 181*, 414

RS 3: nos. 62, 436

SOLO ADULT MALE PORTRAIT
WITH SPEECH GESTURE (11)

RS 1: nos. 101, 629, 708, 756, 771, 795, 801

RS 2: no. 149

RS 3: nos. 428, 548

---

1. Excludes two embedded female biblical figures with speech gestures: Samaritan woman (RS 1, no. 650) and Thecla (RS 3, no. 297).
2. * = "partial" speech gesture: two fingers at top of scroll

Istanbul Musei: fifth-century tomb of Flavius Eutyches (not listed in RS)[3]

COUPLE PORTRAYAL: FEMALE SPEECH GESTURE (5)

RS 1: nos. 120, 241, 811

RS 2: no. 12*

RS 3: no. 51

COUPLE PORTRAYAL: MALE SPEECH GESTURE (22)

RS 1: nos. 39*, 40*, 42, 43, 44*, 188*, 385, 435, 650, 778*, 1010

RS 2: no. 12*, 20, 102, 103, 148

RS 3: no. 38, 40*, 41, 49*, 77*, 203

MALE CHILD WITH SPEECH GESTURE (3)

RS 1: nos. 143, 662, 823

(I did not find any female child portraits with a speech gesture.)

UNCERTAIN IDENTITY (5)

RS 1: no. 135, 636

RS 2: nos. 180*, 182, 952

---

3. Dal Santo, "Bishops and Believers," 253–54.

TABLE 6.12: STATISTICAL OUTCOMES FOR ADULT SOLO PORTRAITS WITH SPEECH GESTURES BY GENDER

Hypothesis: All male and female portraits on Christian tombs have an equal chance of being shown with a speech gesture.

FINDINGS

1. 22 of 60 solo female non-*orans* portraits were depicted with a speech gesture, and 11 of 35 solo male non-*orans* portraits were depicted with a speech gesture.

2. Under the hypothesis of equal proportions, the estimated overall proportion is $(22 + 11) / (60 + 35) = 33/95 = 0.347$, or 34.7 percent.

	Speech	No Speech	Total	Proportion with Speech
Female	22	38	60	0.367
Male	11	24	35	0.314

Solo female non-*orans* portraits were 1.17 times as likely as solo male non-*orans* portraits to be depicted with a speech gesture.

Fisher's Exact test determined that the two-sided P-value for testing an association between gender and speech gesture is 0.660. This indicates that there is no statistically significant difference in the proportions of solo male depictions shown with a speech gesture compared to solo female depictions with the same gesture.

Appendix H: Table 6.13: Both Scroll and Speech Motifs by Gender with Statistical Outcomes

SOLO FEMALE WITH BOTH SCROLL AND SPEECH GESTURE (20)

RS 1: nos. 14, 25, 33, 83, 85, 143, 147, 176, 221, 443, 621, 629, 838, 982, 985

RS 2: nos. 105, 123, 181, 414

RS 3: no. 436

SOLO MALE WITH BOTH SCROLL AND SPEECH GESTURE (9)

RS 1: nos. 629, 708, 756 (male over bust of woman), 795, 801

RS 2: no. 149

RS 3: nos. 305, 428

Istanbul Musei: fifth-century tomb of Flavius Eutyches (not listed in RS)[1]

---

1. Dal Santo, "Bishops and Believers," 253–54.

COUPLE PORTRAYAL: FEMALE WITH BOTH SCROLL AND SPEECH GESTURE (3)

RS 1: nos. 120, 811

RS 2: no. 12

COUPLE PORTRAYAL: MALE WITH BOTH SCROLL AND SPEECH GESTURES (22)

RS 1: nos. 39, 40, 42, 43, 44, 188, 385, 435, 650, 778, 1010

RS 2: nos. 12, 20, 102, 103, 148

RS 3: nos. 38, 40, 41, 49, 77, 203

MALE CHILD WITH BOTH SCROLL AND SPEECH GESTURE (3)

RS 1: nos. 662 (inscription says five years old), 823 (inscription says six years old), 143 (? embedded son)

(I found no artifacts of female children with either scrolls or speech gestures.)

UNCERTAIN IDENTITY (5)

RS 1: no. 135, 636

RS 2: nos. 180, 182, 952

TABLE 6.13: STATISTICAL OUTCOMES FOR SOLO ADULT PORTRAITS WITH BOTH SCROLL AND SPEECH GESTURE BY GENDER

Hypothesis: All male and female portraits on Christian tombs have an equal chance of being shown with both a scroll and a speech gesture.

FINDINGS

1. 20 of 60 non-*orans* solo female portraits contained both scroll and speech configurations, and 9 of 35 non-*orans* solo male portraits contained both scroll and speech configurations.

2. Under the hypothesis of equal proportions, the pooled estimate of the common proportion is $(20 + 9) / (60 + 35) = 0.305$, or 30.5 percent.

	Scroll and Speech	No Scroll or Speech	Total	Proportion with Scroll and Speech
Female	20	40	60	0.333
Male	9	26	35	0.257

Solo female non-*orans* portraits were 1.3 times as likely as solo male non-*orans* portraits to contain both scroll and speech configurations.

Fisher's Exact test determined that the two-sided P-value for testing an association between gender and scroll/speech configurations is 0.495. This indicates that there is no statistically significant difference in the proportions of solo male depictions shown with both a scroll and speech gesture compared to solo female depictions.

Appendix I: Table 6.14: Statistical Computations for Scroll-Speech Iconography as a Representation of Religious Authority

Hypothesis: All figures with scroll-speech iconography have an equal opportunity to be shown in the midst of two biblical figures.

1. Of 20 female scroll-speech portraits, 10 are shown in the midst of 2 or more biblical scenes. Of 9 male scroll-speech portraits, 1 is shown in the midst of 2 or more biblical scenes.

2. Under the hypothesis of equal proportions, the overall estimated proportion is $(10 + 1) / (29) = 0.379$.

	Scroll-Speech with Two or More Biblical Scenes	Scroll-Speech—Not Two or More Biblical Scenes	Total	Proportion—Two or More Biblical Scenes
Female	10	10	20	0.500
Male	1	8	9	0.111

The two-sided P-value for Fisher's Exact test in this case is 0.096. This is greater than the commonly used threshold of 0.05, indicating that the two proportions are not statistically significantly different.

Conclusion: Even though there is no statistically significant difference between female and male religious authority depictions, it is notable that female portraits with scroll-speech iconography are 4.5 times as likely to be shown in the midst of two or more biblical figures compared to male portraits.

Appendix J: Table 6.15: Listing of All Portraits with In-Facing "Apostle" Figures by Gender with Statistical Computations

FEMALE ADULT CENTRAL: NON-*ORANS*. (7)

RS 1: nos. 80, 397, 682, 982, 176

RS 2: no. 151

RS 3: no. 201

FEMALE ADULT CENTRAL: *ORANS* (43)

RS 1:[1] nos. 6, 11, 39, 67, 77, 107*, 206, 222, 225, 240* (x2), 376, 565, 608, 672, 694 (artist places Moses and Abraham as in-facing?), 722, 770, 787*, 877, 900*, 974, 995*

RS 2: nos. 101, 105

RS 3: nos. 22, 34, 35, 37, 57, 69, 70, 75, 170, 218, 352, 355, 359, 368, 460, 479, 511, 514

---

1. * = just one in-facing figure is visible due to damage

FEMALE ADULT CENTRAL *ORANS*:
"PROBABLE PORTRAIT" (23)

RS 1: nos. 75, 117, 555, 560, 566*, 652, 670, 763*, 771, 775*, 855, 919, 979*, 1007

RS 2: nos. 58, 93, 96, 118, 119*, 146, 153*

RS 3: nos. 146, 515

MALE ADULT CENTRAL: NON-*ORANS* (3)

RS 1: no. 226

RS 3: no. 548

Istanbul Musei: fifth-century tomb of Flavius Eutyches (not listed in RS)[2]

MALE ADULT CENTRAL: *ORANS* (6)

RS 1: no. 364

RS 2: nos. 68 (male carved onto female figure; all three figures originally female), 106

RS 3: nos. 36 (male carved onto female figure), 493, 500

MALE ADULT CENTRAL: *ORANS*
"PROBABLE PORTRAIT" (1)

RS 1: no. 827

2. Dal Santo, "Bishops and Believers," 253–54.

MALE-FEMALE COUPLE WITH IN-FACING "APOSTLE" FIGURES (3)

RS 1: 678 (*dextrarum iunctio* depiction)

RS 2: 103*

RS 3: 211

FEMALE CHILD *ORANS* CENTRAL (2: ONE RELIEF WITH IN-FACING PARENTS, NOT "APOSTLES")

RS 1: no. 9

RS 2: no. 34 (parents are in-facing figures)

MALE CHILD *ORANS* CENTRAL (4)

RS 1: nos. 4 ("probable portrait"), 534*, 951

RS 2: no. 32

RS 3: no. 296

(*I found no non-*orans *child figures depicted with in-facing "apostle" figures.*)

UNCERTAIN GENDER

RS 1: 536 ("probable portrait"), 675

FEMALE PORTRAITS WITH SCROLLS AND/OR *CAPSA* AND IN-FACING "APOSTLE" FIGURES (11)

RS 1: nos. 80, 176, 397, 682, 979, 982

RS 2: no. 105

RS 3: nos. 37, 70, 75, 355

MALE PORTRAITS WITH SCROLLS AND/OR *CAPSA* AND IN-FACING "APOSTLE" FIGURES (3)

RS 1: no. 226

RS 2: no. 106

Istanbul Musei: fifth-century tomb of Flavius Eutyches (not listed in RS)[3]

TABLE 6.15: STATISTICAL FINDINGS FOR SOLO ADULT PORTRAITS WITH IN-FACING "APOSTLE" FIGURES BY GENDER

Hypothesis: All solo adult portraits have an equal opportunity to be depicted with in-facing "apostle" figures. If this hypothesis is correct, we could expect male portraits with in-facing "apostle" figures to be proportionate to female portraits in this configuration.

FINDINGS FOR ALL SOLO ADULT PORTRAITS WITH IN-FACING "APOSTLE" FIGURES

1. Of 156 solo female adult portraits, 73 had in-facing "apostle" figures. Of 47 solo male adult portraits, 10 had in-facing "apostle" figures.
2. Under the hypothesis of equal proportions, the estimate of the common proportion is $(73 + 10) / (156 + 47) = 0.409$, or 40.9 percent.

	In-Facing	Not In-Facing	Total	Proportion In-Facing
Female	73	83	156	0.468
Male	10	37	47	0.213

3. Dal Santo, "Bishops and Believers," 253–54.

Fisher's Exact test determined that the two-sided P-value for testing an association between gender and in-facing "apostle" figures is 0.002. This indicates that the proportions of in-facing "apostle" figures for females and males in the population of portraits represented in this sample are statistically significantly different. In fact, the proportion for females is greater. The likelihood that this highly significant finding is due to chance is 2 in 1000. Solo female portraits with in-facing "apostle" figures were 2.2 times as likely as solo male portraits to contain in-facing "apostle" figures.

FINDINGS FOR ALL SOLO ADULT PORTRAITS WITH IN-FACING "APOSTLE" FIGURES: "PROBABLE PORTRAITS" EXCLUDED

1. Excluding "probable portraits," of 115 solo female adult portraits, 50 had in-facing "apostle" figures. Of 44 solo male adult portraits, 9 had in-facing "apostle" figures.

2. Under the hypothesis of equal proportions, the estimate of the common proportion is $(50 + 9) / (115 + 44) = 0.371$, or 37.1 percent.

	In-Facing	Not In-Facing	Total	Proportion In-Facing
Female	50	65	115	0.435
Male	9	35	44	0.204

The two-sided Fisher's Exact test P-value in this case is 0.01, which is less than the commonly used significance levels of alpha = 0.05. This indicates that even when excluding all "probable portraits," the proportions for female and male portraits with in-facing "apostle" figures are statistically significantly different. In fact, the proportion for females is larger. The likelihood that this finding is due to chance is 1 in 100. Solo female portraits were 2.13 times as likely as solo male portraits to contain in-facing "apostle" figures.

FINDINGS FOR ALL SOLO ADULT *ORANS* PORTRAITS WITH IN-FACING FIGURES (NON-*ORANS* PORTRAITS EXCLUDED)

1. Of 156 solo female adult portraits, 66 were *orans* figures with in-facing "apostle" figures. Of 47 solo male adult portraits, 7 were *orans* figures with in-facing "apostle" figures.

2. Under the hypothesis of equal proportions, the estimate of the common proportion is $(66 + 47) / (156 + 47) = 73/203 = 0.359$, or 35.9 percent.

	In-Facing	Not In-Facing	Total	Proportion In-Facing
Female	66	90	156	0.423
Male	7	40	47	0.149

Fisher's Exact test was used to determine that the two-sided P-value for testing an association between gender and in-facing "apostle" figures is less than 0.001. This indicates that the proportions of in-facing "apostle" figures for female *orans* and male *orans* in the population of portraits represented in this sample are statistically significantly different. In fact, the proportion for females is greater. This is a highly significant difference since the likelihood that this finding is due to chance is less than 1 in 1000. Female *orans* solo portraits were 2.84 times as likely to have in-facing companion figures compared to male portrait tombs.

FINDINGS FOR ALL SOLO ADULT *ORANS* PORTRAITS WITH IN-FACING FIGURES: "PROBABLE PORTRAITS" EXCLUDED

1. Excluding "probable portraits," of 115 solo female adult portraits, 43 were *orans* figures with in-facing "apostle" figures. Of 44 solo male adult portraits, 6 were *orans* figures with in-facing "apostle" figures.

2. Under the hypothesis of equal proportions, the estimate of the common proportion is $(43 + 6) / (115 + 44) = 49/159 = 0.308$, or 30.8 percent.

	In-Facing	Not In-Facing	Total	Proportion In-Facing
Female *orans*	43	72	115	0.374
Male *orans*	6	38	44	0.136

The P-value for Fisher's Exact test is 0.004, which is less than traditional significance levels of 0.05. This indicates that even when "probable portraits" are excluded, the proportion of female *orans* with in-facing "apostle" figures is greater than the proportion of male *orans* with in-facing "apostle" figures at statistically significant levels. The likelihood that this highly significant finding is due to chance is 4 in 1000. Female *orans* solo portraits were 2.74 times as likely to have in-facing companion figures compared to male portrait tombs.

Appendix K: Table 6.16: Christ Reliefs with In-Facing "Apostle" Motifs and a Comparison of In-Facing "Apostle" Characteristics on Portraits with In-Facing "Apostle" Characteristics on Christ Portrayals

MAGISTRATE: DEPICTIONS OF CHRIST ON A THRONE OR A MOUNTAIN WITH IN-FACING FIGURES OFTEN DESCRIBED AS PETER AND PAUL (48)

RS 1: nos. 25, 28, 57, 58, 193, 200, 241, 627 (damaged per RS 1), 676, 677, 678, 679, 680, 684, 724, 1008

RS 2: nos. 10, 123, 150, 152, 376, 379, 381, 382, 389, 390

RS 3: nos. 25, 26, 32, 65, 120, 291, 292, 298, 299, 300, 302, 303, 315, 411, 428, 429, 465, 470, 487, 499, 593, 642

NON-MAGISTRATE: CHRIST WITH IN-FACING FIGURES—EXCLUDES DEPICTIONS OF CHRIST ON A THRONE OR A MOUNTAIN WITH IN-FACING FIGURES OFTEN DESCRIBED AS PETER AND PAUL (118)

RS 1: nos. 6, 7, 8, 10, 11, 12, 14, 15.2, 20, 21, 30, 39, 40, 41, 42, 43, 44, 45, 47, 51, 135, 146, 152, 189.1,2, 220, 376, 556, 621, 622, 625, 665, 691, 694, 720, 755, 770, 772, 807, 840, 841, 900, 919, 965, 984, 987, 1007, 1010

RS 2: nos. 11, 12, 20, 33, 58, 59, 60, 74, 79, 97, 101, 102, 108, 111, 149, 250, 413

RS 3: nos. 22, 30, 31, 34, 35, 36, 37, 38, 40, 51, 53, 56, 61, 76, 77, 80, 81, 118, 126, 160, 178, 215, 218, 220, 221, 222, 269, 271, 352, 357, 359, 364, 365, 373, 387 (some damage), 388, 389, 410, 427, 440, 453, 479, 494, 500, 512, 514, 515, 517, 518, 519, 548, 579, 591, 592

TABLE 19: STATISTICAL COMPUTATIONS FOR IN-FACING "APOSTLE" CHARACTERISTICS OF DECEASED PORTRAIT AND CHRIST PORTRAYALS

COMPARISONS OF ALL-CHRIST CENTRAL PORTRAYALS

1. Learned in-facing figure (figure holds a scroll): there is no statistically significant association between the male, female, and Christ figures and the presence or absence of a scroll.

2. "Apostle" or "Peter and Paul" descriptor: there is no statistically significant association between the male, female, and Christ figures and the presence or absence of this descriptor.

3. Recommendation or introduction gesture: there is a statistically significant association between the type of figure and the presence or absence of the recommendation or introduction gesture. The proportion for all Christ is substantially lower than the proportions for females and males. This finding indicates that in

Christ-central portrayals, sarcophagi artists did not show companion figures with introduction or recommendation gestures at the same rate as male- and female-central portrayals. This further suggests that to fourth-century Christians who commissioned these tombs, Christ figures literally needed no introduction (by in-facing companion figures or anyone else), while male and female deceased did require them.

The chi-squared statistic is 35.23 on 2 degrees of freedom. The P-value is less than 0.001, which indicates that there is a statistically significant association between the type of figure and the presence or absence of the recommendation/introduction gesture. The likelihood that this finding is due to chance is less than a 1 in 1000.

	Present	Absent	Total	Proportion Present
Female	26	47	73	0.356
Male	3	7	10	0.300
All Christ	10	156	166	0.060

4. Speech gesture: there is no statistically significant association between the male, female, and Christ figures and the presence or absence of a speech gesture.

5. Acclaim gesture: there is a statistically significant association between the type of figure and the presence or absence of the gesture. The proportion for all Christ is substantially higher than the proportions for females and males. This finding indicates that in Christ-central depictions, sarcophagi artists portrayed in-facing figures with acclaiming gestures at a higher rate than in male and female central depictions. This further suggests that to the fourth-century Christians who commissioned these tombs, acclaiming gestures for Christ figures were more popular than for male and female central depictions.

The chi-squared statistic is 9.69 on 2 degrees of freedom. The P-value is 0.008, which indicates that there is a statistically significant association between the type of figure and the presence or absence of the gesture. The odds that this finding is due to chance are 8 in 1000.

	Present	Absent	Total	Proportion Present
Female	8	65	73	0.110
Male	1	9	10	0.100
All Christ	47	119	166	0.283

FINDINGS FOR COMPARISONS OF NON-MAGISTRATE CHRIST CENTRAL PORTRAYALS

1. Learned in-facing figure (figure holds a scroll): there is no statistically significant association between the male, female, and non-magistrate Christ figures and the presence or absence of a scroll.

2. "Apostle" or "Peter and Paul" descriptor: there is no statistically significant association between the male, female, and non-magistrate Christ figures and the presence or absence of this descriptor.

3. Recommendation or introduction gesture: there is a statistically significant association between the type of figure and the presence or absence of the recommendation or introduction gesture. The proportion for non-magistrate Christ is substantially lower than the proportions for females and males. This finding indicates that in Christ-central portrayals, sarcophagi artists did not show companion figures with introduction or recommendation gestures at the same rate as in male and female central portrayals. This further suggests that to fourth-century Christians who commissioned these tombs, Christ figures literally needed no introduction (by in-facing companion figures or anyone else), while male and female deceased did seem to require them.

	Present	Absent	Total	Proportion Present
Female	26	47	73	0.356
Male	3	7	10	0.300
Non-Magistrate Christ	6	112	118	0.051

4. The chi-squared statistic is 30.39 on 2 degrees of freedom. The P-value is less than 0.001, which indicates that there is a statistically significant association between the type of figure and the presence or absence of the recommendation/introduction gesture. The likelihood that this finding is due to chance is less than 1 in 1000. The chi-squared statistic is 6.29 on 2 degrees of freedom. The P-value is 0.043, which indicates that there is a statistically significant association between the type of figure and the presence or absence of the gesture. All three of the proportions seem somewhat different from each other.

	Present	Absent	Total	Proportion Present
Female	18	55	73	0.247
Male	3	7	10	0.300
Non-Magistrate Christ	14	104	118	0.119

5. Acclaim gesture: there is no statistically significant association between the type of figure and the presence or absence of the acclaim gesture. This finding suggests that by excluding magistrate portrayals, an increased proportion of acclaiming in-facing figures were also excluded.

Appendix L: Table 6.17: List of Images for Scroll-Capsa Learned Portraits with In-Facing "Apostle" Figure with Statistical Computations

FEMALE PORTRAITS WITH SCROLLS AND/OR *CAPSA* AND IN-FACING "APOSTLE" FIGURES (11)

RS 1: nos. 80, 176, 397, 682, 979, 982

RS 2: no. 105

RS 3: nos. 37, 70, 75, 355

MALE PORTRAITS WITH SCROLLS AND/OR *CAPSA* AND IN-FACING "APOSTLE" FIGURES (3)

RS 1: no. 226

RS 2: no. 106

Istanbul Musei: fifth-century tomb of Flavius Eutyches (not listed in RS)[1]

(For non-magistrate Christ images, see appendix K.)

1. Dal Santo, "Bishops and Believers," 253–54.

TABLE 6.17: SUMMARY OF STATISTICAL COMPUTATIONS COMPARING IN-FACING "APOSTLE" CHARACTERISTICS ON LEARNED AND NON-LEARNED PORTRAITS BY GENDER AND CHRIST PORTRAYALS

FEMALE LEARNED, NON-LEARNED, AND NON-MAGISTRATE CHRIST CENTRAL FIGURES

1. In-facing learned: there is no statistically significant association between female learned, female non-learned, and non-magistrate Christ portrayals and the presence or absence of a scroll or *capsa* in in-facing "apostle" portrayals.

2. "Apostle" or "Peter and Paul": there is no statistically significant association between female learned, female non-learned, and non-magistrate Christ portrayals and the presence or absence of this descriptor.

3. Recommendation or introduction gesture: there is a statistically significant association between female learned, female non-learned, non-magistrate Christ portrayals and the presence or absence of the recommendation/introduction gesture. The odds that this finding is due to chance are less than 1 in 1000. The chi-squared statistic is 34.41 on 2 degrees of freedom. The P-value is less than 0.001, which indicates that there is a statistically significant association between the type of figure and the presence or absence of the recommendation/introduction gesture. The proportions for all three types of figures seem to be quite different from each other. The chi-squared test does not indicate specific significant differences between the proportions, just that there is an association between the type of figure and the presence or absence of the recommendation/introduction gesture. That all three proportions seem quite different from each other is all the specific information that can be determined.

	Present	Absent	Total	Proportion Present
Female Learned	2	9	11	0.182
Female Non-Learned	17	22	39	0.436
Non-Magistrate Christ	6	112	118	0.051

4. Speech gesture: There is no statistically significant association between the female learned, female non-learned, and non-magistrate Christ portrayals and the presence or absence of the gesture.

5. Acclaim gesture: There is no statistically significant association between female learned, female non-learned, non-magistrate Christ portrayals and the presence or absence of the gesture.

MALE LEARNED, NON-LEARNED, AND NON-MAGISTRATE CHRIST CENTRAL FIGURES

(Note: Because of small numbers, in all cases, the conditions for inference are not satisfied, so results of each statistical test "are questionable at best.")

1. In-facing learned: there is no statistically significant association between male learned, male non-learned, and non-magistrate Christ central figures and the presence or absence of a scroll or *capsa* in in-facing "apostle" portrayals.

2. "Apostle" or "Peter and Paul": there is no statistically significant association between male learned, male non-learned, and non-magistrate Christ central figures and the presence or absence of this descriptor.

3. Recommendation or introduction gesture: there is a statistically significant association between male learned, male non-learned, and non-magistrate Christ central figures and the presence or absence of the recommendation/introduction gesture. The proportion for male non-learned is substantially higher than the other two proportions. The chi-squared statistic is 7.93 on 2

degrees of freedom. The P-value is less than 0.020, which indicates that there is a statistically significant association between the type of figure and the presence or absence of the gesture. The proportion for male non-learned is substantially higher than the other two proportions. The conditions for inference in this case are not satisfied, and so the results of this statistical test are questionable at best.

	Present	Absent	Total	Proportion Present
Male Learned	0	3	3	0.000
Male Non-Learned	2	4	6	0.333
Non-Magistrate Christ	6	112	118	0.051

4. Speech gesture: there is no statistically significant association between male learned, male non-learned, and non-magistrate Christ central figures and the presence or absence of the speech gesture.

5. Acclaim gesture: there is no statistically significant association between male learned, male non-learned, and non-magistrate Christ central figures and the presence or absence of the acclaim gesture.

Conclusion: For our purposes, it is helpful to find that there were no statistically significant associations between male learned and female learned central figures and in-facing "apostle" characteristics. This suggests that the Christians who commissioned these tombs applied in-facing "apostle" characteristics to learned male and female portraits indiscriminately. It may also be that any deceased Christian depicted with a scroll in such in-facing configurations was less likely to have an accompanying "apostle" with a recommendation/introduction gesture.

Appendix M: Table 7.1: Portraits of Couples (n=64)

MAN AND WOMAN IN SAME *CLIPEUS* (28)

RS 1: nos. 39, 40, 42, 43, 44, 112, 187, 241, 385, 435, 625, 650, 689, 778, 1010

RS 2: nos. 6, 12, 20, 102, 103, 108, 150

RS 3: nos. 38, 40, 41, 83, 203, 211

EACH IN SEPARATE *CLIPEI*, *PARAPETASMA* ON LID OR CASKET PORTRAYAL (8)

RS 1:[1] nos. 120*, 220*, 772*

RS 2: nos. 148, 375

RS 3: nos. 49, 77, 555

DEXTRARUM IUNCTIO (MARRIAGE ICONOGRAPHY) (8)

RS 1: nos. 86, 678, 952

1. * = indicates *orans* figure

RS 2: nos. 148, 149, 151, 245

RS 3: no. 51

MARRIED COUPLE WORSHIPPING AT BASE OF TRIUMPHANT CHRIST (11)

RS 1: nos. 241, 675, 679

RS 2: nos. 102, 149, 150

RS 3: nos. 25, 80, 81, 291, 428

OTHER COUPLE PORTRAYALS (END FIGURES OR STANDING FIGURES) (8)

RS 1: nos. 680, 747*

RS 2: nos. 12, 298, 379

RS 3: nos. 51, 607*, 642

EMBEDDED COUPLE/FAMILY PORTRAYAL (1)

RS 3: no. 323

FEMALE-MALE ROLE REVERSAL? (7)

RS 1: nos. 120, 811

RS 2: nos. 12, 123, 148

RS 3: nos. 51, 77

ADDENDA *(ALSO INCLUDED ABOVE)*

COUPLE PORTRAYALS WITH FEMALE *ORANS* (4)

RS 1: nos. 220, 747, 772

RS 3: no. 607

COUPLE PORTRAYALS WITH MALE *ORANS* (2)

RS 1: nos. 120, 220

Appendix N: Listing of Dates of Christian Portrait Sarcophagi

THIRD CENTURY (N=9)

Second third of third century (n=1)	RS 3: no. 108
Last third of third century (n=4)	RS 1: nos. 747, 778, 811, 985
Last quarter of third century (n=1)	RS 1: no. 914
Late third century (n=2)	RS 1: no. 768
	RS 2: no. 6
End of third–early fourth century (n=1)	RS 2: no. 95

FOURTH CENTURY (N=218)

Fourth century (n=4)	RS 1: nos. 225, 536, 652
	RS 3: no. 201
Around 300 (n=2)	RS 2: nos. 242, 420
Beginning of the fourth century (n=8)	RS 1: nos. 46, 67, 83, 120, 820
	RS 2: nos. 93, 180
	RS 3: no. 18

First decade   RS 2: no. 10
of the fourth
century
(n=1)

Up to 330   RS 3: no. 37
(n=1)

300–325   RS 1: no. 6
(n=1)

310–20 (n=1)   RS 2: no. 245

310–30 (n=1)   RS 2: no. 96

320–30   RS 2: no.32
(lower
casket) (n=1)

Around 325   RS 3: no. 38
(n=1)

Around 330   RS 3: no. 33
(n=1)

Around or   RS 2: no. 102
shortly after
330 (n=1)

First quarter   RS 1: nos. 4, 7, 9, 33, 73, 75, 85, 99, 143, 144, 226, 364, 435, 526,
of the fourth   534, 565, 621, 625, 629, 636, 662, 720, 731, 756, 774, 787, 795, 801,
century   823, 836, 896, 919, 951, 952, 972
(n=40)
    RS 3: nos. 32, 305, 352, 479, 644

First third of   RS 1: nos. 11, 13, 14, 15, 17, 39, 40, 77, 86, 101, 107, 130, 176, 177,
the fourth   187, 220, 221, 241, 443, 566 (descriptor only), 622, 664, 670, 672,
century   674, 692, 693, 694, 708, 770, 771, 772, 803, 807, 838, 855, 877, 900,
(n=47)   991

    RS 2: nos. 12, 60, 101, 181, 182

    RS 3: nos. 36, 436, 601

320–40 (n=1)   RS 2: no. 33

Around   RS 3: no. 40
340–50 (n=1)

Second   RS 1: nos. 37, 41, 42, 43, 44, 222, 376, 385, 389, 560, 695, 722, 776,
quarter of   841, 990, 1010
the fourth
century   RS 2: nos. 20, 34, 58, 103, 105
(n=25)
    RS 3: nos. 34, 35, 146, 359

First half of the fourth century (n=4)	RS 1: nos. 763, 1007
	RS 2: no. 298
	RS 3: no. 555
Mid-fourth century (n=9)	RS 1: nos. 60, 80
	RS 2: nos. 11, 68
	RS 3: nos. 62, 69, 170, 203, 366
Last half of the fourth century (n=4)	RS 1: nos. 47, 172, 206
	RS 2: no. 107
Second third of fourth century (n=21)	RS 1: nos. 25, 45, 112, 135, 188, 195, 397, 555, 608, 682, 974, 995
	RS 2: nos. 62, 118, 119
	RS 3: nos. 41, 70, 75, 218, 368, 511
359 (n=1)	RS 1: no. 680
350–70 (n=1)	RS 2: no. 123
366 (n=1)	RS 2: 106
Third quarter of the fourth century (n=3)	RS 1: no. 650
	RS 2: no. 108
	RS 3: no. 118
Last third of the fourth century (n=11)	RS 1: nos. 147, 293, 638, 679
	RS 3: nos. 49, 51, 355, 460, 493, 497, 642
380–400 (n=1)	RS 2: no. 150
392 (n=1)	RS 1: no. 240
Around 390 (n=1)	RS 3: no. 83
Last quarter of the fourth century (n=6)	RS 2: nos. 71, 153
	RS 3: nos. 57, 68, 160, 500
End of the fourth century	RS 1: nos. 675, 678
	RS 2: nos. 146, 148, 149, 151

(n=16)
RS 3: nos. 24, 65, 77, 80, 81, 211, 291, 297, 304, 428

Well after RS 2: no. 236
Constantine
(n=1)

FIFTH TO EARLY SIXTH CENTURIES (N=14)

End of the fourth/early fifth century (n=2)	RS 1: nos. 133, 843
Fifth century (n=3)	RS 2: no. 375
	RS 3: no. 607
	Istanbul Musei: fifth-century tomb of Flavius Eutyches
Beginning of the fifth century (n=1)	RS 3: no. 296
First quarter of the fifth century (n=1)	RS 2: no. 379
First third of the fifth century (n=4)	RS 3: nos. 221, 271, 514, 515
First half of the fifth century (n=1)	RS 2: no. 414
Second third of the fifth century (n=1)	RS 3: no. 548
Last quarter of the fifth century (n=1)	RS 3: no. 22

UNCERTAIN—EARLY SIXTH CENTURY (N=1)

(ca. 524?) RS 2: no. 256: "holy/saint Proscodimus, bishop and confessor"

DATE NOT LISTED IN REPERTORIUM (N=5)

RS 1: nos. 689, 736, 936, 979, 982

Bibliography

Aldrete, Gregory S. *Gestures and Acclamations in Ancient Rome*. Baltimore: Johns Hopkins University Press, 1999.

Apostolic Constitutions. Translated by James Donaldson. In *Ante-Nicene Fathers*, vol. 7. Edited by Alexander Roberts, James Donaldson, and A. Cleveland Coxe. Buffalo, NY: Christian Literature, 1886. Revised and edited by Kevin Knight for New Advent. http://tinyurl.com/y96at8mb.

Aristides. *Apology*. Translated by D. M. Kay. Early Christian Writings. http://tinyurl.com/y8w4qy9f.

Arlandson, James Malcolm. *Women, Class, and Society in Early Christianity: Models from Luke-Acts*. Peabody, MA: Hendrickson, 1997.

Asia News. "Pope: History of Christianity Would Be Very Different without Women." February 14, 2007. http://tinyurl.com/yb2v3e6s.

Bal, Mieke. *Reading Rembrandt: Beyond the Word-Image Opposition*. Cambridge: Cambridge University Press, 1992.

Barrow, R. H. *Slavery and the Roman Empire*. New York: Barnes & Noble, 1928.

Birk, Stine. "The Christian Muse: Continuity and Change in the Representations of Women on Late Roman Sarcophagi." in *Akten des Symposiums Römische Sarkophage. Marburg, 2.-8. Juli 2006*, edited by Karin Kirchhainer, Heidemarie Koch, and Guntram Koch, 63–72. Marburger Beiträge zur Archäologie 3. Marburg: Eigenverlag des Archäologischen Seminars der Philipps-Universität, 2016.

———. *Depicting the Dead: Self-Representation and Commemoration on Roman Sarcophagi with Portraits*. Aarhus, DNK: Aarhus University Press, 2013.

_____. "Sarcophagi, Self-Representation, and Patronage in Rome and Tyre." In *Patrons and Viewers in Late Antiquity*, edited by Stine Birk and Birte Poulsen, 107–33. Aarhus, DNK: Aarhus University Press: 2012.

_____. "Using Images of Self-Representation on Roman Sarcophagi." In *Using Images in Late Antiquity*, edited by Stine Birk, Troels Myrup Kristensen, and Birte Poulsen, 33–47. Philadelphia: Oxbow, 2014.

Bisconti, Fabrizio, and Donatella Nuzzi. "Scavi e restauri nella regione della 'Velata' in Priscilla." *Rivista di archeologia cristiana* 77 (2001): 7–95.

Bodel, John. "From Columbaria to Catacombs." In *Commemorating the Dead: Texts and Artifacts in Context; Studies of Roman, Jewish, and Christian Burials*, edited by Laurie Brink and Deborah Green, 177–242. New York: de Gruyter, 2008.

Bopp, Linus. *Das Witwentum als organische Gliedschaft im Gemeinschaftsleben der alten Kirche: Ein geschichtlicher Beitrag zur Grundlegung der Witwenseelsorge in der Gegenwart*. Mannheim: Wohlgemuth, 1950.

Borg, Barbara. *Crisis and Ambition: Tombs and Burial Customs in Third-Century CE Rome*. Oxford: Oxford University Press, 2013.

Borg, Marcus J., and John Dominic Crossan. *The First Paul: Reclaiming the Radical Visionary Behind the Church's Conservative Icon*. New York: HarperCollins, 2009.

Brandenburg, Hugo. "Osservazioni sulla fine della produzione e dell'uso dei sarcofagi a rilievo nella tarda antichità nonché sulla loro decorazione." In *Sarcofagi tardoantichi, paleocristiani e altomedievali: Atti della giornata tematica dei seminari di archeologia Cristiana, École Francaise de Rome, 8 maggio 2002*, edited by Fabrizio Bisconti and Hugo Brandenburg, 1–34. Vatican City: Pontificio Istituto di Archeologia Cristiana, 2004.

Brock, Ann Graham. *Mary Magdalene, the First Apostle: The Struggle for Authority*. Cambridge, MA: Harvard Divinity School, 2003.

Brown, Peter. *The Body and Society: Men, Women, and Sexual Renunciation in Early Christianity*. New York: Columbia University Press, 1988.

_____. *The Rise of Western Christendom: Triumph and Diversity AD 200–1000*. Oxford: Blackwell, 1996.

Brown, Raymond E. *The Death of the Messiah: From Gethsemane to the Grave; A Commentary on the Passion Narrative in the Four Gospels*. Vol. 2. New York: Doubleday, 1994.

Brown, Raymond E., and Raymond F. Collins. "Canonicity." In *The New Jerome Biblical Commentary*, edited by Raymond E. Brown, Joseph A. Fitzmyer, and Roland E. Murphy, 1036. Englewood Cliffs, NJ: Prentice Hall, 1990.

Brown, Raymond E., D. W. Johnson, and Kevin G. O'Connell. "Texts and Versions." In *The New Jerome Biblical Commentary*, edited by Raymond E. Brown, Joseph A. Fitzmyer, and Roland E. Murphy, 1083–112. Englewood Cliffs, NJ: Prentice Hall, 1990.

Brubaker, Leslie. "Memories of Helena: Patterns in Imperial Female Matronage in the Fourth and Fifth Centuries." In *Women, Men, and Eunuchs: Gender in Byzantium*, edited by Liz James, 52–75. New York: Routledge, 1997.

Burrus, Virginia. *Chastity as Autonomy: Women in the Stories of the Apocryphal Acts*. Lewiston, NY: Edwin Mellon, 1987.

_____. "The Heretical Woman as Symbol in Alexander, Athanasius, Epiphanius, and Jerome." *Harvard Theological Review* 84, no. 3 (1991): 229–48.

Buttrick, George A. *Interpreter's Dictionary of the Bible*. 5 vols. Nashville: Abingdon, 1962–76.

Cardman, Francine. "Women, Ministry, and Church Order in Early Christianity." In *Women and Christian Origins*, edited by Ross Shepard Kraemer and Mary Rose D'Angelo, 300–329. New York: Oxford University Press, 1999.

Carletti, Carlo. *Iscrizioni cristiane inedite del cimitero di Bassilla ad S. Hermetem*. Vatican City: Tipografia Poliglotta Vaticana, 1976.

Castelli, Elizabeth A. "Gender, Theory and the Rise of Christianity: A Response to Rodney Stark." *Journal of Early Christian Studies* 6, no. 2 (1998): 227–57.

Chadwick, Henry. *The Early Church*. London: Penguin, 1967.

Christern-Briesenick, Brigitte, ed. *Frankreich, Algerien, Tunesien*. Repertorium Der Christlich-Antiken Sarkophage 3. Mainz am Rhein: Philipp von Zabern, 2003.

Clark, Elizabeth A. *Ascetic Piety and Women's Faith: Essays on Late Ancient Christianity*. Lewiston, NY: Edwin Mellen, 1986.

_____. "Ideology, History and the Construction of Woman in Late Ancient Christianity." *Journal of Early Christian Studies* 2, no. 2 (1994): 155–84.

_____. *Jerome, Chrysostom, and Friends: Essays and Translations*. New York: Edwin Mellen, 1979.

_____. *Women in the Early Church*. Message of the Fathers of the Church 13. Wilmington, DE: Glazier, 1983.

Clark, Elizabeth A., and Diane F. Hatch. *The Golden Bough, the Oaken Cross: The Virgilian Cento of Faltonia Betitia Proba*. Chico, CA: Scholars Press, 1981.

Cloke, Gillian. *This Female Man of God: Women and Spiritual Power in the Patristic Age, AD 350–450*. New York: Routledge, 1995.

Comparetti, Domenico. *Vergil in the Middle Ages*. Translated by E. F. M. Benecke. London: S. Sonnenschein, 1908.

Corley, Kathleen E. *Private Women, Public Meals: Social Conflict in the Synoptic Tradition*. Peabody, MA: Hendrickson, 1993.

Cornelius Nepos. *On Great Generals. On Historians*. Translated by J. C. Rolfe. Loeb Classical Library 467. Cambridge, MA: Harvard University Press, 1929.

Corrigan, Kevin. "Saint Macrina: The Hidden Face Behind the Tradition," *Vox Benedictina* 5, no. 1 (1988): 13–43.

Dal Santo, Gitte Lønstrup. "Bishop and Believers—Patrons and Viewers: Appropriating the Roman Patron Saints Peter and Paul in Constantinople." In *Patrons and Viewers in Late Antiquity*, edited by Stine Birk and Birte Poulsen, 237–57. Aarhus, DNK: Aarhus University Press, 2012.

D'Angelo, Mary Rose. "(Re)Presentations of Women in the Gospel of Matthew and Luke-Acts." In *Women and Christian Origins*, edited by Ross Shepard Kraemer and Mary Rose D'Angelo, 171–95. New York: Oxford University Press, 1999.

Davies, Stevan L. *The Revolt of the Widows: The Social World of the Apocryphal Acts*. London: Feffer & Simons, 1980.

Davis, Glenys. "Before Sarcophagi." In *Life, Death and Representation: Some New Work on Roman Sarcophagi*, edited by Jaś Elsner and Janet Huskinson, 21–53. New York: de Gruyter, 2011.

Deichmann, Friedrich W., Giuseppe Bovini, and Hugo Brandenburg, eds.

Rom und Ostia. Repertorium Der Christlich-Antiken Sarkophage 1. Wiesbaden: Franz Steiner, 1967.

Denzey, Nicola. *The Bone Gatherers: The Lost Worlds of Early Christian Women.* Boston: Beacon, 2007.

Didascalia Apostolorum. Translated by R. Hugh Connolly. Oxford: Clarendon, 1929. Reprinted in Early Christian Writings. http://tinyurl.com/ydefsawf.

Dresken-Weiland, Jutta, ed. *Bild, Grab und Wort. Untersuchungen zu Jenseitsvorstellungen von Christen des 3. und 4. Jahrhunderts.* Regensburg: Schnell & Steiner, 2010.

_____. *Italien: mit einem nachtrag; Rom und Ostia, Dalmatien, Museen der Welt.* Repertorium Der Christlich-Antiken Sarkophage 2. Mainz am Rhein: Philipp von Zabern, 1998.

Egeria. *Diary of a Pilgrimage.* Translated by George E. Gingras. Ancient Christian Writers 38. New York: Newman Press, 1970.

Eisen, Ute E. *Women Officeholders in Early Christianity: Epigraphical and Literary Studies.* Translated by Linda M. Maloney. Collegeville, MN: Liturgical Press, 2000.

Elsner, Jaś. "Image and Rhetoric in Early Christian Sarcophagi: Reflections on Jesus' Trial." In *Life, Death and Representation: Some New Work on Roman Sarcophagi,* edited by Jaś Elsner and Janet Huskinson, 359–86. New York: de Gruyter, 2011.

_____. *Imperial Rome and Christian Triumph.* New York: Oxford University Press, 1998.

_____. Introduction to *Life, Death, and Representation: Some New Work on Roman Sarcophagi,* edited by Jaś Elsner and Janet Huskinson, 1–19. New York: de Gruyter, 2011.

_____. "Visualising Women in Late Antique Rome: The Projecta Casket." In *Through a Glass Brightly: Studies in Byzantine and Medieval Art and Archaeology,* edited by Chris Entwistle, 22–36. Oxford: Oxbow, 2003.

Elsner, Jaś, and Janet Huskinson. *Life, Death, and Representation: Some New Work on Roman Sarcophagi.* New York: de Gruyter, 2011.

Epp, Eldon Jay. *Junia: The First Woman Apostle.* Minneapolis: Fortress Press, 2005.

Ewald, Björn Cristian. *Der Philosoph als Leitbild. Ikonographische Untersuchungen an römischen Sarkophagreliefs.* Mainz: Philipp von Zabern, 1999.

Février, Paul-Albert. "Les peintures de la catacombe de Priscille: deux scènes relatives à la vie intellectuelle." *Mélanges d'archéologie et d'histoire* 71 (1959): 301–19.

Frier, Bruce W. "Roman Life Expectancy: Ulpian's Evidence." *Harvard Studies in Classical Philology* 86 (1982): 213–51.

Gafney, Wilda C. *Daughters of Miriam: Women Prophets in Ancient Israel.* Minneapolis: Fortress Press, 2008.

Gardner, Jane F. *Women in Roman Law and Society.* Bloomington: Indiana University Press, 1991.

Gillman, Florence M. *Women Who Knew Paul.* Collegeville, MN: Liturgical Press, 1992.

Grant, Robert M. "The Social Setting of Second-Century Christianity." In *The Shaping of Christianity in the Second and Third Centuries,* edited by E. P. Sanders, 16–29. Vol. 1 of *Jewish and Christian Self-Definition.* London: SCM, 1980.

Gryson, Roger. *The Ministry of Women in the Early Church.* Collegeville, MN: Liturgical Press, 1976.

Harley, Felicity. "Christianity and the Transformation of Classical Art." In *A Companion to Late Antiquity,* edited by Phillip Rousseau, 306–26. Oxford: Wiley-Blackwell, 2012.

Harris, William V. *Ancient Literacy.* Cambridge, MA: Harvard University Press, 1989.

Hickey, Anne Ewing. *Women of the Roman Aristocracy as Christian Monastics.* Ann Arbor, MI: UMI Research Press, 1987.

Hirschfield, Amy K. "History of Catacomb Archaeology." In *Commemorating the Dead: Texts and Artifacts in Context; Studies of Roman, Jewish, and Christian Burials,* edited by Laurie Brink and Deborah Green, 11–38. New York: de Gruyter, 2008.

Hopkins, Keith. "Rome, Taxes, Rents and Trade." In *The Ancient Economy,* edited by Walter Scheidel and Sitta von Reden. Edinburgh: Edinburgh University Press, 2002.

Hunt, E. D. "Palladius of Helenopolis: A Party and Its Supporters in the

Church of the Late Fourth Century." *Journal of Theological Studies* 24, no. 2 (1973): 456–80.

Huskinson, Janet. "Degrees of Differentiation: Role Models on Early Christian Sarcophagi." In *Role Models in Ancient Rome: Identity and Assimilation*, edited by Sinclair Bell and Inge Lyse Hansen, 287–99. Ann Arbor: University of Michigan Press, 2008.

_____. "*Habent sua fata*: Writing Life Histories of Roman Sarcophagi." In *Life, Death and Representation: Some New Work on Roman Sarcophagi*, edited by Jaś Elsner and Janet Huskinson, 55–82. New York: de Gruyter, 2011.

_____. *Roman Strigillated Sarcophagi: Art and Social History*. Oxford: Oxford University Press, 2015.

_____. "Women and Learning: Gender and Identity in Scenes of Intellectual Life on Late Roman Sarcophagi." In *Constructing Identities in Late Antiquity*, edited by Richard Miles, 190–213. New York: Routledge, 1999.

Irvin, Dorothy. "The Archaeology of Women's Traditional Ministries in the Church 100 to 820 AD." In *Calendar 2003*. St. Paul, MN: Self-published, 2003.

_____. "The Archaeology of Women's Traditional Ministries in the Church 300–1500 AD." In *Calendar 2004*. St. Paul, MN: Self-published, 2004.

_____. "The Archaeology of Women's Traditional Ministries in the Church 60–1500 AD." In *Calendar 2005*. St. Paul, MN: Self-published, 2005.

James, M. R, trans. *The Apocryphal New Testament*. Oxford: Clarendon, 1924.

Jensen, Robin Margaret. "Dining with the Dead: From the Mensa to the Altar in Christian Late Antiquity." In *Commemorating the Dead: Texts and Artifacts in Context; Studies of Roman, Jewish, and Christian Burials*, edited by Laurie Brink and Deborah Green, 107–43. New York: de Gruyter, 2008.

_____. *Living Water: Symbols and Settings of Early Christian Baptism*. Leiden: Brill, 2010.

_____. *Understanding Early Christian Art*. London: Routledge, 2000.

Johnson, Elizabeth A. *Truly Our Sister: A Theology of Mary in the Communion of Saints*. New York: Continuum, 2003.

Jones, Leslie Webber, and C. R. Morey. *The Miniatures of the Manuscripts of*

Terence Prior to the Thirteenth Century. 2 vols. Princeton: Princeton University Press, 1930–31.

Jongman, Willem. "Slavery and the Growth of Rome: The Transformation of Italy in the Second and First Centuries BCE." In *Rome the Cosmopolis*, edited by Catharine Edwards and Greg Woolf, 100–122. Cambridge: Cambridge University Press, 2003.

Jurgens, William A. *The Faith of the Early Fathers: A Source-Book of Theological and Historical Passages.* 3 vols. Collegeville, MN: Liturgical Press, 1970–79.

Just, Felix. "The Deutero-Pauline Letters." Catholic Resources for Bible, Liturgy, Art, and Theology. February 17, 2012. http://tinyurl.com/yc5x5fce.

Justin Martyr. *The Second Apology of Justin for the Christians.* In *Ante-Nicene Fathers.* Vol. 1, *The Apostolic Fathers.* Edited and translated by Alexander Roberts and James Donaldson. Buffalo, NY: Christian Literature, 1886. Republished on Early Christian Writings. http://tinyurl.com/yd6ese5f.

Kelly, Joseph F. *The World of the Early Christians.* Collegeville, MN: Liturgical Press, 1997.

Kirsch, Johann Peter. "St. Petronilla." In *The Catholic Encyclopedia.* Vol. 11. New York: Robert Appleton, 1911. Reprinted by Alphonsus Maria Arata Nunobe on New Advent. http://tinyurl.com/yd3ykj7x.

Koch, Guntram. *Sarkophage der römischen Kaiserzeit.* Darmstadt: Wissenschaftliche Buchgesellschaft, 1993.

Kraemer, Ross Shepard. *Her Share of the Blessings: Women's Religions among Pagans, Jews, and Christians in the Greco-Roman World.* Oxford: Oxford University Press, 1992.

———. "Jewish Women and Women's Judaism(s) at the Beginning of Christianity." In *Women and Christian Origins*, edited by Ross Shepard Kraemer and Mary Rose D'Angelo, 50–79. New York: Oxford University Press, 1999.

Kraemer, Ross Shepard, and Mary Rose D'Angelo. *Women and Christian Origins.* New York: Oxford University Press, 1999.

Lampe, Peter. *From Paul to Valentinus: Christians in Rome in the First Two Centuries.* Minneapolis: Fortress Press, 2003.

LiDonnici, Lynn R. "Women's Religions and Religious Lives in the Greco-

Roman City." In *Women and Christian Origins*, edited by Ross Shepard Kraemer and Mary Rose D'Angelo, 80–101. New York: Oxford University Press, 1999.

MacDonald, Margaret Y. "Reading Real Women through the Undisputed Letters of Paul." In *Women and Christian Origins*, edited by Ross Shepard Kraemer and Mary Rose D'Angelo, 199–220. New York: Oxford University Press, 1999.

Macy, Gary "Women Deacons: History." In *Women Deacons: Past, Present, Future*, by Gary Macy, William T. Ditewig, and Phyllis Zagano, 9–39. New York: Paulist, 2011.

Madigan, Kevin, and Carolyn Osiek, eds. *Ordained Women in the Early Church: A Documentary History*. Baltimore: John Hopkins University Press, 2005.

Maier, Harry O. "Heresy, Households, and the Disciplining of Diversity." In *Late Ancient Christianity*, edited by Virginia Burrus, 213–33. Minneapolis: Fortress Press, 2005.

_____. "Religious Dissent, Heresy and Households in Late Antiquity." *Vigiliae Christianae* 49, no. 1 (March 1995): 49–63.

Malone, Mary T. *Women and Christianity*. Vol. 1, *The First Thousand Years*. Maryknoll, NY: Orbis, 2001.

Mancinelli, Fabrizio. *Guide to the Catacombs of Rome*. Firenze: Scala, 2007.

_____. *The Catacombs of Rome and the Origins of Christianity*. Firenze: Scala Group, 1981.

Marucchi, Orazio. *Manual of Christian Archaeology*. Translated by Hubert Vecchierello. Patterson, NJ: St. Anthony Guild Press, 1935.

McDonald, Dennis Ronald. *The Legend and the Apostle: The Battle for Paul in Story and Canon*. Philadelphia: Westminster, 1983.

McGinn, Sheila E. "The Acts of Thecla." In *Searching the Scriptures*, edited by Elisabeth Schüssler Fiorenza, 800–828. New York: Crossroad, 1994.

_____. *The Jesus Movement and the World of the Early Church*. Winona, MN: Anselm Academic, 2014.

McKenna, Mary Lawrence. *Women of the Church: Role and Renewal*. New York: P. J. Kenedy, 1967.

McLeod, Frederick G. "Apophatic or Kataphatic Prayer?" Dominican Central Province. January 13, 2015. http://tinyurl.com/y9c8vh2g.

Meeks, Wayne A. *The First Urban Christians: The Social World of the Apostle Paul.* New Haven: Yale University Press, 1983.

Meier, John P. *A Marginal Jew: Rethinking the Historical Jesus.* Vol. 1, *The Roots of the Problem and the Person.* New York: Doubleday, 1991.

_____. *A Marginal Jew: Rethinking the Historical Jesus.* Vol. 3, *Companions and Competitors.* New York: Doubleday, 2001.

Meinecke, Katharina. "Invisible Sarcophagi: Coffin and Viewer in the Late Imperial Age." In *Patrons and Viewers in Late Antiquity*, edited by Stine Birk and Birte Poulsen, 83–106. Aarhus, DNK: Aarhus University Press: 2012.

Miles, Margaret R. *Image as Insight: Visual Understanding in Western Christianity and Secular Culture.* Boston: Beacon, 1985.

Murphy-O'Connor, Jerome. "Prisca and Aquila: Traveling Tentmakers and Church Builders." *Bible Review* 8, no. 6 (December 1992): 40–51, 62.

Newby, Zahra. "In the Guise of Gods and Heroes: Portrait Heads on Roman Mythological Sarcophagi." In *Life, Death and Representation: Some New Work on Roman Sarcophagi*, edited by Jaś Elsner and Janet Huskinson, 189–227. New York: de Gruyter, 2011.

Neyrey, Jerome H. "What's Wrong with This Picture? John 4, Cultural Stereotypes of Women, and Public and Private Speech." In *A Feminist Companion to John*, vol. 1, edited by Amy-Jill Levine with Marianne Blickenstaff, 98–125. Cleveland, OH: Pilgrim: 2003.

Oakman, Douglas. "The Countryside in Luke-Acts." In *The Social World of Luke-Acts: Models for Interpretation*, edited by Jerome H. Neyrey, 151–79. Peabody, MA: Hendrickson, 1991.

Osiek, Carolyn. "Roman and Christian Burial." In *Commemorating the Dead: Texts and Artifacts in Context; Studies of Roman, Jewish, and Christian Burial*, edited by Laurie Brink and Deborah Green, 243–70. New York: de Gruyter, 2008.

_____. *Women in the Ministry of Paul.* Cleveland: FutureChurch, 2010.

Osiek, Carolyn, and David L. Balch. *Families in the New Testament World: Households and House Churches.* Louisville: Westminster John Knox, 1997.

Osiek, Carolyn, and Margaret Y. MacDonald, with Janet Tulloch. *A*

Woman's Place: House Churches in Earliest Christianity. Minneapolis: Fortress Press, 2006.

Patterson, Orlando. *Slavery and Social Death: A Comparative Study.* Cambridge, MA: Harvard University Press, 1982.

Pergola, Philippe. *Christian Rome: Early Christian Rome; Catacombs and Basilicas, Past and Present.* Rome: Vision, 2000.

_____. "'Petronella martyr': une évergète de la fin du IVe siècle?" In *Memoriam Sanctorum Venerantes: Miscellanea in onore di Monsignor Victor Saxer,* edited by Eugenio Alliata, 627–36. Vatican City: Pontificio Istituto di Archeologia Cristiana, 1992.

_____. *Roman and Italian Catacombs: Domitilla.* Vatican City: Pontificia Commisione di Archeologia Sacra, 2002.

Philo. *On the Decalogue. On the Special Laws, Books 1–3.* Translated by F. H. Colson. Loeb Classical Library 320. Cambridge, MA: Harvard University Press, 1937.

Radbill, Samuel X. "A History of Child Abuse and Infanticide." In *Violence in the Family,* edited by Suzanne K. Steinmetz and Murray A. Straus, 173–79. New York: Dodd, Mead, 1974.

Raming, Ida. *The Exclusion of Women from the Priesthood: Divine Law or Sex Discrimination? A Historical Investigation of the Juridical and Doctrinal Foundations of the Code of Canon Law, Canon 968,1.* Translated by Norman R. Adams. Metuchen, NJ: Scarecrow, 1976.

Rawson, Beryl. *Children and Childhood in Roman Italy.* Oxford: Oxford University Press, 2003.

_____. "Roman Concubinage and Other De Facto Marriages." *Transactions of the American Philological Association* 104 (1974): 279–305.

Rebillard, Éric. "The Church, the Living, and the Dead." In *A Companion to Late Antiquity,* edited by Philip Rousseau, 220–30. West Sussex: Wiley-Blackwell, 2012.

Ruether, Rosemary Radford. "Mothers of the Church: Ascetic Women in the Late Patristic Age." In *Women of Spirit: Female Leadership in the Jewish and Christian Traditions,* edited by Rosemary Radford Ruether and Eleanor McLaughlin, 71–98. New York: Simon & Schuster, 1979.

Riley, Henry Thomas. *The Comedies of Terence.* New York: Harper & Brothers, 1874.

Rossi, Mary Ann, and Giorgio Otranto. "Priesthood, Precedent and Prejudice: On Recovering the Women Priests of Early Christianity." *Journal of Feminist Studies in Religion* 7, no. 1 (1991): 73–94.

Russell, Ben. "The Roman Sarcophagus 'Industry': A Reconsideration." In *Life, Death and Representation: Some New Work on Roman Sarcophagi*, edited by Jaś Elsner and Janet Huskinson, 119–47. New York: de Gruyter, 2011.

Salisbury, Joyce E. *Church Fathers, Independent Virgins*. New York: Verso, 1991.

Saller, Richard. Introduction to *Commemorating the Dead: Texts and Artifacts in Context; Studies of Roman, Jewish, and Christian Burials*, edited by Laurie Brink and Deborah Green, 1–7. New York: de Gruyter, 2008.

Salzman, Michelle Renee. "Aristocratic Women: Conductors of Christianity in the Fourth Century." *Helios* 16, no. 2 (1989): 207–20.

Scheidel, Walter. "Germs for Rome." In *Rome the Cosmopolis*, edited by Catharine Edwards and Greg Woolf, 158–76. Cambridge: Cambridge University Press, 2003.

Schlosser, Hanspeter. "Die Daniel-Susanna-Erzählung in Bild und Literatur der christlichen Frühzeit." In *Tortulae: Studien zu altchristlichen und byzantinischen Monumenten*, edited by Walter Nikolaus Schumacher, 243–49. Rome: Herder, 1966.

Schüssler Fiorenza, Elisabeth. *In Memory of Her: A Feminist Theological Reconstruction of Christian Origins*. New York: Crossroad, 1983.

Shaw, Brent D. "Seasons of Death: Aspects of Mortality in Imperial Rome." *Journal of Roman Studies* 86 (1996): 100–138.

Sivan, Hagith. "On Hymens and Holiness in Late Antiquity: Opposition to Aristocratic Female Asceticism in Rome." *Jahrbuch für Antike und Christentum* 36 (1993): 81–93.

Smith, Kathryn A. "Inventing Marital Chastity: The Iconography of Susanna and the Elders in Early Christian Art." *Oxford Art Journal* 16, no. 1 (1993): 3–24.

Society of Saint Pius X. "Historical Notes about St. Peter's Tomb." Accessed November 2, 2016. http://tinyurl.com/yawyatqj.

Sozomen. *Church History*. Translated by Chester D. Hartranft. In *Nicene and Post-Nicene Fathers, Second Series*, vol. 2. Edited by Philip Schaff and Henry Wace. Buffalo, NY: Christian Literature, 1890. Revised and edited by Kevin Knight for New Advent. http://tinyurl.com/y7rn4sv7.

Spier, Jeffrey. *Picturing the Bible: The Earliest Christian Art.* Fort Worth, TX: Kimble Art Museum, 2007.

Stark, Rodney. *The Rise of Christianity: How the Obscure Jesus Movement Became the Dominant Religious Force in the Western World.* San Francisco: HarperCollins, 1996.

Steinberg, Faith. "Women and the Dura-Europos Synagogue Paintings." *Religion and the Arts* 10, no. 4 (2006): 461–96.

Stewart, Peter. *Statues in Roman Society: Representation and Response.* Oxford: Oxford University Press, 2003.

Streete, Gail Corrington. "Women as Sources of Redemption and Knowledge in Early Christian Traditions." In *Women and Christian Origins,* edited by Ross Shepard Kraemer and Mary Rose D'Angelo, 330–54. New York: Oxford University Press, 1999.

Thompson, Mary R. *Mary of Magdala: Apostle and Leader.* Mahwah, NJ: Paulist, 1995.

Thurston, Bonnie. *Women in the New Testament: Questions and Commentary.* New York: Crossroad, 1998.

Torjesen, Karen Jo. *When Women Were Priests: Women's Leadership in the Early Church and the Scandal of Their Subordination in the Rise of Christianity.* San Francisco: HarperSanFrancisco, 1993.

Treggiari, Susan. *Roman Marriage: Iusti Coniuges from the Time of Cicero to the Time of Ulpian.* Oxford: Clarendon, 1993.

Trout, Dennis E. "Damasus and the Invention of Early Christian Rome." In *The Cultural Turn in Late Ancient Studies: Gender, Asceticism, and Historiography,* edited by Dale B. Martin and Patricia Cox Miller, 299–315. Durham, NC: Duke University Press, 2005.

———. "Inscribing Identity: Latin Epigraphic Habit in Late Antiquity." In *A Companion to Late Antiquity,* edited by Philip Rousseau, 170–86. West Sussex: Wiley-Blackwell, 2012.

Tulloch, Janet H. "Art and Archaeology as an Historical Resource for the Study of Women in Early Christianity: An Approach for Analyzing Visual Data." *Feminist Theology* 12, no. 3 (2004): 277–303.

———. "Family Funerary Banquets." In *A Woman's Place: House Churches in*

Earliest Christianity, edited by Carolyn Osiek and Margaret Y. MacDonald, with Janet H. Tulloch, 164–93. Minneapolis: Fortress Press, 2006.

———. "Visual Representations of Children and Ritual in the Early Roman Empire." *Studies in Religion/Sciences Religieuses* 41, no. 3 (2012): 408–38.

Vagaggini, Cipriano. *Ordination of Women to the Diaconate in the Eastern Churches*. Edited by Phyllis Zagano. Collegeville, MN: Liturgical Press, 2013.

Vatican. "The Basilica: The Tomb of the Apostle." The Papal Basilica: St. Paul Outside-the-Walls. Accessed November 2, 2016. http://tinyurl.com/ydewucce.

Weisen, David S. "Virgil, Minucius Felix and the Bible." *Hermes* 99, no.1 (1971): 70–91.

Wijngaards, John. *Women Deacons in the Early Church: Historical Texts and Contemporary Debates*. New York: Crossroad, 2006.

Wild, Robert A. "The Pastoral Letters." In *The New Jerome Biblical Commentary*, edited by Raymond E. Brown, Joseph A. Fitzmyer, and Roland E. Murphy, 891–902. Englewood Cliffs, NJ: Prentice Hall, 1990.

Winter, Bruce W. *Roman Wives, Roman Widows*. Grand Rapids: Eerdmans, 2003.

Witherington, Ben, III. *Women in the Ministry of Jesus*. New York: Cambridge University Press, 1984.

Zagano, Phyllis. Introduction to *Ordination of Women to the Diaconate in the Eastern Churches*, by Cipriano Vagaggini, vii–xiii. Collegeville, MN: Liturgical Press, 2013.

———. "It's Time: The Case for Women Deacons." *Commonweal* 139, no. 22 (December 21, 2012): 8–9.

Zanker, Paul, and Björn C. Ewald. *Living with Myths: The Imagery of Roman Sarcophagi*. Translated by Julia Slater. Oxford: Oxford University Press, 2012.

Index